# Why Not?

## A MEMOIR

Migration Journeys, Melodic Strides,
and
Quests for Meaning

Renato Wakim

191 Bank Street
Burlington, Vermont 05401

Copyright © 2020 by Renato Wakim

All rights reserved. No part of this publication may be reproduced, distributed, or transmitted in any form or by any means, including photocopying, recording, or other electronic or mechanical methods, without the prior written permission of the publisher, except in the case of brief quotations embodied in critical reviews and certain other noncommercial uses permitted by copyright law.

Onion River Press
191 Bank Street
Burlington, VT 05401

ISBN: 978-1-949066-40-1
Library of Congress Control Number: 2020900920

Publisher's Cataloging-in-Publication Data:
Names: Wakim, Renato, author.
Title: Why not? A memoir: migration journeys, melodic strides and quests for meanings / by Renato Wakim.
Description: Burlington, VT: Onion River Press, 2020.
Identifiers: LCCN: 2020900920 | ISBN 978-1-949066-40-1
Subjects: LCSH Wakim, Renato. | Brazilian Americans--Biography. | Vermont--Biography. | Voyages and travels. | BISAC BIOGRAPHY & AUTOBIOGRAPHY / Personal Memoirs
Classification: LCC CT275.W23 A3 2020 | DDC 973.931/092--dc23

Book cover and layout design by Bianca Lima in Vermont, USA
Typefaces: Questa Grande, Questa Sans, GaramondFBText, Garamond
Paper: Crème stock
Weight: 50 lb / 74 gsm
Printed by: IngramSpark

*To the memory of my father*
*To the child within ourselves*

# Contents

| | | |
|---|---|---|
| | Prologue | 13 |
| 1 | The Storm Is On and It's Not Pretty | 17 |
| 2 | Going to California | 20 |

Perspective in Place: São Paulo, 1979 · Breakaway
Language and Growth · Telegraph Avenue
More Than a Garage · Waking Up Our Minds
Political Science · 'Being There' · Plasma and Emeralds

| | | |
|---|---|---|
| 3 | Staying or Not Staying? | 39 |

The Good Earth · Let's Go!

| | | |
|---|---|---|
| 4 | Life is... | 49 |

Dad, Mom ·...Good: Love and Loved Ones
...Beautiful: Horizons · ...Truth: First Encounters
Escape Valve Diary · "I May Make You Feel but I Can't Make You Think" · Challenges Abound · Growing Pains: From Crossroads to Seizing the Moment · Refuge on Books and More Troubled Waters · Learning a Lesson at Every Corner
A Minor Reflection

| | | |
|---|---|---|
| 5 | Life is Sensation: Getting Out There | 83 |

The Chase for Experience · Off to The Old World
London, the Smoke · Liège, Les Rouches
Paris, Les Arennes de Lutèce · The Cheshire Cat Dilemma
La Grande Motte · Barcelona, Ninth Boat
Monaco, The Principality · Genova, La Superba
Bergamo, Citta' Dei Mille · Florence, the Cradle
Rome, Caput Mundi · Dozza, Bologna
Venice, La Serenissima · Zürich, Little Big City
Munich, Toy Town

Innsbruck, Capital of the Alps · Vienna, City of Music, City of Dreams · Budapest, The Pearl of the Danube
A Short Journey Through the Balkans · Athens, The City of the Violet Crown · Israel and the Kibbutz Experience
Sha'ar Ha'amakim · Jerusalem, Hierosolyma, Urusalim
Egypt, Gift of the Nile, Land of the Pharaohs
Cairo, City of Thousand Minarets
Luxor and Karnak, Palaces and Temples
Hello, Goodbye

**6      Belonging                                    143**

Holding My Skin · Back to School and Beyond
Literature and Experimentation · Johannesburg, then Rio
Honey Bees... · ...And Master's Degree

**7      The Search                                   165**

**8      Lightning Strikes                            171**

Passed the Elements · 'You Become Responsible, Forever, For What You Have Captivated' · Change, The Only Constant

**9      Alchemy                                      181**

The School · Being Here

**10     Trial and Error Amidst the Essential         185**

Seven Years + One · One Precious of Many Special Wedding Gifts · Mutual Love for Travelling
The Flåm Railway · Stop and Go, Then Push Forward
The Princesses · Plainfield, VT
Back in Midtown

**11     Reality Hits                                 202**

Imponderables · The Thirty-Year Phases - I

**12     Far Away                                     206**

The Country of the Future · Down Under
Compiling Business Possibilities · Off to Sydney, The Harbor
City · A Special Moment

| | | |
|---|---|---|
| **13** | **Not So Far Away** | **218** |

Pulling the Plug, Plugging It Back In · The Waters of the Atlantic
Ocean · Porto, A Invicta · Packing Up and Landing
Signs of an Unforeseen Major Obstacle · Navigating the Waters

| | | |
|---|---|---|
| **14** | **Back Home but Not Quite** | **233** |

Trembling Days · Pindorama, Land of the Palm Trees
Fortaleza, Land of Light · A Change of Heart
Jericoacoara · Unfolding Change Favors Opportunity
Catching Up with What Matters · Self-Knowledge in a Bottle
Sayonara · Nihon, Land of the Rising Sun
Grasping Japan · Karaoke
The Program · Kyoto, Tokyo and Cultural Experience
Now, Solo

| | | |
|---|---|---|
| **15** | **A Change is Gonna Come** | **258** |

James, Tricia, and the Dunes · A Thought About Complacency
'Why Has Brazil Never Taken Off as a Country?'
Collision Course

| | | |
|---|---|---|
| **16** | **Why Not?** | **268** |

'There's Nothing in a Caterpillar That Tells You It's Going to Be
a Butterfly' · 'Every Cause is the Effect of Its Own Effects'
Acting On · The Real Why Yet to Be Revealed
Signals · The Family Stays

| | | |
|---|---|---|
| **17** | **It's All About Them** | **276** |

Ben & Jerry's Town · The Vermonter
The Why Explained and Interpreted · Grand View Heights

| | | |
|---|---|---|
| **18** | **Music, Lyrics & Lessons from Songwriters** | **283** |

Lyrics and the Voices of the Soul

**19    Mirrors and The Present                          295**

Development of the Seven Years Cycles

**20    A Job is a Job is a Job?                         300**

Making a Living in the Green Mountain State
'Every Job You've Held, Every Relationship You've Forged, is a Kind of Key That Unlocks an Opportunity'
Caring for the Indispensable · Faith, Freedom and Open Mind

**21    The Big Things. And The Small Things             308**

A Job · Two Jobs? · 50 Golden Years
A Dark Cloud in the Neighborhood
'Every One We Meet is Fighting a Battle We know Nothing About'
He's Gone Away · The Journey Southbound · A Talented Artist
Learning to Navigate the Unknown · Reality Sinks In
A Story Like No One

**22    They Come and Go in Waves                        334**

Processing the Upcoming Changes · Born in Belgium, a Friend of the World · Closure · Staying Whole · Uphill Battles
Global Sturm Und Drang · In Waves They Come and They Go
Project Bona Fide · Hitting the Rowdy Road

**23    Oh, The Things We Do!                            354**

Teaching a Path for Development · Becoming a National
If It's Not Fun... · Elements of the Equation
West Bound · On the Ramp, Off to the Skies
Rejoicing the Day · With Traveling Revisited, a Fresh Look at Things · A New Career – I · Vermont Council on World Affairs
Mr. Ambassador · A New Career – II · Joyful Reunions

Surprise, Surprise · Amsterdam, Venice of the North
The Evergreen State · Ready for a New Beginning
Dreaming of Venice, The Real One
High Living Costs and Cold Weather: Time for Change?

**24     A Hard Rain's a Gonna Fall                         378**

One Man in The Station · The Thirty Year Phases - II
'What Wisdom Can You Find That is Greater Than Kindness?'
Charlotte, NC · Unpulling the Trigger · Acts of Love – I
Acts of Love – II · Acts of Love - III

**25     What Do We Do? Where Do We Go?
        Things Will Never Be the Same                        389**

Nailing Down Options

**26     Taking Action as The Universe Conspires              392**

Silver Linings · Stephen
For the Love of Acting · Acquiring the Taste
Modena, Land of Engines
Puerto Rico, The Island of Enchantment

**27     Where is home?                                       403**

Berlin, Paper City · 9.0
The Dot · Soil vs. Soul · Phoenicians
The Legend of the Phoenix ·Living the Legend
Seven Women · School-Planet
The Willow Tree · Wrapping Up

Epilogue                                                    417

Acknowledgements                                            420

Background Reading, References, Favorite Tunes              424

# Prologue

Much of this memoir is a collection of anecdotes swirling around this short existence of ours, and the way I see it, contextually. The result: my aim is to portray reflections around the phases of life and the quests for home, belonging, and their meaning, associating true stories and realities to observations of my own and of other peoples' life experiences, from a particular time of rupture, to this day.

The idea of writing a book has been dwelling on my bucket list for a while. For most people, their memoir is their first book. I hear it's like taking off your clothes and reading it in public. Probably. I'll go for it. Coincidence or not, I began an intensive thought process accompanied with jotting notes after a significant transformative event – the destruction of my house by fire. This life changing experience prompted me to come up with the structure of the book in a few hours, just about a week after its occurrence. In many ways, it helped me order my mind around the situation I knew would linger, and also drag myself and my family for quite some time.

Hence, my main purpose is to group parts of my life together in themes, followed by highlighting periods, passages and lessons learned, so that family and friends can get to know me a little better. Especially, when most of us – and I include myself – get sucked into the universe of social media and its distractions, where dialogues and discussions become secondary in our day-to-day lives, and we ignore our own stories.

Call it a memoir, an autobiography, or slices of my life story, I do not mind if it does – or does not - get categorized. An active and yet contemplative character, I relay my experiences with components of deliberation and many times utilize others' thoughts to describe what I feel, and what I am going through. I like to think that that helps intensify the dimension and the level of intimacy I try to convey to the reader, while I share the light and not-so-light moments of my journey. The takeaway: you the reader, will find out if it's worth it for you – I hope so.

Then, there's music. I will allude to it in virtually every chapter of this book. Here my purpose is to demonstrate its importance in raising one's mood, and ultimately the mechanism that allows us to feel much, or possibly, most of the emotions that we experience in our lives. Music, a language in itself, for some people it is a way to escape from the pain of life. For myself, I can't think of a better way to bring people together and create more potential for increased empathy, social connection and cooperation.

At last, as I reflect on our historic pandemic moment, I can only imagine what multitudes of people are going through at this very minute. Unthinkable for the common citizen, this is indeed a strange and consequential time for the planet. More specifically, to us humans: the vast majority of us have not experienced or even thought about going through an endemic of this magnitude during our lifetime. The planet itself, as it relates to the environment, seems to be getting a deserved break from the everyday frantic action characteristic of our modern era. Yet, it's all change and inconclusive. For us, as it refers to our own microcosms - and our families', friends', co-workers', neighbors' and acquaintances' - we are far from knowing the limits and the unfolding of the crisis. Nonetheless, one can only wish and trust that there's a purpose behind this planetary experience. Without it, we are only half-way through our journeys.

# 1

# The Storm is On and It's Not Pretty

*"And I'll tell it and think it and speak it and breathe it*
*And reflect it from the mountain so all souls can see it*
*Then I'll stand on the ocean until I start sinkin'*
*But I'll know my song well before I start singin'."*
A Hard Rain's A-Gonna Fall
– Bob Dylan

SUNNY AND PLEASANT, that Tuesday morning started out with the temperature much warmer and more humid than usual. Still agreeable since the forecast was for 93 degrees, a little lower than the previous first two days of July, which had already reached 96 and 97 degrees for this time of the year, respectively. With July 2018 having been officially considered the hottest month the Burlington area had seen since the National Service in the Queen City began keeping records in 1892, the always expected 4th of July holiday promised to be an eventful but toasty day all over New England.

I hadn't seen James and Tricia Meade in about a year when I picked up the phone to eagerly hear that they were in town. The 2018 World Soccer Cup was taking place in Russia and moving along; I must admit that I had never been so disinterested in the sport, particularly at this cup. And I knew why. Cheering for both the US and Brazil, with the US not qualifying for attendance and Brazil being politically marred by unending scandals of all sorts, my mood was to marginally look at the results and rarely watch a match on TV. Besides, work was picking up and keeping me busy. James and I set up to quickly meet at the Home Depot parking lot in Williston by mid-morning, as both of us needed a couple of things from the box store. It was great to see my best buddy back in Vermont. After spending several months in Australia following one of their last and longest housesitting journeys, there was a lot to catch up. However, we managed to get together for a few minutes just enough to set up a lunch gathering in downtown later on.

Back in the office for another hour or so, I then drove to downtown Burlington to drop off a proposal at a customer located on packed Church Street prior to meeting with James and Tricia for lunch at Rí Rá, at 12:15p. Rí Rá is quite an interesting spot. A "unique and genuine pub located in the heart of Burlington" on Church Street, it is situated in a "historic bank building, designed by Boston based Harper & West, that was completed in 1931. The pub opened for the first time in March 1999, and was extended in 2002 with the addition of the Library area. In February 2012, The Whiskey Room opened its doors.

As you enter Rí Rá, you can imagine yourself walking through a door that leads you across the pond to experience the best pubs of Ireland. The pub interiors were salvaged and restored in Ireland prior to being shipped to Vermont," reveals Rí Rá's web page.

Summertime in Burlington is always a great season to enjoy, which makes it even more enticing a place to be in the middle of a major worldwide sports event. There we were watching half of the game between Sweden vs. Switzerland, the first of the Round of 16 matches. We got a pretty good table and rapidly ordered our food. The restaurant was jammed; we were lucky to have found a spot right at the beginning of the game. The downside was that it was noisy and soon I would have to get back to work. Still... life is about to take a turn to the unknown. One of those big moments was in course and I was totally oblivious to what was about to happen. The moment we got our plates served and got ready to savor the food, my phone ringed. It was Silvia. With the background call unusually noisy, my wife's voice sounded shattering and desolating. This was the call I never wanted to receive. And I wish no one would ever have to go through such a thing. "Renato," my wife was desperate, "our house is on fire!!!" Silvia's tone of absolute despair was something I had never experienced before. "Catherine Bianca just called me, she's at the house in tears surrounded by ambulance, fire fighters and trucks, I am on my way to the house now!!!"

What ensued was the battle of the mind versus the physical world. My heart pumped at high speed, all kinds of thoughts and assumptions crossed my system. "Is my girl hurt? How badly? How serious is the fire? Will it spread to the next door's neighbors' houses? Or to the neighborhood? Is my wife going to lose her mind and possibly make things worse? Like, crash her car by driving heedlessly? As for myself, am I going to lose my mind by neglecting the steps between getting conscious of what's happening and keeping my cool?"

Amidst an intense shivering sensation, I managed to carefully drive over to the house. For a moment, the strange experience was that time seemed to stand still. Was this for real?

# 2
# Going to California

*"Standing on a hill in my mountain of dreams,
telling myself it's not as hard, hard, hard as it seems."*
*Going to California* – Jimmy Page/Robert Plant

BERKELEY, 1980. It was the urge to safeguard my intent that did it. After a multitude of attempts to turn the assets I had invested for this project into actual resources in order to sufficiently fund it, I got stuck. The project, originally conceived to be a one-month intermediate English course, got deflected to an open-ended travel experience. At least temporarily, the assets felt more like liability to me and, as a consequence, my funds would be virtually running out of steam in a few weeks. Therefore, I needed to act quickly and had to somehow come up with a creative idea. How?

The clinic, although certified, reasonably clean and seemingly safe, is less than a desirable public place to be, let alone being a source for socializing or generating income. As I crossed the white entrance door under the purplish neon lights signage, I entered the small reception area. From there, I could peek into the large gray room. Screening the ambiance for some kind of identity, I looked around and saw multiple unfamiliar faces – men and women, some aloof, others battered, a few restless – laid down the blue vinyl beds. Some were waiting for their turns; others were in full collection progress.

Traditionally, I learn that this is an industry in which its business model depends on there being plenty of people. Of vital importance, it's an industry that helps heal patients, but it's also one that, to keep blood flowing, depends on the existence of a large group of people desperate for cash. In other words, individuals seeking to make up for low wages or small benefits checks; or even as their only source of cash income during a spell of poverty – so long as they weighed more than 110 pounds and were in good health. Contrary to simply donating blood, which takes about thirty minutes, plasma donation may take a one-and-a-half to a three-hour procedure; so, patience and resignation go a long way.

I felt uncomfortable but intrigued to be there. Yet, I was up for the experience. And for the $10 payout, which would buy me a decent meal - or two - until I could figure things out. The nurses come and go, it's a once, perhaps twice a week undertaking. Pure choice and, in most cases, necessity. And, for some individuals, quite a thrill; donating blood and plasma – "the gift of life," I learned before even starting – could be addictive, whether or not a myth.

The Plasma Center is located at the heart of what is known as the birthplace of the 1960 Free Speech Movement. My new friend Françoise, a smart, full of life smiley-red-haired Belgian girl and a student at the UC, is herself a twice-a-week plasma donor. Knowing my predicament but yet determination to make it on my own, Françoise suggested that I take the chance. I pondered for a day. What was I getting into? Did I really need this? Would I do it at home? What could possibly go wrong?

# PERSPECTIVE IN PLACE: SÃO PAULO, 1979

At 21, I was fully engaged in finishing up my four-year college studies in Economics at *Universidade Mackenzie*, with one more year to go. My days were filled with an intensive full time internship at the Marketing Chemicals Dpt. of a major multinational enterprise. There I found a promising career outlook starting as an aspiring business development exec at the end of the internship, which would coincide with college completion. The pay was above market standards, especially for a pre-employment position. Besides, the opportunity to work with smart and qualified professionals – locals and ex-pats – provided for quite an interesting career perspective. The downside was the long hours plus evening classes at school, from Monday thru Friday, some Saturday mornings too. And the nonsensical, crushing, merciless, out of control traffic of this hugely sprawled, urbanistically challenged, yet amazing, megacity called São Paulo. My direct manager was an expatriate, competent professional and leader, and most importantly a good man, with both Peruvian and American backgrounds. Thomas Irving Betts, known by all as Tom Betts.

The year was 1979, when political unrest was boiling behind the scenes in a country that had been through a period of dictatorship[1] that had exceeded by far the expectations of the society which, itself, allowed it and, to an extent, claimed it to take place. That was a golden decade in terms of economic development and middle class affluence. Politically speaking, a disaster when it comes to democratic freedoms and achievements. This

---

[1] "In 1964, Brazil suffered a military coup that established a dictatorship in the country until 1985. During this period, the armed forces used unrestrained violence to suppress the opposition, and the government placed a heavy censorship on the media and the arts. Music was a targeted area due to its great influence on society, especially on the youth, and many songwriters and singers were exiled. In order to escape from the censor and still be able to convey a revolutionary message to the people, they had to use different literary devices and create new methods of writing. It was in this context that a new and unique segment in Brazilian music emerged – the so-called "protest songs." Fernanda Rezende: The influence of the Brazilian Dictatorship on Brazilian Music: A Rhetorical Analysis of Protest Songs, 2008, Senior Thesis, Liberty University.

was a country known and, more precisely, perceived internationally for its "incredible vastness, natural wealth and beauty, and for its amazing people," quoting an article I read at a somewhere forgotten Life magazine about the Brazil of the 1950s.

In college, the focus was on developing my studies towards a hopefully auspicious career and yet on understanding the intricacies of relationships and their relevance for success. As a largely parochial environment, besides being good at what one does, most attractive opportunities revolve around the people you know and the doors that can get open as a result of an efficient networking context.

## BREAKAWAY

Looking at one's biography from a philosophical but yet practical standpoint, there are a good number of authors that break down our lifespan in phases. One particular author, Bernard Lievegoed, a Dutch medical doctor and psychiatrist from which I will make multiple references in this book, is most famous for establishing a theory of organizational development, and also devoted his time and research to bringing an integrated perspective around what he calls "Spiritual Rhythms" in childhood and adulthood. At that time, not yet being exposed to those theories and thoughts, my search was for answers to questions not fully clear in my mind but in a process of revealing themselves as I allowed them to manifest. Therefore, I needed exposure. Disruption. A breakaway from status quo. Escaping from comfort and the illusion of permanency.

As much effort as one puts toward a mindful reaching for new experiences, there is nothing like physical and adventurous journeys. Especially at a time, described by Lievegoed in *Phases*, as the sensation period, "the start of contemplating something of the future, a strong drive towards expansion in multiple fields." The challenge was ahead, waiting to be uncovered: to pursue the path of a career development right after graduation in order to respond to my own self-imposed repository of expectations – which imply family, friends and colleagues, society in general – or simply, harness and navigate the unknown. In this context, music is a major source of inspiration and will be extensively referenced in this memoir. It brings glimpses of ideas and heartened refuge, thereby allowing for impressions to be moveable and dynamic. Yet, truthful and realistic when lyrics and harmonic frequencies unveil the deepest echoing in one's soul.

## LANGUAGE AND GROWTH

My knowledge of the English language was good at this time but limited to where I wanted it to be, although I had been studying it from an early age. For one to develop a solid foundation on a specific language, especially when its roots are different and only partially grammatically related, it takes a lifetime. Both languages share Latin roots – there are many English/Portuguese cognates, which may facilitate the acquisition of a good academic vocabulary with a small overlap in everyday lexicon. However, as an example, being Portuguese a phonetic language, native speakers have significant problems spelling English words found first in spoken language and pronouncing words encountered first in written language. Also, English prepositions are difficult for Portuguese learners since Portuguese has far fewer, and there is no simple correspondence between those that do exist and their English equivalents. Challenging, to say the least, leading to occasional mistakes. Aiming at improving my skills, a natural choice would be to immerse in a minimum of a one-month ESL – *English as a Second Language* – program in the US and get the best out of it. Tom Betts, my manager at Dow Chemical, had welcomed and encouraged my initiative: he would become a key facilitator in this process. Not only Tom agreed that I would spend this one-month of school vacation period away from the internship program – obviously, it would benefit both parties that I got a boost on the language – but he voluntarily reached out to his equivalent in the company in San

Francisco – the spot I had chosen – for arrangements within his team for a volunteer host to offer me room and board, at a modest and almost symbolic cost. I couldn't be more grateful for what would pave the way for the initial steps of a major life change experience.

## TELEGRAPH AVENUE

Berkeley in 1980 was not the same bohemian hub of civil unrest of the 60s. Yet, it was a great place to be for its progressive thinking in direct contrast with the shallow and obscure days of a democracy in disguise and its consequences in and to the society I experienced back at home. As one of the top spots in town, Telegraph Avenue is home to many restaurants, exquisite bookstores and clothing shops, along with street vendors occupying wide sidewalks. As a magnet for international students, here Telegraph Avenue entices a diverse audience of visitors, tourists, artists, street punks, eccentrics, and the homeless. I was attracted to its ambiance without even planning on it. In fact, I must admit that culturally speaking I still knew little about Berkeley's past and its relevance around the not so long ago history of the country. Especially during and after the Vietnam war, which some call "the torpid experience," referred to by Walter Cronkite as "the living-room war."

The San Francisco Bay Area is a busy spot but not quite as São Paulo, the largest city in the Southern Hemisphere. Now I was detached from the high-speed and heavy hours of the work week. As I took the initiative to go from Walnut Creek – where I was initially staying at my host, Dow's Carlos Nuila's apartment – towards the bay, this one fine and bright sunny Sunday afternoon would stir the pot quite significantly. In search for emulating the delight of having spent many significant weekends with groups of friends strumming the popular chords of the day – and many tunes of the past, back in São Paulo – here I found myself, along with my new friend Bob Liu, at the International House, Berkeley. The I-House[2] – a multi-cultural residence and program center serving students – seeking an acoustic guitar. It was almost as if I were looking for a password to mingle with the people I had not yet met in that campus environment which appealed to me instantly and so intensely. My hope was that finding a guitar could lead to another guitar player which could lead to a group of people looking for fun and purpose.

Magically and in a matter of minutes, after a few phone calls, I got invited to one of the student's bedroom surrounded by a handful of avid listeners. Monica Gavrielides, a Brazilian student from Rio de Janeiro, a *carioca*, herself a cheerful music lover, enthusiastically facilitated the gathering and got me an acoustic guitar. This is an instrument which is universally known to bring people together. Romantic at its best, the acoustic guitar – *o violão* – is a versatile instrument. Back home, it allowed me to play the *samba* and *bossa nova* genres I was so fortunate to grow up with; it also gave me the opportunity to learn and acquire the taste of quality pop music, folk, country, blues, prog-rock and classical genres, in addition to extending the *bossa nova* rhythmic tunes to jazz as both overlap and collaborate beautifully.

My skills at the guitar were self-developed but lacked technical nuances. Although my curiosity was large enough to make me a little dangerous on the strings, I was never a virtuoso and probably never wanted to devote a great deal of time to become one; therefore, I was nearly illiterate as I could not read a single chord, only the tabs. But I had good ears, which helped me with the playing and singing of the ballads my generation loved so much. At the dorm, Monica introduced me to Françoise Havelange and Marco Katz, two students from Liège and Brussels, respectively. The first one, a popular student with an immediate smile and a seemingly universal soul; the latter, an

---

2      According to the International House, its mission is to foster intercultural respect, understanding, lifelong friendships and leadership skills for the promotion of a more tolerant and peaceful world.

acoustic guitar player and lover of the great tunes. Funny, joyful and extremely communicative, they made that night memorable along with another dozen or two happy local and international students. Accompanied by Bob Liu, who brought me to the I-House and saw my intent to undertake the important decision of not going back to my internship any time soon, I did take the chance. And Bob too would play a key role in this journey.

## MORE THAN A GARAGE

"Fifty dollars," was the figure I got from Bob. "Really?" I reply without hiding my disbelief. "That's right, fifty bucks a month." After suggesting I should move to Berkeley, that was the deal I got from Bob to stay in this two-car finished garage at the pleasant Bonita Avenue house of his parents. This could not be more convenient, as it was located at an eight-minute walking distance from Sather Gate, the iconic gateway at the heart of the campus. The two-car garage/apartment was fully carpeted, insulated and detached from the house, with a bathroom in the back. Besides a small fridge I had to purchase, my bed was a sleeping bag, just enough to give me a little cushion. Previously referred to as a predicament, my intent now was to figure out how to survive for at least a year with the money I had brought to San Francisco – designated for a month's stay. Not that I had not planned to stay longer – in fact I did, and my certainty was so keen that that was going to happen that I managed to sign a power of attorney to a school's registrar's office acquaintance at *Universidade Mackenzie* in order to delegate him the ability to interrupt my studies for at least a year, should my decision go through.

Although my upbringing allowed me to be a domestically well-traveled and pretty independent young man, I had never left the country until that year. This was a big deal for me. And I knew it would be a big deal for my parents too. Not uncommon, but not usual for a city individual surrounded by friends, family and opportunities. Yet, I needed the experience. My aim was, by all means, not to ask for a penny from my family while being away. And this could last, at minimum, a year. With the concealed goal in mind and wondering how I could get financial backing for this project, added to my savings, I looked for some unorthodox advice. Days before leaving for the US, a seasoned and savvy cousin, Alfredo Hamam, versed on the gem business, gave me the hints I needed to embark on this journey with the promise that the Bay Area consumer market could offer good chances for selling precious stones, such as aquamarines, emeralds, topazes and amethysts. With the idea of attempting to pay for at least the airline ticket, some of the stones I did purchase from him, some were given to me in consignation. The challenge was to find the right consumers. It didn't take long to learn that it was not going to be an easy task.

My days soon after the decision to stick around were filled with satisfaction, a feeling of being proud of myself for walking an important step and a strong sense of fulfillment. The pursuit for accomplishment was yet to be uncovered, but the outlook was in front of my eyes. Here I found myself writing many letters and post cards – yes, we did write letters back then! – to family and friends communicating my determination to try something new, out of the ordinary. To my surprise, Mom, Dad and sisters supported my deliverance wholeheartedly. As for Tom Betts, he probably realized I needed more time to experience the new environment to develop my language skills and assured me that my internship would be there when I got back. Little did he or I know what was ahead to unfold. Now, it was hands on.

A combination of developing the language, meeting like-minded people, getting to know places – preferably in contrast with what I had been exposed to as a dweller of a big city – and possibly making some cash by doing an occasional menial job were all in the mix. And, most importantly, was the possibility to experience the campus life, not in a traditional way of becoming a formal student – albeit I would have liked it very much – but attending classes as an auditing student, thanks to my friend Françoise's creative and expeditious ideas. With the proper permission from teachers, I bought books and participated in the classes I deemed important for my complementary education.

Freedom and purpose are major aspects of my seeking. As a student of Economics, beyond being "a social science concerned chiefly with description and analysis of production, distribution, and consumption of goods and services" (*Merriam-Webster's*), I was a firm believer that it was primarily the science of social wellbeing, or what it ought to be. Therefore, understanding the world, its peoples and the development, structure and functioning of human society became a primordial objective, whether I knew that consciously or not.

## WAKING UP OUR MINDS

"Our biography is our most precious and intimate possession, yet how many of us can make head or tail of it? How much do we really know about ourselves and the complex construction of our own life story? Psychology tells us that we have a Self, a center that we call 'I.' But our waking mind, stumbling its way through time as if suspended in a dream, barely detects its presence, let alone its influence on our yesterdays and tomorrows." In his book *The Veiled Pulse of Time, An Introduction to Biographical Cycles and Destiny*, author William Bryant depicts the importance of examining our biographies as a major element of growth as men and women. "Not only from an empirical, graphical and statistical standpoint, but also and after all, that we are more than the sum total of events and experiences that comprise our biography." Especially at times when we are porously more vulnerable to absorb the influences we choose, deliberately or not, to be a part of this process. More specifically, honing in higher intelligences – be them philosophical, scientific or artistic, or a fusion of all – that could help shape us into more fully developed individuals.

Music is probably the earliest exposure to art we have as human beings. Those fortunate enough to have had at an early age a highly talented and artistic mother, as well as a caretaker, as I was, can assign to that. The early tunes, the lullaby songs, are powerful for babies and toddlers for their development and growth. A sensory-engaging musical environment can greatly contribute to a child's cognitive and sensory development. More than we will ever know. Here are 11 quotes and their respective authors referring to the importance of music to the individual:

*"Music is the universal language of mankind."* – Henry W. Longfellow

*"Through music we may wander where we will in time, and find friends in every century."* – Helen Thompson

*"He took his pain and turned into something beautiful. Into something that people connect to. And that's what good music does. It speaks to you. It changes you."* – Hannah Harrington

*"Music is the language of the spirit. It opens the secret of life bringing peace, abolishing strife."* – Kahlil Gibran

*"Music is the great uniter. An incredible force. Something that people who differ on everything and anything else can have in common."*
– Sarah Dessen

*"When I hear music, I fear no danger. I am invulnerable. I see no foe. I am related to the earliest times, and to the latest."*
– Henry David Thoreau

*"Without music, life would be a mistake."* – Friedrich Nietzsche

*"A man should hear a little music, read a little poetry, and see a fine picture every day of his life, in order that worldly cares may not obliterate the sense of the beautiful which God has implanted in the human soul."*
– Johann Wolfgang von Goethe

*"I see my life in terms of music."* – Albert Einstein

*"No matter how corrupt, greedy, and heartless our government, our corporations, our media, and our religious & charitable institutions may become, the music will still be wonderful."* – Kurt Vonnegut

*"Music in the soul can be heard by the universe."* – Lao Tzu

## POLITICAL SCIENCE

Back at Bonita Avenue, coming across Bob Liu's collection of vinyl records felt like a good refreshing material compared to mine at home – it actually did reinforce my taste for good contemporary and improvisational jazz, especially related to Brazilian-American fusion. On the instrumental music side, Bob enjoyed Sergio Mendes, Airto Moreira, Flora Purim and Chick Corea whereas my preferences revolved around Miles Davis, John Coltrane, Egberto Gismonti and Keith Jarrett, and the genius of Weather Report, to name a few mostly instrumental performers. Until I stumbled into the out of the ordinary music and lyrics of Randy Newman. Newman's songwriting was a total surprise and somewhat disconcerting. His depiction of the human soul in its bare bones manifestation is as refreshing to one's self-discovery process as it is to one's awareness of the unexplored and at times obscured facets of our personalities. While he writes caustic, ironic, pungent songs that virtually broach all themes of the American cultural and social fabric, and well beyond borders, many times touching on even existential issues, he is capable of writing beautiful chromatic twists worthy of George Gershwin and Kurt Weill. His work, I learned, is vast and encompasses memorable albums as a composer and songwriter, with accomplished awarded works in film and theater as well. Here are excerpts of the lyrics of a very controversial track, "Political Science" from *Sail Away*, a 1972 album:

*No one likes us, I don't know why*
*We may not be perfect, but heaven knows we try*
*But all around, even our old friends put us down*

*Let's drop the big one and see what happens*

*Boom goes London and boom Paree*
*More room for you and more room for me*
*And every city the whole world round*
*Will just be another American town*
*Oh, how peaceful it will be, We'll set everybody free*

*They all hate us anyhow*
*So let's drop the big one now*
*Let's drop the big one now*

This song is, for some perhaps not so obvious, a satire of a particular part of American culture and history. In going along with the theme of the rest of the album, the lyrics are uncomfortable, certainly reflecting a side of the foreign policies at the time. The unnamed narrator describes the state of the world, and suggests, "Let's drop the big one and see what happens." Far from taking sides for wrong and right, what struck me about the songwriting was Newman's genius and daringness to portray that aspect and vision of the culture – as he does to basically all his 'theme' albums: *Good Old Boys*, *Little Criminals* and *Bad Love*, to name just a few. Multiple times misinterpreted, he is first and foremost a story teller of the human nature. An observer of humanity in its essence, I was immersed in Newman's song lyrics universe. Don Henley (Eagles) has quite an opinion about the artist: "Randy Newman is a national treasure. He's a songwriter's songwriter; a musician's musician. He's also probably the most misunderstood and underappreciated recording artist alive."

Part of my pursuit during this period was to not only understand why we do the things we do – and the way we do – but also, what makes the birthplaces where we are brought up to be the way they are. Once again, Françoise suggests with her keen understanding of the Human Sciences – herself at the early stages of what would become a devoted life to justice and human rights issues – that I join one of her classes and take a Political Science grade about Brazil and India – a political, economic and social comparative study on the two promising developing countries (actually, at that time they were still called Third World countries...) The class itself had an intriguing theme.

The boiling frog fable is a good analogy to describe my own ignorance about the country I was raised in. The premise is that if a frog is put suddenly into boiling water, it will jump out, but if the frog is put into tepid water which is then brought to a boil slowly, it will not perceive the danger and will be cooked to death. The story is often used as a metaphor for the inability or unwillingness of people to react to or be aware of sinister threats that arise gradually rather than suddenly. It is said that while some 19th century experiments suggested that the underlying premise is true if the heating is sufficiently gradual, according to contemporary biologists the premise is false: a frog that is gradually heated will jump out.

Whether or not fully aware of the social disparities of my upbringing, now I was exposed to a study that suggests, among multiple other considerations, that both countries face a similar problem translated into what is known as 'castes systems.' Mind boggling to me. While India's caste system is a social structure that divides different groups into ranked categories – where members of "higher" castes have a greater social status than individuals of a "lower" caste, the Brazilian caste system is camouflaged and rarely admitted by its individuals. The reality is that economics creates the primary caste system. When we hear of a caste system we think of India, a strict hierarchy that does not mix, with jobs expected to be done by specific castes; It is not exactly the same reality in Brazil. But it's true that the upper class is predominantly white, as well as the upper middle class. From this perspective, I could see the potential for the gap between classes as well as economic inequality being widened if the issues were not properly dealt with by current and future generations.

Affirmative action is relatively recent in Brazil and it started to show its impact on social class only in the last two decades or so, with all the political consequences and distortions which polarize society. Yet, black and brown people are mostly low middle class and poor; though there are whites in that condition also, inequality is high enough for poverty to strike all colors of skin. The public educational system is not good enough to offer the opportunity of education needed for well payed jobs. Governments, although they seem to try, traditionally do not have people's genuine wellbeing at heart. Political corruption and indifference is usually the norm, sadly, to this day, with the possibility for change.

## BEING THERE

In March, 1980, I attended the *premiere* of *Being There* at the Landmark's California Therater, in Berkeley. In it, "Middle-aged and simple-minded Chance lives in the townhouse of an old, wealthy man in Washington, D.C. He has spent his whole life tending the garden and has never left the property. Other than gardening, his knowledge is derived entirely from what he sees on television. When his benefactor dies, Chance naively tells the lawyers that he has no claim against the estate and is ordered to move out.

"Chance wanders aimlessly, discovering the outside world for the first time. Passing by a TV shop, he sees himself captured by a camera in the shop window. Entranced, he steps backward off the sidewalk and is struck by a chauffeured car owned by Ben Rand, an elderly business mogul. In the car is Rand's much younger wife, Eve, who mishears "Chance, the gardener," in reply to the question who he is, as "Chauncey Gardiner."

"Eve brings Chance to their home to recover. He is wearing expensive tailored clothes from the 1920s and '30s, which his benefactor had allowed him to take from the attic, and his manners are old-fashioned and courtly. When Ben Rand meets him, he takes "Chauncey" for an upper-class, highly educated businessman who has fallen on hard times. Rand admires him, finding him direct, wise and insightful.

"Rand is also a confidant and adviser to the President of the United States, whom he introduces to "Chauncey." In a discussion about the economy, Chance takes his cue from the words "stimulate growth" and talks about the changing seasons of the garden. The President misinterprets this as optimistic political advice and quotes "Chauncey Gardiner" in a speech. Chance now rises to national public prominence, attends important dinners, develops a close connection with the Soviet ambassador and appears on a television talk show. During the latter, Chance goes into detail about what a serious gardener should do and is misunderstood as giving his opinion about what would be his presidential policy, given the chance.

"Though he has now risen to the top of Washington society, the Secret Service and some 16 other agencies are unable to find any background information about him. During this time Rand's physician, Dr. Allenby, becomes increasingly suspicious that Chance is not a wise political expert and that the mystery of his identity may have a more mundane explanation. Dr. Allenby considers confiding this to Rand but, realizing how happy Chance is making him during his final days, he decides not to.

"The dying Rand encourages Eve to become close to "Chauncey." She is already attracted to him and makes a sexual advance. Chance has no interest in or knowledge of sex, but mimics a kissing scene from the 1968 film *The Thomas Crown Affair*, which happens to be on the TV. When the scene ends, Chauncey stops suddenly and Eve is confused. She asks what he likes, meaning sexually; he replies "I like to watch," meaning television. She is momentarily taken aback, but decides she is willing to masturbate for his voyeuristic pleasure, thereby not noticing that he has turned back to the TV and is now imitating a yoga exercise on a different channel.

"Chance is present at Rand's death and shows genuine sadness at his passing. Questioned by Dr Allenby, he admits that he "loves Eve very much." and also that he is just a gardener. When he leaves to inform Eve of Ben's death, Allenby says to himself,

"I understand," but it is left to the viewer to work out exactly what that means.

"At Rand's funeral, while the President delivers a speech, the pall-bearers hold a whispered discussion over potential replacements for the President in the next term of office and unanimously agree on Chauncey Gardiner as successor. Oblivious to all this, Chance wanders off through Rand's wintry estate. He straightens out a pine sapling flattened by a fallen branch and then walks off across the surface of a lake. He pauses, dips his umbrella deep into the water under his feet (confirming for the viewer that it is not just a skim of water on the ground), then continues on, while the President is heard quoting Rand: "Life is a state of mind."

I stand up along with the audience to enthusiastically applaud what would be one of Peter Sellers' last movies. Gone too soon a few months later, to me this one's his best. The innocence and mystique of the main character is showered by an outstanding soundtrack, with original music by Johnny Mandel and the major *Gnossiennes* No. 4 and No. 6 by Erik Satie. And, also, the exquisite jazz/funk arrangement by Eumir Deodato of the open fanfare from *Also Sprach Zarathustra*, by Richard Strauss. 'Being There' is a majestic example of the unintended. Low-keyed black humor, it is full of witty comments on American life in the television age. It had a great effect on me exactly for the wrong reasons. Who exactly Chance represents, I ask myself? A bit of a blessed dupe, one who knows nothing and, yet, knows it all. A resemblance of each one of us as individuals when facing our inner wisdom; itself, almost never achievable since oblivion surpasses our conscious minds. Film critic Roger Ebert writes, "The movie presents us with an image, and while you may discuss the meaning of the image, it is not permitted to devise explanations for it."

## PLASMA AND EMERALDS

Washing hundreds of plastic bottles, containers designated

to cultivate mushrooms, for $0.10/ea. over weekends at the Shitake Factory in Oakland where Bob was the General Manager, wasn't exactly destined to last. It did help me build the character I needed to put in motion the path that was ahead of me. It wasn't fully clear yet, but somehow I could sense what was taking form and in a latent state. Combined with the twice a week plasma donation and the sale of a few of the least expensive stones, I took opportunities to make a few bucks at the I-House playing and singing – solo and along with Marco Katz – the great tunes of songwriters we so much enjoyed performing – Cat Stevens, Carole King, Simon & Garfunkel, James Taylor, Joni Mitchell, Crosby Stills, Nash & Young, Stevie Wonder, Elton John, The Beatles and others, while carrying over my roots and performing Tom Jobim, Dorival and Dori Caymmi, Milton Nascimento, Luis Bonfá, Baden Powell, Chico Buarque, Caetano Veloso, João Bosco, Toquinho, Ivan Lins and other great songwriters from Brazil, the country I now found myself more distant from but yet strongly connected to. It could not be different.

American self-made multi-millionaire and philanthropist Percy Ross once said "You've got to ask! Asking is in my opinion the world's most powerful – and neglected – secret to success and happiness." Scheduled for another session of plasma donation, it crossed my mind during the transfusion to offer the director of the Plasma Center the two more valuable stones, the emeralds, I still had put away and waiting to be commercialized. After an arduous period of months without succeeding to market them through acquaintances and other professionals in the business, here I went again. To my surprise, this lady is eagerly open to looking at the gems. I finished up the session, hop into my 1970 green Skylark Buick I had purchased for $500 and drove over home to pick them up. As I grabbed the stones, my recently installed brown phone rings: a position is open for a dishwasher at my favorite restaurant in downtown Berkeley. The manager wanted to see me. Soon. The Good Earth had the best selection of salads, omelets and healthy choices in town, only behind, of course, Alice Water's acclaimed flagship Chez Panisse. I set up the time for late afternoon. In the meantime, I drove back to the Plasma Center and anxiously waited for the director to see me. In my mind, this could truly be a turnaround opportunity. She showed up. I opened the white paper-cotton packaging and showed her the deep green emeralds. Known as "the stones that nurture the heart," it is believed that "its soothing energy provides healing to all levels of the being, bringing freshness and vitality to the spirit. Also perceived as a stone of inspiration and infinite patience, embodying unity, compassion and unconditional love." She looked at them, her eyes glowed enthusiastically. And, she sighed. "Oh my God, I love them!"

# 3
# Staying or Not Staying?

*"Thinking he is quite alone, he enters the room as if it were his own, but ripples on the sweet pink water reveal some company unthought of."*
*The Lamia* – P. Gabriel / M. Rutherford/P. Collins/S. Hackett/
T. Banks

THE NEWLY ACQUIRED DENIM SHIRT I had bought from an overstuffed used clothes store on Shattuck Avenue has the right sleeve dripping in blood. Pretty messy, this was due to a sloppy bandage from what became the last plasma donation in my life. All of a sudden, now I had in my bank account the equivalent of the round-trip ticket I had purchased back home to fly for almost half of the Americas for an entire year! Besides, I took the position of dishwasher at The Good Earth. Not a glamorous job, nor did I care. My goal was to stay healthy and eat well and, if possible, without having to spend too much. The 200-seat popular café, originally founded in Reno, Nevada, by William and Nancy Galt, offered a great menu and, to my amazement, free food for its entire 90-employee staff during its multiple work shifts. With most of the franchised restaurants located throughout California, during the period of its operations, the Good Earth was "probably the most prominent chain example of a health-food concept" in the 1970s, according to industry trade journal *Nation's Restaurant News*. It was purchased by General Mills in 1980. Taking advantage of my student visa which allowed me to a certain extent to be a legal worker, the hourly pay was nothing special but a few percentage points above the minimum wage of $3.10/hr. But I would put long hours and would get paid overtime, which became an incentive to work more hours and possibly save some money for a larger project. In my mind, my experience began to evolve: I was still meeting great people at school and at work and broadening my view toward what would become a new focus of this journey.

A pleasant and unexpected surprise came about when Françoise, Monica and other friends offered me as a birthday present a long weekend paid trip to Yosemite Park with a group of U.C. Berkeley students. I couldn't refuse it. My passion for visiting National Parks had just started. A good size group of international students from countries as diverse as Algeria, France, Egypt, Italy, Chile, Brazil, Greece, Iran, Monaco, Lebanon, Belgium, and of course the US among others, took off to what became an indelible visit to the California's Sierra Nevada mountains. Yosemite is famed for its giant, ancient sequoia trees, deep valleys and magnificent waterfalls. Not to mention the Half Dome, a natural wonder. Thanks to John Muir, "John of the Mountains" and "Father of the National Parks," the influential naturalist from Scotland, author, environmental philosopher, glaciologist, and early advocate for the preservation of wilderness in the US, which in 1868 set eyes on the Valley stating: "No temple made with hands can compare with Yosemite."

After a few months figuring out what to make out of this project, that trip to Yosemite reminded me of the myriad of possibilities of traveling. To which a couple of weeks later catapulted part of this small group of friends to broaden the spectrum:

a new journey to Vancouver, Canada.

The van had been rented, the itinerary had been laid out, each one would share the overall travel cost. The upside was that the vehicle was comfortable enough to get the six of us – Thiago, a Brazilian Phd. student, Marie, a Parisian and Thierry from Gent, Belgium plus Françoise, Monica and myself. The downside was there was only one tent to accommodate three people and therefore, the other three would sleep in the van. Northbound, the days are sunny and pleasant. The nights were chilly for my standards even in the month of May where in California, Oregon and Washington the Spring should have been well under way. Setting apart each other's idiosyncrasies – *Tu est incorrigible!*, the trip was a collection of great and lousy laughs alternated by more than frequent stops to photograph the stunning West Coast. We'd photograph every worthy scenario. *"Un photo, arrêt!"* Designed to be run through to Vancouver via the back roads by the ocean shore, the trip elapses without any major incidents. A significant highlighting experience was Crater Lake, in Oregon. The mountains still covered in snow, the lake with its deep blue color water partly fills a deep caldera formed thousands of years ago by the collapse of the volcano Mount Mazama. No rivers flow into or out of the lake, the deepest in the country – incredible 1,949 feet (594 meters).

As we dug into what our short passage allows us to learn about the traditions of the local inhabitants, we got a glimpse of the past: "The Klamath tribe of Native Americans, whose oral history describes their ancestors witnessing the collapse of Mount Mazama and the formation of Crater Lake, regard the lake as "an abode to the Great Spirit." Of sacred significance, Klamath oral history tells of a battle between sky god Skell and the god of the underworld Llao. Mount Mazama was destroyed in the battle, creating Crater Lake. The Klamath people used Crater Lake in vision quests, which often involved climbing the caldera walls and other dangerous tasks. Those who were successful in such quests were often regarded as having more spiritual powers. The tribe still holds Crater Lake in high regard as a spiritual site."(2)

Without warning, the first several days of our trip with no occurrences, other than the group itself trying to get the most out of the journey, gave way on a massive, monumental scale. After visiting Vancouver, Canada, we begin our trip back to Berkeley, at this time not via the back roads but through Interstate 5. Speed and time are now the factors to be managed. The day was May 18th, a day after we crossed the border from Washington into Oregon State. The morning was cool and crisp. We walked into a café on the side of the road for breakfast. On a stand at the café's entrance door, we spotted in capital letters the first page of the local newspaper: it is breaking news revealing what would become the deadliest and most economically destructive volcanic event in the history of the United States. *Louwala-Clough,* or Mount St. Helens – which we drove by and extensively photographed the day before, hours actually – became notorious for its major 1980 eruption where fifty-seven people were killed; hundreds of homes, bridges, many miles of railways, and a couple hundred miles of highway were destroyed. It was the largest known debris avalanche in recorded history. "The collapse of the northern flank of St. Helens mixed with ice, snow, and water to create volcanic mudflows. For more than nine hours, vigorous ash erupted reaching 12 to 16 miles above sea level. In total, Mount St. Helens released 24 megatons of thermal energy, 7 of which were a direct result of the blast. This is equivalent to 1,600 times the size of the atomic bomb dropped on Hiroshima." A daunting day in the life.

## THE GOOD EARTH

At the I-House, I would frequently gather with Marco Katz to play at small venues after school and sometimes during evening cultural events. Marco had just composed a song we would perform at the dancing/gym room, "Space Invaders" – "... they're flying to Earth, they're coming to look at the color of the skies..." He must have smoked a joint when he wrote it, some would argue... By then, as our Argentinian friend Alejandra Cisneros would put it, I had become 'an honorary member' of the place. We had so much fun.

At The Good Earth, the work in the dishwashing room and kitchen area was heavy and mostly suitable for young men and women. Fast paced, I would easily put 10-12 hours a day on what seems to be the proper way to keep my project alive: saving, eating good food and meeting interesting people. In his book *Down and Out in Paris and London*, George Orwell portrays his experience working as a dishwasher in a French hotel in 1929. Basically, he describes the job, the interactions with other employees, and his thoughts on the place of a *plongeur* in society. From my perspective, I took the opportunity to dive into the culture, practice my language, do some work out and get to know the lingo of multiple work environments within the business. Kitchen, dining room, supplies, receiving and management all focused in one key player: the customer. Besides, at the dishwashing room I had the freedom to do what I enjoyed doing: singing. The environment was loud enough to handle the exercise of expression without affecting the service to clients; and my co-workers did not seem to care. I must admit that at home this type of work is considered as a 'second class job' or whatever that means. The fact is, in the more just society of the US of the early 80's – I know, things have changed in the past 2-3 decades – virtually every student would embrace work. To a great extent, it still remains to this day – although some of the millennials may think differently...

At work, I made friends with Craig, Layla, Mike, April and Rose. The latter was one of the four managers at the restaurant working in multiple capacities. These are people that would teach me not only how the restaurant business works but also how Berkeley is situated in terms of its relevance in Northern California. It's not by coincidence that during the 1970s and 1980s activists increased their influence in local government spheres and also saw major developments in the city's environmental and food culture. As for myself and my co-workers, we truly enjoyed going out and about the city watching open concerts at the Hearst Greek Theatre, a magnificent 8,500-seat amphitheater adjacent to the campus and operated by the UC. There I saw for the first time Chick Corea, one of the most important instrumentalists of the history of jazz. Already significantly revered, it was through this same group of people that I was introduced to the music of young Pat Metheny, who would evolve to be my favorite jazz musician of all time. Pat will be extensively mentioned on Chapter 18 as he would have an impact in my life later on.

Rose and April were keen on perceiving how engaged and at ease I was with the Bay Area, particularly the Berkeley lifestyle, and the people in general. And how I would appreciate to be a student at the University if I had an opportunity to become one. At this time, I had already been promoted to bussing tables, which significantly contributed to my savings since cash gets added to the hourly wage – and the tips were good. Craig, a veterinarian student at UC Davis living in Berkeley before going back to school, volunteers to host an internship colleague from Dow in São Paulo, Fernando Paolone. This really makes me feel a part of a special community, be it at the I-House with unique international friends as well as with the locals. Quite a change from home. Two months on the job, I began to have the impression that I could broaden the perspective. It was at this moment in time that I had the offer from Rose which would spin my head toward accelerating a decision that was in the works and waiting to be embraced.

## LET'S GO!

Bob Liu had already been married twice when I met him for the first time. My sister Liliana and her husband, Marcos Scheliga, both living and going to school in St. Cloud, Minnesota at that time, introduced me to Bob. Born in Hong Kong, Bob Liu had lived in São Paulo for several years and studied at the Graded School, an English speaking school system which would typically be the harbor for families with children of expatriates like my manager at Dow, Tom Betts. There, expats would take their children for the duration of one's tenure at a given organization and be able to keep the same schooling equivalence without compromising their grades once back in the homeland. Bob Liu and I would have long discussions after work and through the night about everything: politics, business, sports, art and music in general, and travel. Of course, always accompanied with pots of coffee and tobacco at the overnight cafés to keep us awake. A heavy smoker, Bob was street-smart and savvy. A few years older than I, he was an autodidact: an accomplished chef, restaurant and manufacturing manager, skilled in the trades, his knowledge and opinions about the world in general impressed me from day one. A big heart, Bob Liu was nostalgic about his years in Brazil and the friends he left behind. Moreover, practicing his Portuguese, I would imagine – he had also been my brother-in-law's roommate – was desirable and vital for his maintaining of the language alive.

In music, a transition is a passage of music composed to link one section of music to another. Therefore, it can be said that transitions often function as moments of transformation. Throughout our lifetime, noticeably or not, the analogy can be drawn, as depicted by Lievegoed: "At 21, the individual has reached adulthood and is responsible for his own actions. This long-standing legal position is the concrete result of a judgment about responsibility which is itself founded in the pre-scientific knowledge. And although the moment is not really a moment at all, but a process of transition and subject to individual and political influences, it is nevertheless well chosen as a fixation point, both biologically and psychologically. In dividing life into phases we run up against a problem: it is not possible to determine a *moment* of transition from one phase to the next. As has been remarked elsewhere, it is like the change from day into night. Adolescence slides gradually into adulthood until the characteristics of the latter predominate. Inwardly, the beginning of adulthood is experienced in a positive sense; after the doubts and transience of adolescence the individual begins to be able to see something of the future. There is a powerful vital drive towards expansion in many directions. The foundation of the person's own living unit in the beginning of a career are the two most important aspects for the man. For the woman, it is the acquisition of a responsibility for shaping an environment which is usually most important. Where this moment is postponed because of external circumstances, it is felt inwardly to be a deprivation, and is repressed. But in each instance, creativity of no mean proportions has to be developed." *Lievegoed, Phases, Early Adulthood – The Twenties*

Whether or not I was fully aware of the phase I was going through, my instinct drove me to look into options. And that particular moment pushed me to make an important decision that may define the years to come in more definitive ways. Through Bob Liu, I learned that a common practice among young aspiring immigrants of the 70s and 80s, – until the US government deepened cracking down on it in the next decade – marrying nationals was an easy route for citizenship. That would take shape in multiple ways. Other than the mutual love and agreement type of union, one of the ways to obtaining citizenship would be to exchange cash for a legal marriage. "Have you thought about it?" Bob asked. As much as the idea of having the choice to get a permanent work visa and, more remotely, to become a U.S. citizen, appealed to me, paying for such an enterprise was not something I would consider. Notwithstanding, a similar and out of the blue situation came about to rock my boat: one fine afternoon at a walk at Crescent Park at the UC, when contemplating the subject of remaining in Berkeley for a longer period of time to my friends Rose and April, Rose simply stated: "If this is something that would allow you to fulfill your dream of having the choice to become a citizen, I could marry you." Pause. More pause. "Seriously?" I replied.

Of course, that came as a shock: not necessarily Rose's offer – she, like the other co-workers, were special friends and meant well. The dilemma had sunk in as nothing but a great opportunity. But...is that what I wanted to do? To leave everything behind at home – college, career, family and friends - and grasp that chance? Then what?

A couple of experiences with earthquakes considered to be minor – 3.4 and 5 on the Richter scale – would not deter me unless I really had my mind set up for a greater project. Harvard Student Agencies' Student Travel Guide's Series book, *Let's Go: Europe* had fallen on my lap days before Rose's gracious willingness to help me redirect my life in the San Francisco Bay Area. A compendium of precious information to facilitate one's incursion into the Old World put together in an objective, practical and informative way, the book was – and still is – a jewel for backpackers and travelers in general. "The Bible of the budget traveler" or "The granddaddy of budget guides," this was the book of the day for planning short and/or long traveling periods. Today the series added digital coverage in much more and sophisticated detail, country by country, whereas at that time there was one single heavy book which encompassed all Western Europe, some of the Eastern European countries, plus Israel and Egypt.

The world in 1980 had a complex geo-political structure. At the peak of the Cold War, events such as U.S. President Jimmy Carter signing a bill requiring 19-and-20-year-old males to register for a peacetime military draft in response to the Soviet invasion of Afghanistan took place that year. Another relevant event, followed by the Shah of Iran escaping in exile the year before, this same country saw the return of Ayatollah Khomeini to a greeting by several million Iranians. Some of my acquaintances and new friends from Iran, like Ateshé Firouz, a smart and bright young lady, would see the transformation of her country before her eyes in the next six months. As for myself, not quite used or exposed to an international scenario back home except via studies at school, newspapers and television, the inner calling to cross borders was much stronger than simply switching one environment to another, i.e., exchanging my roots in São Paulo to settling down in the Bay Area. Therefore, the decision became mature enough to not only be thankful and decline Rose's offer but to design the next several months' journey: Europe.

Backpack ready. Unchained. No boundaries. Open for change. Azimuth inspired. Free spirit-driven.

# 4
# Life is....

*"When you're falling awake*
*And you take stock of the new day*
*And you hear your voice croak*
*As you choke on what you need to say*
*Well, don't you fret, don't you fear*
*I will give you good cheer*
*Life's a long song*
*Life's a long song*
*Life's a long song*
*If you wait then your plate I will fill."*
*Life is a Long Song* – Ian Anderson

THE IMPORTANCE OF SOCCER in the Brazilian culture is well-known worldwide. As in North America, when compared to baseball and football, its impact goes beyond a favorite pastime but transcends it into bringing its citizens together in ways hard to imagine. For my father René, in his twenties, it was not much different. FIFA World Cup, Rio de Janeiro, Brazil x Uruguay. This was the decisive match of the final group stage played at the *Estádio do Maracanã* in the then-Brazilian capital of Rio de Janeiro on 16 July 1950. With Brazil one point ahead of Uruguay going into the match, Uruguay needed a win while Brazil needed only to avoid defeat to claim the title of world champions for the first time. Brazil took the lead shortly after half-time, only to be equalized by Uruguay midway through the half. Then the unthinkable strikes. Ghiggia, the Uruguayan-Italian right winger, scored the winning goal with 11 minutes remaining in the match, resulting in one of the biggest upsets in soccer history.

The specialized press and the general public had already started declaring Brazil the new world champions for days prior to the final match, and they had reasons to do so. Brazil had won their last two matches with a very attack-minded style of play against which all efforts had proved fruitless. Uruguay, however, had encountered difficulties in their matches with Spain and Sweden, managing only a draw against Spain and a narrow victory over Sweden. When those results were compared, it seemed that the Brazilians were set to defeat Uruguay as easily as they had dispensed with Spain and Sweden.

Twenty-two gold medals were made with each player's name imprinted on them and the mayor of Rio delivered a speech with the words: "You, players, who in less than a few hours will be hailed as champions by millions of compatriots! You, who have no rivals in the entire hemisphere! You, who will overcome any other competitor! You, who I already salute as victors!" A victory song, *"Brasil Os Vencedores"* ("Brazil The Winners"), was composed and practiced, ready to be played after the final.

Then the unthinkable. As Uruguay scored the second goal, the crowd was virtually silent until the referee signaled the end of the match with Uruguay winning 2–1. The Uruguayans had become World Champions for the second time.

René was 25 when he, along with 220,000 crestfallen fans, walked out of *Maracanã* Stadium in 1950. For years, possibly decades, my Dad and the 'country of football' were embittered by that defeat. To say that Brazilians love soccer is an understatement. Just like the Italians, the Argentinians and the British do, it is a big deal in people's lives. It was not until 1958, a couple months after my birth, that the national team would win its first World Cup, this time in Sweden, establishing itself from then on as one of the major squadrons in soccer history. As I grew up and began to understand my world, I learned that that year was a significant and happy time for my Dad: after two girls, not only a new member, a boy finally joins the crowd.

## DAD, MOM

Alice's fourth and youngest child was not even four years old when his father Elias, my grandfather, passed away peacefully on the morning fall of May, 10th 1929. The next few years would prove to be difficult for this young woman, mother of four – Lourice, Eduardo, Theodoro and Dad. Struggling to keep her children together and to survive, Alice would remarry a few years later and have two more children – Yemen and Sergio. At age 7, René began working at his already wealthy uncle's socks manufacturing unit. Inevitably, this propelled him to mature and grow up faster than other kids of his age. The tallest and physically strongest of his siblings, he at times would be intimidating and help get them out of trouble when bullied by other boys of the same age. By inheriting a sum from the sale of the family's farm at 19, he and his brother Theodoro set up a fabrics/textiles distribution business in the nervous but prosperous center of São Paulo's commercial hub. These two young men ventured their business relentlessly to safeguard them the means to support their mother and later on, to care for their own families. Both married in their mid-to-late twenties, the two brothers were close. Although not always sharing the same interests and at times differing on the method of running the business operation, they managed to develop a successful and trusting relationship. Theodoro had three boys and a girl; his brother, three girls and a boy. Sons of immigrants, both their parents and respective families had left Mount Lebanon in the

1910s running away from the domination of the Ottoman Empire which lasted until 1918, during the hardships coming from the "war to end all wars," the bloody World War I.

Guardini, in his book "*The Periods of Life*," beautifully portrays a wealth of carefully formulated human wisdom and intimate perception. "Man characterizes himself again and again, and still it is always the same man living in each phase. The person is conscious of himself and has to account for the phases in question. Each phase has its own nature, which can be deduced neither from the preceding nor from the subsequent one."

On my mother's side, my grandfather Aref had already lost a brother to one of the many regional wars when he and his remaining siblings embarked on the journey to South America. Fighting for whatever the cause of the day, with military enrollment mandatory and wars typically the usual senseless ordeal, his youngest brother left home to never come back. Between the 1910s and 1920s, a wave of immigrants fled their countries in the Middle East, particularly Lebanon, in search for the opportunities their own land had denied or could not offer them. France, United States, Canada, Mexico, Australia as well as Argentina and Brazil were major recipients for these people. Word of mouth would run around the communities and spell out the possibilities for a better life. Alexandra, my grandmother, was very young when her family left their homeland for the countryside of the promising State of São Paulo. As her family had already been back and forth, she and Alice had been born respectively in Alexandria and Cairo, Egypt. Both married Aref and Elias at a very young age, as it was a common and acceptable practice in the dawn of the 20th century. My mother, Aref's and Alexandra's second child, Jeritza, a skinny brunette young woman, grew up with her siblings – Zilah, Roosevelt, Marcilio and Gloria – in the countryside and at age 18 was already well on her way to become what she loved to do most: teaching. And what a teacher she was.

## ...LIFE IS GOOD: LOVE AND LOVED ONES

*"What do I do when my love is away? Does it worry you to be alone? How do I feel at the end of the day? Are you sad because you're on your own?"*
*With a Little Help From My Friends* – J. Lennon/P. McCartney

The first seven years of childhood are immensely important as they are seen as the foundation of every individual – "neural connections are like the roots of a tree, the foundation from which all growth occurs," says psychotherapist Hillary Jacobs Hendel. In fact, when it comes to child development, it's been said that the most crucial milestones in a kid's life occur by the age of 7. Born and raised from a balanced and loving family helped me be a secure child. Moreover, to a good extent and at their best, my family's extended family members were affectionate and cared for one another. To make things more interesting when it comes to added support in a household environment, as income and the local and national culture permitted, my immediate family was able to afford a caretaker for myself and my siblings; to which, in exchange, also allowed time for Mom to pursue her career – thanks to Rosa, an African-Brazilian woman whom I adored – loving, humble and dear – from the northeastern State of Bahia. Rosa was also our household's cook and housekeeper for the first 7 years of my life. A great influence on me for being a humane, wise and compassionate individual.

Jeritza was an elementary school teacher; having a career was not a common practice among middle-class families of that time, unless mandatory from an income standpoint. Fortunately, this not being the case, it also allowed her to pursue her artistry skills which later in life would reveal to become successful and, most importantly, provide her with an enriching sense of accomplishment.

Mom was an exceptional story teller. Her sweet voice, either when telling a tale or singing a tune, gave us a *sense of path*, described by William Bryant:

"Why are old stories so durable? What is the reason for their irrepressible vitality? First, just as it is for our children, the pictorial idiom was perfectly suited to the nonintellectual, pre-logical mind of the ancient. Second, the dramatic and emotional content easily engages the attention. Not only does the story stimulate the imagination, it also appeals to the child love of action, and provides healthy emotional exercise. Above all, it implants pictures of the track to independence.

We adults should remember that fences of skepticism and cynicism do not bar the gate to a child's soul. Picture, unlike concepts and cold, hard, indigestible facts, appeal to the child's fantasy and are therefore easily absorbed and digested. The pictures are not obliterated but percolate through layers of memory into interior life, where they become healing, integrating forces that strengthen the emerging personality."

As for Dad – "I want to be proud of you," he once said to me at an early age – his loving presence, sense of humor and easy smile coupled with a practical approach to things, hardworking attitude, wisdom and integrity were attributes visible to the eyes – his utmost second nature qualities.

A generous and magnanimous couple, hanging out with Mom and Dad meant everything to me and my sisters Silvia Regina, Liliana and Cristina. Lovers of exploring the natural beauty of the country along with a genuine curiosity for the culture, traveling was always on the family's agenda. With an astounding percentage of the Brazilian population living 2-3 hours away from the Atlantic Coast – 70%, approximately – an essential and frequent destination during school vacation, holidays and other special occasions was to spend time at the beach. By age 7, I could say that I had been exposed to some of the relevant capitals and cultural spots of the country – Rio, Minas Gerais, Salvador and Recife, among others.

The love of the outdoors once took us on a magnificent trip via "The Princesa Leopoldina." Built in 1962, at the Spanish naval shipyard of Eskalduna, Bilbao – this was known to be the first cruise ship of the famous White Swans fleet to arrive in Brazil: scheduled for about 30 days, the cruise journeyed around almost the entire coast from the southernmost port of Porto Alegre all the way up and down to the heart of the Amazon forest, Manaus, the capital of the State of Amazonas. Navigating the deep blue waters of the Atlantic Ocean was an experience in itself. However, other impressive ones were yet to come: one of them, the encounter of the Atlantic waters at the Amazon Basin. Being the most extensive river system in the world, second in length only to the Nile in Egypt, the waters of the Amazon River allow for countless sights, especially when it comes to the "Meeting of the Waters" with other river systems within and throughout the forest – to me, still vivid in my mind to this day. This is the confluence between the dark (black water) Rio Negro and the pale sandy-colored (white water) Amazon River or Rio Solimões, as the upper section of the Amazon is known in Brazil, upriver of this confluence. For 3.7 miles (6 km) the two rivers' waters run side by side without mixing. The same phenomenon occurs near Santarem, Pará, with the Amazon and Tapajós rivers. Both phenomenon take place due to differences in temperature, speed and water density between rivers. Just as memorable was the rainforest fauna with its unparalleled biodiversity. Last but not least, it is still intense in my mind the memory of the number of tribes which during our stay in the city would occasionally visit the port of Manaus and display their costumes and colorful folklore comprised of tales, traditions, characters and beliefs – an unforgettable experience.

"Childhood is a series of separations," says Bryant. "As we grow, so we gradually lose the union of self, family, and world. This is the only way we can establish a conscious and independent relationship to life. Our early appetite for life urges us to grasp the physical world with our senses. Thus, the joyful imagination of play, touching, tasting, running, speaking, and so on develops our orientation and self-mastery. Likewise, grazed knees, quarrels over toys, and disputes over bedtimes are the collisions with life that engender both a self and a social awareness."

At the dawn of the first seven-year phase, Bryant highlights that "the threshold between six and seven is marked physically by the appearance of the permanent teeth – the densest components in the human body. On the other hand, it signifies the beginning of a new phase of consciousness. According to Rudolf Steiner, the formative activity that has hitherto been involved with building the child's physical body is now partially released from this task to stimulate the development of psychological activity."

## ...LIFE IS BEAUTIFUL: HORIZONS

*"Light their way when the darkness surrounds them; Give them love, let it shine all around them. Bless the beasts and the children; Give them shelter from a storm; Keep them safe; Keep them warm."*
– Barry De Vorzon/ Perry L. Botkin

My siblings and I were raised in the symbolic neighborhood of *Ipiranga*. Our house – next door to our cousins' – was located near where Emperor Pedro I proclaimed the Brazilian independence in 1822 on the banks of the brook of the same name in the Southeast region of the city of São Paulo. There was created the *Museu do Ipiranga*, a monumental building designed to be an "eclectic-styled construction similar to the French Palace of Versailles with impressive and perfectly manicured gardens and fountain." "The 123-meter-long palace was inspired in a Renaissance palace and is considered an example of Eclectic architecture. The museum and the gardens, opened to the public several decades later on September 7th, 1895, six years after the Proclamation of the Republic." This was a frequent area in the neighborhood where my cousin Mauro and I used to visit. When not playing ball at the house, or marbles, ping-pong and *jogo de botão* (button soccer), we would ride our bicycles in and around the museum's trails and perimeter. Second-degree related, Mauro was like a brother to me since we were just about the same age: playing we did all afternoons after school and all day over the weekends as we got along pretty well. The youngest of his family, his older siblings – Sergio Elias, Sandra and Ricardo – also related well to my siblings.

At home, I must admit that I was not always a cool brother to my sisters during my childhood, especially during puberty. I would overhear the adults saying that I couldn't be around them without teasing or annoying them, especially my sister Liliana. True. Not until I learned how good they had always been to me; and how overcoming my ignorance about them as truly loving human beings became prevalent. That's when I started to really appreciate them in meaningful ways.

"Play is older than culture, for culture, however inadequately defined, always presupposes human society, and animals have not waited for man to teach them their playing."

In his 1938 book *Homo Ludens*, Dutch historian and cultural theorist Johan Huizinga discusses the importance of the play element of culture and society. Huizinga suggests that play is primary to and a necessary (though not sufficient) condition of the generation of culture. The Latin word *Ludens* is the present active participle of the verb *ludere* which itself is cognate with the noun *ludus*. Ludus has no direct equivalent in English – perhaps ludic – as it simultaneously refers to sport, play, school, and practice. The author makes clear that animals played before humans. One of the most significant aspects of play – human and cultural – is that it is fun. To which he identifies five characteristics that play must have:

> *"Play is free, it is*
> *in fact freedom*
> *Play is not "ordinary"*
> *or "real" life*
> *Play is distinct from*
> *"ordinary" life both as*
> *to locality and duration*
> *Play creates order,*
> *it is order.*
> *It demands order absolute*

*and supreme
Play is connected with no
material interest,
and no profit can be
gained from it"*

It is typical of Middle-Eastern families and their descendants to congregate in large numbers around food and laughter, where many of the multiple extended families' Sundays were spent at *Jaraguá Clube Campestre,* an outstanding country club with ample space and various scattered pools, waterfalls, small lakes and ponds; well maintained, there were playgrounds and sports courts – with soccer, basketball, volleyball for the youngsters – as well as tennis and bocce for the more seasoned members, the latter a common ancestry from ancient games played in the Roman Empire. The adults would spend time fishing and preparing for barbecuing, anticipating the late afternoons naps laid down on colorful hammocks hooked up on eucalyptus trees, followed by the dreadful playing of cards – boring, for the kids – a high point of the day for the adults, of course – canasta or *buraco,* a most preferred one. Fun on Sundays, for everyone.

Bryant brings up a glimpse of the upcoming phase: "The onset of puberty near the end of the second seven-year cycle is often marked by a loss of natural grace, laughter and openness. Young teenagers become more introverted, hidden, and isolated. Preoccupied with a startling new awareness of themselves, they can be secretive, hostile to criticism, moody, and easily embarrassed. This self-consciousness and sensitivity may well erode the communication between parent and a young person. Our teenagers feel things deeply, and it will take a while for them to become comfortable with themselves. The advent of sexuality makes them acutely aware of their own bodies, but it also signifies 'coming to ground,' the death of childhood and the birth of independence. Even as the body grows stronger, denser, heavier – more and more a prisoner of gravity – the mind is opening to the limitless universe of ideas, ideals, and meaning." This passage of Bryant's book is revealing as it relates to my own experience and to the period I was about to embark on. The shift from puberty to adolescence is like the shedding of a snake's skin. Science tells us that snakes shed their skin to allow for further growth – a snake's skin doesn't grow as the animal grows. The analogy being subtle, it's like reaching a point where further growth is not possible without the skin's replacement. The old skin giving room to the new.

## ...LIFE IS TRUTH: FIRST ENCOUNTERS

*"Was it real or did we dream. The days of children gone.*
*Seagull's scream and pink ice cream and the deep blue sky*
*And the waves seem high and golden sand and the town*
*brass band play on..." Schooldays* – Shulman, Minear, Shulman

"Freedom within this everyday world is constantly threatened by the ancient ethic 'thou shalt and thou shalt not', and by the dogmas of the 'scientifically justifiable' images of man and the world," says Lievegoed in one of his approaches to adolescence. Regardless the cultural background, with few exceptions, pressure from country and society in general – added to family, school, friends – to push the individual to make decisions which will impact his or her future starts early and occasionally carries on unpredictable consequences. Many influences are at play and, instead of offering guidance and discernment, it is the opposite that sometimes prevails.

"It takes a village," teaches the old saying. And I would add a great deal of luck, too. Whereas the two previous phases presented as opportunities to strengthen confidence and character, and therefore produce the equivalent quality of consciousness, this phase seems to put those into question as more is demanded from the individual. "In the years of adolescence everything still has a certain absoluteness, and yet at the same time a certain quality of temporariness – a remarkable and self-contradictory situation," highlights William Bryant.

School at this time played a major impact in my way of seeing, experiencing and behaving in my little world. For good or for bad. The development of adolescence in the culture I was brought up to was fast and chaotic, leading young men, especially, to risks that today's generation are more aware of or, at least, gets exposed to at a later moment: going out without parents, driving without a license and/or recklessly, drinking alcohol, experimenting drugs, dating and sex, were prevalent in the early years after puberty, in which in some cases would bring disruption and unimaginable losses to individuals and families. I can remember at least a dozen situations in which schoolmates – directly and indirectly – lost their ground, in the best of cases and, sadly in some other cases, their own lives. Stupidly. Senselessly. Fully avoidable.

While "young children experience the loss of a parent, a loved one, a friend or an acquaintance on a subliminal, organic and mostly unconscious level, adolescents feel their loss very deeply. In fact, their pain tends to swamp the self, because the emotional reactions in this period are very intense and obvious, ponders Bryant. "Young adolescents are deeply affected by grief, but their awakening thought-life struggles to come to terms with it. Young adults are also engulfed by their anguish, but their consciousness enables them to look more objectively at their own feelings and at the feeling of others. Indeed, their pain may prompt them to explore the mystery of life and death and its philosophical-religious implications."

The aforementioned is a vivid hallmark of the new period to follow. My cousin Mauro and I went to different middle school systems. Whereas his school was nearby our twin houses and he could walk home, other than occasional rides with my parents' and neighbor classmates, I would catch a bus to school, which could take a good 45 to 60-minute ride, depending on traffic. Both of us couldn't wait to get home. After school, we would play soccer at the orange dirt field located half-mile from home, by the Ipiranga Brook, or simply practice on my house's driveway and backyard, which was always available. In fact, I cannot remember a single time when we would play in his backyard. The reason was that Leonilda, an elderly maid of the family, dweller of his house's basement and backyard level, was usually in a terrible mood and would always yell at us if her territory was threatened. Of course, we would laugh at her ways, but no one dared to defy her authority leery of the repercussions.

Our older siblings were influential to us and deserved respect, especially Mauro's oldest brother, Sergio Elias. The eldest of us eight, he was a natural leader and a protector to the younger ones, in which on the other hand demanded more from him, whether he liked it or not. Eight years older than I, he was the first to go to college and away from home – a 5 ½ hour driving distance west of the big city. Inevitably, he was the role model not only for the boys – Ricardo, Mauro and myself – but the girls would see him as a reference, especially when contemplating the critical years ahead of high expectations that they would eventually experience after high-school.

Uncle Theodoro was most of the time a serious and focused individual, both at home and at work. At home, although my Dad could get a little annoyed and yell at us at times, he was much more laid-back than my uncle. We could see *Tio Jujuba*, his nickname, relax only during the weekends when pizza and tap beer were part of the Saturday night ritual along with his wife, Aunt Yacy, and other couples like Uncle Eduardo and Aunt Tica, where laughter and joy would be noticed and heard from our next door distance or at restaurants when the extended family would gather.

"As twenty-one-year-olds, they poised on the launch pad of independent life, bearing the mandate of their own responsibility. In the simplest terms, their individuality has fashioned itself a physical body and psyche that can think, feel, and act for itself. From now on, the process of growth and consciousness reversed. Up to now, most of the formative energy has poured into the unfolding of the physical body. From now on, the body will follow a hardening, devitalizing route while consciousness continually adds to itself through the pursuit of self-knowledge, experience, and the search for meaning." Bryant describes this period brilliantly and I can't think of a better way to see cousin Sergio Elias entering his fourth and last seventh formative year in transition to adulthood.

The day precedes the beginning of *Carnaval* and the preparations for the Brazilian annual festival held between the Friday afternoon before Ash Wednesday and Ash Wednesday at noon, which marks the period of Lent, the forty-day period before Easter. For Sergio Elias, the first and second year of School of Engineering had not been easy and this particular period required him to utilize the holidays in order to catch up and dedicate time to prepare for exams. *Tio Jujuba* had been clear that he needed to improve his grades. Still left for fun was Friday night prior to diving through studying in the next few days to make up for the momentary low marks. Moreover, *Tia Yacy* had been a victim of a car accident a couple of weeks earlier, which forced her to immobilize her neck for several days, therefore influencing Sergio Elias to stick around at home.

Saturday morning was supposed to be a normal play day for me if it weren't for the holidays. Unusually, I woke up earlier this day. Opening my bedroom window, I noticed that it had rained overnight and the ground was still quite wet, hence I would have to push back my plans to play soccer with my cousin for some time later on. I walked down the stairs quietly and perceived that the adults were already in the living room. Unusually silent. As I got closer, I looked at my Dad, thoughtfully seated in the brown velvet chair, in a way I had never seen him before: tension in the air, worried but collected, he seemed very perturbed with the news he had heard overnight. My cousin Sergio Elias, along with friends, had been involved in a horrific car accident. One of his friends had been killed instantly and he himself had been gravely hurt. His life was critically in danger.

The hours that followed were a mix of deep apprehension, sorrow and hope. A sentiment of impotence on every adult's semblance was evidence of the crucial state my cousin found himself in the hospital as he fought for his life. For us teens and younger, we could sense the torpor and trance the adults were going through, which inevitably contributed to our own. The same large number of family members that typically gathered at the country club or at grandma's home around fun, food, joy and laughter over the weekends, now came and went between the two houses facing that harsh reality in a bitterly and emotional state never experienced before. Literally, unchartered territory for all. As the hours went by, I could sense restlessness and desperation. My cousin Sandra, Sergio Elias' sister, was an exception: surprisingly calm and aware of the somber picture, she seemed to bring serenity to the youngsters, which did not go unnoticed. Sitting at the living room floor in a circle, some of us gathered around her. She looked up some of my cousin's notes she had found on his bed and tried to make sense of what she was reading. The writings could be related to past hours, possibly days or even months. As if looking for a connection that could spell some type of early warning, someone, or yet his own reflective thoughts about his present moment. Almost whispering, she paused and shared a devastating writing from his notebook: "I have dreamed I was getting drowned in my own blood."

## ESCAPE VALVE DIARY

*"Grief is not a disorder, a disease or a sign of weakness. It is an emotional, physical and spiritual necessity, the price you pay for love. The only cure for grief is to grieve."* – Earl Grollman

Far from being a diary, I unpretentiously started to jot down notes on an old notebook as several months had been gone by since my cousin's passing. Being one of the oldest boys in the extended family, his legacy left indelible marks, almost as if he had to live and leave his short existence to teach us about the impermanence of things. Family gatherings continued to take place but they were never the same. A dividing line had been drawn between one phase and another. Now at 14, this period was marked by a series of challenges: some of the neighbors also experienced losses; at school, things got interesting as I turned to look at my existence from a different perspective: more introspective, I would hook up with schoolmates that would have more in common. Less concerned with performing good grades, it was music, literature and mingling in general that became more valuable than school demands. Unfortunately, something had to give: at the end of the school year, I failed for the first time. And last. Preceding the outcome, I got caught cheating – through the classroom window and at my request, my buddy classmate Carlos Van Hartog tried to pass me some of the test results - which cost me not only the school year but forced me to leave the school and the classmates I so much enjoyed. It happened at the end of 8th grade, at a final Biology exam; Prof. Morivaldo Krambeck Jr., one of the directors at *Colégio Bandeirantes* and also a superb History teacher, knowing what I had done and that I was having trouble with my grades, suggested I looked into another school. That sank like a bombshell inside me. On top of having a tough year, now I was being invited to withdraw from my school. A disaster. My parents, perceiving the big picture, were supportive and without hesitation helped me look at that moment with some perspective. Yet, not only I admired the professor for his intelligence and vision – every classmate did – but there was more to it: his wife, *Dona Elza*, had been my first and preferred English teacher. At last, his son Rui Fausto was one of my closest classmates – we both loved the same music! Tough luck. I was the only person responsible for that mess. Period.

> *"As the verses unfold*
> *and your soul suffers the long day*
> *And the twelve o'clock gloom*
> *Spins the room, you struggle on your way*
> *Well, don't you sigh, don't you cry*
> *Lick the dust from your eye*
> *Life's a long song*

*Life's a long song*
*Life's a long song*
*We will meet in the sweet light of dawn"*
*Life is a Long Song - 2nd Verse* – Ian Anderson

My cousin Mauro and I grew closer than ever. We continued playing soccer and now added basketball to our practices, mostly influenced by his absent older brother, a talent on the sport. He too failed that year at school as the impact of the loss on him had been obviously magnified. Shattered and picking up the pieces, the twin family next door would struggle to heal for years. I wonder for how long. Now at the same school, we both took the bus or got our parents' rides alternatively. A lot less liberal than the other schools, particularly mine, *Anglo Latino* was a lot more structured and regimented environment. Influenced by the moment when the dictatorship in the country had its strongest grip, school management implemented an almost segregating frame to its modus operandi: although both genders attended classes together, e.g., the stairs that gave access to the playground facilities, as well as the playgrounds themselves, had boys and girls separated. Also, at a time where boys had long hair, the school enforced the use of caps, a laughable and ridiculous mandatory requirement; justified by 'hygiene purposes.' But what struck us the most was the tone used from management on how to impose order. Those were challenging times for the country. A 1970 article of the New York Times properly depicted the moment:

"The military leaders of Brazil, soon to begin their seventh year in power, have slowly changed their role from that of temporary caretakers to stern tutors, with a vision of a disciplined Brazil on her way to becoming an industrial power on the world scene. Since March 31, 1964, the armed forces have put together a regime that maintains, except in periods of political stress, the appearance of an elected Congress. But their domination of almost any phase of national life they choose to control is virtually unchallenged and they have shown that they will not tolerate serious opposition or open defiance."

From a society's perspective, what households and civil institutions wanted was simple: freedom to work and create work, liberty to raise their families and to function decently. Some would argue that the regime, initially supported by a majority of its citizens, had achieved some of their goals; however, at a cost, like everything. As a result, they muzzled their citizens, an entire generation being part of this process.

René and his brother, rarely opinionated about politics, were strongly connected as business partners and would take initiatives and at times embark on almost identical projects. Like the houses purchased at the foundation of their families, it was time for us to move out to a different neighborhood. Logistically more convenient, for work and school, they both purchased two units in an apartment building that took much longer for completion than expected. Finally, leaving the twin houses seemed to be a breath of fresh air – all children had practically been born and raised there. Moving to an apartment had also the purpose of making things more simple, especially in a city prevalent of hi-risers and safety starting to become an issue in many parts of the metropolis.

"I MAY MAKE YOU FEEL BUT I CAN'T
MAKE YOU THINK."
*Thick as a Brick* – Jethro Tull

Every now and then I would be asked by Dad to come help at the store. And I would try to do it most of the time. But sometimes, reluctantly, for what I really wanted to do was to spend my time after school listening and researching new tunes, and refining my guitar playing. In the new home, I truly developed the taste for music, especially for the British prog-rock bands of the day and some of the American as well. An addition to and yet departure from The Beatles and The Rolling Stones, the new bands of the late 60s were now solidly putting a stamp in the history of progressive rock. There will be more references to bands and songwriters at a later chapter but, suffice to say, music helped me acquire the taste for learning the English language in a singular way.

As a way to validate that, much of the influence my household had experienced two years earlier came from hosting a caring and intelligent international exchange student from Scranton, PA. Barbara Ann O'Gorman arrived a little after our extended family's ordeal following my cousin's passing. A project previously planned, I like to think that hosting Barbara worked positively for both herself as a visitor as well as to our family: it encouraged connection in our home and broadened everyone's horizons allowing us to embrace new perspectives. My sisters Silvia Regina and Liliana were excited to receive Barbara for that represented the sharing of our own culture and the chance for her to grasp, and possibly learn, our own language. As a consequence, our daily routine livened up and a more spontaneous effort to develop better understanding among our family members took place. Not to mention, a true exposure to the English language and, to some extent, indirectly to a different culture.

Liliana had already been scheduled for the same Rotary Exchange Student Program the following year, pending confirmation as to where she would be going to. It could literally be any country where English was the first language, such as the UK, Canada, Australia and, of course, the US. As for my little sister, Cristina, still young, she would also ride the same wave. Barbara's first few days were shocking for her. Stranger to the culture, Barbara had never been away from home before. Spending her very first day hiding in bed and trying to figure out the new environment, I could sense that smells, noises, colors, textures and especially people and food would play a challenging adjustment for her. I can still remember as if it were today: among the presents she brought to our household was the newly released album from this whimsical and yet not well known band for us: Jethro Tull – the album, *Thick as a Brick*. Exquisite music. None of us had any idea of its existence and how it would influence our perception of music, especially myself. Another album she brought with her was Alice Cooper's *School's Out*. A lot less subtle, that album would also be influential. Both would open the doors for new winds of musical possibilities.

Barbara was only 17 and her experience in Brazil must have been transformative, both culturally and personally. Along with my Mom and Dad's support, our family tried to provide her with a meaningful travel experience as well as the program itself encompassed multiple interstate excursions along with other exchange students around the country. Also, Barbara truly dedicated time to learn Portuguese and did an excellent job at it. Her program, however, scheduled to last for a year, got cut short by her own decision to go back home, after a little more than six months. She truly missed her family and her boyfriend, Tom. Barbara's experience seemed to have been a rich one, as I could attest to many years later. While gathering my family with Barbara and Tom Kelleher, the same Tom she left Brazil for a few decades earlier, in Philadelphia in 2006 and once again in New York City in 2010, when Liliana, Marco Chiusano and their son René visited us, we had such a wonderful time cherishing great photos, letters and memories. Back then, one of Barbara's last moments at the airport when catching her flight back home had a picturesque and a literally fun story, unthinkable in today's world of all kinds of safety rules and regulations. My American sister's love for tropical fruits pushed her to dare loading a large bag of mangoes into her baggage and try to pass it through security. With all of us cheering for her to succeed, we learned a few days later that Barbara successfully managed to bring the mangoes she so relished – safe and sound – back home.

## CHALLENGES ABOUND

*"As the Baker Street train spills your pain*
*All over your new dress*
*And the symphony sounds*

> *underground puts you under duress*
> *Well, don't you squeal as the heel*
> *Grinds you under the wheels*
> *Life's a long song*
> *Life's a long song*
> *Life's a long song*
> *But the tune ends too soon for us all…"*
> Life is a Long Song - 3rd Verse – Ian Anderson

"...We may see that the central problem of adolescence is: *Who am I? What do I want? What am I capable of?* The individual who has failed to ask these questions in this phase of life – even if only by realizing that he suffers from not knowing the answers – has failed to lay the foundations for the awakening of his psychological being, so that he runs the risk in the important middle phase of life of finding himself stuck at the passionately final stage, an eternal adolescent who in his appreciation of values remains dependent on what the world thinks of him, or who, on account of his own insecurity, continues to kick against the world."

In an effort to contextualize the words behind the aforementioned thought, I must admit that "failing to ask these questions in this phase of life" sounds like a strong statement. It implies rather negative connotations such as to weaken, to fall short and to be unsuccessful. From Lievegoed's perspective, and he is not shy about pointing this out, the individual must go through the process of questioning one's own existence rather earlier in order to liberate oneself from the ties which may later in life define one's own vision of and positioning in the world – and possibly release oneself from the chains of one's own limitations. Adolescence does play a key role and I describe my experience of what I understand the author tries to convey in more detail on what I call "Mirrors and the Present," in chapter 19. As much a monolithic statement as it may seem, he suggests no complacency and, in my opinion, implies that distractions get in the way of self-knowledge and self-discovery. Yet, in my view, there's no failing in this process but rather a sequence of experiences and events that may – or may not – lead to "laying the foundations of one's psychological being." Besides, can we measure consciousness? Or, put an age on one's conscience? There's always time to learn and introject experiences. And the process only ceases to exist once we are no longer here. That too may be questionable...

Now in the new neighborhood, the opportunities for developing new friends became broader. By contrast, at the new home, my parents oscillated from the excitement of moving to a newly large and fresh space to a worrisome experience they had to endure which would mark them for a period of time. My older sister, Silvia Regina, was herself on a quest for finding meaning and purpose for her life. It always seems that the oldest child has a difficult task. In his book *Brothers and Sisters: A Study in Child Psychology*, Karl Konig brings an interesting perspective around and within the family constellation:

"In ancient times, the first-born child was outstanding among other children. And still today the first-born son or daughter is of special value to the parents. The first child has a unique position in life and in the family. The more brothers and sisters that are born, the more obvious the position becomes; they have a link between the parents on the one hand, and his brothers and sisters on the other. A link, however, can be a bridge or it can be a barrier; like a gate that is either shut or open. These are the two characteristics of a first child. They can either bar the way or bridge the past and the future. They have two faces – one is turned to the parents who represent the past, the other looks on to the brothers and sisters, thereby gazing into the future. The position of the first child has a most important function in the whole flow of the river of life."

On her quest for self-discovery, my sister was not necessarily interested in my parents' achievement but rather in finding her 'leitmotif.' "She's leaving home," by The Beatles's finest album *Sgt. Peppers Lonely Hearts Club Band*, would be a good song and lyrics' association to reflect what she was going through. Life in the big city seemed at first to be the reason for her fleeing to the countryside in search for a more natural way of living in connection with her inner self. In exchange, my parents, especially Dad, were most concerned about her whereabouts and how she would do having left home for the first time. And possibly without a clear plan. This was one of the few times I saw him dropping tears of distress and fear for her safeness. Her experience lasted a couple of months until a cousin from out of state, Beto Pietruza, Dad's sister Yemen's oldest son, graciously traveled a thousand kilometers determined to convince Silvia Regina that she didn't belong to where she was. Busy with making friends and adapting to the new neighborhood, I never quite knew in detail what they all went through. But I could read my parents' moods, and their bodies' and faces' languages. Only to show relief by having her back. Safe and sound. A few years later, her influence on myself and on my other siblings would be remarkable as she clearly led a path for investigative research, especially toward a more philosophical examination.

My new friend, Celso, lived in the apartment building next door and, once again, music was the bond that kept on giving. Always exploring new sounds, we had fun together and along with other neighbors. For my birthday, my Dad had agreed to help me acquire this sculptural *Del Vecchio* 12-string guitar I had been flirting with getting it for about a year, as long as I took care of my grades at school. I could do that. Celso and I would spend time on tape recordings and also uncovering new released albums during the decade where the prog-rock was at its excellence and topped the record charts. Great quality bands such as Pink Floyd, King Crimson, Rush, Yes, Genesis, Emerson Lake & Palmer, Gentle Giant all had their peak at that time.

We also liked the outdoors and did go camping several times. *Campos do Jordão*, located in the State of São Paulo's *Serra da Mantiqueira* was one of our preferred towns as it offered hiking, mountain climbing, horseback riding at any time of the year. A unique place to experience the native Brazilian Paraná Pine, the *Araucária*, and home of unique panoramic views, *Man-*

*tiqueira* hosted part of the Atlantic Forest habitat. The high season was at its best during wintertime where the area would see an enormous influx of visitors, due in part to the winter festival of classical music. On that particular season we arrived for a 10-day stay at the end of winter when most of the crowd had already been gone. Therefore, the camp site had about a dozen or so tents scattered throughout a large area. With the 12-string guitar at hand, it was quite easy to meet people as we would stay by the outdoor fireplace until late hours singing and enjoying likeminded people's companies. Cold for Brazilian standards, almost every night different campers would cook meals and slam their pans inviting the few other outdoor lovers to mingle around soup, fresh bread and hot wine.

One particular night was a cold and dark evening as the stars were hiding behind the clouds waiting for the wind to blow them away. Scheduled to go home a couple of days later, we were already feeling nostalgic about leaving this lovely town back to the big city with classes scheduled to start the next Monday. Having cooked a meal for the campers the night before, we heard the calling from a more distant tent telling the 'community' that the soup was ready. Yum! We hastily organized our stuff and quickly fled to mingle with the small group, located at about 500 yards from our tent. After hiking for almost the entire afternoon, we were ready to satisfy our hunger. As we got there I noticed I had forgotten to bring the guitar for the customary night camp serenade. Well, I thought, I will go get it after supper. Meal served and half way through it, a bitter and unexpected moment caught us all by surprise. Loudly, we heard screams blazing that a fire was taking over someone's tent. As we all rapidly stood up and walked out of our host's tent, we could see a tent from afar quickly being consumed by flames. As the group ran over and our hearts speeded up the beat at a faster and excruciating pace, we just wished that nobody was hurt. And we wanted to believe that this was not happening to us. Wishful thinking...although the night was dark, as we got a visual of the scene we already knew that it was our own tent that had caught on fire...ruined...completely destroyed. Nothing left but a pile of ashes.

What to make out of this? My most precious belonging in the tent, the guitar, gone...it did hurt. Needless to say that we didn't try to find which one of the two was responsible for leaving a lighted candle in the tent without the proper support base. Most likely, the rationale was, as the camp site was rather unoccupied, "let's pretend there are people in the tent so that the light would 'shun' unwanted visitors." Not only an innocent idea if it weren't for an even worse outcome: the candle was left on top of a likely flammable surface...lesson learned for the young and inexperienced, the hard way. Back home, my next door neighbor and I would still be good friends. But something had changed in the relationship. Understandably so.

## REFUGE IN BOOKS AND MORE TROUBLED WATERS

The questions now as to *what* and *who I want to become* were a little more complex. On my mid-to-late teens, anxiety and passion got in the way. By observing peers and acquiring the references I needed to shape up my character, although we were told to play safe, I still wanted to take risks. Past and present books such as Mark Twain's *The Adventures of Huckleberry Finn*, Jonathan Swift's *Gulliver's Travels*, Madeleine L'Engle's *A Wrinkle in Time*, Scott O'Dell's *Island of the Blue Dolphins*, Harper Lee's *To Kill a Mockingbird*, George Orwell's *Animal Farm*, John Steinbeck's *Of Mice and Men*, Walt Morey's *Gentle Ben* and Aldous Huxley's *Brave New World* were important influences. So were major core literary works from figures in Brazil, including classic novelists like Machado de Assis, Guimaraes Rosa, Graciliano Ramos, Jorge Amado, Ariano Suassuna and poets such as Mario de Andrade, Manuel Bandeira and Carlos Drummond de Andrade.

It was year's end, another period winding down. From Carlos Drummond de Andrade, considered to be one of the greatest poets in the country's history, typically ironic and pessimist, here's a poem that speaks more positively to his poetic mood, and mine as well:

TIME

*Who had the idea of slicing time into pieces,*
*Which were given the name of year,*
*Was a genius person.*
*Industrialized hope*
*Pushing it to the limits of its exhaustiveness.*
*Twelve months are enough for any human being*
*to get tired and give up.*
*Then comes the miracle of renewal and all stars*
*Once again*
*We pick up another number wishing that*
*From now on everything will be different.*
*…For you,*
*I wish your dreams fulfilled.*
*The love you waited*
*Hope renewed.*
*For you,*
*I wish all the colors of life.*
*All happiness you can smile to*
*All songs you can thrill.*
*For you in this new year,*
*Wish all friends to be better,*
*May your family be more united,*
*May your life be more lived.*
*I would like to wish you so many things*
*But nothing would be enough…*
*So, I wish only that you have many wishes.*
*Big wishes and may they move you further every*
*single minute,*
*On route to your happiness!*
– Carlos Drummond de Andrade

Late 1974, beginning of 1975 was a time I re-encountered a former schoolmate from *Colégio Bandeirantes* which poised a strong sway on me during that phase. Two and a half years older, Octávio Barollo Jr., *Tatá*, a nickname used by his family, was a tall, strong, handsome and energetic young man with a great instinct for the passion of the day: cars. I must say that most boys of my generation could not wait to start driving. However, Barollo, being older and a natural leader, not only was already driving and had his own car but he loved the pleasure and thrill of speeding. A good driver, he could drive fast. It is important to highlight the perils of a big city like São Paulo: urbanistically speaking, with the exception of the more well maintained areas of the megalopolis, it was a challenging environment as multiple road works or traffic rearrangements were always happening simultaneously. Besides, there was also the unfortunate aspect of some driver's lack of discipline – and impunity – which, in many cases, allowed for lack of respect for other drivers and passengers – and for the rules of traffic. Most young drivers, myself included, ran too many risks.

This was a confusing time for its contradiction and drama, only eased by reflections and efforts to understand the turbulent period of our lives we were living in, and also by having fun. Barollo and I lived in the same vicinity and, along with other neighbors, loved playing pool, ping-pong and foosball. But the growing pains were there, waiting to manifest and push us to higher altitudes. Or lower, depending on the perspective. After spending the entire school vacation month of February on the warm seaside along with Barollo's family, it was time for school again. It was a relief to be back for the month had been full of good times and not so good ones. Hormones galore, summertime and the always over the top carnival period, a perfect mix for trouble. To name but a few events during that period, we got involved in a couple of street fights in which consequences could have been terrible and unpredictable. Another one, an overnight ordeal in which his Mom and I drove up and down the coastal mountain road hoping Barollo had not been involved in a car accident, also added to high alarm, only alleviated when we finally saw him the next morning turning the street corner on foot after having walked overnight until he finally caught a ride, exhausted and bitten by insects all night long. As his car broke down at late evening hours, with no telephone readily available, he had not been able to fix it or even tow it away on his way back from the city. The upside of that summer was the good friendships developed during that period, among them Fabio D'Onofrio, himself, becoming our latest new pal.

Already back to school for a couple of months, two other schoolmates and I would take rides every morning with our friend Barollo. It was such a nice time of the year for the weather was not so hot and, although not quite cool yet, we started to feel the winds of fall looming in the air. Now enrolled back in a more liberal school environment – the Anglo Latino experience only lasted a year, thank God – at *Colégio Objetivo* we combined expectations that would drive our High-School studies to a potential career path in contrast with our day-to-day full-fledged adolescent process. Awkward mix. Painful. We didn't have the brains yet. Could somebody help?!!!

Whether or not possessing a clear understanding of growth as a process, I side slipped. "Guardini describes adolescence as the continuation of the crisis of the years of puberty. It begins with the awakening of the person – the experience of consciously wanting to be someone distinct from everyone else," analyzes Leivegoed. "Even the mere choice of a career is always a daring venture. Part of the way in which Guardini orders his problems when referring to the phases of life is his continuous search for that *configuration of values* which controls and guides the phase of life by making choices in a particular direction. It is this configuration that he calls the 'dominant value-centre.' For adolescence, this configuration of values is 'taking oneself upon oneself,' that is, learning to accept oneself and thereby being able to answer questions for oneself (and making choices and decisions). This is the same as being able to start bearing one's own, individual, responsibility. The only condition is that one be willing to learn from them. Yet, Guardini points out with some emphasis that each phase of life has its own task in the development of the individual, and quotes Goethe: 'We travel not only to arrive but to live while traveling." My friend Barollo and I had long discussions around the theme of inner development and our task to achieve it as individuals. It felt like a worthwhile pursuit.

That pleasant and sunny Monday morning in June didn't go quite as planned. Usually on time, Barollo didn't show up, which would be atypical. Celso, Wilson and I tried to call his home number, but nobody answered. Not normal. We ended up sharing a taxi to school thinking he could have had issues with his red GM Chevette, the same car that let him down in the coastal mountains a few months past. As we got to school, our friend was not there. Already late, we went about our classes and hoped to catch up with him at recess. His girlfriend, Selma, would likely have a clue as to where he might be – they would normally spend time together on Sunday evenings at a disco or at the Italian restaurant of their preference. She, also, was not around. Finally, we spotted Selma's sister along with her boyfriend: he was embracing her and looked distraught. Barollo had been involved in a horrendous accident the night before while taking Selma back home for the evening. Selma had had a large but not serious cut on her forehead as a consequence of the Chevette's blowing windshield. For her, it could have been much worse had Barollo not tried to shield her from the inevitable blast on the back of a truck, stuck in the middle of the road waiting to be towed. At a higher speed than the highway curved ramp would allow for, he did not stop the car on time. He himself was at the hospital in critical conditions. At first, it sounded that his life was not in danger. A relief for all of us. The following hours were excruciating. Even if we went to the hospital we would not be able to see him. In a coma, he would stay in the ICU for several days. His parents being divorced, made communications challenging. We would have to wait.

# GROWING PAINS: FROM CROSSROADS TO SEIZING THE MOMENT

Multiple plastic surgeries were necessary to restore Barollo's face originated from the 150+ stitches used to amend his skin and tissues. His surgeon did a terrific job especially reconstructing the surrounding of his eyes and nose, the most affected parts of his face. His memory lightly affected, he looked different but was still the good looking young man of before: a great friend, more inspiring now for his braveness and painful experience. Well, he still loved speed...

According to Bryant, "Between fourteen and twenty-one, the adolescent 'esquire' had to master the social graces of singing, dancing and conversation. Even more important, he was encouraged to deepen his moral awareness and respect for womankind. These disciplines introduced him to the highest ideals of knighthood, while his combat training developed his physical prowess and courage. With the satisfactory completion of his physical, mental and spiritual instruction, the twenty-one-year-old could prepare for the sacred ceremony of initiation. Dressed in white, he affirmed his ideals of his rank and accepted his spurs, gauntlets, shield, mail and lance. The celebration reached its climax when the young knight accepted the accolade and the dedicated sword. Sworn to bring compassion and justice to all evil places in his life's path, and armed with both material and spiritual weapons, he was permitted to leave the sanctuary and follow his quest and destiny."

Bryant brilliantly displays the symbolic rite of passage which adolescent young men must go through in order to cope with the demands of maturity. Not there yet and after agonizing from close relatives' and friends' markedly harsh experiences, added to my own, my next few years' development were not to be a smooth ride. Under different circumstances, up and down romantic relationships coupled with school and career decisions to be made did pose enough drama to the current phase. Choices. Must have choices. School of Engineering? Economics?

Business Administration? Girlfriend? Setting up a band? Job? Sports? Join family business? Travel, perhaps?

Big city, small world. As I took on handball practices, I re-encountered some of my former schoolmates from Elementary, Middle and High School. Also known as European handball, this is a sport in which two teams of seven players each (six outfield players and a goalie) pass a ball using their hands with the aim of shooting it into the goal of the other team. A standard match consists of two periods of 30 minutes, and the team that scores more goals wins. With no protective equipment required, this is an indoor game first played in Denmark, in the late 19$^{th}$ century. The game is fast and packed with action, somewhat keeping a similar speed to basketball. Machi and I had been classmates at Elementary and High School and now joined in one more time in College. Machi and I were tall guys perfectly suited for the sport. He had had the opportunity to play handball for years at the local *Aclimação* neighborhood club and was considered to have one of the best shots – a real powerful sling. I had a lot to learn from him on the sport, which I had been playing only for about two years. He practically grew up in the game and was an excellent player. Freshmen at the college of Economics at *Universidade Mackenzie*, Machi and I drove to school together every day. He had been dating Jane, a beautiful half Vietnamese, half Italian girl since High School and worked part time in his family's business, a jewelry based in downtown São Paulo. With a similar temperament as mine, except while on the court where he would take the game a lot more competitively than I, we had become good friends.

As healthy, formative and disciplinary as it may seem, the culture around handball at Aclimação is one of good and also of sad stories. Once again, we students would hear of bad experiences of others doing drugs and losing grip of their north. As much as schools at that time would have a decent curriculum, drugs were still a taboo and seldom talked about. With rarely a word from teachers, the curriculum would not include any education around drugs whatsoever. Users were discriminated against and marginalized. Yet, families would typically play the most important role in bringing discernment to the pressing issue, to the extent of their understanding. The neighborhood itself was known as lenient and accepting of the use of drugs, from light to heavy ones. Not an insignificant number of excellent athletes with a promising future in the sport had succumbed to using drugs and simply abandoned the sport; even more sorrowful, in a number of cases, some had died of overdose or accident-related situations. Years back, many times I would overhear my Mom on the phone speaking with other parents about common and genuine concerns.

Machi and I had no intention of losing focus on the sport and, along with a number of other peers, we trained consistently in order to competitively dispute tournaments between multiple college teams. We had a lot of fun and loved the freshmen year in college. Of course peer pressure exerted influence on every single teenager and avoiding experimenting drugs was nearly impossible. However, dabbling was not an option and my instincts spoke louder against substance abuse and addiction.

## LEARNING A LESSON AT EVERY CORNER

My phone ringed at the end of one day. I heard Machi's voice greeting me in a lower tone than usual. It's evening, an uncommon time for him to call me, I thought. "Renato, I lost my father." Impeccably composed and serene, I could sense that that message was the reflection of a game changer for my friend. His life turned 180 degrees in a few hours as he made the quick decision to quit college immediately and take over his dad's business. Our daily coexistence would be interrupted for good. For a couple more years, I would stay in touch with this amazing person mostly through my own family as he would assist with occasional minor jewelry purchases and repairs. We remained in touch sporadically until it was my turn to see my life take a different direction. Many years would go by until I would hook up with him again. Come that time, I will be down on my knees when I'm told of an unthinkable, harrowing story.

Referred to as "the college experience teenage minds in the United States were, and still are to this day, typically filled with daydreams of wild parties, endless dates and alcoholic beverages. Whoever came up with this concept and decided that this kind of existence should be the type that a four-year term should consist of made this idea wildly unreasonable and exhausting. In Brazil, this reality would vary from school to school and could apply to some students, especially those that would go to school during the morning schedule and could afford to strictly go to college in pursuit of, best case scenario, preparing for a career. On the other hand, evening students would work full time jobs or participate of some kind of internship in private or public institutions during the day in order to help provide for their families and yet be able to fund their four-year evening course. An arduous task for many young men and women.

My first two years in college were a mix of both, especially as a freshman, but it began to change as my observation of reality began to take shape. I would go to school in the morning, help my Dad two to three times a week in the afternoon, and alternate homework and sports; and, of course, music playing and listening, between afternoons and evenings. Yet, the spectrum of 'finding the proper career path' was always in mind and at some point would become dominant in my system.

## A MINOR REFLECTION

I wouldn't come across the thoughts of Allan Watts until many years after my experience as an early adult. The author of *The Way of Zen*, a book that focuses on philosophical explication and history, puts things in perspective during a broadcast recording when broaching the future. As a young man, it would have been interesting to come across Watts' thoughts:

"My goodness, don't you remember when you first went to school? You went to kindergarten and in kindergarten the idea was to push alarm and go to first grade and then push alarm so you could go to the 2$^{nd}$ and 3$^{rd}$ grade and up and up... then you went to high school, this was a great transition in life and all the pressure is being put on you. You must get ahead, you must go up the grades and finally be good enough to be going to college. And then you get to college, you are going step-by-step, step-by-step up to the great moment when you are ready to go out into the world. Then, when you go out into this famous world comes... the struggle for success in profession or business. And again, there seems to be a ladder before you, something for which you are reaching all the time.... and then.... suddenly, when you're about 40 or 45 years old in the middle of life you wake up one day and say....'Uh? I've arrived. But I feel pretty much the same as I've always felt, in fact I'm not so sure if I feel a little bit cheated because...', you see, you were fooled. You were always living for somewhere where you aren't. And while as I said it is of tremendous use for us to be able to look ahead in this way and plan, there is no use in planning for a future which when you get to it then it becomes a present you won't be there. You will be living in some other future which hasn't yet arrived and so in this way one is never able actually to inherit and enjoy the fruits of one's action. You can't live with all unless you can live fully now." – Allan Watts

# 5
# Life is Sensation: Getting Out There

*"Well I left my happy home to see what I could find out. I left my folk and friends with the aim to clear my mind out. Well I hit the rowdy road and many kinds I met there and many stories told me on the way to get there. So on and on I go, the seconds tick the time out, so much left to know, and I'm on the road to find out." On the Road to Find Out* – Cat Stevens

I HAD BEEN FORMULATING THESE PLANS when I met with Machi back in the beginning of November, 1979. Machi and I got together for dinner after almost a year from the last time we had seen one another. He seemed happy. His wedding was scheduled for the atypical date of February 29th, 1980. With his usual big and easy Italian smile, he was excited to communicate the event and expected me to be one of his best men. I was thrilled for him and just as exhilarated to be invited. There was, however, a caveat which prompted me to reluctantly – and regrettably – decline the invite. Scheduled to fly to New York and then San

Francisco on January 18th, I would most likely make it back on time for his wedding if my trip was to last about a month. If it weren't for my Plan B, which was not to come back to São Paulo any time soon...

My sisters Liliana and Silvia Regina had been married for about two years and one year, respectively. Cristina, my youngest sister, was still in High School and not to leave our parents' home any time in the near future. With the decision to get on the road after spending several fantastic months in the San Francisco Bay Area, with Berkeley as a beacon, I was bound to Minnesota to spend a couple of weeks prior to heading to Montréal, then New York and off to Europe. Married young, Liliana and Marcos had the perspective to finish up studies in a couple more years and then go back to São Paulo to pursue their careers. It was the first time I was seeing members of my immediate family in many months and that felt good. I was happy to be around them and they were also glad to see me. The month was August and it looked like mosquitoes in hot St. Cloud, Minnesota reigned in the air space. Before becoming Quarry Park, the spot was known as one of "The nude beaches in the USA" for being for decades considered to be an unregulated party spot. Today, this area is a magnet for rock climbing, mountain biking, scuba diving, skate skiing and trout fishing. But at the time they and their friends took me to the quarries, the big deal being the 30-45-feet cliff jumping experience – quite a thrill.

## THE CHASE FOR EXPERIENCE

"Does twenty-one signify the end and conclusion of the seven-year progression? There is an overwhelming array of evidence to suggest that this rhythm continues to unfold until death. We should realize, however, that the degree of psychological advancement, especially after twenty-eight, is no longer automatic but depends largely on our own efforts. I do not believe that the development of the psyche ever stops completely, inasmuch as the seven-year cycles continue to regulate the "digestion" of experience, by which the outward experience becomes part of the inward self. But those who strive for self-knowledge and meaning obviously fulfill more of their potential in each seven-year span than those who do not – and they better transform their past experience." – *William Bryant, The Sacred Seven*

Seeking awareness and purpose, the impulse to get on the road was now in full-blown activity. After catching up with my family members in Minnesota, I was off to the Province of Québec. The only predominantly French-speaking population in Canada, its location is unique as it borders with four U. S. states – New York, Vermont, New Hampshire and Maine – and is interestingly surrounded by multiple bodies of water and the eastern provinces of New Brunswick, Newfoundland and Labrador. Montréal was my first destination and there I got the first and condensed glimpse of what this only French territory in this magnificent country of Canada felt like. Youth hostels were the accommodation of choice. With a student card at hand, hostels provided not only budget-oriented but sociable accommodation in a dorm-shared environment usually with a bunk bed, bathroom, lounge and sometimes kitchen. Ideal for travelers and backpackers. Europe being the major focus of the next several months of my journey, Montréal and then Québec City were a perfectly preamble of what to expect in probably the most European-like atmosphere in North America. A three-and-a-half-hour train took me to Québec City where I had my first of many peculiar experiences as a traveler. Before leaving São Paulo earlier that year, my sister Silvia Regina had anticipated one perspective that stuck in my mind: "no matter where you are, you will always find a situation or someone that will provide help when you need it." The month was August and summer was busy all over the place. Energetic Québec City was packed; as I looked for a hostel, I encountered quite a challenge finding a spot. Worst case scenario, I would roll out my tent and sleeping bag and spend the night at a camp or similar site. While I went from one hostel to another, I stored my backpack in one of them and went to a live music bar. There I greeted the bartender and asked for *une bière*. The bartender brought me the beer and, in his broken English, started a conversation following my broken French request. Luc and I engaged in an amicable conversation alternated with his busy shift. Learning that I was a guitar player as I mentioned that it crossed my mind playing in bars, he brought up that his girlfriend was about to finish up her shift – she worked as a waitress across the street and would be coming to join us for a beer, momentarily.

"Travel is fatal to prejudice, bigotry, and narrow-mindedness, and many of our people need it sorely on these accounts. Broad, wholesome, charitable views of men and things cannot be acquired by vegetating in one little corner of the earth all one's lifetime." – *Mark Twain*

I had read Twain's quote in a bookstore in Minneapolis and could not help not taking note of it. Traveling, added to literature and music, make for a complex combination. Impressions are vivid and the emotional component of the experience becomes more meaningful. As Martine arrived at the bar, Luc made the introductions and we chatted for a few minutes. She excused herself and stepped out calling Luc at the corner of the bar counter for a quick discussion. In a few minutes, Martine came back and, to my surprise, tendered their house for me to stay for the period I had planned to visit Québec City, which was about a week. Just like that. I looked at both, almost incredulous with the offer, and saw their honest smiles, as if they were saying: "Hey young man, we know very little about you but you seem a reliable guy. Besides, we have been helped before. Just make sure you'll pass it on."

The intro to my journey while in Canada could not have been more auspicious. It made me realize that the experience of being myself while meeting strangers – real strangers – did support the concept of how things can quickly change in such a positive and least expected way. Here are a few inspirational quotes from anonymous individuals:

"Own who you are."

"In a world where you can be anything, be yourself."

"Just be yourself. Life is too short to be someone else."

"Be yourself. People don't have to like you and you don't have to care."

"When you truly don't care what anyone thinks of you, you have reached a dangerously awesome level of freedom."

"The biggest challenge of life is to be yourself in a world that is constantly trying to make you look like everyone else."

Traveling does take one to unexpected territories. Not only to various physical ones but to subtle inner places as one allows the experience to unfold. It can be lonely too. But that's the opportunity to learn and invigorate oneself with the unknown. Many times challenging and tempting to look back and to look for the safe havens. To keep moving is the motto. And the mojo.

## OFF TO THE OLD WORLD

Laker Airways was a private, British independent airline. Founded in 1966, it was originally a charter airline flying passengers and cargo worldwide. "No frills," as it was known for, the early 1970s saw the airline battle with aviation authorities in the UK and the US to gain approval for a low-cost transatlantic service to link London and New York during the peak summer period from May to September. This was to be marketed as *Skytrain* for £32.50 one-way in winter and £37.50 in summer, clearly a signal that there was a large contingent of people that could benefit from those incredible rates. Skytrain took several years to be approved but finally gained ground at decade's end. I was one of the young travelers that were flying from JFK to Gatwick at those revolutionary rates during that summer of 1980. I am sure I had paid more than that amount seeing that my ticket was to be valid for several months. However, no airline could match those rates. A wide body McDonnell-Douglas DC-10, the aircraft would take close to 400 passengers plus cargo. Humongous. Jammed. Little food and minimum service. But it was worth the shot.

## LONDON, *THE SMOKE*

After crossing downtown from Gatwick on a double-decker, I finally made it to the youth hostel I had picked out of *Let's Go: Europe*. Located at the peripheral part of the city, it was simple and not crowded. Clean, the rates were affordable and exactly what I had in mind to match my daily budget. With plans to possibly work in London, there I set ground with the idea of inquiring about potential job opportunities in places such as restaurants and hotels. I had an excellent letter of reference from the general manager of The Good Earth and thought this should be an easy transition had the decision to stick around taken place. Another idea that crossed my mind was to work on fishing boats from England to Iceland as I had heard there was good money to be made. While working on the perspective for work, Adro and Lucia, Amelia and Stefanie, Francesc and Dolors, and in the last few days, Maurizio, would become exceptional hostel companions for the extension of my stay. The first couple was from a small town near Bologna, the sisters were from Paris, the second couple from Barcelona and Maurizio from Genoa. Of course, there was a guitar available and that made things fun and enjoyable.

Adro and Lucia were an adorable couple. Music was around us all the time as both were singers at their small town choir. Lovers and interpreters of Italian folk music, this style is an important part of the country's musical heritage. Moreover, instrumental and mainly vocal classical music is an iconic part of Italian identity. Both unabashedly expressed that character. "Matona, mia cara," – https://youtu.be/hswJaD3mBUI – was a song of their choice for singing as a duet as we would hang out and about London everyday while visiting the usual tourist sites – e.g., walking by the River Thames or picnicking at the green gardens of the Big Ben. This song got stuck in my mind for decades. Although Portuguese has some similar phonetics and quite a number of vocabulary overlapping to Italian, I had just a minor clue as to what the song was about. Besides, the couple had basic English knowledge and made things more interesting when communicating to us its meaning. Thanks to You Tube and Google, not only did I run by a live performance of the song but I could also do a little research around the lyrics...to my surprise, here are the Italian words followed by the (English) translation:

*Matona, mia cara mi follere canzon*
*(My lady, I'd love to sing a song),*
*Cantar sotto finestra, Lanze bon campagnon,*
*(To sing below your window, I'm a lancer*
*and a good lad)*
*Ti prego m'ascoltare che mi cantar debon*
*(Please listen to me, for I sing well)*
*E mi ti foller bene come Greco e capon*
*(and I love you greatly, as a Greek does his capon)*

*Com andar alle cacce, cacciar, cacciar con le falcon*
*(When I go hunting, hunting with a falcon)*
*Mi ti portar beccaze, grasse come rognon*
*(I'll bring you woodcocks as fat as a kidney)*
*Se mi non saper dire tante belle rason*
*(Though I do not know so many elegant phases)*
*Petrarca mi no saper, ne fonte d'Helicon*
*(and know nothing of Petrarch, or the fountain*
*of Helicon)*
*Se ti mi foller bene mi non esser poltroon*
*(If you'll have me, I'm no laggard)*
*Mi piccar tutta note, urtar come monton*
*(I'll make love to you all night long, thrusting*
*like a ram)*

As per Craig B. Daniel's *Folklore in History* notes, "Matona Mia Cara" was written by Orlande de Lassus, a sixteenth-century composer who was not himself Italian, though the piece was written in that language... badly. The Italian of the lyrics is terrible, and deliberately so. The song's viewpoint character is a German soldier during the Italian Wars, and his words to Matona are full of grammatical errors, faux-unintentional double *entendres*, innuendo, and irony. To an Italian audience of the sixteenth century, presenting this as a serious German love song and then singing *"mi ti portar becazze, grasse come rognon"* would have been the height of comedy.

Craig continues on: "All too often, however, modern audiences are either given a translation into well-written English or no translation at all. But it doesn't have to be this way — I once conversed with a gentleman who had been part of a group which sang the song with somebody holding signs with English subtitles, written in the same style as the original Italian words while translating it more or less accurately. "Me go hunting in woods," they read during one verse. "Me bring you back cock. Me bring you back BIG cock." The audience was in stitches, just like the sixteenth-century ones would have been."

The two French sisters, the Catalan couple and I would look at one another as the Italians would discuss and gesticulate, laughing about the song. As if they themselves were questioning the meaning of the piece they had been rehearsing with the other members of the choir back at home. Hilarious. And they made it sound so good.

"We may call the effervescent cycle between twenty-one and twenty-eight the period of enthusiasm and intemperance. It is the time when we celebrate our liberation from the somber introversion of adolescence by shaking our tail feathers at the world. Regardless of the cost, young adults spend prodigious amount of energy searching for a physical, emotional, and intellectual challenge and stimulation, accepting privation and sacrifice as a matter of course. The experiment with their newfound independence, testing and proving themselves, doing almost any crazy thing in the name of experience. In this process, the newly awakened self, swept along by the winds of optimism, tends to be flooded by a welter of impressions, all of which have to be digested later. At that pace we are easily fooled by the blandishments of pleasure in the counterfeit values of the seductive world. The voice of conscience, though stronger than it was in adolescence, is often smothered by the roar of action. On the other hand, the awakening sense of social responsibility thrives many of flushed knight full tilt at the dragons of injustice and hypocrisy. These radical lances, however, are seldom tempered by perspective and wisdom. It is the exercise and experience of battle that counts as the young ego finds itself by pitting itself against the world." – *William Bryant, The Sacred Seven-2*

Bryant's thoughts could not be more emblematic of the times I was living through, right at the beginning of the fourth seven-year cycle. The excitement of getting on the road was added to iconic London, a city that dismisses intros. London's nickname *The Smoke* comes as a result of pollution from coal fires in homes and factories. The smoke from the fires would mix with the fog that is common in London, and would cover the city. Air pollution laws finally corrected this problem, but the nickname remained. The idea of staying in London, looking for a job and reaching out to the fishing companies ended up never materializing. The aspiration to breathe into the geographical and cultural scene waiting to unfold in front of my eyes was now too strong and, after working hard in Berkeley for the past months, I could do away without settling for a period in the UK. It was time to get going and leaving my London companions was accompanied by the promise we would see each other again. The next stop was Liège, Belgium where I would meet my partner in crime at the Plasma Center, Françoise Havelange. This time I would have to make an important decision as it referred to getting around Europe. While many students and travelers would acquire the Eurorail pass in the US to travel from a period of a couple of weeks up to three months, I choose to do it differently. Instead, Françoise suggested I purchased the Interrail pass, which was the European pass purchased in Europe, which encompassed more countries than the Eurorail pass. My plan was to possibly cross the borders towards socialist countries. For the thrill, during the time of the iron curtain and the Berlin Wall, and, surely, because it was a unique opportunity.

## LIÈGE, *LES ROUCHES*

It was Saturday at noon. I had arrived by train from London the night before at the Liège-Guillemins Train Station, where Françoise and her brother Carl picked me up. In her family's three-story home lived her Mom, Dad, Carl, Isabelle, Françoise's older sister and an aunt. Having been given a single room and fresh linen, it felt like home. Françoise's Mom, whom Françoise resembled, was a joyful lady and her Dad, Mr. Havelange, a focused but playful personality.

Before getting to town, I learned about a mesmerizing historical fact: "Liège has an exceptionally rich history, as well as prehistory, even by European standards. The oldest (pre-)human settlements in Belgium, dating from 800,000 years ago (Homo erectus), were found in Hallembaye, 15km north of the modern city centre. The world's very first Neanderthal skull was found in the suburb of Engis in 1829, i.e. 27 years before the skeletons of the Neander Valley in North Rhine-Westphalia, after which the Homo species was named."

Having grown in a young continent such as South America, the exposure to ancient history was dwarfed when compared to Europe. Inevitably, one sees the reflection of the culture on the people and that makes for a special experience. Once I read: "Culture does not make people. People make culture." After a quick early breakfast, Françoise, Carl and Isabelle took me to Maastricht, Netherlands, for a morning walk. A thirty-minute ride, this is a university city distinguished by its medieval-era architecture and vibrant cultural scene – its quirky cobbled old town brings one back in time, a must-see old and historic gem. Back in Liège, as we sat at the table a little after 12:00p, I was not aware of the household skills and hospitality I was about to enjoy. Firstly, the table was set just impeccably. I had a sense that the Belgian cuisine would be widely diverse with significant regional variations while also reflecting the cuisines of neighboring France, Germany and the Netherlands. It is sometimes said that Belgian food is served in the quantity of German cuisine but with the quality of French Food. This could not be more true. Added to the exquisite dishes and style – and I am not necessarily referring to sophistication – I cannot remember a more pleasant experience, i.e. to be seated at a table with a family that would genuinely enjoy one another's company, stories and laughter. And certainly the food. It felt like time was not a concern. Freshly baked multiple varieties of bread, soft cheese and pate's are on the menu along with delicious Belgian fries and freshly harvested vegetable dishes, with beer and wine, at the table.

The one distinctive aspect about this family started with the name: Havelange. Known by the soccer lovers of Brazil, and to a great extent worldwide, FIFA – Federation Internationale de Football – the organization which described itself as an international governing body of association of all soccer related sports – was currently presided by Jean-Marie Faustin Godefroid de Havelange, or simply João Havelange, a Brazilian compatriot. He became the first non-European to hold the post – which he held it from 1974 to 1998; his tenure as President was the second longest in FIFA's history, behind only that of Jules Rimet. He came to be recognized as a powerful soccer advocate for expanding the sport throughout the globe. FIFA under his watch would be transformed into a multi-billion dollar business and, along with it, also a hotbed for subsequent depravity. Françoise's dad was not too fond of his cousin. "Everything comes with a price," he would say. An honorable man, I knew what he was talking about. Overtime and as the sport multiplied its influence around the world, the effects of corruption in the high ranks of management within the organization would be visible and widespread. Historic debacles would follow in the years to come. Mr. Havelange, the "poor cousin", knew exactly where this was going and was vocal about it.

It was five in the afternoon and we were still at the table degusting chocolate and tartes, two of the best Belgian specialties, laughing and enjoying everyone's stories. Priceless and timeless.

## PARIS, *LES ARENES DE LUTÈCE*

Françoise had finished her Berkeley college term and was off to Paris-Sorbonne University for her master's. Fluent in at least five languages, she had been looking into her career future which, in a few years, would translate into efforts towards the development of marginalized African populations. Quite a goal and task she had ahead of her. As I had been planning for the right moment to kick off my train journey – the *Interrail* was valid for a month – once I stepped into a train wagon the clock would start ticking and in thirty days it would be over. I was well equipped and, most excitingly, her brother Carl was fantastic lending me his Yamaha acoustic guitar for the duration of my voyage. The itinerary I had in mind had started to take shape. I still had most of the month of September to get around and sticking for some time in Paris seemed a good idea. Françoise gave a few phone calls and a close friend, Pascal, graciously offered me to stay at his apartment near *Montparnasse* and the *Cité Universitaire*. I was ecstatic and forever thankful for the opportunity as this would allow me to get around Paris and save precious francs in accommodation, let alone to be able to experience Pascal's routine first hand.

After a couple of weeks, I had already seen a lot of la *Ville Lumière* and spent quality time planning the next several months of my journey. Besides, some of our friends from Berkeley – Marie, Julio and Ateshé – also joined Françoise and me for a great sunny Saturday afternoon at Versailles. Yet, it was not time to jump on the wagon. My next challenge was to get to Southern France and possibly see a friend. This time, hitch hiking was in the works and I hadn't done it before. Europe, probably to this day, allows for a safe hitch hiking experience.

One last time, Françoise and a friend drove me by the Seine River towards the Boulevard Peripherique which would take us to the beginning of *Autostrada A6B*, the road that would take me toward southern France. As we said goodbye, I quickly pulled a good size piece of cardboard and a marker and wrote down in visible letters 'Avignon' on one side and 'Lyon' on the other side, places I had in mind visiting. I thought to myself, hitch hiking will be fun. There I was holding the sign for fifteen minutes. Thirty...forty-five minutes...nothing. The day was cloudy but no rain was on the forecast. What I noticed was that some car drivers and/or passengers would smile at the sign and make comments to one another. An hour. Another half-hour...an hour and forty-five minutes...I started to think, maybe I should pick up the guitar and play while I waited...Two hours, not a chance. "What's the learning lesson here?," I pondered. I got impatient and finally decided to call my friend and ask if I was doing something wrong. *"Alo?,"* "Hi Françoise, I'm still stuck in Paris! Am I doing the right thing?" After I explained my 'procedure' to leave the urban area, she cracked up and said: *"Oh, non!* Just get another cardboard and write *'Sud'*, for South, instead." "That's all?," I asked. In less than ten minutes a young woman driving a miniature Peugeot pulled over and...bingo! I was out of town!

A red wine color station wagon pulling a U-Haul type of hitch was one of the first vehicles I spotted at the parking lot of the ELF gas station where the young lady had so nicely driven and dropped me off, about a half-hour from Paris. My next move was to find a good soul that would take me farther south and, if possible, near to my next destination. There was not what is known today as the European Community, so that made it easy to identify that the wagon's license plate was from the Netherlands. Anthon had left Amsterdam the day before and was on his way to Barcelona, Spain, where he and his family would settle down for the next several years. Driving by himself with the car packed with all kinds of home belongings, he promptly agreed to give me a ride. "An uncertain beginning of the day possibly turned into a lucky one," I thought. He would still grab a bite at the ELF station and invited me to join in, evidently to delve into my intent.

## THE *CHESHIRE CAT* DILEMA

"The Cat only grinned when it saw Alice. It looked good-natured, she thought: still it had very long claws and a great many teeth, so she felt that it ought to be treated with respect."

'Cheshire Puss', she began, rather timidly, as she did not at all know whether it would like the name: however, it only grinned a little wider. 'Come, it's pleased so far,' thought Alice, and she went on. 'Would you tell me, please, which way I ought to go from here?'

'That depends a good deal on where you want to get to' said the Cat.

'I don't much care where –' said Alice.

'Then it doesn't matter which way you go' said the Cat.

' – as long as I get somewhere,' Alice added as an explanation.

'Oh, you're sure to do that' said the Cat. 'If you only walk long enough....''

The analogy I use to describe that portion of my travel experience with Lewis Carroll's classic *Alice's Adventures in Wonderland* – when Alice meets the Cheshire Cat – is one of too many options. In fact, easy to get carried away and at times loose the sense of direction and objectivity. Therefore, my guidance was basically time as opposed to space. And places. I decided that once I started travelling by train I would try to qualitatively cover as much ground as I could. Even if it meant sleeping overnight in transit when going from town to town and from one country to another, which would actually help deflect accommodations costs.

Having passed the 'screening test' during lunch time, the Dutchman and I got on the road and headed down South toward Lyon. He still had another ten hours to arrive in Barcelona. As for me, I began to question the need to stop in Lyon at that time. Down by the ocean near Montpellier, there was a beach town where an almost relative-made-friend was likely to be living with his girlfriend. I thought I should give it a shot and meet them since I had not seen him in years. Seven hundred kilometers later and after second-hand smoking almost half a pack of *Gitanes*, it was almost twilight when Anthon dropped me off at a toll booth and told me that it would be fairly easy to get a ride to the beach resort I had in mind. Our seven-hour drive was fairly pleasant and we enjoyed each other's company. We shared good stories around the remarkable landscape. France's countryside's textures, smells and scenery were indeed spectacular.

## *LA GRANDE MOTTE*

Fabio and Isabelle had met a couple of years before in the beautiful tiny island of Formentera, near Ibiza, off the east coast of Spain. I had not seen Fabio in years, possibly since someone's wedding or a family's event I could not recall. Many years back, Fabio had been a Math private teacher to help me with the challenges I encountered during 6th and 7th grade at *Colégio Bandeirantes*. A strong personality, persistent but stubborn, sometimes quick-tempered, Fabio had always been an articulate and opinionated individual in multiple realms, especially in politics and human matters. In pursuit of his PHD in Project Economics at *L'Université de Montpellier*, they were both living in one of Isabelle's family's apartment in this popular seaside resort and port, built in the 1960s and 1970s. La Grande-Motte, is characterized by its homogeneous architecture, many of the prominent buildings built pyramidal in form. The architect of the project, Jean Balladur, drew inspiration from pre-Columbian pyramids such as Teotihuacan, Mexico; and from the modernist architecture in Brazil, especially the work of architect Oscar Niemeyer. Quite a contrast from the classic architectural environment found in Montpellier. Of last name Chazyn, Fabio's background is an interesting combination of Jewish-Lebanese from father and mother, respectively. Intellectually stimulated, the Fabio I knew and met again after years seemed an enduring, honest and diligent thinker that I allowed myself to be influenced in the way I would look at the humanities. Being myself a student of Economics, it was a matter of time until I got more exposed and open to western philosophies and authors other than the usual classics - Adam Smith, David Ricardo, Karl Marx, John Maynard Keynes and more recently Frederic Hayek and Milton Friedman. The couple offered me to stay in another family's apartment during a visit that lasted for about a week, for which I was grateful. There I could finalize my plans prior to rambling from town to town once I got on a train. Also, I had the chance to immerse in some of the literature that would broaden my universe: In philosophy and politics, I first came in contact with Plato's *Dialogues*, *The Prince*, by Niccolo Macchiavelli and Friedrich Nietzsche's *Beyond Good and Evil*. Enough material for a short period of time but excellent reflections during the alternating sunny and rainy days of the fall season by the ocean. I would stay in contact with this couple for several more years until our lives took different directions.

Perhaps the most interesting piece of literature I came across with during those particular few days, it was on Marcus Aurelius' *Meditations* that I found the inspiration to lay out my next several months on the road: "I travel on by nature's path until I fall and find rest, breathing my last into that air from which I draw my daily breath, and falling on that earth which gave my father his seed, my mother her blood, my nurse her milk; the earth which for so many years has fed and watered me day by day; the earth which bears my tread and all the ways in which I abuse her." – *Marcus Aurelius* – *Excerpts on Meditations*

## BARCELONA, *THE NINTH BOAT*

A legend from the Roman times states that Hercules set out on a sea expedition in search of the Golden Fleece. During the 9-boat voyage there was a huge storm, the first 8 boats escaped without damage, whilst the ninth was lost at sea. Hercules set out to find it and found the boat shipwrecked at Montjuic. The navigators were so taken by the place's beauty that they named it after the lost boat – "Barca Nona" (the ninth boat).

Barcelona was the mark zero choice to kick off my train journey. *RENFE – Red Nacional de los Ferrocarriles Espanoles*, the national railway network of Spain, had been using the same standard gauge to connect with the French trainsets for a few years; therefore, there would be no more changing trains from one country to another. After about four and half hours and once again successfully hitch hiking to the border and through part of the Pyrenees Natural Park, I then arrived to the Catalan capital. It was mid-afternoon and catching a bus to a youth hostel seemed convenient. From there I grabbed my little phone book and aimed at calling a couple I had recently met back in a hostel in Montréal, a month and a half ago. I had always found that going to places where you know locals was rewarding in a sense that, not only I had the opportunity to once again gather with a somewhat familiar face, but the experience of getting around with a local became richer. Biel, a Barcelona native, and Margarida, a Uruguayan-Brazilian residing in Catalonia for years, seemed fairly receptive to my call as we set up a meeting point for late afternoon at an amusement park at *La Rambla*.

PSOE were the initials for the Spanish Socialist Workers' Party. A major gathering of the party's supporters was to take place at that end of September late afternoon where my Catalan acquaintances invited me to meet up. The party's Secretary-General, Felipe Gonzalez, was scheduled to be at the Barcelona celebration on that evening and it looked like my Spanish to-become-friends-with were ecstatic to attend the event. It is important to highlight that Francoist Spain, or the Franco Regime, is the period of Spanish history between 1939 and 1975 when Francisco Franco ruled over Spain as a military dictator. Francoist Spain has been described by scholars as a "semi-fascist" regime and seemingly the Spanish people were ready to elect a Socialist for the next decade or so. At the park, it only took a few minutes for me to find the couple. When I saw them I had a great surprise: another couple next to them, the same Francesc and Dolors I had hung out in London were their...best friends. Talk about coincidence, my stay in Barcelona was off to a great start.

American actor and travel writer Bill Biatrak's depiction of the city is intriguing: "There's a story that one of the kings of Catalonia had a lisp so bad, he said "Ibitha" instead of "Ibiza" and "Barthelona" instead of "Barcelona." To avoid offending him, the people of the area started pronouncing their words the same way. Although the story is probably just a myth, it's still a good one to perhaps partially explain the striking Catalonian accent you'll encounter when visiting Barcelona, the capital of the region."

"Beautiful Barcelona is the second-largest metropolis in Spain and a world class city, vibrant, full of history and a must see on any European itinerary. You may hear people say that Barcelona doesn't feel like the rest of Spain, and this is true — partly because the area is an autonomous region in the country, one in which the Catalonians seem to have created their own version of Iberia with their own language and culture. There's a vibe that gives the city its own identity."

"Unless you've visited Barcelona or studied architecture, you may never have heard of Antonio Gaudi, but Gaudi is considered by most to be the "face" of Barcelona. His inspiring architecture eclipses almost anything you might have seen. His buildings scattered throughout the city are best described as whimsical, organic, Seussical and nonsensical, although there's truly nothing nonsensical about any of his grand designs."

So true. Needless to say that I had a nice time visiting *Barna*, one of the popular colloquial terms distinctly used as a nickname while hanging out with the locals. Luckily, Biel and Margarida hosted me in their home, which enhanced my experience in this outstanding Spanish – but not so Spanish – city. Their young son had just started school and would ask me to walk him to *l'escola*, as proud as he was about beginning the new year. Whether checking out the *Museu Picasso* and *Fundacion Juan Miró*, learning about Barcelona's medieval roots in the maze-like Gothic Quarter, or simply walking by the beach was worth spending several weeks in this amazing area. So much to see...

## MONACO, *THE PRINCIPALITY*

The clock was ticking as I began my thirty-day train blast in Southern Europe. At the station and bound to Monaco, I waved goodbye at *mis amigos de Catalunia*. I had a pretty good idea about the itinerary I was going to go through but kept an open mind in case I needed to change course. Jean-Louis Personnat was a Berkeley contemporary student who once invited me to stop by if I ever went to Monte Carlo, the glamorous city-state situated at the base of the Maritime Alps along the French Riviera. Known as "an international byword for the extravagant display and reckless dispersal of wealth," my goal was, other than to see Jean-Louis, to visit the *Museé Oceanographique de Monaco*, one of the best on the planet. Rising from the cliff side rock of a mountain, The Oceanographic Museum was at the time run by Jacques-Yves Cousteau, which dismissed introductions. A monumental baroque architecture, the museum was home to exhibitions and collections of a myriad of species of sea fauna and a great variety of sea related objects – model ships, sea animal skeletons, weapons, etc. An aquarium in the basement of the museum also displayed a wide array of fauna and flora – featuring Mediterranean and tropical marine ecosystems. Plus, a plethora of artworks.

Jean-Louis met me in downtown and drove us directly to his parents' house, a mansion. I could not imagine what a piece of real estate like that would cost, especially in Monaco. I had an idea of the opulence but experiencing it first hand was quite something. Crowded, noisy but clean, safe and filthy rich – 30% of the population were millionaires – life in that small country was different. While going to places and sharing the same group of people in Berkeley, I saw another side of my friend's lifestyle that didn't quite sit well to my eyes. All perception, for this was his own environment. And not mine. In retrospect, I was not sure I left a great impression during my stay nor did the place play a significant importance for me while being there. Although exhilaratingly beautiful, ostensive luxury, casino and "the good life" was not exactly my cup of tea.

## GENOVA, *LA SUPERBA*

Traveling by train in Europe felt magical. With time to read and reflect upon my experience, every symbol I could attach to my journey made sense, hence recording it on my notebook became inevitable. Here's a meaningful note: "Language...has created the word 'loneliness' to express the pain of being alone. And it has created the word 'solitude' to express the glory of being alone." – *Paul Tillich*

Getting to Genoa's historical port was impressive. Known for its critical role in maritime trade over many centuries, the 'Most Serene Republic' ruled over the Mediterranean waves during the 12$^{th}$ and 13$^{th}$ centuries. Christopher Columbus is its illustrious controversial son. Its old city, a reminder of pre-modern life with its twisting maze of narrow streets, is extensive and intact. Underrated if compared to Rome and Venice, Genoa and the Ligurian region are gems to be experienced. Maurizio had a good voice and did well on the popular tunes our London crew had enjoyed chanting. We were happy to meet one another at the main city train station at *Genova Piazza Principe*. If it wasn't for the size of my backpack and the fact that I was carrying the guitar in an also sizable case, he would have had me hop on his red scooter on our way to his home. We walked about a mile while he pushed his little *motoretta*. His *Mama* had prepared this delicious meal: *spaghetti al pesto* and chopped *insalata*. Both pasta and sauce craftily made at home and veggies freshly picked out in the backyard, lunch was about to be served when we got to his house. Hungry as I was, I felt so pleased to be there.

The fact that I wanted to stay on an average of one to three days in each of the locations I had in mind had an ambiguous effect: for once, it gave me a glimpse of what the city or town looked like. On the other hand, meeting people I knew from previous encounters for only a day or two was just the right amount of time for it didn't disrupt their routines; however, I could only get on the surface of what their lifestyles and neighborhoods, friends and family, as well as getting a sense of their values and beliefs were. The price I had to pay for an intensive schedule and so much to uncover in good Old Europe.

## BERGAMO, *CITTÁ DEI MILLE*

Heading up to Milan, I was a little hesitant to call Enrico in Bergamo, about an hour distant from the multi-cultural capital of *Lombardia*. A nice but intense individual I had met earlier in the year in San Francisco while taking the ESL classes. Ico, as he preferred to be called, was a funny and joyful lover of reggae and everything related to it. A bit too much on the wild side, one of the things that concerned me about hanging out with him was his fondness for recreational drugs – and beyond. In San Francisco, I was never judgmental but yet I would not cave in to joining the crowd, be it from light drugs such as weed up to cocaine or LSD. An occasional beer, glass of wine or even some liquor was just fine for me. From an early age, I have always been an observer of life and its realities and it doesn't take much for me to realize that existence was difficult enough without drugs, let alone, adding them to one's system. Anyway, I liked Ico and wanted to see him, now in his own environment.

On Big Picture Questions.com, "Bridging Science and Spirituality with New Thought," I find the following reflection:

"There are many classes of drugs, which affect the central nervous system (CNS) in different ways, including CNS depressants (e.g. alcohol, heroin, oxycontin, valium), CNS stimulants (e.g. cocaine, methamphetamine), hallucinogens (e.g. LSD, psilocybin, peyote, ecstasy, ayahuasca).

"ALL these agents (whether natural or synthesized) are a mechanical way to achieve a greater level of connectivity, BUT they do it by throwing the soul out of the body!" Whoa, I chew over the idea.

"From the soul's perspective, the body is so disharmonious that the soul cannot stay within the energies associated with the gross physical body or the spiritual-physical or astral bodies. The auric layers split open, and the soul ejects out of the body to a higher level, depending on the type of drug(s) and doses taken. The more drugs are taken (without overdosing), the more disharmonious the body."

There's a lot to say about the text. Whether I believe it or not on the aforementioned statement is irrelevant. I like to keep it in perspective that there are no consequences without causes and that the use of recreational drugs can be, for some individuals, more damaging than for others. Ico had a somewhat complicated family and escaping from that reality was adequate from his point of view. I could see him getting in trouble sooner or later for being audacious. Yet, choice is sovereign. And inalienable.

## FLORENCE, *THE CRADLE*

Arriving in Florence was an experience in itself. The train station, *Stazione Santa Maria Novella*, is an architectural masterpiece. Although built during Italy's Fascist period, it is a great example of Italian modernism from the 1930s. It gets its name from the church of the same name across the *piazza* from the entrance. Impossible to skip it, the church contains a multiplicity of art treasures with frescoes by masters of Gothic and early Renaissance. *Firenze* is home to some of the greatest artists and thinkers of all time. Beyond the monumental buildings like the Old Palace and the *Grand Palazzo Medici*, a humble house is a highlight: *Casa di Dante* (Dante's House), home of Italy's most famous poet. The Renaissance made Florence a cultural hub during the time where architecture, engineering, painting, sculpture, literature, science and mathematics played center stage when Italy was divided into city-states, Florence being one of them. Besides, Dante, Michelangelo, Da Vinci and Donatello were all Florentines.

For the first time in a while, I found myself without knowing anyone while being in this beautiful and poignant city. During the train travel from Milan to Florence I came across a reading that would stick throughout my journey for a long time: It went like this:

> *"That I am a man*
> *This I share with other men.*
> *That I eat and drink and that I walk and sleep*
> *This is what all animals do likewise.*
> *But that I am I is only mine*
> *and belongs to me and to nobody else.*
> *Not to an angel – nor to God.*
> *Except inasmuch as I am one with Him."*
> – Meister Eckhart

From a self-knowledge seeking standpoint, Florence can be inspiring. Thanks to the Medicis who spent lavish sums especially on art, the work produced by the Florentines incited still more creative activity. There I learned that locals and visitors during Renaissance time would mingle and spread knowledge and new thinking, goods and technologies that energized the city. Also encouraged by the freedom of ideas that was the core of humanism, Florentines prized the individual and tried to look with fresh eyes at nature and human society. I could not help but spend a few extra days in an area I knew it would take years for me to go back to – if I ever did.

This city had a great influence in my travel experience in ways that it produced in me a mindset shift. One afternoon, after an extended walk around the multiple historical sites for several hours, I finally reached the contemplating sight of a small mountain range. The Chianti Mountains are located between Florence, Sienna and Arezzo. The territory, largely characterized by cypresses, is rich in river sources. Situated high up on the hilltops are many castles with towers that were once fortresses. There, I got some rest time. Out of the blue and in the quiet, I had the strange sense of...not belonging. Of detachment. A sense of emptiness and neutrality without feeling depressed. Initially having some sensation of sadness, this awkward experience of not belonging anywhere was followed by the amazing experience of belonging...everywhere. A bit hard to describe, it was as though a window had been opened into my soul as a preamble for the things to come. Powerful and yet humbling, I was another man from that time on.

Again, Marcus Aurelius comes to 'rescue' me: "Pick me up and throw me where you will. Wherever I land I shall keep the god within me happy – satisfied, that is, if attitude and action follow its own constitution. Is this present thing any good reason for my soul to be sick and out of sorts – humbled, craving, shackled, shying? Will you find any good reason for that? – *Marcus Aurelius, Meditations, Book 8.*

## ROME, *CAPUT MUNDI*

Longing to one day be able to go back to *Firenze*, I was south bound. The Eternal City is certainly a focus of any serious traveler in Italy. Once again, I knew no one in this global city which dismisses intros. Excited as I was to keep moving, I was not as thrilled to go to Rome as I was to go to Florence. Yet, I was compelled to take the time and effort. Most likely due to the intimidating importance that Rome has historically played in the world stage for many centuries and to this day, with its both oppressive and magnificent influence in Western Civilization. My days were filled with introspection. The sense of grandiosity was extraordinary, reason why visiting it was unavoidable. At least, I did try to do it by skipping the high peak tourist hours and did get to experience places such as The Pantheon, Colosseum and Ancient Rome, the *piazzas*, the Vatican Museums. So much to see and to touch, so little time and...budget. As nice as it was to be in such a magnetic piece of history, my focus was on simplicity among complexity. To which it made me deepen my knowledge about the inspiring figure of Marcus Aurelius:

"In his private entries of his *Meditations*, Marcus Aurelius Antoninus does not conceal from himself the fact that he is the Roman Emperor and one in a long line of emperors. His insistent demand for rational analysis and stripping his human and material environment down to its essentials reveals an essential part of his character. Scattered through his *Meditations* we encounter reflections on his duty to serve, as 'a male, mature in years, a statesman, a Roman, a ruler.' This 'service' is subsumed under his more fundamental duty as a rational human being to benefit and tolerate – perhaps the more difficult task – his fellow human beings. Only once does Marcus Aurelius mention the city of Rome. In the entry that concludes his *Meditations*, he begins: 'Mortal man, you have lived as a citizen in this great city.' The city of Marcus' meditations was his provident Stoic universe, not the city and empire he prudently ruled over for what was, in his view, a brief moment in time."

## DOZZA, *BOLOGNA*

From Rome, I left for this beautiful region known as Emilia-Romana, where a round of seven villages is reachable from major cities like Bologna, Parma and Rimini. Dozza is a tiny *borghi* that has managed to retain authenticity and a slow pace of life. Home to my dear Italian friends whom I met *a Londra* (London) months earlier, Adro and Lucia. Needless to say, our encounter was a delight. As I got to their village from the train station they took me to Adro's home where I met his family and in particular his older brother, a *pianoforte* classical performer. In London, Adro had proudly told me about his brother's talent on the instrument which I thought was just another name for a piano. However, there is a subtle difference. *Pianoforte* designates any piano dating from the invention of the instrument by Bartolomeo Cristofori around 1700 up to the early 19$^{th}$ century. Most typically used to refer to the late 18$^{th}$ to early 19$^{th}$ century instruments for which Haydn, Mozart and the younger Beethoven wrote their piano music. Starting in Beethoven's time, the pianoforte began a period of steady evolution, culminating in the late 19th century with the modern grand piano. The earlier pianoforte became obsolete and was absent from the musical scene for many decades. In the 20th century the pianoforte was revived, following the rise of interest in historically informed performance (period instruments, faithful to the style of the musical era in which a work was originally conceived). *Pianofortes* are built for this purpose today in specialist shops.

To my big surprise, Adro and Lucia prepared my stay carefully. I was taken to an old barn where we gathered with their group of friends and choir. During an entire weekend, people showed up bringing flowers, dishes and local wine. In the barn, I experienced the joy of a small community relishing friendship and laughter, great folk and classical music, and loving care for one another. Magic moments I will never forget. In fact, I had only seen such flashes in films, such as Giuseppe Tornatore's, one of the most notable, *Cinema Paradiso*. Exquisite time.

## VENICE, *LA SERENISSIMA*

The fifth and last of the major cities I wanted to be sure to visit while in and around this exhilarating country, Venice is the capital of northern Italy's Veneto region, built on more than 100 small islands in a lagoon in the Adriatic Sea. After the fall of the Western Roman Empire, barbarians from the north were raiding Rome's former territories pushing frightened men coming from the nearby Italian mainland to be the first people to settle in, beginning around 400 A.D. It has no roads, just canals – including the Grand Canal thoroughfare – and over 400 bridges, lined with Renaissance and Gothic palaces. I got to Venice on a windy rainy afternoon: *Venezia Santa Lucia Railway, la stazione* was cloudy and foggy. Almost like a haunted and spooky feeling-mysterious in a good way. The good aspect about getting to *Venezia* in mid-to-late October was that fewer visitors were in town, so not too many crowded areas throughout. What I did experience was what the venetians call as *acqua alta*, or "high water." This is a term used for the exceptional tide peaks that periodically occur in the northern Adriatic Sea. The phenomenon revolves around the peaks reaching their maximum in the Venetian Lagoon, causing partial flooding of Venice. Colder at night, the morning fog adds to the mystique. Of course, the vaporetti were always crowded. Zipping through the Grand Canal and through the small adjacent water ways, all kinds of boats populated the scenery making *The Floating City* a very special place.

It was easy for me to be mesmerized once in Venice. Its amazing architecture, my walks around the city as well as navigating its waterways allowed my visit to be a unique journey. Especially being there towards the end of the high season, which at that time of the year had more to do with experiencing the local mood than wrestling one's way through the crowds. Quoting Imtiaz Manji: "The whole city is really a monument to human ingenuity, determination, resourcefulness, and artistic passion. It was founded out of urgent necessity and evolved to become a home to some of the greatest art and architecture mankind has ever created. Human beings are like that; we have the ability to invent ourselves out of a crisis, to make the most of what we have and achieve incredible things for the simple reason that we are forced to. And then we emerge from the crisis stronger than ever, and able to apply that newly discovered capacity for greatness to work in new and exciting ways. For the people of Venice, their capacity for survival in the early years is surpassed only by the greatness of their passion for the arts as they flourished."
– Imtiaz Manji

## ZÜRICH, *LITTLE BIG CITY*

After several weeks spent in Latin dominant cultures such as the French, the Spanish and the Italian, which to a good extent were somewhat related to the Portuguese, I finally began heading up to countries with a less familiar structure than I was accustomed to. The last leg of my trip was still geographically distant. Yet, it would be the one that I would spend a great deal of time considering the period I had left. Once again, *Let's Go: Europe* was an outstanding resource for getting acquainted with my next stop: Zürich. Having borrowed the Yamaha guitar was a blessing as during the train travels young men and women would occasionally join in and sing along a tune or two.

Matthias, two other travelers and I had been in the same cabin for most of the time since the departure from Venice. Although reserved, I could tell he had enjoyed the music. As we said goodbye at the arrival to the *Zürich Hauptbahnhof*, I walked into a telephone booth to call a couple of targeted youth hostels to check availability prior to going over. Not knowing the German language, it took me a little while longer to 'decipher' names, meanings and signage. That's when I saw Matthias once again walking towards the booth with a smile as if he had something to say. Opening the door, he let me know that he had reached out to his parents and, if I were fine with that, they had agreed to host me during the couple of nights I had in mind to be in town. Thrilled and humbled, of course I accepted it enthusiastically.

The first thing I learned as we waited for Matthias' Mom to finish up cooking supper was that politics was not first in the household's agenda. Although politically aware, his Dad couldn't care less about politicians, which seemed to be the norm for a country in which its middle class comprises of about 60% of the population. After asking me questions about Brazilian soccer and the geography of "your immense country," we were ready for the meal: the tastiest soup and bread I had in months. Plus, the few hours that I was allowed to partake with a real local family was such a treat for me. The experience I would always aim at since this was the best way to scratch the surface when it came to visiting and learning something genuine about a different country. A few fun facts made Switzerland a unique country, I learned: there were more banks than dentists – this one, not a surprise; it was illegal to have a 'solo' pet – Swiss law does not allow owning pets unless you have a pair, be it a mouse, guinea pig, fish, ferret or canary and, of course, dog or cat. The law assumes isolation of such animals as abuse. In fact, the country even has pet lawyers...; The Land of Lakes – more than 1,500! The Home of the Alps – more than 200 mountains, over 3,000 meters high! And, not to be ignored, a major producer of...chocolate – billions of Toblerone triangles made in a year!

## MUNICH, *TOYTOWN*

October in *"Millionendorf,"* another nickname for this high quality of life and safe city, is synonymous with *Octoberfest*, the big beer festival. Much to my lack of interest – which I later kind of regretted not having experienced – my mind was less on partying and drinking but more on fathoming some of the roots and sources of Europe's past and present. Being in Germany for the first time and headed to Israel as one of the highlights of this journey, I needed to understand some of the facts that brought the world to where it was in 1980: What was this Cold War really about? That this was a state of geopolitical tension between the Soviet Union with its satellite states (the Eastern Bloc), and the United States with its allies (the Western Bloc) after World War II, I had studied at school and knew it from the news. The term "cold" used because there was no large-scale fighting directly between the two sides was also known, with each bloc supporting major regional wars known as proxy wars. The most visible effect of the Cold War was the split of the temporary wartime alliance against Nazi Germany – the latter, where Munich and the Bavarian region were center stage from the very beginning, and the Berlin Wall an icon of divisiveness.

Historically, Munich is where Hitler came to power and where the Nazi Party had its official headquarters. Located at 16 km from the city, Dachau was the concentration camp that was in operation the longest from March 1933 to April 1945, nearly all the twelve years of the Nazi Regime. Initially reluctant but yet firm on my purpose, I made the decision to visit the camp. There I learned that not only Jews and homosexuals were made inmates but also Communists, Jehovah's Witnesses and Catholic priests - together with thousands of German political prisoners seen as enemies of the regime – were the victims of the constant fear of brutal treatment and terror detention. Nearly 32,000 documented deaths occurred at the camp, and thousands more that were undocumented.

The choice to visit The Dachau Camp was deliberate and I knew it would strongly take me out of my comfort zone. Located in the medieval town of the same name, Dachau was opened in 1933 with its purpose enlarged to include forced labor. Reflected throughout the pictures I saw orderly displayed in this historic site, the system grew to include nearly 100 sub-camps which were mostly work camps, spread throughout southern Germany and Austria. One of the camp's despicable functions was to harbor medical experimentation, where hundreds of prisoners suffered and died or were executed. The multiplicity of atrocities was recorded on the site via documents, access to the dorms and gas chambers, books, artistic work and outdoor sculptures depicting the barbarian time. Shocking and at the same time liberating, this dark side of history was indelible to a traveler's eyes. Not to be forgotten in my mind.

## INNSBRUCK, *CAPITAL OF THE ALPS*

Gone from Germany, I headed East. Nestled in the Austrian Tirol, Innsbruck sits in a valley and is surrounded by enormous, snow-capped mountains. Quite a change from the reality-check experience I had in Munich, I was ready for some serious hiking and outdoor endeavor to clear my mind out. "Colorful and picturesque, this is a city with endless views," I read on my travel bible. The youth hostel was located in the Old Town, a compact scenic spot with a stroll of colorful streets. Rather than mingling, I was looking forward to spending time away from tourists and thought that hiking up one of the mountains seemed to be a good option for photographing the astonishing landscape. The humid morning after a light overnight rain made the terrain not ideal but manageable for hiking. Packed with the appropriate gear – or so I thought – I walked out of the Old Town area towards the Inn River where I could see one of the peaks of Nordkette, a range of mountains north of the city. Served by cable car, my goal was to hike it all the way up to the top of the ski area station and from there, either hike back or take the cable car in case I got exhausted.

It was mid-to-late October and the temperature was cool but still pleasant by the river side. The first two of the estimated four-and-half-hour hike went well. With stunning views and the sun up, it made it for a perfect time. I had had experiences before that would remind me that hiking up a mountain was typically better handled by the body than hiking down, especially when one's knees could feel the body weight pressure more strongly. That was my case. Another 1 ½ hour went by and I hit a part of the ground where the snow was packed. Inexperienced as I was on that type of weather, the remaining hour I still had left to climb my way up to the top became a near nightmare. Not only was I cold and beginning to get tired but the snow was getting higher and higher, making it gradually more difficult to cover the ground up as my legs sunk deep into the snow. I could see my destination up the mountain but hiking got rather challenging. What was supposed to take another hour ended up becoming a 3-hour ordeal. In total, 6 ½ hours got me tired, hungry and ready for crashing. Luckily, I found the ski lounge cafeteria still open and was able to get a hot soup just enough to warm me up a bit. My boots and socks were soaking wet. The upside was that photographing the views was such a gift. In the end, it felt like a sense of accomplishment. Next time I would certainly do things differently but for now my day had been a good one.

## VIENNA, *CITY OF MUSIC, CITY OF DREAMS*

A hub was one way that crossed my mind to describe this incredible city. Among the couple of youth hostels I had a chance to drop by and the multiple places where travelers would gather around, Vienna was that unique spot in the Europe of the West and East which shelters people of a wide variety of dreams, anxieties and expectations. Definitely a crossroads. Why is that? Besides being a hub, it was paradoxically a threshold. From there, moving eastbound became unchartered territory. In the train cabins, I could empathize with the gloomy and burdensome faces of folks from Czechoslovakia, Poland and Hungary, to name a few; these people, typically the elderly, would need special permission to leave their countries in order to visit family in Western Europe even for a short period of time. Their countries' regimes, although less restricted than the dominated republics such as Belarus, Ukraine or Moldovia, were still under the Soviet indirect influence and would make all efforts to curtail freedoms. Therefore, for these passengers, going back home from West to East would translate into sad and discouraged semblances visible to inquisitive eyes. For many, this would only start to change with the fall of the Berlin Wall, nine years later.

There's a good reason for Vienna to be nicknamed as *City of Music* and *City of Dreams*. Its artistic and intellectual legacy was shaped by illustrious residents such as Mozart, Beethoven, Schubert, Strauss, Freud, Pulitzer, Schiele and others. It is also known for its imperial palaces, gardens and Baroque castles, as well as for the Museum Quartier district with historic and contemporary buildings. Urban planning, a topic which determines a city's quality of life, makes Vienna well known for regularly hosting international conferences on the subject in which the city is often used as a case study by world-wide urban planners, a high-profile environment for its high-quality standards.

There I had the rare opportunity to go to the Vienna State Opera and see "The Sleeping Beauty" with Rudolf Nureyev, widely regarded as the greatest male ballet dancer of his generation. His great and equally dramatic life story, already one of the best dancers of all time, was one of being the first defection of a Soviet artist during the Cold War, which in the early 60s created an international sensation. He became a citizen of Austria naturalized in 1982.

It was time to move on to the last leg of my train travel with the final destination being Athens, Greece. Less than a week before my *Interrail Pass* would expire, I met at the hostel a group of young travelers discussing the particulars and what they knew from word of mouth of the next step for heading out East. I joined in and tried to get a sense of what to expect once I crossed the border into Hungary. It was as if this group was looking forward to a little push that would allow them to breath in the new adventure. *Let's Go: Europe* had good information and we expected to make the best out of our journeys.

## BUDAPEST, *THE PEARL OF THE DANUBE*

Mark, Jeffrey and Christopher were already seated when I walked into the train compartment. I had seen them briefly as part of the group discussing the eastbound undertaking at the hostel and now, at *Wien Hauptbanhof*, the Viennese central station, we were waiting for the train's departure. The first two from western Canada, the latter, a seer, as he denominated himself, an American from Wisconsin. A seer? I didn't immediately ask him what he meant by that but learned later on that a seer, besides being "one that sees, is someone that predicts events or developments, a person credited with extraordinary moral and spiritual insight," according to the Webster's Dictionary. Fascinating, I ponder. Like myself, they were all apprehensive but excited to have made the decision to go to the *"Heart of Europe,"* another nickname for Budapest. With all of us kind of drinking from the same fountain as it related to where to stay and how to get around the capital, the four of us instinctively stuck around each other at the arrival at *Budapest Keleti* Train Station. Through *Let's Go: Europe* we learned that accommodations could take a more interesting perspective if a traveler chose to be a guest at a local dweller, i.e., spending time with a native family. With Airbnb still at light years from us, it was an exercise imagining how the accommodations would be like. Not surprisingly, it didn't take long for the first offer to come to us. Actually, it happened the moment we stepped into the station. No sooner said than done, this quiet but lovely out-of-the-blue old lady had already figured us out. Savvy, she approached us and with a good knowledge of English she immediately offered us her place at a very reasonable price. Of course, provided we took the offer together and 'as a package.' We looked at one another and smiled. It was a no brainer. *Koszonom*, we thanked her in Hungarian.

Buda on one side, Pest on the other side of the bank. The Danube, second largest river in Europe, cuts through no fewer than ten countries and sixteen cities. In Hungary's capital, it divides the two-city personalities turned into one. Merged in 1873, Budapest sounds more natural than twin cities such as Minneapolis/St. Paul and Dallas/Fort Worth. Buda is situated on a series of hills, Pest is flat and populous, busy and buzzing. After a long tram ride, the five of us got to the old lady's building which seemed to have been built in the 1930s. To get to the apartment, we took turns to ride an antique Otis birdcage-style elevator for backpack drop-off and settling in. The apartment, a large old fashioned ornate wide open environment, seemed a disquiet area with little privacy at first sight. It felt like the space had once belonged to a rich family and overtime changed hands, thereby probably becoming a rental property. The old lady showed us the facility all around and took us to our own private bedrooms, quite a treat from the sharing dorm experience of the youth hostels we had been accustomed in the West.

The silent question we had in our minds was: "Where is the old lady's room? Does anyone else live with her?" As we subtly screened the atmosphere around, we could not physically spot her room until...in one of the corners of the wide open chamber, timidly separated by curtains, there was a small enclosed space. Without verbally manifesting our curiosity, the four of us figured it out. Smart as she was, she came forward and told us that that was the space she shared with her 38-year old son.

Unemployed, we could tell he was there although he would not show up for the length of our stay. In fact, the seemingly wealthy family that once owned that space was actually her own. With Hungary ruled as a socialist republic since 1949, her family basically disintegrated throughout the years. Although she would inhabit that space for many years to come, like many other households in the city, she did make her living out of tourists' acceptance of the condition we were having the opportunity to experience. Good or bad, it seemed irrelevant. Except for, that was the reality of that household.

Evening fell, we quietly walked to a section of the Danube. From Buda's side, we looked across the river where a young couple seemed to be waiving at us as if reaching for contact. Coming to a closer sight, yet on opposite sides, their gleeful behavior attracted us. Certain that we were tourists, they attempted to communicate and acted effusively inviting us to go to the other side of the river. We all agreed and crossed the nearby bridge over to Pest. The young man was holding a bottle of some kind of liquor, whereas the young lady seemed submissive to his initiative. After exchanging incomprehensible words, we unanimously assumed that they wanted us to follow them as they pointed out to the direction of a two-story old house. Dark and built resembling a small castle, they opened the door. A spiral set of iron stairs surrounded by battered walls led to the next level, to which we reluctantly began to climb. Half way through as we followed the young couple, we heard the yelling upstairs of another supposedly young individual most likely censoring his mate's initiative, thus shattering the silent enclosure. For the four of us, the expected mingling with the locals got short-lived as our friendly Eastern European young man turned around and, with a mixed semblance of frustration, disappointment and irony, shrugged and articulated: "Sorry…"

With our evening being over with hopes of grasping some of the Magyar experience, tired and confused, we simply crashed. We woke up the next morning with a feast prepared by our host, ready to be degusted – freshly baked bread, sausages or 'kabanos and beerwurst,' bacon, eggs, pates, cream cheese and cold cuts, accompanied by multiple kinds of fresh vegetables. To die for. All homemade, prepared with love by our lovely harbinger, we silently enjoyed the breakfast before each one of us set out to the next town.

## A SHORT JOURNEY THROUGH *THE BALKANS*

Josip Broz, known as *Marshal Tito*, the benevolent dictator, had died earlier in the year. Viewed as authoritarian but also as a unifying symbol, his policies maintained for decades the relative peaceful coexistence of the nations of Yugoslavia – namely, Bosnia and Herzegovina, Croatia, Macedonia, Montenegro, Serbia and Slovenia. They would be dismembered by horrific ethnic conflicts in the 1990s which culminated in the Yugoslav Wars, first in Croatia and then, most severely, in multi-ethnic Bosnia and Herzegovina. Wars that would leave a dismal long-term economic and political devastation in the region, with unthinkable consequences for the Europe of the end of the 20$^{th}$ century.

With not much time left until my train pass expired, I was now running against the clock and must embark on a twelve-hour travel time to Athens in order to keep my schedule in good shape. Although wanting to experience this diverse cultural scene, I had to make the choice of hopefully learning what I could from the local train travelers. Belgrade, the capital of today's Serbia, then Yugoslavia, a two-and-a-half-hour trip from Budapest, made for a natural stop at the central station where I could get a taste of the local food before switching trains and continuing on towards the Greek capital. As many train stations in Europe, this too had the status of a cultural monument of great importance. Built by a French company to reflect the latest European technical and architectural achievements of the late 1800s, it was a symbol of the royal capital at that time.

Back to the platform and into the next train, the middle-aged man and his daughter joined me in the compartment for what would take the entire traveling time to the border with Greece.

Reserved and conveying a modest behavior, he and his child looked like peasants going back to their rural environment. In my relative ignorance about this multi-cultural and ethnic country which I was only going to spend half a day crossing through, I had already learned that there were no magic formulas that told me how to deal with people the first time I met them. My experience at this point was that it was essential to be courteous, polite, humble and especially show willingness to listen. In a few minutes, I found out that this local traveler, unshaved, simply dressed, with a caring and sincere smile did not speak a word in English. Nor did the ten or eleven-year old girl. I thought to myself, this will be interesting. The often topics of conversations that would typically sit well when meeting new people – regional history and culture, local/international politics, business, agriculture and sports – would rather now give way to silence and observation of the landscape. And to our body language and the subtle eye-crossing ways to communicate when verbal language does not find common ground.

Common ground – the key word for communication and understanding. As this decent, introverted man took the initiative to reach out to a magazine left or forgotten in the train cabin, we began to interact. Images speak for themselves. What is revealed after the interaction begins is the values and attention to detect what seems to be relevant in order to make our mutual experience worth our while. As we looked at my *Let's Go: Europe* maps, I learned he was from the southern part of Yugoslavia: Macedonia, a Slavic country made up of different ethnic groups. In our intent to communicate, family seemed to be most important as he emphasized on the photos: he pointed out to pictures and situations translating into his own language. Just as though he wanted me to learn and acquire the sounds, to which I reciprocated. Particularly, the way they lived, worked, married and carried out daily life.

Our reciprocal efforts to communicate took center stage when he noticed that I had an infection on my left hand ring finger. It was actually rather gross for pus had already been formed around the swollen fingernail tip. He grabbed my hand and with his battered peasant hands examined my finger as if he were a nurse or a doctor. Without hesitation, he calmly pulled a hidden pin out from his coat's lapel, looked at the little girl and showed it to me. Quietly reaching to his pocket, he took out a lighter and igniting it he began to sterilize the pin. Knowing where this was going to go, my confidence in his aptitude was total. My uncomfortable finger pain was relieved almost immediately. Smiles and a sense of duty was transparent in his demeanor; to which, I fully corroborated. A timeless moment of unpretentious kindness and bonding with that individual made it for a meaningful travel journey. Simplicity at its best, a few more hours went by when I gave him and his daughter a hug as we arrived at his destination only to never see him again. And to never forget that moment in time of sheer and genuine joy.

## ATHENS, *THE CITY OF THE VIOLET CROWN*

Athens was the bridge toward my final destination in the Mediterranean: Israel. Even before the start of my train journey, my goal to continue traveling in that part of the world became clearer. However, in my mind I couldn't dismiss the idea that being in that convoluted geographical spot in the Middle East had great significance to me. And the reason was also clear: all my ancestors immigrated to Brazil from Lebanon in the mid-1910s and, for whatever reason, our family simply lost the connection with the land, language, friends and possibly remaining family members. Now, it was impossible to reach Lebanon from Israel. Moreover, the country had been going through a horrific civil war since 1975 with no signs of de-escalation – quite the contrary, the civil conflict would linger until 1990.

As my resources would eventually become scarce, while time was still on my side, the idea of an experience in a *kibbutz* in Israel was real. Highly influenced by anonymous travelers, that seemed to be a good plan: to work and get room and board in exchange. But before I got there, I must get a sense of Socrates' birthplace. There were two possible origins of the nickname for Greece's capital city. The first being a direct translation of Greece's former name Ionia (after King Ion). The word Ion means violet in Greek, and Athens was the city where the King Ion was crowned. Another origin story stems from a line in a surviving fragment of one of Greek poet Pinda's works: "City of light, with thy violet crown, beloved of the poets, thou art the bulwark of Greece."

With some Greek family background – my grandma Alexandra's father was born in Mykonos in the mid-1800s – arriving in Athens felt like an achievement. Not only for being in such an iconic place in world history but because this was my last traveling platform: after an intensive almost three-month voyage throughout the Old Continent, I was ready to spend some time getting around this historic region before moving on to a totally different dynamic across the Mediterranean. Rome, and ancient Greece, with Athens as its centerpiece, laid the roots of western civilization – themselves built on foundations laid in ancient Egypt and Mesopotamia. So much to be absorbed. A center for the arts, learning and philosophy, home of Plato's Academy and Aristotle's Lyceum, it was widely referred to as the birthplace of democracy, largely because of its cultural and political impact on the European continent. In the few days I had planned to stay in Athens, I was able to sightsee some of the 5th century BC landmarks: The Acropolis with the Parthenon Temple; the Acropolis Museum with the National Archeological Museum; Syntagma Square and the Temple of Olympian Zeus plus the Ancient Agora of Athens.

The rise and fall of Athens were engraved in its soil and ruins but many of its monuments stood still. Defeated in multiple wars by Spartans, Corinthians, Macedonians and later on by the Romans, many of its vanquishers refused to allow their soldiers burn or destroy the city itself. At its height, Athens once epitomized the best of Greek virtues and enjoyed such prestige that the Spartans refused to sack the city or enslave the citizens even after the Peloponnesian War. History tells that this set a model that would be followed by future conquerors who would defeat Athens but not decimate it. In the modern age the name Athens still conjures to one's mind words and images of the classical world and the heights of intellectual and poetic creativity. History at its best.

Which led me to a remarkable thought in Marcus Aurelius' *Meditations*: "The universal cause is a torrent, sweeping everything in its stream. So, man, what does that mean for you? Do what nature require at this moment. Start straight away, if that is in your power; don't look over your shoulder to see if people will know. Don't hope for Plato's utopian republic, but be content with the smallest step forward, and regard even that result as no mean achievement." – Marcus Aurelius, Meditations[1], Book 9.

## ISRAEL AND THE *KIBBUTZ* EXPERIENCE

The Olympic Airways flight time from Athens to Tel Aviv took nearly two hours. At the arrival and the plane still on the tarmac, I was puzzled with the question my co-passenger asked me. With an inquisitive look, he worn round glasses and an impeccable grey suit with a yellow bow tie, he fired up: "Why are you going to a *kibbutz*?" As I was glad to manifest my answer that I was going to spend time in a *kibbutz* as a volunteer, the short man in his sixties struck again: "But why are you going to a *kibbutz*?" Not knowing exactly why he would ask me the same question, I assumed he did not understand my answer. So, I paused and brought up the same response. Silence followed suit before he asked the same question once again. It took me an instant to realize that his question had in fact a rather disapproving tone which, at that moment, I had no means to understand why. It would take a few days to fathom the origin of that peculiar approach. My interaction with the man became

---

[1] Marcus Aurelius excerpts, known as the Meditations, are unique in Classical literature. These are writings reflecting personal and philosophical diary notes written in Greek by a man who happened to be an intellectual Roman Emperor. Although he had no intention for these thoughts to be published – they remain of interest and relevance to the modern world.

the very first experience about being in a *kibbutz* without even setting foot in one yet.

It was the last day of October. After getting around Tel Aviv in the afternoon and spending the night in a youth hostel, my focus was to get up first thing in the morning and get to the *Kibbutz* Office in downtown. From there, according to my valuable travel book, I would be directed to one of the 258 *kibbutzim* established throughout the country – provided my application process for a minimum of a two-month stay was satisfactory and I got accepted. The word *kibbutz* in Hebrew means "gathering, clustering." The proper meaning for it is, a collective community. Traditionally based on agriculture, the first *kibbutz* was established in the early 1900s and began as utopian communities, a combination of socialism and Zionism.

Secular or religious, *kibbutzim* were organized around factories and farms, accounting for a significant percentage of Israel's industrial and agricultural output. As a student of economics, learning and experiencing their *modus operandi* was one of the reasons for my efforts to make this volunteer visit a reality. Besides, at that stage of my journey and running a tight budget, volunteering had its benefits: learning multiple working skills, free nutritious food and accommodations and, most importantly, learning and understanding their *modus vivendi* and, to a reasonable extent, the Israeli people. Equally important was the opportunity to meet other volunteers – from many parts of the world.

Application approved, I was bound to northern Israel, near Haifa, about an hour by bus. Intrigued by one of the questions from the *Kibbutz* Officer: "Are you Christian or Muslim?" Being a volunteer from a Christian background involved minimum scrutiny, second only to being Jewish, I learned. Joseph Baratz, one of the pioneers of the *kibbutz* movement back in the early days, wrote a book about his experiences: "We were happy enough working on the land, but we knew more and more certainly that the ways of the old settlements were not for us. This was not the way we hoped to settle the country – this old way with Jews on top and Arabs working for them; anyway, we thought that there shouldn't be employers and employed at all. There must be a better way." The pioneers wanted to farm the land themselves but becoming independent farmers revealed to be unrealistic. Controversial as it may be, I began to understand that the idea about *kibbutzim* revolved around the successful establishment of *Eretz Israel*, the State of Israel[2].

## SHA'AR HA'AMAKIM

Corola had been a *kibbutznik* – a member – for many years at the Gate of the Valleys, the literal translation for Sha'ar Ha'amakim. In her fifties, she was responsible for orientation and guidance for all volunteers enlisted in the collective community. An immigrant from Romania, she showed me the area around where human habitation dated at least as far back as the Hellenistic period, around 300 BC. Founded in 1935 by immigrants from the Balkans, with a population of 650 members, most of the income of Sha'ar Ha'amakim derived from a solar water heater factory as well as agriculture – with orchards producing apples, peaches and pears – and dairy farming. Specialized in the production of sunflower seeds, the *kibbutz* marketed the manufacturing products and produce under its name, both in Israel and for export.

I couldn't help but dive into learning about this unique world of communities: According to the Jewish Agency of Israel, "The *Kibbutz* operates under the premise that all income generated by the *Kibbutz* and its members goes into a common pool. This income is used to run the *Kibbutz*, make investments, and guarantee mutual and reciprocal aid and responsibility be-

---

[2] The Balfour Declaration was a public statement issued by the British government during World War I announcing support for the establishment of a "national home of the Jewish people" in Palestine. Not including geographical boundaries, it also envisioned that "nothing shall be done which may prejudice the civil and religious rights of existing non-Jewish communities in Palestine." Controversies aside, *kibbutzim* played a role in defining the borders of the Jewish state-to-be and also had a prominent military function. Despite growing conflict between Palestinian Arabs and Palestinian Jews, it was not until 1948 that the State of Israel was created.

tween members. *Kibbutz* members receive the same budget (according to family size), regardless of their job or position. In terms of education, all children start equally and are given equal opportunity. The *Kibbutz* is governed by a system of direct participatory democracy, where the individual can directly influence issues and events in the community. In this mostly self-sufficient circle, the collective as well as the work ethic play a major role."

Located near Mount Carmel, Sha'ar Ha'amakim, like most of the secular *kibbutzim*, was a host for volunteers from all around the world. At that time, nationals of Dutch, German, Austrian, French, American, Danish, Australian, Swiss, British, Rhodesian (Zimbabwe), Colombian and South African origin were part of the body of people volunteering from two to six months in multiple capacities. Yehuda, in charge of the children's facilities and their coordination, presented me what would be my job for the first three weeks: from six in the morning to two in the afternoon, with intervals for breakfast, break time and lunch, my task was to load food from the community kitchen onto two wagons attached to a small tractor, drive and deliver the food stored in containers to the multiple children's houses; then, from each house, load up the laundry and drive up the loads for delivery at the *comunas*, the laundry houses which served the community.

Children's housing had strictly to do with communal child rearing, the method of education that prevailed in the collective communities in Israel until about the end of the 1980s. Collective education started on the day of birth and went on until adulthood. At the time, it was considered a natural outcome of the principle of equality, which was part and parcel of the *kibbutz* life. The education authority of the *kibbutz* was responsible for the rearing and well-being of all the children born on the *kibbutz*, taking care of their food, clothing, and medical treatment. Everybody received the same share of everything. Surprisingly, parents were not involved economically in the upbringing of their children.

Children's lives had three focal points: the children's house, parents' house, and the whole *kibbutz*. They lived in the children's house, where they had communal sleeping arrangements and visited their parents for 2–3 hours a day. Non-selectivity was a fundamental principle of collective education; every child got 12 years of study, they took no tests whatsoever, and no grades were recorded. The founders of the *kibbutz* actually aimed at creating the 'new man' of a utopian society.

Yehuda had been clear about the job: "At the end of the third week, there is a man coming from the U.S. that will be taking over the job you will be doing now. James is his name. He had been in the *kibbutz* a couple of times before. When applying this third time, he was adamant about coming back and specifically doing the children's houses' round up operation. Therefore, consider this only as temporary." Without questioning, I promptly agreed and went about learning my duties. One of the interesting aspects of being a volunteer in that environment was that by 2:00 p.m. the work shift was over. From that period on, there was plenty of time to visit the towns around the *kibbutz* – especially Haifa and its districts, like Kiryat Bialik, Tirat Carmel, Nesher and Akko, also known as the Old City of Acre. Or, simply experience other areas in the community complex where volunteers could develop better knowledge of the lifestyle, such as: doing extra activities other than one's own – the dairy farm and the multiple orchards, pottery, the solar panel and boiler manufacturing unit, etc. – visiting the library, as well as simply mingling and relaxing.

Every day, with the exception of the *Sabbath* – a day of observance and abstinence from work kept from Friday evening to Saturday evening – breakfast, lunch and dinner had a specific structure and held up a special moment in the community. There, the 650 members and about 20-30 volunteers gathered as a group. With an impressive organization and providing high quality wholesome food, this collective group gathered in an orderly and respectful manner in the large dining room. It didn't take long to perceive that that area was the heart of the *kibbutz*.

There, a few and brief announcements were conveyed to the community during the meals. After dinner, tea and coffee followed with time spent at the *kibbutz* library.

Oskar had been there for a couple of weeks before I arrived. A volunteer from Austria, I learned from him that he was advised by his family to stay away from his hometown for having gotten in some kind of trouble due to a drug related issue. Apparently friendly, he seemed to be genuinely interested in forging relationships. As long as he was sober. The second night in the *kibbutz* I had the experience first-hand: as volunteers, we were granted free lodging, medical insurance and a small stipend, basically pocket money, to cover for extras such as cigarettes, beverages, etc. It was up to each individual to make the best use out of that resource. In his case, although personable, smart, and communicative, the alcohol effect would play negatively on his behavior once his tolerance was exceeded. For a couple of random evenings, I helped a heavily drunk Oskar put himself together and brought him into our dorm, which we shared with three other guys. My interpretation was that he was happy to be there and alcohol was just a way to celebrate. The next morning, after hangover, he was apologetic and life went on as usual. But the red flag was there.

There is a perception that *kibbutzim* can be compared to a good quality country club with the added bonus of a safety net. Often times, I heard members bragging that not everyone could become a member of a *kibbutz* but any member had the free will of not being a part of it, if that was one's wish. The fact is that it is clear to one's eyes that there is mutual help and responsibility for each other, which reflects the *kibbutz's* sense of community and its effect on the quality of education, environment, space and security. Attractive to a few – only 3% of Israel's population lived in the *kibbutzim* system, the *Kibbutz* has made a dramatic mark on Israeli production and culture. And on ideology, which explains the question I was asked multiple times by the fellow on the flight from Athens to Tel Aviv...

Life in a dorm is not easy when there was uncontrollable and relentless snoring next to you, night after night after night. My poor next-bed neighbor, a young man from Germany, had some kind of a serious nasal septum deviation which was driving me bananas. Besides, helping carry Oskar back into the dorm every other night was getting old, not only for me but for other volunteers as well. There was clearly a problem that sooner or later would have to be dealt with. Aiming at finding a way out for a better quality sleeping, I had no choice but to be on the lookout for other possible dorm arrangements.

It was Friday afternoon and the *kibbutz* was winding down the work week, ready for the *Sabbath*. Volunteers out and about, I see from a distance the emergence out of nowhere of this Jesus-like thin-completion figure; as he approaches, the tall, blue-eyed, bearded and long hair individual arrived with a rather small backpack. Compared to mine, it looked like he was going to be there for a week or so. I carefully observed his screening of his own possibilities around accommodations. It was mid-November and a number of European and American volunteers were arriving every day in search for warmer days. Even though it was wintertime in the Mediterranean, the days were pleasant and the nights were just nicely cool. Volunteers roaming around, I took the initiative and introduced myself to the newcomer: "Nice meeting you too," he reservedly answered, "I'm James Meade." He stepped out and I continued to watch his next move. Perceiving he spotted a vacant little house detached from the dorm area, which I had no idea was available for volunteers until that very moment, I took action to ask: "Are you planning on moving into that house?" Restrained, he answered: "Maybe." Decisively, I took a shot: "Would you mind if I join you?." Not convincingly but in a positive manner, after being quickly measured up, I got a: "Yeah. Ok." Up until that moment, the only thing we had in common was the job I was about to relinquish and pass on to him. Other than that, we were both volunteers and knew nothing about each other.

My next job was at the solar water heater factory where most of the male volunteers work. A manufacturing unit environment and completely different from what I was doing before, I rapidly adapted to the new routine and was glad to be learning new skills. Diversity dictated the capacity for survival of the collective community at Sha'ar Ha'amakim. Therefore, Israel being a small country, the economic activities of the *kibbutz* also revolved around extending sales to the export market. Yet, it was impressive to see that virtually every house roof throughout the country had a solar panel system, which attested to the innovative, self-sufficient and forward-thinking spirit of the Israelis.

James and I worked hard cleaning up the entire little house and its surroundings. The white wooden dwelling surrounded by trees looked like it had been built in the 1930s. Separated from the dorms, the tiny house had no bathroom, so we still used the dorm facility regularly. But it was a relief to get a break from the typical drama of multiple foreign personalities, each trying to figure out how to make the best out of their time in a place unlike their own. The average age of the volunteers was probably 25 or less, which frequently prompted singles to start dating and sooner than usual move in together. In general, not a conservative environment, the *kibbutz* mentality was one of a community with focus on the collective but yet tolerant to individuality. Quite a liberal model, this is the reason why it attracted a sheer number of people every year.

It was in one of those gathering nights during a *Sabbath* that a rather dramatic scene happened at our door steps. The group of volunteers was peacefully laughing and singing by our porch. James had worked several hours at the pottery house building jars and bowls, which brought him great satisfaction. It also happened to be his birthday, and one of the girls had brought him homemade cookies, with which he gladly filled one of his recently made bowls and started to pass it around. All were happily assembled until Oskar, once again beyond his limits on alcohol, when given the bowl inexplicably threw it on the ground smashing it into pieces. Silence and disbelief took place. The grumpy party pooper had just ruined the gathering. Worse than that, it ruined James' time of celebration. "What did you do that for?" James inconsolably yelled at him. With an ironic smile, Oskar responded in a noxious drunk tone: "I don't know." James' reaction was surprising to me. He hastily stood up and, without saying a word, went into the house not to leave until the next morning.

The drama was not over yet. A confusing yelling and arguing time ensued as that harmonious moment vanished. I knew Oskar well enough to predict that his demeanor would cause him trouble. That time seemed to have arrived. When confronted by another volunteer as to why he behaved like that, Oskar bent to the ground, grabbed a rock and was about to throw it at the same young man, when I quickly intervened: as an adult, this was the first and last time I punched somebody in the face. Knocked out, Oskar would not see me until the next morning as we came across the dining room entrance. Escorted by two of the members, his face was significantly swollen around the right eye. Yet, he found a sarcastic moment to smile at me, saying: "You did a good job." It was also the last time I saw the man. His irascible, inconsequent irrational behavior put an end to his volunteer time at the *kibbutz*. Not proud of what I did, I felt sorry for him for I still think he was not a bad person.

There were no consequences to me for having used physical force during that sad event. I guess the *kibbutz* management interpreted it as an act of protective self-defense, or what not. Things could always get better and they could always get worse. For most of the volunteers, life in the *kibbutz* was back to 'business as usual.' For most, it was a relief to stay away from that persistent theatrical stage.

## JERUSALEM, *HIEROSOLYMA, URUSALIM*

New York City, December 8th, 1980. This larger than life figure had been living quietly in the city with his wife and had just made his comeback after five years away from the studio. Five gunshots rang out at the entrance of his building in New York City ending the life of one of the world's most influential musicians of all time. As the police arrived at the scene within two minutes, his killer was cuffed and two officers hoisted the musician on to their shoulders and placed him in the back of a squad car. One of the officers asks: "Do you know who you are"? As he slipped away, he nodded and moaned. "Yes." It is the last thing that John Lennon ever said.

The news ran around the world in a flash. Being in the *kibbutz* surrounded by young foreign nationals was daunting as that was a generation that grew up listening to his music, embodied by The Beatles. For me, it has a significant effect as I particularly loved, sang and played many of the band's tunes. The mood was somber and a sense of melancholy penetrated most minds. My roommate was not happy and I knew why. A fierce opponent to any kind of violence, I could tell he was not in a good place and reconciling that moment must have been difficult for him. After being in the *kibbutz* for over a month, I planned my first trip to iconic Jerusalem the next day. Bus ticket and accommodations previously booked, I left the next morning.

Jerusalem is one of the oldest cities in the world, and is considered holy to the three major religions – Judaism, Christianity and Islam. Both Israel and the Palestinian Authority claim Jerusalem as their capital, as Israel maintains its primary governmental institutions there and the State of Palestine ultimately foresees it as its seat of power; however, neither claim is widely recognized internationally.

A few months earlier, Israel's Knesset (equivalent to Congress) enacted the symbolic 'Jerusalem, Capital of Israel' Law, much to the world's annoyance and blisteringly to the Arabs, particularly to the Palestinians. Combined with an amendment to the law adopted two decades later, the Jerusalem Law declared, among other things, that the city would remain unified in the borders that the Israeli government determined following the Six-Day War, and that no part of the city could be transferred to a foreign government or body.

What "Basic Law: Jerusalem" did not do, and what Israel had not done in 1967 either although it is a common misconception that it did was to annex East Jerusalem by law to the state. That remains the case today. Jerusalem's status had remained unresolved both before and following the 1948 War of Independence. In its partition decision the year before, the United Nations determined that the city would remain a separate body under international supervision – a distinct entity belonging to neither Israel nor the Arab state to be established. A provision never accepted by either side.

Contemplating the Temple Mount and the Dome of the Rock from afar was more than a unique experience. As the most important religious site in the Old City of Jerusalem, it had been used for thousands of years. And yet, it is center stage for much of the historic conflicts in the world – with no end in sight. However, at this time and incorporating the spirit of an aspiring world traveler, it was hard to fathom why the parties involved would dwell on the physical aspect of it. Or, any considered religious site, for that matter. It would take a few more years for me to find answers to those questions. At that moment, a song and its lyrics flashed through my mind and it could not be more meaningful: Lennon's *Imagine*.

Besides visiting some of the multiple sites in the city, a highlight of my trip to Jerusalem was the Hebrew University, particularly, the Hadassah-Hebrew University Medical Center where the *Windows of Jerusalem* lithographs are portrayed. Some of the most important of Marc Chagall's works, they showcased the beauty and intricacy with which Chagall designed an architectural masterpiece in the stained glass windows. The accumulation of years of labor, this lithograph series portrays Chagall's passion for religious narration – representing the twelve tribes of ancient Israel - and the inescapable draw that everyone had to his dreamy interpretation of them.

## EGYPT, *GIFT OF THE NILE, LAND OF THE PHARAOHS*

Back at Sha'ar Ha'amakim, I started working on the beginning of the end of my travel time before I headed home. With still a month to go, I wanted to go to Egypt before initiating the long process of return. James had been incredibly kind to lend me some money that would make the trip to Cairo and Luxor possible, and some of it would allow for the rest of the journey to be a little more comfortable since I had had no chance to get compensation in the past two months, as a volunteer. Wolf and Manfred were two German inseparable friends which I got along with well enough to undertake the trip across the Sinai. Inconspicuous by nature, the two guys were good humored and easy to be with. They probably saw me the same way as we envisioned this next step of the trip would require some flexibility of behavior. We heard all kinds of stories about the adventure and wanted to make it a good experience.

We left early in the morning for Tel Aviv aiming at getting to Cairo by day's end. Catching the bus from Tel Aviv to Eilat, the smooth ride took about 5 hours. The Taba Border Crossing with Egypt was just a five-minute drive from the city center and from there we expected to quickly cross into Egyptian soil. With a distinctive but relatively easy scrutiny at the border from the authorities, our goal now was to find a ride which would take us through the Sinai Desert towards the Suez Canal. As the buses were crowded and would take much longer to get through the desert, the alternative was to take a taxi. An old beat-up yellow Mercedes Benz, large enough to accommodate six people comfortably, was the vehicle that would take us to the Canal. Beyond the regular capacity, instead we were eight people in the car including the driver, with travel time estimated to take place in 4 ½ hours. Luckily.

The driver was focused but showed some signs of uneasy behavior, probably due to the pressure on the job and its time constraints. It was a fascinating journey, as we passed through stunning scenery; the downside being the road conditions and the predictable reckless driving we experience en route to the Suez. Somewhat turbulent, a close call in one critical occasion got the passengers terrified with the thought of imminent crash: "This is it, goodbye world," I pictured. Miraculously, as the taxi driver audaciously attempted to pass a number of slow vehicles, the truck in the opposite direction abruptly stopped just in time to avoid what would have been the end of everyone's wishes to go from point A to point B. Seated on the front passenger seat along with another soul, the mix of relief, sunny blue skies and sand swirling around like mini-tornadoes gave me the surrealistic impression that this would be an eventful not-a-dull-moment type of trip to my destination. If we all ever made it safe and sound.

As we finally reached the Suez, with every passenger dusting off their bags and belongings, distress and anxiety were quickly replaced by the silent ride of the boat crossing of the Canal. A moment of peace, compared to surviving the taxi desert rally. At the sea-level waterway connecting the Mediterranean Sea to the Red Sea, the boat took a small number of people into Adabiya where we expected to get another and last ride to the heart of Cairo. This time, we were lucky to have a more conscientious driver who got my German travel companions and me safely to the capital. It was already dark and half way through the evening when we found a decent hotel just ready to crash.

## CAIRO, *CITY OF A THOUSAND MINARETS*

Aware that tap water drinking quality anywhere in Cairo was shady, we were off the next morning to find a bottled alternative as well as a good breakfast choice. Wolf and Manfred were bound to the streets in downtown as I headed out to the American University of Cairo and then to the Egyptian Museum. In a moment of reflection, I wished I could have communicated with the locals in their own language. Even though my grandmother Alice was born and raised in Cairo until leaving with her family for Lebanon and then Brazil between ages 12 and 14, none of her offspring ever learned Arabic. Regrettably, the reason was simple: dominated at the time by the Ottoman Empire, many migrants from Lebanon went to Brazil and other recipient countries. With their passports showing Ottoman/Turkish identity, they would be called Turks by the uninformed and culturally uneducated locals. But...they were not very fond of the Turks, to be diplomatically correct. Therefore, speaking the language was restricted to the households and the passing of the teaching and learning experience never took place. Nor did the culture. All for the sake of not being considered what they were not. My Dad and Mom, although somewhat familiar with words and expressions, could not speak more than a few words. My sisters and I are completely ignorant of the language.

My Iranian friend Ateshé Firouz had been going to school to finish her graduate studies at the American University. I had met her in Berkeley earlier in the year and saw her again in Paris along with Françoise and other friends prior to kicking off my European journey. With the high tensions between the U.S. and Iran, I was not sure how her family was doing. On top of the armed conflict with Iraq, the Iran hostage crisis[3] was in full swing. I tried to call her in the morning but she seemed to be in class. Knowing that the University would be at a 30-minute walking distance from the hotel, I set out on foot and tried to get familiarized with the streets in hopes I could hang out with Ateshé at the end of the day.

From the school, I was off to the magnificent museum. Containing most of the important pieces of Egyptian history, the latest version of The Egyptian Museum was established in Tahrir Square very early in the 20th century. It housed the largest collection of Pharaonic antiquities. One can spend days between its two main floors looking at the myriad of statues, tables

---

3    The Iran hostage crisis was a diplomatic standoff between Iran and the United States. Fifty-two American diplomats and citizens were held hostage for 444 days from November 4, 1979, to January 20, 1981, after a group of Iranian college students belonging to the Muslim Student Followers of the Imam's Line, who supported the Iranian Revolution, took over the U.S. Embassy in Tehran. It stands as the longest hostage crisis in recorded history.

and sarcophagi, as well as papyrus and coins collections in multiple metals, including gold, silver and bronze. An archeologist's dream of a place and a privilege for a layman to get a glimpse of human history. I vowed that I would go back one day for another round of this part of the world civilization's narrative.

I got to the Pyramids by early to mid-afternoon. Wolf and Manfred had just arrived at the meeting point, on schedule. Located in Giza, on the outskirts of Cairo, the pyramid complex is an archeological site on a plateau of the same name. The three Great Pyramids – Khufu/Cheops, Khafre/Chephren and Menkaure – and the Great Sphinx are majestically located in the Western Desert, approximately 5 miles west of the Nile River and about 8 miles southwest of downtown Cairo. This monumental site has "historically been emblematic of ancient Egypt in the Western Imagination," stated the great Spanish traveler Pedro Tafur, in 1436 in his *Travels and Adventures*. Khufu is the first and the only one of the Seven Wonders of the Ancient World still in existence. A shocking reality.

The German travelers and I were in awe at what we saw. An experience which is hard to describe, we were almost paralyzed by such significance and enormity. I had read as much as I could about the possible process of construction of the Pyramids, which probably contributed to my wonderment. That admiration didn't help me deepen my knowledge about the inner complexity of the Giza Pyramids for I never got inside of them. One of a few things I regret not having done. Well, maybe one day. Twilight approached and we found ourselves sailing at the margin of the Nile. The sunset was mesmerizing and breathtaking.

Back in town, it was dark and once again from the hotel I was bound to walking over to the University, as I did in the morning. Over the phone, Ateshé was glad to learn I was in Cairo and we set up a time to meet up for tea. *Let's Go: Europe* warned me about the potential for being ripped off by taxi drivers once they found out you were not a local. Therefore, my option was walking instead. Half hour down through the sidewalks of the insane

Cairo rush hour, with street kids stopping me at every corner asking for *basksheesh* (small sum of money or tips), jewelry and perfume merchants chasing every prospect (I guess I seemed to be a promising one), I was finally...lost – of course. It got very difficult to recognize the same spots I had been throughout the day; firstly, because of the intense and chaotic rush hour traffic and secondly, due to darkness which dramatically changes perception. It was about 6:30 p.m. and some commercial spots were still open. I walked into a general store, which reminded me of one of the miscellaneous stores in downtown São Paulo, and asked how far I was from the American University. "Not too far, sir. About 10 minutes," I was told. It feels like an eternity when you can't wait to get to your destination. "And how much should I pay for a taxi to take me over there?" I ask again. "About twenty-five piastres, no more than that," the attendant at the counter replied. One Egyptian Pound is the equivalent to 100 piastres, to which a quarter of it seemed a reasonable amount. I decided, what the heck, I'm already late, I am taking a taxi.

It took about 2-3 minutes for a taxi driver to pull over with two passengers in the back. Well, I thought, this may be usual in this culture, I'm in. At the front passenger seat, I asked the driver to take me to my goal. My co-passengers in the back seat, a nice and groomed looking couple, translated my request to the taxi driver. Lucky me, I thought, I'm on my way. It didn't take 5 minutes to get to where I recognized was one of the entrances to the university. After a hectic and tiresome day, I was happy to have arrived. Excited, I looked back diagonally at the male passenger and inquired: "How much is it, sir, if you don't mind asking the driver?" Without hesitation, the driver himself responded in Arabic. Silence followed. My back seat co-passenger looked at the driver, then immediately looked at me, evidently embarrassed, and responded: "Two pounds." Silence followed again. Have I understood it correctly? Two pounds is...eight times more than what I had been told to pay for the ride! Blood boiling, I looked back, astonished. And at the driver, with mixed feelings of annoyance and contempt. "Two pounds," I repeated twice looking out and through the window. What followed was a scene of a Buster Keaton or Charlie Chaplin movie as I embodied a stoic, deadpan expression of "I-must-do-something-about-it." Opening the car door in a flash, I stormed off and began running over and through the University gate. Not surprisingly, the driver ran after me and the comedic situation ensued. As I swore all kinds of words I know of – possibly even in Arabic, as swearing was the only thing I knew in the language – he probably did the same. I was determined to give him a hard time, and so was he to get paid for the despicable ride. After a long and excruciating one to two-minute flight, I finally slowed down and imagined the possible confrontation about to take place. He reached me, we began yelling and sort of slapping one another until it got to the point that it became just too... funny! As we looked at each other, we started laughing. Aiming at putting an end to the scene, I opened my wallet and pulled out one Egyptian pound bill. He hastily grabbed it, smiled at me sarcastically and walked away...

Ateshé could not help but crack up at my sloppy taxi ride time. "That's part of the Cairo experience!" she said. She would not be there for very long as her semester would end up in a couple of months. But one thing was for sure: as much as Ateshé loved her birth country, she would not be coming back to its soil anytime soon. The Iran after the revolution became a sealed off country to most of the world. And the following years would be very hard on their people too. Hoping to take advantage of Iran's post-revolutionary chaos, neighbor Iraq had just recently invaded the country in a war that would carry on for 8 years: massive civilian loss, economic problems, war-weariness, decreased morale, repeated military failures on both sides, use of weapons of mass destruction and lack of international sympathy would tear down both countries. Ateshé and her family were fortunate to stay away from Iran as they would be able to find refuge somewhere in Europe, like a number of the more privileged and fortunate families did during that time.

## LUXOR AND KARNAK, *PALACES AND TEMPLES*

"The world's greatest open-air museum," is how Luxor is known. My German comrades and I embarked on what would become the strangest and yet most fascinating portion of our travel to Egypt. The distance from Cairo is about 410 miles and we chose to do it this time by...train. Little did we know that traveling by train in that part of the world would be quite an adventure. From the Ramses Station in Cairo – a magnificent iconic building, the historic entry point into Cairo after arriving in Alexandria by ship - it took us about an hour just to get the train tickets. Traveling economically, we opted out to take the sleeping night train only on the way back. The way to Luxor would be a normal ride with the locals. And normal would become wishful thinking very quickly.

Contrary to the expected privacy found in a sleeping cabin, the economy class is an all-open wagon where privacy is a luxury one can only wish for. Instead, the overnight ride was to be shared with several hundreds of peasants going back to their homes in the countryside after trading their goods to the capital and subsequently acquiring the provisions needed and not available in their areas south of the Nile. Marked by the harsh work characteristic of their agricultural efforts to provide for their households and small communities, the exposure to sun and sand, day after day, year after year, makes these people to look much older than they really are.

Not surprisingly, the train was late. At around 10:00p, the station was packed. That time of the year was a busy period of preparing to provide for the ongoing winter, however mild by European standards. It was the second season from November to April alternating with the hot summer from May to September. In the wagon, the scene was a mix of dramatic reality with surreal imagery: literally – lots of people jammed sharing the wooden seats and also spaces between themselves – and with animals too – goats, chickens, pets, caged birds – and all kinds of stuff, from old used furniture, to food, to provisions in general, you name it. As the train finally left the station, the initial turbulent noise gradually gave way to grasping whether the train will make it to its destination. An old wagon, it was poorly preserved, dirty, some glasses on the windows are missing or broken, therefore contributing to drafts. The restroom, forget it; the toilet was a pit and the water dripped from the faucet sink. A chilly evening, our clothes were the bare minimum to resist the dropping temperature.

The passengers are the simplest of people; most are *fellah*, hard-working peasants which most likely did the itinerary at least once a week. Serene and humble, they were enigmatic. These were farmers or agricultural laborers, as they were known in the Middle East and North Africa. The word derives from the Arabic word for "ploughman" or "tiller." The *fellahin* make up a significant part of the Egyptian population in both Lower and Upper Egypt, leading humble lives and continuing to live in mud-brick houses like their ancient ancestors. Their percentage was much higher in the early 20th century, before the large influx of Egyptian fellahin into urban towns and cities. In 1927, anthropologist Winifred Blackman, author of *The Fellahin of Upper Egypt*, conducted an ethnographic research on the life of Upper Egyptian farmers and concluded that there were observable continuities between the cultural and religious beliefs and practices of the *fellahin* and those of ancient Egyptians.

None of the locals would speak English but crossing glances, eye-contact and body expression speak more than anything. Demonstrating curiosity to know where we could be from and what we would think about their country, they would share their bread with us and offer dried fruits or candies of their consumption. As always, we had a number of uproarious travel episodes: more than once and half-way through, while most were trying to rest with eyes closed, the railroad felt more like a bad bumpy dirt road. Instead of smoothly rolling over the tracks, the sensation was that we were in a bus driving over a poorly covered cobblestone road. Just enough to see bags falling off the racks, jars breaking down from friction, animals screaming and the ludicrous reaction of the locals. All we could do was to laugh uncontrollably for a good several minutes, which led us to deep sleep for a few hours before dawn.

Daylight allowed us a fascinating glimpse of rural Egypt. Modest squared and rectangular mud brick houses and walled compounds; camels munching on the bushes and children riding donkeys. Fields of wheat and alfalfa shaded by scattered date palm trees, with mango orchards dotted between the field crops. No wonder the Nile is so revered, nothing would be possible without its offerings.

In Luxor and Karnak, I was bedazzled with their monumental palaces and temple complexes, which rank among the world's greatest ancient sites. In terms of artistic achievement, they are Egypt's finest; in scale, its most impressive. Beautiful artefacts found on site were displayed in two worthwhile museums. The stunning Avenue of the Sphinxes, Luxor Museum and the unmissable Valley of the Kings with its tombs and historic facts – all made this trip extraordinary. Must go back to hectic Cairo on my way to Haifa, now. Time to ride in the sleeping car, just for a change.

## HELLO, GOODBYE

It was late evening and I couldn't see any volunteers around on my return to Sha'ar Ha'amakim. Back in the dorm I shared with James and now with Peter, a new volunteer recently arrived from Maine in the U.S., I learned that many of the young men and women had gone to Bethlehem, the city where Jesus was born. It was Christmas Eve and there were Christian celebrations all over town turning the city into a major event. Although the day of the week was a Wednesday, the *kibbutz* had allowed for the Christians to celebrate, the Eve and Christmas Day as a holiday. Quite a nice treat. I suddenly realized that my family in Brazil would also be celebrating the day along with friends and loved ones; quickly, I reached out to the *kibbutz* office in search of a phone. It took me a few phone calls to finally fathom that they must have left town or be somewhere I would not be able to find them. Oh well, it was late, I was exhausted and it was time for bed – Merry Christmas!

Paradoxical and confusing at times, yet deep and meaningful as it relates to understanding the determination of the Jewish people and the complexities of settling in that part of the world, my learning experience at Sha'ar Ha'amakim[4] was unique. By all means, my aim was simply to acquire knowledge and life lessons. Not for everyone, the *Kibbutzim* assumed prominent roles in almost every sphere of developing Israel. Although encompassing only a small percentage of Israeli society, the *Kibbutz* movement would be undergoing a process of change. Some aspects that in the past were included in the public domain would be under the care and responsibility of each member of his or her family. Somewhat romanticized in the past, the *Kibbutz* of the late 20th and beginning of the 21st century would evolve dramatically and the focus of *Kibbutz* life on society would substantially diminish.

My journey back home began a couple of days after the New Year's celebration. I was packed and ready to go. Would I ever come back to Israel? Would I ever see these people again? James and I promised one another to be consistent in writing letters. He would stay there for a few more months before returning to Philadelphia – or elsewhere on the East Coast. With a long way to go, my experience in that part of the world had been incredibly enriching and proven to be personally transformative in the years to come.

*Shalom, Lehitra'ot. Marhaba, Maa Salama.*

---

4    Sha'ar Ha'amakim* - It was not until a few months before I started writing this memoir that, when looking for information online on the present-day status of this particular place in Israel, that I've come to learn that Senator Bernie Sanders had coincidentally volunteered in the same *kibbutz* for a few months back in 1963. Controversies apart, his experience is said to have influenced the Senator from Vermont in his political views. Maybe yes, maybe not. Here's a link from an Israeli Newspaper from 2016 which tells some of the story of that time: https://forward.com/news/israel/332946/revealed-at-last-inside-the-*kibbutz*-where-bernie-sanders-lived-and-learned/

# 6

# Belonging

*"And as you cross the circle line,*
*the ice-wall creaks behind --- You're a rabbit on the run.*
*And the silver splinters fly in the corner of your eye ---*
*Shining in the setting sun.*
*Well, do you ever get the feeling that the story's*
*Too damn real and in the present tense?*
*Or that everybody's on the stage, and it seems like*
*You're the only person sitting in the audience?*
*Skating away, skating away, skating away*
*on the thin ice of the new day."*
*Skating Away* – I. Anderson

YET TO COVER A LOT OF GROUND, I flew from Tel Aviv over to Athens and then to Geneva where I took a night train to Paris. This would happen in a couple of days as my destination in Europe was London, where I would fly again to New York's JFK. In Paris I got to see my friends Françoise and Pascal, as well as sisters Amelia and Stephanie. Françoise couldn't believe I brought the guitar back as her brother Carl never expected to see it again, she confided to me. What great human beings these people are. I was so humbled by their kindness and friendship. Off to London's Gatwick, I took a most needed shower at the airport and waited to catch the Laker's flight to JFK – another dose of squeezed seats and happy backpackers.

The next two weeks were particularly interesting. A mix of mental preparation before getting back home and yet, always in the mood to keep traveling and seeing new places. This final leg took me from New York down to Miami and then New Orleans. My uncle Roosevelt and his wife and son, Wilneide and Rogerio, were visiting the Big Easy and seemed happy to see me in downtown New Orleans; jazz jamming was already taking place at Sunday brunch time, where we gathered for a Louisiana Creole cuisine experience accompanied by traditional Dixieland jazz. Likewise, I was glad to meet family as a prelude to returning home. There I also met a couple of traveler companions I had come across in Austria and was pleased to get a little taste of the South from the locals' perspective.

Mexico was my last stop. I was excited again to see aunt Gloria and Nico, who had visited me earlier in the year in Berkeley along with Grandma Alexandra and their children, Nicholas and Alessandra. I had a great time getting around Mexico City, Cuernavaca and even flying to Tabasco State, where Nico had a cattle business. Definitely a family reintroduction to the reality I had been used to prior to that entire year away from home. In many ways, I was the same affectionate individual when it came to meeting and visiting with loved ones. The question in my mind was whether returning to the same big city, lifestyle, friends, school, career perspective and, most importantly, values were still in my veins. I had to face it, and that would be my choice.

It felt good to be back in the country I was born and raised. Different, but still a good sensation. A year may not be a long period of time; however, the intensity of my experiences and exposure made it feel much longer. It is summertime and my immediate family was spending time in Guarujá, a resort beach town about sixty miles from São Paulo. After landing at Congonhas Airport from Rio and finding my way through to the bus station, it would still take me 2-3 hours to knock on the door of the house my parents had rented for the summer. And what a joy it was to see my Dad, Mom and my little sister! I had not told them the day I was going to come back, so it was a surprise for them to see me arriving unannounced. Full circle, I would restart my life from where I had left.

## HOLDING MY SKIN

Whether I was aware of the upcoming hurdles of having acquired a different conscience about things, people, places and myself, only time would tell. As I write this memoir, I come across the text below, a precious excerpt I've found from an article from the blog site, Alternate Dimension – alternatedimension.wordpress.com, that well describes how and where I found myself after a year of consistent movement and change:

*"I'm a misfit. I fit nowhere and everywhere all*
*at the same time.*
*To give a proper definition, misfits are individuals*
*who do not fit into any social groups quite right,*
*not even the outcasts, but may have qualities*
*of each one.*
*You can be geeky but don't quite fit in with*
*the hardcore geek.*
*You can be sporty but don't quite fit in with the*
*hardcore athletes or fitness people*
*You can like arts but don't quite fit in with the*
*hardcore artists*
*You can like fashion but don't quite fit in with*
*the hardcore fashionistas*
*You can be all for justice but don't quite fit in with*
*the hardcore justice warriors*
*You can be spiritual but don't quite fit in with*

*the hardcore spiritual people*
*The outcasts think you're too conformed,*
*the conformists think you're an outcast*
*The introverts think you're too extrovert,*
*the extroverts think you're too introvert*
*The party animals think you're too philosophical,*
*the philosophers think you're a riot*
*The suits think you're too much of a hippie,*
*the hippies think you're too much of a suit*
*The rebels think you're too proper and mild,*
*the pacifists think you're too crude and wild*
*People of your culture think you're an alien,*
*people outside of your culture think*
*you're a stereotype*
*People of your age think you don't act like*
*people of your age*
*People outside your age think you act too much*
*like someone of your age*
*Whatever the case may be, it seems you*
*are basically*
*a bit of everything and everyone, but not enough*
*of everything and everyone.*
*This always makes you stand out, no matter where*
*you go and no matter how much you try to fit in*
*with the rest.*
*If you relate to what I'm saying right now,*
*I'm talking to you. I want to tell you something*
*important that will probably change your life.*
*You are not a mistake.*
*There is no mistake in this Universe.*
*You are exactly how you are meant to be. It was*
*probably never intended for you to quite fit in.*
*It was probably meant for you to standout and live*
*your own truth.*
*You are luckier than the rest because you are*
*not tied down like they are. You are more*

*open-minded than the average human being.*
*Matter of fact, you are way too opened to enclose*
*yourself in a box.*
*While everyone is one-dimensional in their way of*
*perceiving the world, you are multi-dimensional.*
*You have a bird-eye view.*
*You have the freedom to create your own identity.*
*Take what works and roll with that.*
*The Universe has blessed you with individuality.*
*It's a gift. Embrace it. You're free.*
*I choose to embrace it and no longer feel misplaced.*
*I am right where I should be and I'm exactly who*
*I should be, which is myself.*
*Infinite love, health, healing, wealth,*
*success, happiness, awareness, peace*
*and wisdom your way."*

I wish I had read this by the time I got back home, many moons ago. Not that I hadn't read multiple and good related writings, but this information is condensed and critical for those in the middle of asking: "Who am I?" It just provides for a little break, a breathing moment away from the constant inquiring and inquisitive seeking that young men and women go through from time to time. One sip at a time feels just right.

## BACK TO SCHOOL AND BEYOND

*"Education is the leading of human souls to what is best and making what is best out of them."* – John Ruskin

Years earlier at *Colégio Anglo Latino*, when I was still in my mid-teens, one of the few positive aspects of my experience at that school was keeping a dear friendship that remains to this day. Luiz Eugenio Rubbo, *Gaucho*, and I stayed in contact throughout the years. With both of us then at the School of Economics at *Universidade Mackenzie*, prior to getting on the road to the U.S., then Europe and the Middle East, I had considered embarking on an experience as a volunteer at what is known as *Projeto Rondon*, a program oriented by democratic principles, of social responsibility initiatives and in defense of national interests, aiming at two major goals: the formation of young college students and the sustainable development of needy communities. Instead, as much as I nurtured the idea of diving into this valuable program, I never joined it and ended up getting on the road. But my buddy Gaucho did. I know it was a meaningful experience for him.

Getting around São Paulo became an exercise of observation. And comparison. In my mind, my mood was still on the experience of returning, and the first months reflected the adjustment I would have to delve into in order to work on my options. Walking was my way of preference to go from one part of the city to another. Sometimes short, sometime long distances. It felt that my senses were demanding a slower and more cadenced speed, although I knew that covering long hauls on foot was a non-practical mode of locomotion and hence would only be temporary. Coupled with touring the few nice parks along with my year-old niece Sofia, I found some amusement in being back to the city I grew up in. São Paulo was and has been the fastest growing city in South America for decades, a city in which the numbers speak in volumes: largest - in the Southern Hemisphere - wealthiest – the 10th richest in the world, most industrialized with a population of 12 million, etc., etc. Along with all the supposedly positive superlatives come the negative ones: crime and safety, enormous traffic jams, rampant real estate activity and irrational sprawling, internal migration issues and serious infrastructure challenges. These were factors impossible to ignore and comparing them with cities of other countries' *modus vivendi* I had been exposed to was inevitable.

Focusing on finishing up college was now a priority. Introspective, I enjoyed catching up with only a few of my old colleagues and friends. However, I was a stranger to some and felt that the other way around was also real – I no longer valued some of the ethos of my generation prior to traveling abroad. At home, I was fortunate and no longer took for granted having my own room. As part of a cultural factor, many of the responsibilities like cleaning, cooking, ironing, etc. were done by a maid, as 100% of the households with an equivalent family income could afford to. Yet, my mindset had changed in regards to that way of living. Demand for privacy, silence and for the need to assert my individuality were growing stronger. *You've got to get in to get out*, the chorus line for "Carpet Crawlers," by Genesis, had been in my mind. In a matter of a couple of months, I managed to rent a small apartment and, again, I was out of my parents' house. Nothing atypical for American and European households, but not common for my cultural background. Objections and awkwardness ensued. Nonetheless, I was pretty determined to make it happen.

Funding for my new project would not come for free. To provide for the new convenience, I committed to work at my Dad's business every afternoon, between my senior year's morning and evening classes. Rent fees were ok, the budget tight, but doable. My first week in the new spot felt good. In the same neighborhood, the apartment building was located at the end of a dead end street, which contributed to the quiet and no traffic whatsoever. To furnish the space, I purchased some modular used furniture and modestly equipped the apartment with the basics.

"During the twenties, and especially in the second half of the twenties, the individual's inner, psychological life takes on its first personal shape." This is the shape which Rudolf Steiner calls the 'sentient soul' and Martha Moers the 'vital-mental strivings.' Moers characterizes these by saying that it is not until now that the individual's mind becomes a closed unity capable of being experienced as such: "These, the vital-mental strivings, cannot be explained as a simple intensifying or sublimation of the biological drives, but represent something that is specifically a new, leap forward in mental development that far transcends what is biologically logical and hence also the sphere of drives and instincts."

Lievegoed's description of this period on his book *Phases: The Spiritual Rhythms in Adult Life* is paramount to explain the last leg which anticipated the beginning of my adulthood. It was as if I had to build a laboratory, real and at the same time imaginary: the specialty equipment, like burners and microscopes, needed to operate in the specific conditioning chamber of my new space. The analogy would soon reveal the changes in mindset and habits in which I would undergo. While still tasting my Mom's delicious dishes a couple of days a week during dinner time, I started to develop some cooking and baking practices. Along with related recipe books, I began to perceive that buying, manipulating and cooking certain foods like meat became an unpleasant obligation when trying to emulate the prescribed food combinations. On the other hand, while exchanging ideas with my sisters Silvia Regina and Cristina, the first one a vegetarian for years, the latter having recently adopted the new diet, I was intrigued. "Isn't meat the real deal? I've always loved meat, why is it that I feel disgusted when preparing my own food with that component?" Confused and yet excited with the new perspective of a habit change, I was bound for diving a little deeper into the subject.

One of my favorite classes at the School of Economics was The History of Economic Thought, not only because of its broadness but also because Professor Antonio Carlos Borges had an excellent way of communicating such a complex theme. It was from his classes that I heard for the first time the thought: 'Economics is the Science of Social Wellbeing.' *The Economist* magazine describes Economics, or Social Science Economics, as "the study of social behavior guiding in the allocation of scarce resources to meet the unlimited needs and desires of the individual members of a given society." Which, to me, implied that social wellbeing did start with individual wellbeing – and not the other way around. Hands on, here I went on looking for literature on the relevance of vegetarianism. Not as abundant back then as they are today, I came across a number of books and writings on the subject, some scientifically-driven, others focused on preventive health and even tying in to religious and spiritual purposes. Diet and everything related to eating habits is such an important subject, therefore requiring one's full commitment to understanding and experimenting.

It's worth remembering that years back my sister Silvia Regina began experimenting with Macrobiotics at around age 19. Needless to say that she became the object of joking and laughter in our household for a while. Brown rice, spelt, burdock, *gersal* (sesame seeds and sea salt), tempeh, seaweed, lotus root, millet, rye, buckwheat and the awkward tofu and miso contributed to free entertainment. As many morons in their unintended ignorance would react to the new and unconventional, I was not an exception. The fact was that the food didn't quite taste good and together with the boring approach to health, it didn't look appealing either. Yet, my sister managed to withstand the pressure, shrugged off criticism and moved on to find out what was best for herself. It would not take too long for Silvia Regina to evolve on her convictions and end up adopting vegetarianism as her diet of choice. My Mom, always the gatherer of the family, with her artistry and manifested cooking skills, would develop creative ways to keep the family together by combining and adapting recipes. Which, when hosting a Saturday late lunch or a special occasion dinner time, to the eyes of the guests, the table would look and taste great: veggie options for the "sick ones" on one end, "normal" food on the other end. The result: food for everyone, with no (or little...) discrimination.

## LITERATURE AND EXPERIMENTATION

History has plenty to offer when it comes to the primordia of vegetarianism. According to non-sourced citations on the web, it has its roots in the civilizations of ancient India and ancient Greece. Those regions of the old world along with peoples in southern Italy, show the earliest records of vegetarian diet as a concept and practice. Closely connected with the idea of nonviolence toward animals (*Ahimsa* in India), it was promoted by religious groups and philosophers. The Christianization of the Roman Empire in the 4$^{th}$–6$^{th}$ centuries brought the practice in Europe near to extinction, restricting it to monks in medieval times. Re-emerging during the Renaissance, it became again widespread during the 19$^{th}$ and 20$^{th}$ centuries. In the United States, small groups of Christian vegetarians were found in the 18$^{th}$ century. Among the best known was Ephrata Cloister in Pennsylvania, a religious community founded by Conrad Beissel in 1732. Curiously, Benjamin Franklin became a vegetarian at the age of 16, only to *reluctantly* return to meat eating later on as an adult (*Iacobbo p.1-2*). It was the same man that introduced tofu to the American colonies in 1770 (*Mother Nature Network, Robin Shreeves*)– tofu lovers and haters, you can thank or blame it on good old Ben Franklin. It was during the Age of Enlightenment in the England of the 19$^{th}$ century that vegetarian ideas were more welcome than anywhere else in Europe. The English vegetarians were particularly enthusiastic about the practical implementation and their principles, although still in small numbers. The popularity of vegetarianism grew during the 20th century as a result of nutritional and ethical concerns, when Mahatma Gandhi would have quite an impact in the Western world for being a strong advocate of nonviolence toward animals as the Indian concept got more and more acceptance.

As for my experimentation, although beginning to acquire glimpses of sympathy in favor of a healthier diet while in Berkeley, it wasn't until reading a tiny book called *What's Wrong with Eating Meat*, by Vistara Parham, in the early 1980s, that the concept would strongly resonate in my system. The author's approach and detailing the reasons not to think of animals as 'something for one's plate' and the consequent ending of its practice, such as animal disease and world hunger, to name a few, is riveting:

As Parham points out, "From the beginning of recorded history, we find that the vegetarian diet was regarded as the natural diet of humanity. The early Greeks, Egyptians, and Hebrews described man as a fruit eater. The wise priest of ancient Egypt never ate meat. Many great Greek wise men – including Plato, Socrates, and Pythagoras – were strong advocates of the vegetarian diet. The great civilization of the Inca Indians was based on vegetarian diet. In India the Buddha urged his disciples not to eat flesh. The Taoist saints and sages were vegetarians; the early Christians and Jews were also vegetarians. The Bible clearly states: And God said, 'Behold, I have given you every herb-bearing seed, which is upon the face of the earth, and every tree, in which are fruits; for you it shall be as meat.'

As much as I appreciated the historical facts, it isn't until Parham's observations on the economics of food that my curiosity kicked in: "But how does vegetarianism relate to food shortage? The answer is simple: meat is the most uneconomical and inefficient food we can eat; the cost of one pound of meat protein is *twenty times higher* than equally nutritional plant protein. Only 10% of the protein and calories we feed our livestock is recovered in the meat we eat, that is 90% goes down the drain." Then, the striking reality: "Vast acres of land are used to raise livestock for food. These acres of land could be utilized far more productively if planted with grains, beans, and other legumes for humans to eat directly. For example, one acre used to raise a steer will provide only about one pound of protein; but this same land planted with soybeans will produce 17 pounds of protein! In other words, to eat meat, we need to use 17 times as much land as the amount needed to plant soybeans. In addition, soybeans are more nutritious, contain less fat, and are free from the poisons of meat."

Coupled with finally abandoning the nasty habit of tobacco smoking and well over a year into adopting the new practice of removing red meat and pork from my diet – I kept eating fish and chicken for another year – I was almost done with college and still had a couple of classes which would take me through the year. Now my focus was somewhat idealistic with the intent of utilizing practical knowledge and experience on the subject.

The gift I had received in Florence, Italy – the key to opening and shutting the doors of this dilemma of 'belonging or not belonging' to multiple places, environments, groups, stereotypes, thoughts and frames of mind – should be put to work. The key – or I should call it, a developing skill – was a work in progress and meant to be used; whereas, the learning curve would be a constant throughout the years. If not a lifetime.

## JOHANNESBURG, THEN RIO

"I'll be there by mid-May!" James and I had been pretty consistently exchanging letters. The news of his visit was simply electrifying. James was not only a great friend. He was one of the most important links I had to this period of discovery and awareness acquired during the long and preceding travel period. It was as if the cultivating and nurturing of our friendship was a preparation for the ever expanding opportunities of growth ahead, present and future. I drove to Rio to pick up James at Galeão International Airport where he flew directly from Johannesburg, after visiting a friend. James' open mindedness to visit South Africa felt like a pretty bold move to me since *apartheid* was still very much enforced on the South African people. Back in San Francisco two years earlier, I had seen Peter Gabriel's memorable concert in June, at The Warfield. The hit "Biko" was the highlight of the concert (Richard Attenborough's movie *Cry Freedom* – which delves into South Africa's segregation and discrimination system, political corruption, and the repercussions of violence - would not be released until 1987). Gabriel's "Biko" is an anti-apartheid protest song, more like a musical eulogy inspired by the death of the black South African activist Steve Biko in police custody on 12 September 1977. A powerful statement that would help undermine apartheid and add to the myriads of efforts to end this sad chapter in human history several years later, Gabriel wrote the song after hearing of Biko's death on the news. Here are some of "Biko's" lyrics:

*September '77*
*Port Elizabeth weather fine*
*It was business as usual*
*In police room 619*
*Oh Biko, Biko, because Biko*
*Oh Biko, Biko, because Biko*
*Hiromija, Hiromija*
*The man is dead, the man is dead*
*You can blow out a candle*
*But you can't blow out a fire*
*Once the flames begin to catch*
*The wind will blow it higher*
*Oh Biko, Biko, because Biko*
*And the eyes of the world are watching you now*
*You gotta waken up, you gotta face up*
*I think you gotta open up*

Soon after its release, a copy of "Biko" was seized by South African customs and submitted to the Directorate of Publications, which banned the song and the album on which it was featured for being critical of apartheid, calling it "harmful to the security of the State." The song received strongly positive responses from critics, and it was frequently cited as "so honest you might even risk calling it truth." Biko had an enormous political impact. It has been credited with creating a "political awakening" both in terms of awareness of the brutalities of apartheid, and of Steve Biko as a person. It greatly raised Biko's profile, making his name known to millions of people who had not previously heard of him, and came to symbolize Biko in the popular imagination. Ingrid Bianca Byerly, in her "Musical Markers as Catalysts in Social Revolutions: The Case of Gabriel's Biko" writes that it was an example of the "right song written at the right time by the right person"; it was released in circumstances of social tension that contributed to its popularity and influence. It triggered a rise in enthusiasm for fighting against apartheid internationally, and has been described by Byerly as "arguably the most significant non-South African anti-apartheid protest song."

Thrilled to see my friend from Philadelphia after two years since Israel, we stayed in Rio, The Marvelous City, for a couple of days and headed 400 km (250 miles) southbound via the coastal area. First stop was Angra dos Reis, then Paraty and finally Ilha Bela, where we stayed in picturesque hostels, *pousadas*, before we got to São Paulo. The days were kind of wet, so not a chance to fully enjoy the beaches. In SP, we gathered with multiple of my friends and family – my opportunity to introduce James to everyone. After a few days of gastronomical experiments at my Mom's and at the Italian-Japanese-Arab food circuit which so easily puts SP within one of the best routes for quality cuisines in the Western World, we headed to a friend's family farmhouse in the countryside. *"Uma família quatrocentona"* or a "top social four-hundred-year old family," was a term coined in the middle of the 20th century around the celebration of the four hundred years of the founding of the city of São Paulo, on January 25, 1954. It basically designates a family as belonging to the traditional São Paulo elite, that is the São Paulo aristocracy and oligarchy – most of them from Portugal, among some of Spanish, French, Belgian and Flemish origin. A beautiful 1850s farmhouse, this was a property situated nearby mountains, lakes, stables, coffee plantation and vegetable gardens within its grounds. Not quite a *Gone with the Wind* experience, a famous 1939 movie depicting the eve of the American Civil War at a family's cotton plantation environment, but there was certainly a colonial feel with its wooden floors and fireplaces and white sash windows framing stunning views of the verdant countryside. Educational for myself, let alone for James.

A once-in-a-lifetime event was scheduled to take place a few months after James' departure from this majestic but at times erratic country. With so much fun already experienced during his two-week visit, James had planned to take a bus from Central Station down to southern Brazil and seize the opportunity to experience Iguazu Falls as well as another natural marvel while still in existence before its doomsday: *Sete Quedas*, or, Seven Falls. (7) This would be celebrated as an epic event later in the year, but for the wrong reasons. Guaíra Falls were a series of immense waterfalls on the Paraná River along the border between Brazil and Paraguay. The falls ceased to exist in October 1982, when they were inundated by the impoundment of the Itaipu Dam Reservoir. Guaíra's Falls flow rate was among the greatest of any then-existing falls on Earth. The falls comprised 18 cataracts clustered in seven groups—hence their Portuguese name, *Sete Quedas*. The falls were located at a point where the Paraná River was forced through a narrow gorge. At the head of the falls, the river narrowed sharply from a width of about 380 m (1,250 ft) to 60 m (200 ft). The total height of the falls was approximately 114 m (375 ft), while the largest individual cataract was 40 m (130 ft) high. The roar of the plunging water could be heard from 30 km (20 mi) away.

The falls were completely submerged under the artificial lake created by the Itaipu Dam, linchpin of the world's largest hydroelectric project to date upon its completion in 1982. The building of the dam, authorized by a 1973 bilateral agreement between the Brazilian and Paraguayan regimes of the time, marked a new era of cooperation between the countries, both of which had claimed ownership of Guaíra Falls as its own.

Brazilian poet Carlos Drummond de Andrade wrote a poem expressing his dismay at the destruction of Guaíra Falls. Set in large type, the poem filled an entire page in the *Jornal do Brasil* newspaper:

> *"Here seven visions, seven liquid sculptures*
> *vanished through the computerized calculations*
> *of a country ceasing to be human*
> *in order to become a chilly corporation,*
> *nothing more. A movement becomes a dam."*
> – Carlos Drummond de Andrade, *"Farewell to Seven Falls" (excerpt, translated from the Portuguese)*

# HONEY BEES...

At the end of 1982, I began to drive my attention to learning about the fascinating world of bees. Following the idealistic instinct of doing something good out of my focus on health – which comes from my acquired vegetarian dietary habit and its consequential benefit - the universe of beekeeping echoed deeply into the logic of health-diet-wellbeing. While still working a six-hour shift per day at my Dad's business, I could manage to take care of studying for the two classes I still had left to finish up college and yet develop correlated interests to my academic field. Although I knew that my Dad would like to see me joining the business at some point on a full time basis – my cousins had already joined it a few years back – I was not so sure that that was what I wanted to do for my career. Increasingly interested in how Economics could harbor social-wellbeing, I began developing my own view of how I could contribute to it. Academics seemed to be the answer and therefore I started saving money prior to enrolling on a two-year master's degree in Agricultural Economics at the renowned *Universidade de São Paulo*, starting the following year.

"Beekeeping is a very old activity, plunging its origins into pre-history. Famous are the drawings discovered in caves of Spain, showing the primitive man harvesting honey from a swarm, with the aid of a rope ladder attached to the top of a ravine. Ancient records from Egypt, Mesopotamia and Greece describe facts about bee breading. The Bible makes numerous references to honey and swarm of bees. Therefore, man and bees have known each other for many centuries."

The aforementioned is an excerpt from APACAME's web page, an organization founded in 1979 in São Paulo with its denomination standing for 'Paulista Association of Beekeepers, Breeders of European Honey Bees.' Its motto, "Bees in Service of Agriculture" and its goal, "To Assemble beekeepers, technicians and amateurs for technical, social and cultural exchange, aiming at the diffusion and improvement of rational beekeeping." Besides, "stimulating the production of wax, royal jelly, honey, pollen, propolis, venom, swarms and selected queens, equipment and materials for beekeeping, use of bee products in natural food, apitherapy and cosmetics." Among other goals, APACAME had a very ambitious objective: to be able to cope with the 'africanization' of the European bees in Brazil – a problem that concerned many people due to the complexity of handling the aggressive bees from Africa. The blurb on African Bees, from the association's perspective, is as captivating as it is controversial:

"In 1956, Dr. Warwick Estevam Kerr brought from Africa and introduced in Piracicaba, São Paulo, 51 queens of Apis mellifera adansoni and Apis mellifera capensis. For Rio Claro, 27 matrices of African queens were transferred, of which 26 were swarmed, running away from the technicians. From then on, African bees crossed the existing European ones and spread rapidly through Brazil and South America, then to Central America and North America…" "The Africans bees…did not arrive in Canada due to the intense cold in that northern region of the continent. They spread throughout the southern and western US, passing through the states of California, Oregon, New Mexico, Texas, reaching as far as Miami, if they did not go any further."

African bees were basically demonized. On the other hand, from an economic standpoint, there was a perk. "Brazil's annual honey production from the European honey bees was just 15 million pounds in 1956. Brazilian agriculture was expanding and needed a tropical honey bee for pollination and honey production. After the African bees arrived, Brazil's beekeepers produced 110 million pounds" – numbers of 1994. "Brazil went from 43rd in the world to 7th largest honey producer."

On his *Bad Beekeeping Blog*, American-Canadian beekeeper and scientist Ron Miksha begins describing Dr. Warwick Estevam Kerr, as "the man who made the Killer Bees." Surprisingly, he shifted his focus and brought up what to me was a 180-degree view of what I had learned about the introduction of the

African Bees in the country and, most interestingly, who the man really was: "Just like his bees, Kerr comes from hot, tropical Brazil. And just like his bees, Dr. Kerr had been much maligned and misunderstood in the popular press. But Kerr did more to help his country's agriculture than perhaps any other individual."

Miksha goes on to argue that "When the Africanized hybrid honey bee entered our awareness in the 1970s, the bee was described as a *killer bee* (in Brazil, they called it *the assassin*). The man who brought African honey bees to South America was turned into a mysterious friend who had "disappeared from sight" after "he turned killer bees loose." Well, he did disappear for a while. He was in prison. But not for any reason you might guess. First, some background."

"What was Kerr's crime?" inquires Miksha in his blog.

"Dr. Kerr brought Africanized genetic stock to South America in 1956. In today's context, importing an alien creature from another continent seems horribly reckless. In Dr. Kerr's day, the importation of bees from Africa was hardly daring. First, recall that all honey bees in the Americas are imported from somewhere else. Honey bees are not native to the western hemisphere. Second, Kerr was not introducing a new *species*. The African bee (*Apis mellifera scutellata*) is a cousin of a common European honey bee, *Apis mellifera iberiensis*, which was in Brazil when the African queen bees arrived. Kerr's importation of 26 queen bees from Tanzania is in league with importing Clydesdales long after Arabians and Morgans were already established. Kerr's goal was to improve the non-tropical honey bees which farmers were using in Brazil. He rightly assumed that tropical genetic stock would be more successful in his tropical country."

Amidst all quarrels, it is particularly what follows that becomes the most revealing of the facts about this controversial scientist: "Warwick Kerr's sour reputation came directly from the Brazilian government. Although he was a geneticist and was at first entrusted with developing a better bee for Brazil's farmers, the Brazilian military dictatorship attacked Kerr's stand on civil rights. He was imprisoned in 1964 when he publicly fought government corruption. In 1969 he was re-arrested, this time for protesting that Brazilian soldiers who had raped and tortured a nun went unpunished. Sister Maurina Borges, who ran the Ribeirão Preto Orphanage, was an activist; the soldiers were part of Brazil's military dictatorship, committing crimes encouraged by the government. Most of the western press didn't bother to investigate the reasons behind the Brazilian government's dismissal of Kerr's work and his qualifications."

It was publicly acknowledged that Warwick Kerr was largely responsible for establishing the study of genetics in Brazil. His work as an entomologist spanned decades, with research that included genetics of honey bees and native Brazilian bees. Far from taking this or that side, if the above story is true, it is just mind-bending to observe how distorted the facts can get and consequently attempt to destroy one's reputation. Undoubtedly, his scientific contribution has remained and continues to be recognized.

APACAME's aspirational goal was to relieve the impact of 'Africanization' and promote the 'Europeanization' of bees. I dove deeply into the subject and learned a lot about beekeeping, which prompted me to assemble a number of beehives at my sister Silvia Regina's and brother-in-law Georg's ranch near Tatuí, outside of São Paulo. Beekeeping not only involved my dedication to learning the history and theory behind the activity but it became an interactive experience. For instance, it started with choosing the spot for the beehives, if possible surrounded by trees, where they could fly over from the beehives to the feeding sources and vice-versa. The ideal situation is that the bees had the least interference to perform their noble work of collecting all of the amazing complex substances so critical for their survival – and, indirectly, our own. As an example, an environment immediately next to the beehives which posed noise coming from machinery and/or animals were deterrents to an excellent beekeeping culture. Other aspects, such as a rich flowering surrounding culture, are key to the production of not only good honey – the most immediately recognized item –

but other products no less important such as nectar, beeswax, pollen, bee bread, propolis and royal jelly, not to mention the bee's venom, known since millennia for being capable of providing phenomenal therapeutic effects. Also, as bees rarely spontaneously come to beehives, the chasing for bee swarms or wild nests is probably one of the most challenging steps towards the enhancement of beekeeping, especially, when dealing with 'africanized' bees, known for their aggressiveness and challenging handling. I have a number of memories of calling friends to help me out with 'hunting' for bees and subsequently transferring the wild bees into the hives: a fun, smoky, messy, - and sometimes painful – experience. For some, a one-time initiative...

For years, I had great pleasure and fulfillment in the activity. There's a great deal to be learned from these amazing creatures and their collective organization which, today, are being threatened in its very existence by corporate greed and ignorance.

## ....AND MASTER'S DEGREE

Excited about finally concluding college, I was ready for the next chapter. The last year had been intensely dedicated to studies and to figuring out what to do with my degree in Economics. Although business had been front stage of my experience and what I saw as career possibilities given the broad aspect of it, I made the venturesome decision to enroll on a Master's Degree at USP – *Universidade de São Paulo*. Enrollment plus the very first class fees were supposed to be paid upfront and took almost all of my savings. "It'd better be what I have in mind," I told myself. My advisor was a renowned scholar and had provided me the necessary support. Classes started out and the program in its broad spectrum seemed to be promising. The course revolved around economics related to agricultural production and the use of natural resources; the focus was on the knowledge and understanding of industry potential in energy and socioeconomic analysis of the impacts of the sector.

As much as I perceived the pragmatism around techniques and innovations for productivity enhancement and scientific development in agriculture, I couldn't afford not to be an observer of the politics behind it. And that had to do with what Vistara Parham called the "Politics of Hunger":

"According to a widely accepted myth about world hunger, the world does not have the capacity to feed its people. Everyone is doing the best they can, so the story goes. 'There is simply not enough to go around. The hungry masses are rapidly multiplying, and if we are to avert disaster, a concerted effort to control population must be vigorously pursued.' Parham emphatically contradicts the statement: "However, a rapidly growing number of renowned scientists, economists, and agricultural experts are expressing their strong disagreement with this. 'It is patently false – a myth,' they say. 'Actually there IS enough to go around, and then some. Any scarcities are due to wasteful utilization of resources and their irrational distribution. According to Buckminster Fuller, there are enough resources at present to feed, clothe, house, and educate every *human being on the planet at American middle class standards!*"

It was a matter of time until I started questioning the Masters' program and its orthodox structure. And along with it, the decision to pursue an academic path. My attempt to instigate discussions in class around the debate of a better and more rational utilization of resources in agriculture[1] – and my reality pointed out to the principles of vegetarianism as a problem solver – did not resound within that rigid program. In retrospect, my point was to find out if there were spaces I could explore in order to bring sense to the momentum and experience I was living through. Short lived, the sense vanished and I was bound to pursuing a path I had no clue as to where and how to find it.

Dropping out of the Master's program and, consequently,

---

[1] The idea about methane gas emitted by cows and other livestock having a significant impact on the amount of greenhouse gases in our atmosphere was not even on the radar at that time. Considered to be one of the main culprits behind climate change and global warming, this is a controversial issue but cannot be ignored today if a serious debate around the subject is to take place.

giving up the idea of following an academic path, was not that difficult, although frustrating. However, swallowing the fact that my decision to go that route was less than proper hit me a little harder. Why in the world had I not seen it? Now, not only was I not sure what to pursue but my savings were gone. Disappointed in myself, I had been withdrawing from my Dad's business, rent was about to be raised, and I began to face the fact that if I wanted to remain independent I would have to strive to get a position in an unfriendly and complex job market or yet, go back to my parent's house until I could figure out my next move.

# 7
# The Search

*"Just take a pebble and cast it to the sea*
*Then watch the ripples that unfold into me*
*My face spills so gently into your eyes*
*Disturbing the waters of our lives."*
Take a Pebble, Greg Lake – ELP

"INITIALLY THESE POWERS are still very much directed at themselves, and are experienced above all in feelings, but they are already leading to the need to occupy oneself with spiritual problems and to see oneself in a development which spans the entire arc of life." – *Lievegoed, Phases, The Course of Life.*

The above thought was symbolic of the days I lived through in 1983. It was on one of those weekends – dedicated to hunting bees in the wild, turning them into the wooden beehives I would frequently acquire at APACAME, and acclimating them in and around the spot in the woods chosen to shelter the apiary – that I ran into one of the most intriguing books of my young adulthood. A couple of years earlier, American author

Marilyn Ferguson, "described her first glimmers of what she called 'the movement that has no name' – a loose, enthusiastic network of innovators from almost every discipline, united by their apparent desire to create real and lasting change in society and its institutions." Her attempt to compile and synthesize the patterns she was seeing eventually led her to develop The Aquarian Conspiracy (J.P. Tarcher, 1980), the seminal work that earned her a lasting global reputation.

Clearly, her ideas resonated to me in opposition to an academic approach. "The book's title led to some confusion, having to do with astrology only to the extent of drawing from the popular conception of the "Age of Aquarius" succeeding a dark "Piscean" age. The word conspiracy Ferguson used in its literal sense of "breathing together," as one of her great influences, the philosopher Pierre Teilhard de Chardin, had done before her." That same year I had come across an influential text by the same philosopher which resonated deeply in me. Pierre Teilhard de Chardin was a French Jesuit priest, theologian, philosopher and paleontologist who tried to construct an integrating vision between science and theology. His view on Religion and Spirituality:

> *"Religion is not just one, it's hundreds.*
> *Spirituality is just one.*
> *The religion is for those who sleep.*
> *Spirituality is for those who are awake.*
> *Religion is for those who need someone to tell*
> *them what to do and want to be guided.*
> *Spirituality is for those who pay attention*
> *to their Inner Voice.*
> *Religion has a set of dogmatic rules.*
> *Spirituality invites you to reason about everything,*
> *to question everything.*
> *Religion threatens and frightens.*
> *Spirituality gives you Inner Peace.*
> *Religion speaks of sin and guilt.*

*Spirituality tells you to "learn with error".*
*Religion suppresses everything, makes you false.*
*Spirituality transcends everything,*
*makes you true!*
*Religion is not God.*
*Spirituality is All, and therefore it is God.*
*Religion invents.*
*Spirituality discovers.*
*Religion does not ask or question.*
*Spirituality questions everything.*
*Religion is human, it is an organization*
*with rules.*
*Spirituality is Divine, without rules.*
*Religion is the cause of divisions.*
*Spirituality is a cause of union.*
*Religion seeks you to believe.*
*Spirituality you have to seek it.*
*Religion follows the precepts of a sacred book.*
*Spirituality seeks the sacred in all books.*
*Religion feeds on fear.*
*Spirituality feeds on Trust and Faith.*
*Religion makes one live in thought.*
*Spirituality makes Living in Consciousness.*
*Religion is concerned with doing.*
*Spirituality is concerned with Being.*
*Religion feeds the ego.*
*Spirituality makes us Transcend.*
*Religion makes us renounce the world.*
*Spirituality makes us live in God,*
*not renounce Him.*
*Religion is worship.*
*Spirituality is Meditation.*
*Religion dreams of glory and of paradise.*
*Spirituality makes us live the glory and*
*the paradise*
*here and now.*

*Religion lives in the past and in the future.*
*Spirituality lives in the present.*
*Religion enclaves our memory.*
*Spirituality frees our Consciousness.*
*Religion believes in eternal life.*
*Spirituality makes us aware of eternal life.*
*Religion promises to after death.*
*Spirituality is to find God in Our Inner Life.*

*"We are not human beings going through a*
*spiritual experience ...*
*We are spiritual beings going through a*
*human experience..."*

Marilyn Ferguson stated that "although her book was not explicitly political, it expressed early enthusiasm for the radical centrist perspective." Here is an excerpt of The Conspiracy:

"A leaderless but powerful network is working to bring about radical change in the United States. Its members have broken with certain key elements of Western thought, and they may even have broken continuity with history. This network is the Aquarian Conspiracy. It is a conspiracy without a political doctrine. Without a manifesto. With conspirators who seek power only to disperse it, and whose strategies are pragmatic, even scientific, but whose perspective sounds so mystical that they hesitate to discuss it. Activists asking different kinds of questions, challenging the establishment from within."

Ferguson based her studies and research in her own country and spoke about a paradigm shift, especially as it related to education. "...the Aquarian Conspiracy is a different kind of revolution, with different revolutionaries. It looks to the turnabout in the consciousness of a critical number of individuals, enough to bring about a renewal of society...."

| OLD PARADIGM OF EDUCATION | NEW PARADIGM OF EDUCATION |
|---|---|
| Emphasis on content, acquiring a body of "right" information, once and for all. | Emphasis on learning how to learn... pay attention to the right things, be open to and evaluate new concepts, have access to information.... |
| Hierarchical and authoritarian structure. [Teachers teach facts!] | Egalitarian. Candor and dissent permitted. [Teachers facilitate class dialogue] |
| ...emphasis on the "appropriate ages for certain activities" | Flexibility and integration of age groupings. |
| Emphasis on external world. Inner experience often considered inappropriate in school setting. | Inner experience seen as context for learning. Use of imagery, storytelling, dream journals, "centering" exercises, and exploration of feelings encouraged. |
| Emphasis on analytical, linear... thinking. | Augments left-brain rationality with holistic, nonlinear, and intuitive strategies. |

"The crises of our time, it becomes increasingly clear, are the necessary impetus for the revolution now under way. And once we understand nature's transformative powers, we see that it is our powerful ally, not a force to be feared our subdued. Our pathology is our opportunity."

Almost reaching my mid-twenties and having been exposed to a multiplicity of images, thoughts, peoples, my own and, most significantly, other people's experiences, it was impossible to ignore Ferguson's call. Which was not a call for militancy or activism, but a call for inner exploration into the existing unknown. Sounded like an oxymoron, and I suppose it was. Adding to the search, where the searcher becomes a seeker, I couldn't find a better analogy for this life journey and self-discovery:

"The Tree of Life"

"What life is could be illustrated by the example of a tree. All the various attributes of the outer aspect of the tree—trunk, branches, leaves, flowers, and fruit—together with the various attributes of the inner root, go to make up the whole life of the tree. But when we look more closely into the life of the tree we find that, although the root is the basis of the outer tree, it has no absolute, independent status. The root depends upon the nourishment, or sap, that comes from the area outside the root itself. This sap is the essence of the entire tree. It makes the root and, passing through the root, gives rise to the various aspects of the tree. We thus find the tree is nothing but the nourishment that comes from outside the boundary of the individual tree. The tree is obviously limited within the bounds of the root and outer tree, but its basis is outside these bounds." – Maharishi Mahesh Yogi

*The Aquarian Conspiracy* became the emblematic gateway of my investigation. An eye-opener for new possibilities. From there, I would set out my path on waters I had not navigated before. New people and groups were now part of my circle, as well as books and authors I had not yet been introduced to.

Philosophers, scientists, and educators who had proposed theories of spiritual evolution would include Lao-Tzu, Paracelsus, Francis Bacon, Helena P. Blavatsky, Rudolf Steiner, Annie Besant, J. Van Rijckenborgh, Sri Aurobindo, Pierre Teilhard de Chardin, J. Krishnamurti, G.I. Gurdjieff, Joel Goldsmith, Allan Watts, among others. Their works would offer me enough material for a lifetime of research – to which I would spend a significant amount of time in the next several years.

# 8

# Lightning Strikes

*"At my request you take me in
In that tenderness I am floating away
No certainty, nothing to rely on
Holding still for a moment
What a moment this is
Oh for a moment of forgetting
A moment of bliss."*
– In the Blood of Eden, Peter Gabriel

*May 25th, 1983*

*My dearest friend James,*

    Yes, a year ago we were saying goodbye after getting together for a real short three weeks. It feels like those three weeks became a key part of the history of our friendship, like a bridge that joins our spirits throughout our lives. My soul gets richer every time I hear from you. God bless you man. I'm happy to learn you're doing fine up there with a very original way of living Mother Nature has preserved for all of us, in spite of what we're giving Her back. Hopefully more and more people will get aware of the state of the world and its needs in order to maintain, or should I say, to recover the balance it once had. Mankind has somewhat lost its bonds. But not all humans.

Soon wildflowers will be welcoming you and your roommate Peter and I'm glad for that. This time of the year brings hope and joy for it's supposed to be really cold in winter months, as I understand. Well, as you noticed by my delaying in writing back to you, my mind is in confusion again. I quit graduate studying, no comments. Practically, I'm doing nothing except for some sporadic artistic work, playing the guitar – and now the piano - and thinking too much. I'm even considering going back to Israel, and spend some time in the kibbutz where I could get some experience in sustainable agriculture, apiculture and dairy-farming. It is as paradoxical as it can be: Brazil is supposed to be an agricultural country, isn't it? I feel kind of obstinate to get out of this town. Needless to say, it's crazy living here. I'll take my time and find out how to do it, no matter how long it's going to take.

Tomorrow I'll be going to the 7th Encounter of Rural Communities, which is supposed to be an attempt to organize people around the difficulties predicted to happen in the coming years. It may sound nonsensical, but the country is emerged in great economic difficulties; politicians don't give a damn to social problems. Still drained in their struggle for and to stay in power, they insist in neglecting the population's needs for decent survival. We'll see what happens.

Please still consider my wish to visiting you in the U.S. sometime this year. When would be a good time? How long will you be there? Be sincere and let me know. My rent will be over in August and I'm no longer planning on staying here. This is all for now my friend. I'm happy to know you are content, well you always are, and that's great. My love to you and your family, to your friend Pete, and the chicks, the dog, the cat...I miss you too.

Renato

"It's all about change." I don't think I will ever forget the first time I heard this. It took me a while to accept the fact that carrying on the lifestyle I had created as ideal for my development as an individual was getting more and more difficult to sustain. Per my letter to James, the economy had been in recession for a couple of years, I was now actively looking for a job and my savings had gone down the drain. Mom and Dad, once again, with their wisdom and understanding of the phase I was going through, opened their arms and offered me back the room where I spent a meaningful part of my adolescence. Grandma Alexandra was not only getting old but starting to show signs of acute senility, therefore requiring close care. Both my parents wholeheartedly embraced and provided her the appropriate assistance in the same apartment space.

Cristina had become a beautiful young woman. My little sister had always been a cheerful, smart and communicative girl and watching her grow up was a delight. With my two older sisters married and out of the house for some time now, we had become very close since my return from overseas and nurtured long and deep conversations about behavior, psychology and existentialism. Besides, as Silvia Regina did a few years earlier, she joined a group of young individuals with likeminded ideas and purpose. I was happy to see her flourish and express her potentialities.

The day was a Saturday, June 18th late afternoon-evening, when Cristina planned a gathering of young friends and relatives to celebrate her 19th birthday. June is a festive month all over the country. *Festas Juninas* (June Festivals), also known as *Festas de São João* for their part in celebrating the nativity of St. John the Baptist, (June 24), are the annual Brazilian celebrations adapted from European Midsummer that take place in the southern midwinter. These festivities, which were introduced by the Portuguese during the colonial period (1500-1822), are celebrated during the month of June nationwide. The gathering had no intention of characterizing the festivity, which typically takes place outdoors. However, the mood for celebration was in the air depicting joy as it is also a month to honor rain, the harvest season and marital union. This gathering had a special meaning for me as I got to meet a fine group of youngsters and converse with a number of young relatives I had not seen in years.

With a few romantic relationships going nowhere in recent years, the pursuit for finding the right companion was and had always been there. Needless to say that a particular girl, part of Cristina's group, stood up in my eyes. An encounter that would change my life forever. And hers too. While mingling and chatting with several people throughout the party, I didn't quite have the opportunity to speak with her – yet, she did not go unnoticed for the length of the celebration. Half way through the party, the expected 'Happy Birthday' singing was about to take place around the dining table. With the always delicious homemade strawberry cake covered in whipped cream, the nineteen candles were lit up and about to be blown by my little sister. Exactly when this young woman standing up across the table – tall, elegant, long brown-haired, her eyes as sweet as a honey bee - smiled a smile at me I could not quite fathom. Silvia was her name and what follows was a moment of mystery and revelation. Similar to the unique experience I had in Florence a few years back, it was as though time had stopped for a fraction of an instant. Slow motion, as I looked at her, singing and expressing her presence at that moment, the sensation of a silent thunder following lightning crossed my brain and my entire system. A voice, clear and undisturbed, cool and serene, one of those things that come from the other side, spoke to my mind: "this young woman, right in front of your very eyes, will one day be your wife."

## PASSED THE ELEMENTS

Sunday a.m. The effects of 'lightning striking' must have been properly neutralized since I woke up in that cool morning, whole and ready for the day. I was unusually curious but calmly waiting for Cristina to wake up and inquire about that young woman. "Who was that?" I think to myself. "Ok Cris, tell me all about your friend." Without disclosing the revealing experience I had the night before – which was yet to come as proof to me – I began to walk a pathway of patience and perseverance until the opportunity to see Silvia again presented itself. It was quite a moment to internalize and I wanted to nurture it the proper way.

An intriguing thought of one of my favorite thinkers depicted my momentum: "There is no such thing as being isolated. To be is to be related and without relationship there is no existence. What do we mean by relationship? It is an interconnected challenge and response between two people, between you and me, the challenge which you throw out and which I accept or to which I respond; also the challenge I throw out to you. The relationship of two people creates society; society is not independent of you and me; the mass is not by itself a separate entity but you and I in our relationship to each other create the mass, the group, the society." – J. Krishnamurti

As I hoped that I would get to meet Silvia again in the near future – after all, she belonged to my sister's group of friends - my attention was also focused on the possibilities for self-realization. Not only was I diligently investigating a course of action for a potential career, but I also allowed myself to come across discussions, people and literature that helped me understand the opportunities associated with that self-realization path. The economy was trying to come out of the recent recession years and jobs seemed to be more available; yet, I intensified research on what this group of youngsters was striving to get accomplished.

Year's end during a family event, I ran by my Mom's younger brother, Marcilio. This was a man with incredible business acumen, energy, intelligence and an acute sense of opportunity. His business was flourishing: *Arquetipo* manufactured glazed aluminum curtain wall products and supplied them to the always increasingly growing and demanding construction industry in São

Paulo. His company had just recently closed large contracts and he was looking for a professional he could rely on to help further grow his organization. Although I did not quite possess the profile of a seasoned professional, he saw in me someone he could trust to closely work with him on the execution of the contracts which literally knocked on his door due to the quality and reputation of his work.

Silvia and I randomly came across one another at the school – *The Lectorium* – where weekly classes took place in the same neighborhood where we both lived in. She had been studying music for years and played the piano beautifully, helping support the activities of the school from an early age. With a solid foundation in classical music, she could play and interpret almost anything written by Brazilian classical composers such as Heitor Villa-Lobos, Francisco Mignone, Ernesto Nazareth and Radames Gnatalli, all the way to the well-known masters – Bach, Handel, Haydn, Mozart, Beethoven, Chopin – the latter, one of her favorite composers – Schumann, Debussy, Satie and many others. This was a time which coincided – really? – with my developing the taste for classical music in a strong way.

As I accepted my uncle's offer to join him at Arquetipo in January, I continued to occasionally run by the young woman I had met several months before. Every now and then I gave her a ride home after class – to which her brother Sergio also showed up to sometimes. The school was located right next to *Parque da Aclimação*, a jewel of a park adjacent to downtown, enclosed in the middle of a neighborhood surrounded by high-rise buildings. Long walks, joggling, standing still; old trees with rich greenery surrounding the park's pond and lots of people were part of the scenery seven days a week. I had basically spent my adolescence visiting that park and found great solace being there.

At work, there was much to learn. The company was going through growing pains and it was not always easy working with Marcilio. My brilliant uncle had too much on his plate, added to the major responsibility of raising a family. His children,

Marcelo, Rodrigo, Ana Paola and Marina, the latter one my goddaughter, were younger but very close to me. Their mom, Silvia Chazyn, had a strong personality but was a warrior when it comes to keeping the family whole while giving her husband enormous support for his business initiatives and outstanding creativity. Marcilio's dominant and charismatic personality portrayed the necessary leadership across the organization, however at a cost. As for myself, in general we got along and communicated with each other well. At home, however, there was reason for concern. One evening, waiting for a bus ride home, I coincidentally ran by my cousin Ricardo and learned the regrettable news that uncle Theodoro has cancer. Its progression could be unpredictable and treatment was about to get started. As I reached out to my father, typically discrete in situations of family members' illnesses, I perceived his effort to keep his cool; however, I knew my old man: internally, he is worried about his brother's wellbeing and possibilities for a successful treatment.

"YOU BECOME RESPONSIBLE, FOREVER, FOR WHAT YOU HAVE CAPTIVATED."

*The Little Prince* – Antoine Saint-Exupery

Silvia was on my mind and I tried to make sure that I was on hers as well. "In the minds of men and women two different force-fields play a part. From within the biological drives various impulses and longings penetrate the soul - from within the spiritual strivings there is in *equal measure* a problem of individuation. Since the human being is a trinity of body, psyche and spirit, the spiritual path, of individuation, will follow different paths in men and women. At the same time, each individual is unique and equal, even where there are differences in the level of spiritual development and moral quality. Where the individual is along the path of development does not determine the value of the individuality, just as an old man is not superior or inferior to a child. The person who has acquired a certain insight has more responsibility in his wrestling with moral and social problems and problems of knowledge. It is for this reason that I talk of the equivalence of individualities as beings with aspirations. As I have said elsewhere: 'The human mind is a citizen of two worlds, a spiritual one and a biological one.' Because of the latter the soul-life of men and women differs." *Bernard Lievegoed – Male and Female Development – Phases*

Bernard Lievegoed's thoughts are not of easy absorption, especially as it relates to the role of men and women. In fact, if the spiritual problem – an appropriate way to address spirituality – was simple, there would not be so much conflict and misunderstanding in our planet.

Livegoed goes on to say "Each man seeks his Eve, each woman her Adam. Deep in the soul there is an ideal picture which completes the individual's own soul. Will he meet the right person or will he have to make do with the first one to correspond roughly to the ideal? When the first relationship has been established it becomes a practice-ground for further development, so that, however it may end, both parties end up richer than when they started." Lievegoed goes beyond and states that "even those who believe in the predestination of two people for each other will have to develop the maturity necessary for the recognition of the future marriage partner."

Silvia had no idea about my experience at the birthday party nor did I dare to share it with her. At least, for the time being. I would be the one to carry on this intuitive momentum and find possible reciprocation if we were to build something out of it. As it happened before in different life situations, I had good reasons to be confident that we would be together. Hence, I let it run its natural course. Besides, there was family and friends involved - it would help big time to count on their support.

From the time we first met to the time we started dating it basically took a year. Silvia was about to start college; therefore, we had quite some time to get to know one another before committing to a more serious relationship. As much as I perceived her as being a mature young woman – her demeanor at home and at the school, *The Lectorium*, her exposure to life's challenging situations – she was still young. Besides, there was a component in her upbringing that made all the difference in the way she was: her parents, Mauricio and Elvira, although not quite socializing like my parents, were extremely good creatures. Far from sentimental, there was an aspect of intelligence that attracted me about her family, and Silvia would portray that to me in her own joyful, sincere and authentic way.

## CHANGE, THE ONLY CONSTANT

Six months had passed since I started the job at *Arquetipo*. Work was going well and I liked what I did. With multiple moving targets, it felt that I had learned the job quickly and was contributing to the business as there were many challenges to overcome. However, things were about to change again. It was a cloudy early Sunday morning in July and my sleep had been interrupted a few times throughout the night. The last leg of my sleep was quite shocking and I woke up compelled to share my experience with my Dad. Scheduled to travel to Europe for a month's stay in a few weeks for the first time since I had been back from the long trip of three and a half years earlier, my dream was accompanied by a decision. "Dad, could we talk for a moment?" That weekend, we had the visit of Gloria and Nico from Mexico, which was always a delight having them around. My Mom and Dad took pleasure in hosting friends and family and were busy with the hospitality. "Sure, son. Let's step out into your room." What follows was a moment of introspection and apprehension: I told my Dad that I dreamed that his dear brother would not be alive when I came back from Europe. My Dad was a good listener and waited for me to finish up my thought. "I know you have been worried about *Tio Jujuba's* health and also how work is of your concern once he is no longer around. Therefore, if this is of any help, once I am back from this trip I am committed to rejoin you at the store." The news is bittersweet for my Dad. He's always hoped that I would join the family business again. Under the circumstances, he welcomes my decision but knows that my statement about his brother's condition could well have that outcome. However, he seems disturbed just to think how soon this can happen. He and my uncle worked together for their entire adult lives. Their connection is profound: above all, there is great trust and respect for one another.

After breakfast, I picked up the phone and called Silvia to tell her of my dream and decision. As always, she was very supportive and helped me figure out a few things in preparation for what's to come. The upcoming trip to Europe was of great significance to me as I was scheduled to visit countries I had been before but now under totally different circumstances – The Netherlands, Belgium, France, Germany and Switzerland, with the purpose of visiting the temples and symbolic sites associated with the activity of the school, known and described in the next chapter as *The Lectorium*, in Utrecht, The Netherlands and beyond, such as *The Goetheanum*, in Dornach, Switzerland. Silvia's dad, Mauricio, is also in the same group – it would be a good opportunity to get to know him a little and let myself be known.

# 9
# Alchemy

*"And the people bowed and prayed to the neon god they made*
*And the sign flashed out its warning in the words that it was forming*
*And the sign said "The words of the prophets are written on the subway walls*
*And tenement halls and whispered in the sound of silence."*
*Sound of Silence* – Paul Simon

"IT WAS THE EXPERIENCE OF MYSTERY – even if mixed with fear – that engendered religion. A knowledge of the existence of something we cannot penetrate, of the manifestations of the profoundest reason and the most radiant beauty, which are only accessible to our reason in their most elementary forms – it is this knowledge and this emotion that constitute the truly religious attitude; in this sense, and in this alone, I am a deeply religious man." – Albert Einstein

The excerpt is from Einstein's book *The World as I See It* which I had come across a few years earlier. Composed of assorted articles, addresses, letters, interviews and pronouncements, it includes Einstein's opinions on the meaning of life, ethics, science, society, religion, and politics. For the most part, it is a magnificent and yet simple piece of literature accessible to 'common mortals' since his theories of relativity and universal gravitation are generally regarded as inaccessible to the ordinary person. His opening vision is straightforward and yet deeply touching:

"What an extraordinary situation is that of us mortals! Each of us is here for a brief sojourn; for what purpose he knows not, though he sometimes thinks he feels it. But from the point of view of daily life, without going deeper, we exist for our fellow – men – in the first place for those on whose smiles and welfare all our happiness depends, and next for all those unknown to us personally with whose destinies we are bound up by the tie of sympathy. A hundred times every day I remind myself that my inner and outer life depend on the labors of other men, living and dead, and that I must exert myself in order to give in the same measure as I have received and am still receiving. I am strongly drawn to the simple life and am often oppressed by the feeling that I am engrossing an unnecessary amount of the labor of my fellow-men. I regard class differences as contrary to justice and, in the last resort, based on force. I also consider that plain living is good for everybody, physically and mentally."

Einstein's words are inspiring and influential to an entire generation, and well beyond. His own experiences and disillusionment, first renouncing his German citizenship – not only once but twice – due to the actions of Nazism, and later on becoming drawn, against his own intention, into the whirlpool of political passions and the contemporary history of his time.

## THE SCHOOL

My interest in the subject of spirituality developed spontaneously during and after being in contact with Marilyn Ferguson's *The Aquarian Conspiracy*. Now, my visit of approximately four weeks to Europe has a specific objective: to allow myself to deepen the knowledge on the philosophical aspects of my interests, particularly as it relates to truth, freedom and understanding of humankind. As I bumped into books and seminars provided by this philosophical school, it became clear to me that I was a beginner, seeker of the unknown, looking for answers to the questions of one's existence and its purpose. As a briefly description of the school and its meaning, here are basic and synthesized excerpts from Wikipedia:

The School, *"The Lectorium Rosicrucianum*, (8) is a philosophical entity which considers itself a worldwide school of Esoteric Christianity. It was founded in 1924 by Dutch mystics Jan Van Rijckenborgh, his brother Zwier Willem Leene and Catharose de Petri. The school teaches a form of modern Christian Gnosticism which is based upon the ideas and iconography of *Rosicrucianism*, the beliefs of the Cathars and other forms of religio-mystical thought such as Hermetism and Alchemy.

"Although it was suppressed by the Nazis during World War II, the *Lectorium Rosicrucianum* now counts about 15,000 members and has branches in countries all over the world, including Europe, North America, South America, Africa, Australia, New Zealand and the UK.

"The teachings of the organization are based on the New Testament (especially the Gospel of John and the Apocalypse), Catharism, the Corpus Hermeticum, the dualistic Gnosticism of the first centuries and the German literature of the first Rosicrucian trend, including Paracelsus.

"The school has a "particular version of Christian Gnosticism" which includes the fundamental teaching of the concept of the 'two nature orders': First, there is the material nature order, which includes the dead as well as the living, and everything in this nature order is subject to the cycle of being born, living, dying, and being born again. Secondly, there is the original, divine, spiritual nature order. The first domain of existence is the world of perishability, of rising, shining, and fading, or 'dialectics' the second is the world of imperishability, or 'statics,' which in the Bible is called 'the kingdom of heaven.' A last remnant of the second nature order, called a 'divine spark' or 'rose of the heart', is latent in the heart."

The timing and importance of this trip would shape up my

actions for many years to come. There, just as I had come across likeminded individuals in my own country, I get to meet with a serious group of people from many corners of the world aiming at similar goals. What are the goals and which actions are to be shaped up? In my heart and mind, the answer was to gradually acquire what was referred to as self-knowledge and to expand awareness and understanding of the world. A priceless experience, not intellectual, not mystical, but a practical experience of co-existing with multiple persons from dozens of countries sharing a similar purpose.

## BEING HERE

Once again, I looked for reflection and found it through Krishnamurti's lenses: "A religious man does not seek God. The religious man is concerned with the transformation of society which is himself. The religious man is not the man that does innumerable rituals, follows traditions, lives in a dead, past culture, explaining endlessly the Gita or the Bible, endlessly chanting, or taking sannyasa—that is not a religious man; such a man is escaping from facts. The religious man is concerned totally and completely with the understanding of society which is himself. He is not separate from society. Bringing about in himself a complete, total mutation means complete cessation of greed, envy, ambition; and therefore he is not dependent on circumstances, though he is the result of circumstance — the food he eats, the books he reads, the cinemas he goes to, the religious dogmas, beliefs, rituals, and all that business. He is responsible, and therefore the religious man must understand himself, who is the product of society which he himself has created. Therefore, to find reality he must begin here, not in a temple, not in an image — whether the image is graven by the hand or by the mind. Otherwise how can he find something totally new, a new state?" – J. Krishnamurti

# 10

# Trial and Error Amidst the Essential

*"Now as the river dissolves in sea,*
*So Neptune has claimed another soul.*
*And so with gods and men*
*The sheep remain inside their pen,*
*Until the shepherd leads his flock away.*
*The sands of time were eroded by the river of constant change."*
*Firth of Fifth* – Genesis

THE YEAR WAS 1968. It's vivid in my memory the curiosity, importance and attention I gave to the act of working:

"Are you sure?" Mom asked me.

"Yeah, that's what I want to do, Mom" I answered without hesitation.

My Mom conceded to my determination and finally agreed upon reaching out to the corner store's management nearby our house where they provided the neighborhood with office supplies and toys. At age 10, properly authorized by my parents, I got my first job during Christmas season. My task was, among other responsibilities, to watch the store front doors so that no minor or grown up thief would take advantage of grabbing easy-to-reach items and running away with them. Also, I would help with restocking items, packaging and assisting the managers on various requests. What I loved about this store was the variety of choices, especially during year's end shopping season. Done with school – in the Southern hemisphere school year ends up around the Summer Solstice in December – I could work for a few weeks before our usual summer vacation. But what I liked most was the idea of interacting with the public, the experience of servicing and observing one's satisfaction. Probably anticipating the early stages of what would be a career in business development and consulting. Throughout my teenage years I would have multiple experiences, e.g. buying and selling shoes directly from manufacturers or customizing tape recordings of the musical hits of the day then selling or bartering them at school; and, of course, my Dad being a mid-size business man would allow me to exercise the taste for helping people at the counter. Fun and educational, rewarding and dynamic as I would be in contact with people and learn from multiple interactions.

Fast forward to August 1984, a few days after my dream and just before leaving for Europe, I had to face my uncle Marcilio and tell him I would not be coming back to Arquetipo. Although he was not very happy with the news – he needed help and trusted I could be instrumental to assist his company to go to the next level – Marcilio understood my quagmire and promptly supported my decision.

After four weeks and back in the country, my Dad was happy to see me but saddened by a double loss experience: His loving brother had passed – uncle Theodoro could not resist and perished from a painful and long period of illness. As well, one of my Dad's favorite cousins, Omar, a true best buddy, occasional business partner, companion of traveling, camping, hunting, fishing and, most importantly, of playing cards, himself also fighting a long and debilitating illness process, had left us only days apart from *Tio Jujuba's* decease. Dad, being a cerebral character, as much as he would miss the two individuals for the rest of his life, had his focus on the present day. For sanity, he knew this was the wise thing to do: to continue to be joyful and good-natured, he was ready to move on.

## SEVEN YEARS + ONE

The next period of my life would be permeated by deep learning. Parallel to the activity of *The Lectorium* where Silvia and I were actively engaged in the Youth Work, my learning curve was, to a great extent, about how to contribute to the business my Dad and his brother had created in their early twenties. My cousins Ricardo and Mauro had joined the business a few years before, had been married and had already started constituting their families. Our upbringing had a strong component to the potential success of our partnership: we grew up like brothers and trusted one another – half the battle right there. Coupled with a strong model – partly selling fabrics for seamstresses, small retailers and resellers in general in exchange for cash, partly financing small to mid-size resellers and apparel companies by supplying fabrics offering a limited line of credit – the business was solid and had potential for growth and innovation.

1985. Democratic winds were finally looming in a country that so anxiously aimed at becoming more socially just and economically developed. The economy, however, had adjustments to be made and one could only understand its critical aspects by looking at the past. In an overview of the multiple attempts to miraculously address the economic issues of the day, by the mid-1980s, domestic debt nearly displaced foreign debt as Brazil's main economic problem. During the high-growth 1970s, a significant portion of foreign borrowing had been by state enterprises, which were the main actors in the import substitution industrialization strategy. Initially, they borrowed to finance their investments. Nonetheless, towards the end of the decade, with the acute shortage of foreign exchange, the government forced state enterprises to borrow unnecessarily, therefore markedly increasing their indebtedness. Their situation worsened with the sharp rise in international interest rates in the late 1970s, the devaluations of the austerity program, and the decreasing real prices of goods and services provided by the public enterprises stemming from price controls. Because the state enterprises were not allowed to go bankrupt, their debt burden was gradually transferred to the government, further increasing public debt. This, and a growing disorganization of the public sector, transformed the public debt into a major economic problem. By the mid-1980s, the financial burden stemming from the debt was contributing decisively to its rapid expansion.

What did the above scenario have to do with microeconomics, where small to mid-size companies like ours would find themselves? Almost everything, unfortunately. During the second half of the 1980s, it became increasingly clear that a large-scale fiscal reform, one that enabled noninflationary financing of the public sector, was needed not only to control inflation but also to restore the public sector's capacity to invest. Both are essential for an economic recovery; however, political obstacles prevented the reform from materializing. And, because inflation has become the most visible symptom of the public-sector imbalance, there were several attempts to bring inflation under control through what came to be known as "heterodox economic shocks."

Those "shocks" although initially perceived and supported as inevitable remedies aimed at correcting the economic challenges faced by a malfunctioning system, would work for some time but eventually turn into devastating consequences for the economy and society. Especially, for those less protected from their effects: the usual suspects, the middle class and the poor, always more vulnerable and susceptible to economic downturns.

Meanwhile, the private sector would follow along and would be typically sensitive to economic shifts, especially in Brazil, where the presence of the government and the state are usually prevalent. Our business was doing well, despite the economic hick-ups. We had diversified our distribution channels by creating multiple product lines and began to implement a manufacturing component to the business. On a personal level, Silvia and I got engaged and planned our wedding in about 6 months. This period coincided with a spike in inflation levels which demanded urgent decisions by the government.

One of those "shocks" baptized as *Plano Cruzado*, named after the new currency name, its main objective was to eliminate inflation with a dramatic blow. Between 1980 and 1985, inflation escalated from 86.3% to 248.5% annually. A few months later, early in 1986, the situation would become desperate, prodding the implementation of the plan. Its main measures would be a 'general price freeze, a wage readjustment and freeze, readjustment and freeze on rents and mortgage payments, a ban on indexation, and a freeze on the exchange rate.' What? Unthinkable for a first world economy given the magnitude of its interventionism, it would seem well thought out for the country's standards and would promise to provide staggering results. Meanwhile, amidst all decisions and events during that period, with Christmas approaching, I got a letter from the northern hemisphere:

*One night in December 1985*

*My dearest friend,*

*Just a short note to you to let you know that I'm thinking of you – missing you a lot!*
*A new life for me here in Vermont. I have moved from the farm for many reasons, & now live on another beautiful hill in a place which reminds me a lot of the kibbutz. Maplehill Community is a home for 8 teenagers who cannot live at home for one reason or another. Some have been abused, some are in trouble with the law, most have problems at school, & all are in need of a lot of love. This is a place of love – like no other place I've ever been. 6 adults "work" & live here & care & love*

*& share & support each other in a way I've never before experienced. A lot is given, a lot is expected & a lot is shared on a very sincere level. I love it here & feel that I have much to give & much to receive.*

*Time will tell. Winter has come north, & I'm sure you are now warm. How are you? I yearn to spend time with you, to talk and laugh like old times. Maybe 1986 will be a year when we can find a way to be together for a while. It's a plan and I want to make it true.*

*My love to everyone, I hope you are happy.*

*Merry Christmas,*

*James*

Pumped up by my friend-turned-brother's letter, I continued on this life phase determined to build my future.

Implemented in February 1986, the plan's immediate results were spectacular: the monthly rate of inflation fell close to zero, economic growth surged upward, and the foreign accounts remained under control. With the initial success of the economic plan, improving demand and the apparent control of inflation, there was plenty of optimism.

Business plans came out of the drawers and so did personal plans. Our wedding was set up for June. Besides our own thrill, this was an exciting time for my parents and siblings: Cristina and Carlos had their wedding in late 1985 and Silvia and I would stick to our plan. Getting married, as big a deal as it is and coupled with economic uncertainty, could be challenging. Nevertheless, we trusted our good foundations and were confident about the major step we wanted to undergo.

ONE PRECIOUS OF MANY SPECIAL WEDDING GIFTS

William Bryant on *The Veiled Pulse of Time* has an enlightening description of the twenty-eighth year – the seven-times-four threshold: "For most people, the crucial years between twenty-eight and thirty are particularly trying and can be a time of disorientation, stress, or even dramatic change. We enter a phase of *contraction*, and our inward-looking self-assessment primes us for the vital expansion that takes place close to the thirtieth year. Opportunities seemed to appear out of thin air in the previous cycle, but now life demands more exacting and thought-filled decisions in keeping with our emergent sense of self and our social responsibilities. The realization that we are now much more dependent on our own inner resources may make us anxious and unconfident for a time. Although we get less help from the external world, some kind of inborn stimulus in the psyche exhorts us to face ourselves on a deeper level. We are forced to reconsider our position: how and where do we fit into life? Are we on the right course?"

Nathalia Kolosuki was a dear friend of both Silvia's family and mine. From my end, I did not know her well but she seemed an honest and true individual. She had known my sisters Silvia Regina and Cristina for years and was also a customer of our store, from which she frequently purchased fabrics to utilize them as raw materials for the fine sewing services she provided for her clients. From Silvia's end, there was a greater connection there as she had known both Mauricio and Elvira for many years, even before Silvia was born. It was May, 1986. Nathalia showed up at the store for a minor purchase one fine early afternoon, just about a month before our wedding. Always a pleasant personality, I was happy to see her. We chatted for a moment and I helped her find the proper fabrics she was looking for, measured, cut and wrapped them up, then calculated out and presented her the bill. Once she was all set, out of the blue, she asked me: "Would you buy me a cup of coffee?" Surprised but immediately receptive, I replied: "Of course, Nathalia. Let's go to the café next door, they make a good espresso."

Nathalia was an immigrant from Poland and was in her mid-sixties, although she looked older. White-haired, her small, angelical blue eyes were deep and reflected the semblance of someone who may have had a rough life. Yet, her smile was noble and captivating and she meant nothing but well. As she slightly touched my hand after a few sips, with her soft voice, she went: "You and *Silvinha*" – kindly referring to Silvia using the diminutive variation, as she had known her for all her life –"you two will be getting married in a few weeks and I wanted to share something with you."

Wide open to her words, I said: "Sure Nathalia, please" "I love *Silvinha* and her family and I've known your Dad and your sisters for some time now. I hope I can convey this to you properly." Looking straight at me in the eyes, she proceeded: "I am a firm believer that life does prepare us for the difficult things. In other words, I think we come to our existence somehow ready to go through the tough times. Big events such as death, illness, major losses of all kinds – these are the big things every human being will go through, sooner or later. Yet, somehow we are equipped to withstand these hard experiences. However, on the other hand, I don't think we are always fit to deal with small things or situations. As an example, circumstances that get us involved in bickering, petty arguments and undesirable acts may escalate if we don't pay attention to as to how to deal with them. And these things, the little details that we tend to overlook in relationships of all nature – at work, in friendships, at home with siblings and parents and, most importantly, in a marriage – are the very things that undermine the same relationships and more than often bring them to an end. Sometimes amicably, sometimes loaded with anger, mistrust and hatred. Only because we tend to ignore the little things."

Her message was clear: work out differences before they build up to a point of no return. Nathalia knew what she was talking about. Many years later I would learn that she herself had gone through significant disenchantment, having experienced an unhappy marriage and troubled relationships. She had learned it the hard way and now felt compelled to subtly get that off her chest. As for myself, although not yet fathoming the profoundness of her message, I cannot think of ever having received a better advice.

It is said that a good night's sleep is what it takes to let experiences sink in before we incorporate them into our system. From the moment I heard those words and after the next few days, I must say that her message entered my brain and there it stayed. Days, months and years would go by – it became part of my repository and could be accessed at any moment through the course of my existence.

Silvia and I were fortunate. Our families, friends and community gave us remarkable support to start our lives together. And I mean beyond material support. We were blessed with their love and affection and that meant a lot for the bedrock of our relationship. Besides, as both of us being pretty independent, we learned to give one another the proper space from the very beginning while yet capable of acting interdependently. A promising start.

## MUTUAL LOVE FOR TRAVELLING

*Pico da Agulhas Negras*, translated as Black Needles Peak, is the fifth highest mountain in Brazil, standing close to 10,000 feet (2,800 meters) above sea level, making it one of the highest in the Brazilian Highlands. Our two-stage honeymoon was planned initially in the beautiful *Itatiaia* National Park, in the *Serra da Mantiqueira*, a range bordering the states of Rio de Janeiro and Minas Gerais. *Itatiaia* and *Penedo*, the latter one a district in the municipality, was the first Finnish colony in the country. The two picturesque towns where we chose to spend time right after our wedding, were the preamble for the larger travel time we had already booked along with a group of *The Lectorium*. Silvia was aware of my fondness for getting on the road and she herself had an open mind for the same travel interest.

Our trip to Europe would happen a few weeks after the short honeymoon trip and would encompass The Netherlands, Belgium, Germany, France and more. This time, Scandinavia was the region we wanted to visit beyond the usual conference centers, where we as pupils gathered for studies. We were truly excited and somewhat let planning run a little loose prior to embarking on our trip by train. From Amsterdam we headed up to Norway's Bergen and Flåm, the latter a special spot in the world.

## THE FLÅM RAILWAY

We were beyond enthusiastic to visit the fjords and that part of the world, as we read on the travel booklet: "This is one of the most beautiful train journeys one can experience once in Norway." The train ran from the end of Aurlandsfjord, a tributary of the Sognefjord, up to the high mountains at Myrdal station. The journey featured the finest aspects of the stunning scenery of Western Norway. Over the course of one hour, the train took us from sea level at the Sognefjord in Flåm to the Myrdal mountain station, situated at 867 meters above sea level. Myrdal was also a station on the Bergen Line, meaning the Flåm Railway connected with trains running between Bergen and Oslo.

The Flåm Railway is one of the steepest standard gauge railway lines in the world, with 80% of the journey running on a gradient of 5.5%. The train ran through spectacular scenery, alongside the Rallar Road, vertiginous mountainsides, foaming waterfalls, through 20 tunnels, and offered so many viewpoints. A single trip up and down was not enough – back one day, who knows?

The experience of visiting the fjord and its beauty was indescribable. For Silvia, it was as if she had detached herself from reality, given the breathtaking uniqueness of its nature. From Norway, we headed to Sweden's Stockholm and Malmo where we stayed with local friends, then Finland's design and musical marvel's Helsinki, and finally a short stop in Denmark's Copenhagen before getting back to Amsterdam. Music, art, nature and a taste of how the locals lived made our travel time unforgettable. Silvia was hooked on the travel band.

## STOP AND GO, THEN PUSHING FORWARD

As the rubber hits the road, where macro influences micro, the economic plan's heterodoxy began to show signs that it would not prevail over reality. By the end of 1986 the plan would be in trouble. The wage adjustments were too large, thereby increasing aggregate demand excessively and creating inflationary pressures. Moreover, the price freeze was maintained for too long, creating distortions and leading to shortages of a growing number of products. Translating: Silvia and I would have to be patient in order to equip our little apartment until some normalcy between supply and demand in the economy got reinstalled. An odd time for getting married? Maybe. Yet, worth the trouble.

What Lievegoed calls the organizational period, the next phase, beginning towards the end of the twenties and lasting until the mid-thirties, is of quite a different character from the previous one. "Youth is now past, the serious business of living has finally begun. This fact becomes evident in many ways. The changes of job in previous years now cease. Now the challenge is to push in order to make a firm bond with one's work, and to find within it either a means of rising towards or to the top, or at least to some broadening of responsibility. The individual's attitude is now more intellectual; the expansionary drive is still there and is still carried along by considerable vitality, but now it is the intellectual aspect that is beginning to predominate."

Imbued by a strong sense of accomplishment, we implemented discipline and diligence at work. Dad, cousins and myself, although not always in the same boat, wanted to push our business forward as the potential for growth was imminent. We liked to think that we had good ideas; our customer base had been established, the firm was financially sound and we all wanted to fulfill a social responsibility, thus allowing our efforts towards the creation of jobs and wealth. As the country went through another economic hick-up in 1987, mostly affecting the infamous public sector, the next three to four years revealed to be of great progress to our business. Given the nature of our industry, where textiles were considered commodities, the only way to differentiate our business was to add a design component that would translate into a good degree of customization to and for our clients. With a number of strategic partnerships with key manufacturers, we catapulted our business significantly: our physical space grew, specialized professionals joined our team, research travels and understanding of the most relevant international textile markets added to the objectives we were pursuing. Moreover, technology via CAD systems applied to the industry promised to revolutionize the textile sector.

We ran the business as if all the pieces of the puzzle were to be put in place. At this time, I embarked on a graduate school specialized in Marketing and Advertising – ESPM – which would add to the knowledge of strategy and business administration, a field which my major in Economics had slightly broached when I was in college. Erratic an economy as Brazil was and always has been, we did venture in believing the winds were to blow favorably for sustainable growth and innovation. With elections scheduled for November 1989, tensions were high between left and right, as usual. After a bitter pre-election process, the country would end up electing Collor, a populist who would overcome both the left and the right. The country, once again, would be in political turmoil, once again the economy would live the cyclical helter-skelter.

## THE PRINCESSES

It didn't take long for us to navigate the waters of parenthood. Our lovely Catherine Bianca was born in 1987 and a new baby was expected in July of the same election year of 1989. Silvia and I were now the proud parents of a beautiful girl, and her upcoming little sister Diana Louise – GG – would make things even more cheerful and exciting – but challenging too. Life was indeed getting pretty darn serious and, of course, parenting is no easy task. But, we both enjoyed the outlook. James was once again scheduled to be in São Paulo after seven years from his first visit – I could not be more thrilled. I would see my friend again and Silvia would finally have the opportunity to meet the man.

He got to the city and we basically travelled the next day to the coast where we would stay with friends for about ten days – it was late February and end of summer, life is good. *Juquehy* is located at about 100 miles from São Paulo. Considered part of the north shore, it is one of the best beach towns in the area – with fewer dwellings and people, somewhat secluded, the water is calm, clean and clear; the sand thin, the beach flat and suitable for long walks, perfect for family vacation. Our lovely one-and-a-half-year old little girl would go, from a very young age, anywhere with us without constraints of weather or temperature. Accepting of travel distances, she would get used to our excursions to multiple places – coast, mountain, caves, you name it – as we would take every opportunity to get out of the big city.

The year of 1989 started out strongly and promised to be an eventful period; At work, my cousin-partner Ricardo and I planned a trip between mid-March/early-April to research ways to improve our business aiming at perfecting what we were doing well. In previous years, my Dad would go to Europe for ideas on design and printing. However, this trip was different. First stop would be the U.S., then Germany and finally Italy. In New York we would meet with Professor Allen Cohen at F.I.T. – Fashion Institute of Technology, an author of an all-encompassing study about the industry: *Marketing Textiles: From Fiber to Retail*, had provided deeper intellectual knowledge of the textile sector and its many ramifications. In the Big Apple, we met with multiple *converters* – fabric resellers which would add their own unique design component to their business – and had lunch with Professor Cohen, who gracefully gave us free consulting on the direction we were headed, which reinforced our convictions. Later on we would recommend him to a large and relevant manufacturer in Minas Gerais, to which he did end up providing exceptional consulting services.

## PLAINFIELD, VT

James had a good time while visiting us. In fact, my perception was that he was good at enjoying himself everywhere he went. At work, with a busy work schedule ahead of us in March/April, I had told my friend that I'd give my best shot and try to fly for the first time over to Vermont during my stay in New York City. James had been living in the Green Mountain State since 1982 and loved the change of scenery from New Jersey's Stone Harbor, where he had spent a great deal of time in the last few years. After a full week of appointments and extensive research in the textile industry environment in NYC, and with the following week yet reserved for flying overseas for fabric trade shows in both Frankfurt and Lago di Como, located in the Milan's fashion belt, I took the chance and bought a ticket to Burlington for the weekend. It was Friday late afternoon, with yet cool temperatures, – I should say cold for my standards – heavy rain was on the schedule. We were staying at The Roosevelt in Midtown East, and cousin Ricardo decided to stay at the hotel – he had himself the beginning of a cold. Walking the streets of Manhattan proved to be challenging as the weather, with frigid winds and rain, was much colder than we had expected for the end of March.

After an hour's flight, James picked me up at the Burlington International Airport on Friday evening. The weather was awful; torrential rains almost cancelled the flight from La Guardia and that was the only window of time I would have available to make it happen – I was happy to be with my buddy after only a month from his visit, now under completely changed circumstances. It was Easter weekend and his schedule was full. His little apartment in Plainfield makes it convenient to go to work and dedicate his time to what he loved to do – James teaches Math at Maplehill.

"Maplehill School and Community Farm is nestled in the

hills of Central Vermont. Grounded in a deep commitment to nurturing authentic relationships between students, staff, volunteers and community members, the Maplehill School and Community Farm offers young people unique opportunities to learn in either small groups or through individualized learning opportunities."

The school served both male and female students between the ages of 12 and 22 in grades 7-12. "Whether they were applying mathematics concepts to garden planning, learning biology through animal chores, or discovering the history of the region through community projects with the local senior center, Maplehill School students were nurtured to develop their interests, skills and talents through a wide range of activities and community connections."

With some snow still on the ground, we woke up in the morning to get breakfast and then headed out to Maplehill. There we got together with a group of young men and women and stuck around for a couple of hours. As a working farm, Maplehill featured school time and programs for homeschoolers as well as a summer camp. The staff seemed outstanding and all of them were expected to work exceptionally well with children and young adults. There was also a program for at-risk teens that was part of the school curriculum and it appeared to be working well. On that morning, I met Patricia Persons, Tricia, as James liked to call her. Previously arranged, after mingling with the group, we drove through the capital, Montpelier, on our way to lunch at Wanda's, Tricia's mom, in Waterbury. Curiously, spelled with one "l" only as opposed to France's southern city of the same name, it is the least populous state capital in the United States. With fewer than 8,000 dwellers, the daytime population grew close to 20,000 due to the large number of jobs within the city limits. Besides the capitol building being one of the few in the country to have a golden dome, to this day Montpelier is the only U.S. state capital without a McDonalds. It sure does speak a lot about this town – and I seemed to like it.

Wanda's background family was Lebanese and it was hard

not to expect a table with the greatest Mediterranean dishes. Describing food is not as easy as it would seem. How many ways could I say something was really tasty? Not enough to keep one interested in the writing...Tricia's mom, reminded me my Dad's mom, Grandma Alice. Besides the great food and hospitality, we had loud laughs on that Saturday early afternoon in Waterbury along with Tricia's sisters – Theresa, Georgeanne and Maryanne - and their significant others, Gordie, Don and Jeffrey. I was pleased to have met those people for we would become good friends in the years to come.

The next day was going to be a short one as I would have to fly back to New York late afternoon. James gathered Tricia along with the Maplehill co-workers and we headed over to the Burlington area. Located in Winooski, the group had booked the Easter Lunch at Waterworks, a unique spot situated by and partially 'floating' over the Winooski River falls. Located at the historic old Champlain Mill building, this was a construction completed in 1912 as part of American Woolen Company's expansion. Built in the Italianate style with brick from Drury Brick and Tile Company of Essex Junction, it was the last of the four textile mills at Winooski Falls. Coincidentally, a former textile environment which sheltered great historic activity. It felt good to have visited this landmark of Vermont along with thoughtful and purpose-driven people. And great food!

## BACK IN MIDTOWN

Named in honor of President Theodore Roosevelt, the hotel located at 45 East 45th Street, opened on September, 1924. Ricardo and I had been there for about a week, and three more days would close our intensive research on the role of *converters* in the textile industry of New York City before leaving for Europe. Besides being a setting for a number of music videos, The Roosevelt had been and would become the stage for well-known movies such as the *French Connection, Wall Street, Maid in Manhattan, The Dictator and Man in Black 3*, among several others.

With its elegant architecture – astounding high ceilings with majestic chandeliers, its rooms decorated with mahogany wood furniture and light-colored bed coverings – the hotel is linked with Grand Central Terminal by way of an underground passage that connected the hotel to the train terminal. At minutes from Times Square, getting around was convenient and made our stay in the city very productive.

# 11

# Reality Hits

*"Though I saw it all around*
*Never thought that I could be affected*
*Thought that we'd be last to go*
*It is so strange the way things turn*
*Drove the night toward my home*
*The place that I was born, on the lakeside*
*As daylight broke,*
*I saw the earth*
*The trees had burned down to the ground."*
Don't Give Up – Peter Gabriel

EXPERIENCING THE TEXTILE TRADE SHOWS in Frankfurt and Lago di Como gave us the certainty that our initiatives to further develop our already established business were the right path for success. Besides, we had the opportunity to deepen our understanding of what the new technologies applied to design could do to boost marketing, sales and services in our industry. Back home, we had work to do. The original business was now more structurally organized and ready to give way to the newly created division of customized fabrics for the apparel and retail industries. Besides, a new component of CAD technology could open new avenues of opportunities once the foundation of the business was solidified. Sales were excellent and we more than doubled distribution and market share. In the spring of the same year, we inaugurated a new space off-downtown. With the help of my cousin Sandra Trentini – an interior designer with great experience in remodeling homes and offices in São Paulo – a show room was created to provide an exciting design-oriented environment to both our clients and our own team – designers, textile techs, sales and marketing.

## IMPONDERABLES

November, 1989. The newly elected President Collor promised to fix the economy, fight corruption and cope with the malaise of the public sector and its bizarre behavior. The very day he took office, the emboldened politician launched *Plano Collor*, implemented by his finance minister. The plan attempted to reduce the money supply by forcibly converting large portions of consumer bank accounts into non-cashable government bonds, while at the same time increasing the printing of money bills, a counterbalancing measure to combat hyper-inflation. Needless to say that while the economy had major challenges to overcome, life would obviously not stop for civilians; therefore, basic needs such as jobs and job creation, housing, education, safety and general infrastructure continued to demand attention. Once again, the country would go through a period of major changes, what ISTOÉ magazine called an "unprecedented revolution" in many levels of public administration: "privatization, opening its market to free trade, encouraging industrial modernization, temporary control of hyper-inflation and public debt reduction."

In the month before Collor took power, hyperinflation was 90 percent per month and climbing. All accounts over CR$50,000 (cruzeiros, about US$500 at that time), were frozen for several weeks - unimaginable. He also proposed freezes in wages and prices, as well as major cuts in government spending. The measures were received unenthusiastically by the people, though many felt that radical measures were necessary to kill hyperinflation. Within a few months, however, inflation resumed, eventually reaching rates of 10 percent a month.

During the course of his government, Collor was accused of condoning an influence peddling scheme. The accusations weighed on the government and led Collor and his team to an institutional crisis leading to a loss of credibility that dramatically reached his finance minister.

This political crisis had negative consequences on his ability to carry out his policies and reforms. *Plano Collor I*, would be renewed with the implementation of *Plano Collor II*; the government's loss of prestige would make that follow-up plan short-lived and largely ineffective. The failure of *Plano Collor I* led to its substitution by a new finance minister and his plan tried to correct some aspects of the first plan, but it was too late. Collor's administration was paralyzed by the fast deterioration of his image, through a succession of corruption accusations.

During *Plano Collor*, yearly inflation was at first reduced from 5,000% in 1990 (Collor's first year in government) to 400% in 1991, but then climbed back up to 1,020% in 1992. Hyperinflation at its best.

## THE THIRTY-YEAR PHASES – I

Bryant's description of this critical life cycle is surgical: "The thirty-year cycles are often the most dramatic of all the cycles. This means that our thirtieth and sixtieth years, along with the midpoint at forty-five are likely to be scored by crucial incidents or a change of pace, direction, and emphasis. There is much evidence to support the view that each climatic predicament typical at these times summarizes the previous cycle and provides the impetus and opportunity for important experiences to come. These are the principal turning points where time and destiny focus on the present. A change of some kind is demanded - an adjustment to jerk us back on course, a course known only to the psychic center of our being." – William Bryant, *The Veiled Pulse of Time, The Chronos Cycle*.

We had heavily invested in the business with the promise of wealth creation, development and growth to nurture what we understood was our social responsibility. Three years into venturing our projects, we were forced to go back to where we were by the time I had joined the company, eight years before. But there were multiple aggravating variables: drowned in economic and political difficulties, the country's condition now put a heavy toll on the private sector, a lot more vulnerable this time, leading to a general disarray of the civil sector. From our family business perspective, at one time we had almost sixty employees working in multiple areas of the company. This number, after the economic debacle, shrunk down to about ten. From a household perspective, our families now had grown – each of the partners had two children and my Dad's retirement would have to be pushed back to a few years down the road. The silver lining for me was still at a distance: I simply cannot not find myself and my family cell continuing to live in São Paulo. Big cities pose a mix of allure and simultaneous brutality. Culture, family, friends, people, food, amenities in general intermix with lack of safety, traffic, pollution and impersonal interactions. Weighing it in, as difficult as it was to live in such an unstable country and its environment, coped with the problems of a monster city, I found myself getting to unfamiliar terrain.

Silvia and I brought back long discussions about quality of life, simplicity, purpose and outlook. Especially with the girls at ages four and two, their future was at stake. We had to be creative and find alternatives to accommodate the new reality. The reality of scarcity, despair, lack of motivation and perspective. I needed to find a way out and for several weeks I just simply didn't have the tools. Yet.

# 12

# Far Away

*"Travelling around sure gets me down and lonely.*
*Nothing else to do but close my mind*
*I sure hope the road don't come to own me*
*There's so many dreams I've yet to find."*
*So Far Away* – Carole King

JOHN TUCKER WAS A STUDENT of *The Lectorium* and was visiting Brazil for the first time. Like we did when we visited the multiple conference centers of the school in Europe, John was touring around – from the Southeast to the Northeast of this immense territory, and the many places in between, he was amazed at what he had seen so far. John was an Aussie. Australians are considered to be great travelers and they love to travel. Known worldwide for it, every other traveler you meet – and most locals in any given country – will recognize that, along with people from New Zealand, Australians are probably the most prolific travelers on the globe. It's in their blood and it is part of their nature. Why is that?

There are multiple reasons. One is financial: It's one of the richest countries in the world; Another is time: people get a minimum of four weeks holiday a year; Geography: they live a long way from most countries, which means they're used to going a long way to get anywhere; Immigration: almost all Australians have cultural and familial roots in another country, therefore adding motivation to leave and investigate other lands. There is a real attraction for travelers to go overseas. And they do it passionately and enthusiastically, uninhibitedly and adventurously.

I met John in September, 1991, about a year before the political snafu which would cost the sitting president his job and basically bring the country to its knees. The economy showing subtle signs of decline and unbalance, it would take a few months for the economic agents to perceive its mixed messages and to fathom what to do with them within their own environments. For us, it started out with a spike in interest rates which brought us financial concerns as to how to deal with inventory and committed orders. The result by year's end was that the design division I had created suffered severe major order cancellations due to uncertainty, to the point that we had to close the show room, cut down our team dramatically and pull the plug on the technological initiatives which – ironically – could probably rescue us in the coming years from our current condition: a textile industry in decline, already starting to suffer from stringent competition from Asian countries, especially China. There was an additional challenge: the future was way too volatile and abstract, we had to deal with the reality of the present. To make things more interesting, Ricardo and I had been undergoing a simultaneous construction of two new apartments for our respective families, which contributed to our financial vulnerability. In those days, there was not such a thing as a mortgage system – I doubt if there's one today that works – to support housing acquisition for the population. Either you could afford to pay cash – or pay as you build, as we did – or not. Otherwise, you would just pay rent until better winds arrived.

Which, for most people, is the only option.

## THE COUNTRY OF THE FUTURE

My generation, and probably my parents' too, grew up hearing that Brazil was the country of the future. From the early 1990s, a time when the country was 'threatening' to become a stable and powerful economy, dark humor took place born from the following years of political and economic turmoil. We – the locals – would repeat the curious expression over and over... now, with a more dramatic connotation, "Brazil is the country of the future – and always will be." For me, that was hard to swallow. I was not going to sit and watch the washout in front of my eyes. I needed the present and I was going to find it, no matter what.

At that point, my presence in the business became marginal and I began to sense that I was being a burden to its financial health. While I initially cogitated to get back in the market place – my focus was clear and my assessment right to the point: "This is the country of the future with no present." With silent resignation, Silvia and I agreed to expand the horizon. I picked up the phone and called John Tucker, now back in Australia, to share my current situation. John himself was no stranger to tough times – he had been married before and was now rebuilding his life with Pam Wattie and her daughter Shawnie. As I bring up the idea to travel to Melbourne and investigate the radical idea of immigration, he immediately offered their home to assist me in the research. My determination for change was imperative. Silvia and I had two cars and we agreed to sell one of them to finance the trip. Much to the opposition of our extended families' wishes, I set the plan in motion.

After I put the letter in the mail I had written to James to tell him about my momentum, I had a couple more days before embarking on the journey. In Vermont, James and Tricia had been married for about three years and now had a little girl, Gabriela. He had been in Australia before and would most certainly understand and appreciate my initiative. I just wished that the conditions would be different and that the pressure was not so pervasive. But, I had no choice but to pursue this new and unfamiliar life experience. At home, the plan was that Silvia hunkers down with the girls until I got back. I knew that my initiative may have sounded for some like escaping, for others bold and for other people even ridiculous. I simply didn't care and was too independent to give ears to criticism. Or compliments.

## DOWN UNDER

This trip was like no one I had done before. Firstly, the circumstances. Secondly, the massive distance between the two countries. From São Paulo to Buenos Aires, the flight's destination before crossing the ocean over the South Pole was Punta Arenas, Chile at a short distance from Ushuaia, *The End of the World*, the capital of *Tierra del Fuego*, the most extreme city in Argentina. From there, the long haul to Auckland, New Zealand, before catching a flight to Sydney and finally Melbourne. Altogether, thirty hours. The upside was my willingness and sheer determination. The downside, well, it was a killer trip. During one of my air travels, I learned from flight attendants that what makes one tired about flying from point A to B, especially on long runs, is that the air quality breathed inside an economy class cabin is by far inferior than in business class, let alone in first class. In other words, e.g., while a specific square footage accommodates, let's say 20 people in first class, the same space may squeeze in 45-60 or more people in economy. Therefore, it's easy to perceive how dramatic it is to 'share oxygen' with so many more people. Multiplied by the number of hours, the temporary damage in the body is done. Truth or myth, the fact is that I felt like I was run over by a bus when I got to Auckland. I was so ready to stretch and breathe real air!

John Tucker picked me up at the airport in Melbourne on a beautiful Sunday early afternoon. As much as I was tired, I could not conceal my excitement. Derived from the country's position in the Southern Hemisphere, at the antipodes of the UK, Australia is colloquially known as "the Land Down Under." At first glance, I was impressed with Melbourne's cleanliness, lush green trees and parks, and inner-city neighborhoods; but one aspect did call my attention: the variety of cars was understandably concentrated on Japanese makers and many of them seemed to be well preserved old models. Datsuns, Toyotas, Hondas, Subarus, Mazdas, Daihatsus, Suzukis, Isuzus, and Mitsubishis occupied the traffic landscape. Those cars were so well built that old models still ran pretty well. Whether the climate was a contributing factor, it also attested to the non-discarding mentality of 'use it and toss it', which prevails in other countries, especially the US and to some extent in Brazil.

John drove us from Melbourne to Emerald, where he and Pam had rented a house not too long ago. It was the month of June and fall was beginning to give way to winter quickly. Melbourne temperatures were warmer than up towards the Dandenong Ranges. Emerald is a suburb in the Greater Melbourne area, about less than 30 miles south-east of the city. The population was minuscule compared to the big city I grew up in, and that alone was a major factor of attraction for me. Though it would take me two to three days to start getting used to the time zone and sleep adjustment, I would typically navigate well when dealing with the expected jet-lag. Nevertheless, I was glad I took the initiative and was eager to start the process of getting to know the people, culture, geography, and, most importantly, the conditions that could eventually favor and simultaneously justify myself and my family to becoming potential migrants.

The chance to experiment a household routine in a different country and culture was and always will be of high value for me. John, Pam and Shawnie were affectionate human beings. Yet, males typically would shake hands at a distance, with no physical contact, and it was no different with John and I. With Shawnie being about twelve, the attention and support was focused on her: I loved the fact that every night before bed time, Shawnie would give us all an individual deep and long hug.

Quite distinct from my culture, though also affectionate, it was nice to be a part of that special good night moment along with my new friends.

The time frame I had in mind to visit this unique country was rather extensive: 30 to 45 days, depending on the unfolding of the research. My certainty was that only Silvia understood what was in my mind and therefore approved of this project. The sole purpose was to find out everything I could about immigrating: with a 'business skilled' migrant status in mind, a few of the preliminary conditions revolve around the following: being under 45 years old; possessing a college degree; good knowledge of English; settling down with spouse and child(ren); and, not less importantly, to be capable to invest a minimum required AU$400K dollars, at a ratio of US$1 = AU$0.75, give or take. All checked, with the latter yet to be figured out, the opportunity was there to be tapped into.

Under normal circumstances, I would tour a given country and get to see much of its nature while exploring the landmark areas. However, my mood was for enduring this experience. My routine varied from accompanying Pam and Shawnie to school first thing in the morning; then, I would catch a bus and head over to downtown Melbourne in order to interview with immigration agents; collect informative material and documentation as to how to proceed once back in my country of origin, where an application should eventually originate from; the critical factor, as it related to qualifying as a business skilled person, was exactly proving that this was to effectively take place: either by setting up my own business, or by acquiring an existing business. The latter seemed more plausible and I began by focusing on the multiple opportunities.

Nature in Australia is beyond extraordinary. To explore the vastness and beauty of this country, it would take years and resources. As my time and available means allowed me to be in Victoria only and eventually visit other friends for a few days in Sydney, once I was headed back home, I alternated my research with a keen observation of the landscape. John was a master when it came to offering this outlook during our daily walkabouts. Victoria's flora and fauna is mind-blowingly diverse. The distinct scenes of this unique and varied state were home to a plethora of wildlife, much of it rare or endangered. From the wet temperature rainforest to the dry gigantic eucalyptus forests, and from the coastal heaths to the soaring granite ridges, this region is home to a truly formidable range of species, many of which are not found anywhere else on the planet. In the suburbs, magpies, king parrots and cockatoos were seen everywhere. But it was the Kookaburra bird that I couldn't ignore because of its loud distinctive laughing sound. Hard to spot the bird at first, its sound reminded me of monkeys in the Brazilian forests or the echoing of human laughter. A truly intriguing bird, sized between 11-17 inches.

Melbourne's suburbs were true gems. From quiet hills to clean communities, they felt like open air bed-and-breakfast environments all of the time. Besides, they were a haven for tens of thousands of wild animals, due to a combination of permanent water, varied landforms and plant species. On the weeks riding the bus from Emerald to Melbourne and back, I systematically stopped by every town in between: Olinda, Mount Dandenong, Belgrave, Gembrook, Sassafras, Ferntree Gully and beyond Emerald, other villages like Monbulk and Mount Evelyn. The winding roads and walking paths that crisscross the region took me to some of the world's most intriguing animal and plant life. All it took was to keep eyes, ears and mind wide open. Aware of that at times, I did take some time out to explore the environment there and at times was rewarded with wildlife encounters: a wombat crossing the road like a sultan, completely oblivious of the surroundings; a running possum-like animal zipping through towering tree ferns; mother koala carrying her baby up high on a small eucalyptus tree; the myriad of birds flying the immediate skies, and even getting a short distance visit from small wallabies, kangaroo's closest cousin. Most of them Australian native species which spent thousands of years in isolation and, consequently, extremely shy.

## COMPILING BUSINESS POSSIBILITIES

Narrowing my options down to two industries, which seemed the proper thing to do at this stage of the process, the small town environment enticed me to look into a couple of franchising possibilities. The first one, crafts and fabrics stores. To my surprise, the local culture still accepted and got inspired by craft assortment such as the use of yarns, needle arts, paper crafting, jewelry making and cake decorating. Getting to know a little bit of that region reminded me of the type of lifestyle my ancestors had experienced 30, 40 or 50 years ago in small town environments. It made me feel that I was the one missing something of the essential there...Another industry of my great interest, this one spoke strongly due to its future perspective, was the natural food business. I was fascinated with the quality and diversity found in the several stores I had visited, which spoke to the local people's mindset. Here, at least in Victoria, Australians were way ahead of many countries when it came to the use of alternative medicine and healthy lifestyles. Much to my delight since I had an open mind to the novelties in that field and did appreciate to see my family continuing to refine our lifestyle.

Never too advanced in my own way of looking at things, I frequently reached out to John and Pam for advice. They had truly been incredible supporters of my initiative and I made sure to tread lightly on their day-to-day lives. I also had a good friend who had been living in Melbourne for years, which happened to be the daughter and sister of very influential teachers and a classmate during middle school, at *Colégio Bandeirantes*: Silvia Krambeck, Prof. Morivaldo's and Prof. Elza's daughter, Rui Fausto's sister. Coincidentally, Silvia had gone to school with my sister Liliana in São Paulo back in the day and, most interestingly, had met her husband in a *kibbutz* in Israel years ago. For years, Silvia Krambeck has been a curator with great experience in collections management, art historical and cultural heritage research within the art museum and local governments in Australia.

Small world indeed, we gathered along with my friends during a weekend and caught up after many years. A great time.

After several weeks of research, understanding and gathering material about the Melbourne area's business outlook, I had a lot on my mind and was ready to start heading back. My wife and I nurtured an intensive exchange of letters, photos and booklets, to which I could get a sense of what she liked or did not like. Housing being a major concern for Silvia, I was not sure she was as totally excited as I was with the perspective of living a countryside-like lifestyle. Yet, with smart phone technology light years still ahead of us, there was only so much I could convey of this experience.

## OFF TO SYDNEY, THE HARBOUR CITY

Yet at the *City by the Bay*, I took the time to visit the Royal Botanic Gardens Victoria and a few cultural and historical sites in Melbourne. After five weeks, I was ready for the next part of my journey before heading back. With my mindset divided between my family business's momentary hardship for the second time – the first one during a major flooding in the 1960s – and the country's economy and politics, for the *nth* time, I did my best to learn as much as I could on what I had determined to be the focus for this trip. Forever grateful for John, Pam and Shawnie, I said goodbye at the Melbourne Central Railway Station. There, I caught the night train through the New South Wales corridor to Sydney. Mostly wondering whether this whole radical initiative would have any future or if this was just an escape from reality. Whichever the case, I needed perspective and this was the process I chose to live through in order to heal from the transitory professional and financial losses at home.

Having arrived in *The Emerald City*, I couldn't wait to see my friend Fabio D'Onofrio, from São Paulo. We had been best music buddies for years, since the early stages of Prog-Rock during the seventies. For similar reasons – the job market depleted in our home country – Fabio had a close friend in Sydney and had arranged to spend a few months with him until some normalcy was back in place. Professionally, Fabio was connected to the high-tech industry. The future was bright – *oh, the future*. We spent an entire day visiting the shores in, around and outside the bay and, of course, the exquisite surroundings of the Sydney Opera House before heading out to dinner at another friend's house, where together we spent a lovely evening. I rented a Mitsubishi Eclipse and wanted to experience what it was like driving on the left. No surprises, just that the brain quickly adapts to the new orientation. After spending great quality time with Fabio, we said good bye and looked forward to catching up again.

The next morning after breakfast, I was bound to visit new friends I had not met before – like John and Pam, the Dutch couple Thijs and Naomi were serious about developing the work of *The Lectorium* in and around their area. Still incipient and nothing yet like the dynamics found in Europe and Brazil, these were pioneers of the work and were somehow inspired by having me visiting them aiming at the possibility of Silvia and I helping at the school, especially with the Youth Work, if our project was to materialize. Thijs, Naomi and their little girls lived in one of the suburbs of Sydney, their house located in a land surrounded by multiple ancient caves.

Suburban Sydney was stage to Aboriginal rock art sites, believed to be tens of thousands of years old. In fact, the only surviving record of Aboriginal culture by the Aboriginal people themselves was contained in their art, found on rocks and in caves around the country. Thijs explained to me that there were main categories or sites, each one peculiar: economic sites (campsites, showing evidence of occupation); sacred sites (areas reserved for religious ceremonies, initiations); meeting sites (where groups met to trade and partake on festivities); and burial sites (members of a tribe buried or cremated, where spirits were freed to travel to the skies). Sydney's Aboriginal Heritage is profound. It is believed that the Aborigines of Australia first arrived in the continent some 25,000 years ago from Southeast Asia or by the submerged land access which once joined Australia to mainland Asia. Thijs was very proud and protective of these areas, like most of his fellow men and women.

For decades, Australia had been focusing their attention on major issues such as climate change, land clearing, soil and water shortage and degradation. The latter, a massive concern. Resulting from widespread droughts, there were several restrictions enacted in many regions, making this the driest inhabited continent. Usage of water at John's and Pam's house was one of the aspects of great concern for this family, the same for the Dutch household. Dishwashing, clothes washing, showering, all accompanied with usage techniques that I would make sure to apply when I got home.

## A SPECIAL MOMENT

Although not a great friend of zoos – justifying a life of captivity for so many wild creatures is not easy for me – I was highly encouraged to visit the Sydney Taronga Zoo. Unlike a number of cultures that mistreat animals in zoos in exchange for the economics behind it only, Australians in general tend to be thoughtful toward safeguarding animal welfare, especially in the unique environments and ecosystems such as those found in Oceania. I realized that nowhere in the world would I find such a combination of wild life and decided to take the chance. Besides, this was my last day in the city before riding the plane back to the South American continent.

Few destinations in the world compare to Australia. As I dove into the culture, I found the writing from a booklet of the Australian Government Dept. of Foreign Affairs and Trade, as part of the large material I was taking home: "The Australian coat of arms consists of a shield containing badges of the six Australian states symbolizing federation, and the symbols of the Golden Wattle, the kangaroo and the emu. By popular tradition, the kangaroo is accepted as the national emblem." The kangaroo being the symbol of this massive country was not to be disputed; this was something kids grow up knowing about. To me, once again, the kookaburra was a mystery. And it became an experience once I spotted this rather sizable bird from a distance. Perching on a 6-feet tall tree log behind a wired fence, I was immediately attracted to it, and I decided that I wanted to approach it and, if doable, come as close as possible. Laughing kookaburras have prominent brown eyes with dark stripes extending through them. As I walked towards this strange bird, I could tell he noticed my presence from afar and locked eyes with me. Then, I think, being close to the fence as he was, he was going to vanish once his territory got threatened. Not at all. I walked over another step, two, three, four and...he was still there. Behind the fence, of course, less than a yard distance, he sat fearless. Impassive. Looking at me in the eyes, like pets typically do. For minutes that I didn't bother to count, I admired this longish, red rusty tail in color with dark brown barring and white feather tips. His disproportional large head, with heavy and boat-shaped beak makes the kookaburra the largest of the kingfishers; kookaburras mate for life and live in pairs of small family groups. And laugh, as though they're having a lot of fun.

# 13

# Not So Far Away

*"But what I'd like to know*
*Is could a place like this exist so beautiful,*
*Or do we have to find our wings and fly away*
*To the visions in our minds?"*
*Visions* – Stevie Wonder

WITH A STOP IN BUENOS AIRES overnight on the flight back, I was moderately confident that the project Silvia and I had agreed upon investing in could bear an interesting perspective for our household. However, the reality was that Australia being remote as it is, the act of moving from one continent to another would be massive. Could we do it? I had no doubt about that. Would it be simple? Definitely not. Would we find the right conditions? Many were already in place, however, resistance from our extended families was the question mark. The ingredients and resources necessary to make the idea into a plan were there: we were still relatively young, the girls were young enough to adapt to the change and Australia welcomed the type of immigrants we could become, therefore fitting into the category. And, we were open to learning the new lifestyle and making the best out of the opportunity.

By phone and via letters, Silvia had already briefed me on the ongoing tension. My Dad was not happy with the signals I had been sending during my stay in Melbourne. Additionally, Silvia's Mom was far from excited about our initiative and would certainly put some psychological pressure if we were to follow through on this project. As I got home after weeks of imagining and planning the steps, I was beyond happy to be back and see my wife and the little girls. Going through the process of telling the stories about the experience was the best part of it. Now, off to making the case.

Our family business was hurting, as was the industry, the economy and the country. My disillusionment was real and I knew that enduring this moment was inevitable. But I could work on the perspective of inducing change as opposed to just navigating the storm until it got over. Crisis and opportunity go hand in hand, as the Chinese teach – or we, as Westerners, interpret it. The more appropriate translation to this would be: to 'turn danger into opportunity,' the danger of complacency, which in my view was a malaise in the Brazilian culture. Whether or not we know, understand and accept it.

After a few days of my return, we got together with our extended families and explained how we felt about the project and the rationale behind it. Needless to say that our views were in clear conflict with our parents' generation: They had seen and lived more than we had, therefore they had reasons to think that this was another temporary situation that at some point would go away. The difference, clear in my mind, was that Brazil has a structural problem. I could be dead wrong but this cycle could repeat over and over again. Besides, structural problems take decades to be addressed, if not many generations. There was a pervasive cultural component which individuals alone cannot solve. And I felt powerless. It's difficult enough to change one's own circumstances, let alone cultures behind behaviors. I will go into more detail in a later chapter as the stories unfold.

Determined to move ahead, one of the first actions I put in place was to reach out to a realtor. Our property was new as we had been there for only six months after construction was complete. Yet, we furnished the space with the basics and would need a long time and extra funds for completion. Most of the resources to make the Australia project viable would have to come from the sale of our home. This would generate enough finances to undertake the process and yet be able to make a significant down payment on a property in the suburbs of Melbourne. While the process moved on, I continued to work in the store almost every day: unmotivated but consistent, I knew that that was a temporary condition and a matter of time until change could take place. But change would not come without action on my part. While I reached out to John and Pam for a heads up on the progress in Australia, I was also starting to hear back from my previous initiatives from contacting employers and head hunters, a grinding process of expectations that normally gets to dead ends until a favorable moment or situation materializes.

The phone ringed, the realtor wanted to bring a potential buyer. Our apartment, located in a sought after part of the city, had been built by a reputable developer and was likely to go quickly – provided we found the right buyer. Not an easy chore in recession periods, especially during a 'buyer's market.' We set up the appointment, the visit came about, and the real estate agent promised to get back to me within the next day or two. At the end of the same day though, we already had a proposal and the feedback that the buyer had simply 'fallen in love' with the property. The numbers were where we needed them to be. This was a scary moment from which Silvia and I might have to make a big decision. My wife loved the place; I liked it but could not care less about continuing to live in São Paulo, a city which I had deepened such aversion due to its irrational ways – extensively described in previous notes.

My Dad got nervous when I shared the possibilities with him. As much as he opposed my initiative, I knew he did it particularly silently. And that was a problem for him. My Dad had had stomach ulcers throughout his adult life. Besides being a gourmand, which particularly contributed for him to developing gout the same year I was born, he also suppressed his feelings – which, in my opinion, didn't help him over the years from acquiring cardiac problems. In fact, a year earlier he underwent a preventative open heart surgery which especially depleted his health condition in the short term. Silvia's Mom, Elvira, became insecure and was not comfortable with the idea either. My Mom and Mauricio seemed to be more neutral in the process.

## PULLING THE PLUG, PLUGGING IT BACK IN

A voice message was on my phone mailbox from the realtor that brought us the business. He needed to hear from us rather quickly. Silvia and I looked at one another and found his tone to be of concern. As I reached back to him, I learned the unpleasant news that the buyer decided to pull the plug on the purchase. Our minds were blown: As I pushed the individual for an explanation, he told me that the buyer had decided to pick up another unit in the same building. "Ok. Do you know what triggered the buyer to change his mind? And who is the realtor involved?" His twofold-answer is exasperating: "Well, he got a better deal and...I have to be honest with you, I am the one who sold him the unit."

Stabbed in the back by both the 'honest' realtor and the aspiring buyer, I felt I had been used. Not fun. The clock was ticking, the bills were piling up, we were back to square one. Moreover, I knew that this is the best realtor for the type of property and the "fool-me-once-shame-on-you, fool-me-twice-shame-on-me" sentiment was there to test me. With a sour taste in my mouth and, knowing myself, I did not plan to pick up the phone if he called again. At this point, I could not afford to watch my Dad run the risk of deteriorating his heath. As well, Elvira felt the same way about the whole thing. We had to think about a different project. As I called John and Pam, they were also not excited about my doubts about the viability of all that effort. Our friendship was the important aspect of understanding the turn of events but yet, disappointment was inevitable.

I began to think that if that step was too big for us, at least for the moment, we could try exiting the metropolis toward the countryside. The thought was, if we were to stick around, we could always try to make it better. Not necessarily conforming but enough to provide us with a better outlook. There are excellent smaller size cities – still a significant move for what I had envisioned us for a change in lifestyle – but smaller in scale to allow us the experience of a simpler but more promising future. The 80-mile radius from São Paulo has good options. Now, it was finding a job and tying it up with a decent housing option within a good school system. Doable, although it might take some time.

Just when we started getting excited with what we saw, I got an out-of-the-blue phone call. It was a headhunter. Curiously, it was not one out of the dozen plus headhunters to whom I had mailed out my resume in the past several weeks. I found out that a recipient of my resume had forwarded my profile on to another firm. Appointment set up, I was there the next day.

## THE WATERS OF THE ATLANTIC OCEAN

Intriguing. This could be a game changer. A real one. Passed the formal initial interview scrutiny and advancing on discussions, the position was for the professional to be the front man for the largest manufacturer of cotton and poly-cotton yarns in South America to represent them in Europe. Based out of...Portugal. "Really?" I internalized my excitement with caution. As one of the first sequential links from "Fiber to Retail," cotton was historically the protagonist of the textile industry. In Brazil, this is an industry that is most profitable when marketing the products to the internal consumption market. For unmistaken reasons: the industry is protected and indirectly subsidized by tariffs charged to entrants in the market. In other words, by having little to no competition the only competitors are the local manufacturers. No competition? Not really, but little competition. Prices can be manipulated to 'acceptable' levels.

From my experience in the family business, founded and operating as a reseller throughout the years, I knew the predicament of no external competition as it relates to supply choices. One of the few virtues of the exiting populist president – threatened by impeachment from Congress followed by his resignation the same month of the starting of my interviewing process, after a painful and traumatic judicial mess – is the vision behind the attempt to modernize the overall Brazilian industry, starting with automobiles all throughout higher technology. It was a recipe for disaster if not implemented, as it had happened a few years earlier when a number of careless entrepreneurs fell into temptation to develop the Personal Computer industry internally. A terrible error of judgement, if one is to consider it the best case scenario; or madness, for lack of a better word – a negligent move that dragged the economy backwards for years. Possibly decades.

*TBM* S/A. – Textile Bezerra de Menezes was a successful family business based out of Fortaleza, State of Ceará, located at 2,400 miles north of São Paulo. A large city with more than two million people, the capital of the state is a beautiful coastal tourist spot for nature lovers. It is known for its beaches, which are punctuated by red cliffs, palm trees and lagoons. Its name is an allusion to Fort Schoonenborch, which gave rise to the city, built by the Dutch during their incursions in the area in the 17$^{th}$ century. Fortaleza had big plans to boost its existing status of a regional power house in multiple strategic industries, from tourism, commerce, textiles and garment manufacturing, to fruits and cashew nuts, fishing, leather and is one of only three states which together produced the world's entire supply of

Carnaúba wax. The ambitious goal was also to become a future global technology attraction hub. *TBM* was already a major producer; with the economy momentarily tanking and the export market functioning as an escape valve, the company's higher management wanted to plant a permanent professional in Portugal, one of the major producers and distribution garment centers for Europe.

As I got to meet with the top executives and discussions evolved for an offer, the perspective opened up an unexpected window of opportunity: besides the possibility for a professional turnaround coupled with financial relief, there was the potential for a new experience for Silvia and the girls, still five and three years old; and for myself, a solid way out from the reality of the country I was so disappointed with. After negotiations revolving around income, fringe benefits and timing for the move, I accepted the offer. The downside was that they wanted me in Portugal quickly. In less than a month time frame, they expected me to hit the ground running. It didn't seem to be a problem – I was ready for work. The caveat: I had to be in the City of Porto for about four to five weeks before my family could join me.

For over a year I had silently debated with myself the idea of stepping out of the family business. What was I to do but to find the best for my immediate family? For both Dad and myself, this was a difficult moment. He nurtured the idea of passing the baton to his son as a legacy of his decades of hard work. Now, although the firm had been steady and in recent years temporarily successful, the reality was that this situation was at a point of no return.

My partners, Dad, Ricardo and Mauro, would hold the business for a couple more years until there was no justification for continuation. The solace, if any, was that many firms were on the same boat and the industry sector itself was in free fall. The internal market overlap, added to the Asian factor – Koreans and Chinese, later the Indians – were indelibly taking over the show, marketing and selling their highly competitive products directly to the apparel and retail industries.

## PORTO, *A INVICTA*

Oporto is another name by which the second largest city in Portugal is known. Located along the Douro River estuary in northern Portugal, Porto is one of the oldest European centers, and its historical core was proclaimed a World Heritage Site by UNESCO in 1996. The western part of its urban area extends to the coastline of the Atlantic Ocean. Its settlement dates back many centuries, when it was an outpost of the Roman Empire. Its combined Celtic-Latin name, *Portus Cale*, has been referred to as the origin of the name "Portugal," based on transliteration and oral evolution from Latin. In Portuguese, the name of the city is spelled with a definite article *o Porto*; consequently, its English name evolved from a misinterpretation of the oral pronunciation and referred to as *Oporto* in modern literature and by many speakers.

I got to the city at the end of October, 1992. After weeks of meetings with higher management, specialists and also spending a week in Fortaleza to get acquainted with *TBM's* exporting and importing systems and its multiple product lines, I was back in São Paulo boarding a *TAP Air Portugal flight*. Along with me and leading the initiative, was the architect of the idea, Byron Queiroz. This was a man with prominent performance records. His previous executive achievement was of successfully leading a conglomerate of twenty-eight companies in his native State of Ceará; now, a recently nominated VP and minority partner of the Bezerra family in the organization, he wanted to shake things up. An individual of strange behavior and a few words, he was an intellectual of management and a man of action. Known and respected as a high achiever, he was my new boss. Dr. Byron, as I was supposed to address him.

For about a week, together we cover the most important clients and business relationships. Exports had been historically good for the company, although not as lucrative as selling the goods in the Brazilian market. Yet, there are many benefits in exporting as it brings balance to manufacturers, especially those, like *TBM*, dependent on the combination of locally produced raw material and imported cotton from sources such as California and the Bible Belt states in the US, certain African countries such as Egypt, and other producers from countries like Uzbekistan, China and India. Other sources as well, besides Brazil, are Turkey and Pakistan. With the executive back in the headquarters, I was on my own and responsible for managing the relationships from now on.

My temporary home was the downtown Sheraton Hotel for about a month. From there, I managed to travel on a daily basis to the towns nearby and up to the north of the country – Famalição, Matosinhos, Barcelos, mainly Braga and Guimarães, and other smaller villages. Located in these towns are the garment manufacturers, producing clothing made out of cotton and poly-cotton yarn for key European players and brands such as Benetton, H&M, Marks & Spencer, to name a few. *TBM's* plan was to keep me in Portugal for at least five years and direct a significant portion of its output for exports; therefore, I simultaneously began to look for an apartment while performing my daily visits. Silvia and the girls would be getting to town in a few weeks – we needed a new home.

## PACKING UP AND LANDING

Organizing the move by herself back in São Paulo was no easy task for my wife. With the girls still young and the clock ticking, she needed to find a tenant, rent the apartment, pack up the furniture and all the stuff accumulated during our six years of marriage and then arrange it to be sent to a storage place. Silvia was up to the job and I liked to think that that helped her develop skills she had not been exposed to before. The upside of this whole project was that we could keep our property for the time we are away from the country and, if things didn't go well for a reason, we could always come back, a reassuring thought for herself and for our extended families. And for me, to a certain extent; however, not in my plans unless for visiting our loved ones.

Antonio Carlos Borges was my preferred teacher in college. As I reached out to him right before taking off to Porto, he graciously gave me a name he thought may be a good contact in town once I got established. Borges was still a teacher at the School of Economics at *Universidade Mackenzie* but his main job was as the Executive Assistant to the President at the powerful FCESP – *Federação do Comercio do Estado de São Paulo*, the organization that regulated commerce in my native state. São Paulo's economic engine is massive, and recently he participated in an official encounter in Porto where he met a brilliant attorney, Rui Peixoto Duarte. Borges highly recommended that I reach out to him.

The views from the windows of the recently rented apartment were stunning. From there, I had an overall sight of the *Foz do D'Ouro*, where the encounter of the sea coastal waters took place with the River *D'Ouro*. Also visible was the *Ponte Vila Nova de Gaia*, a bridge connecting Porto with the next door city of the same name. After looking at multiple properties, this was the best I could find in a very decent residential area. Lucky to have this unit available, the apartment was sizable and modern considered the real estate environment in a city where pretty much everything looks old. I knew my wife would be pleased. Moreover, Dr. Rui Peixoto Duarte, now a true friendship in the works, had recommended the spot – he was also a neighbor in the same development – the Foz neighborhood. A year younger than me, Rui and his wife Fatita had a couple of kids aged the same as our little girls. A promising and lasting relationship to be nurtured.

Vivid in my mind was the image of Silvia, Catherine Bianca and GG arriving at *Aeroporto Francisco Sá Carneiro*, Porto International Airport lounge. It was the beginning of December and also the start of the winter in the northern hemisphere. My three girls were wearing clothes that I had not seen before, appropriate for the new environment we were going to build our lives from now on. Silvia looked beautiful in her long burgundy trench coat, an elegant well – designed English cut. From a distance, the little girls seemed so enthused with the new scenario – flying over the Atlantic didn't seem to have put a heavy toll on their moods. Kisses and hugs properly addressed, we were ready to explore places.

## SIGNS OF AN UNFORESEEN MAJOR OBSTACLE

Quality of life in Porto was excellent. Safety, traffic, school system, dwelling, the arts and, most importantly, the people, all contributed to a great initial experience. The city, and the country as a whole, was undergoing an extensive revamping of its infrastructure, thanks to German monies provided via agreements as part of the European Community (EC) for development and homogenization of its members. Portugal's heavy-handed era, during the corporatist authoritarian government period under Antonio de Oliveira Salazar, ended about two decades earlier. Salazar's rule was conservative and nationalist in nature. Governing for stability and not for democracy, Portugal under his 48-year dictatorship remained poor as Europe flourished in the 1960s and 1970s. Focused on controlling the many colonies, he spent large sums on the military, rejected goals such as modernity and progress, and liberalism in favor of tradition; it revealed to be a losing battle, thus contributing to years of mismanagement and neglect. Isolated and backwards, the country only started to experience slow change in 1974, the year of the Carnation Revolution – the 25$^{th}$ of April. In Spain Franco had promoted economic progress despite his iron fist ruling. Whereas in Portugal, I once heard this expression, "Salazar had a peasant mentality for governing" and, therefore, blocked the country from advancing in many fronts.

My first four months at work were dynamic and allowed me to utilize the time to develop good connections and understanding of the market, the garment industry and the current perspectives for *TBM* with an eye into the future. At trade shows, I could appreciate learning that our product was widely accepted and its quality consistent with European standards, a fact that I embraced way back in the beginning of my interviewing process. However, something seems to be working behind the curtains. In certain situations, I overheard discussions from our reps and even customers with rumors that the European Community may apply sanctions against exporters if proven that there was practice of dumping. As I began to understand the issue, I learn that "A standard technical definition of dumping is the act of charging a lower price for the like product in a foreign market than the normal value of the product, for example the price of the same product in a domestic market of the exporter." This is often referred to as selling at less than "normal value" on the same level of trade in the ordinary course of trade. In other words, the term dumping refers to the illegal practice of fabricated pricing of given goods in order to make a certain industry – represented by one or a pool of exporters – more competitive.

I bring this up to my higher management which did not deny nor admitted there was something in the works of that nature. This, by itself, was not good news. Six months on the job, what I saw coming appeared to be a jolt, explained on information I collected from a Portuguese newspaper: "The WTO – World Trade Organization - agreement allows governments to act against dumping where there is genuine ("material") injury to the competing domestic industry. To do so, "the government has to show that dumping is taking place, calculate the extent of dumping (how much lower the export price is compared to the exporter's home market price), and show that the dumping is causing injury or threatening to cause injury." That was to say, a stalemate is installed for yarn exporters from Brazil to the EC as it turns out that the practice of dumping has been verified and currently under an international judicial process. What that meant to *TBM* was that sales would simply stop, at least temporarily. What it meant to me was that my role could become significantly reduced until counter-legal actions could prove the contrary. Which can take several months. Even years.

## NAVIGATING THE WATERS

Our girls loved their school, *O Cantinho Escolar*, The Little School Corner. Silvia and I alternate taking them to and back from school. In Portugal, a typical elementary school schedule starts a little later in the morning and went up to mid-afternoon. Silvia enjoyed some free time, which she could dedicate to teaching piano classes and to developing better skills in the English language. We had good friends and coincidentally run by old classmates from *Colégio Bandeirantes*, whom I had met almost two decades earlier, Luiz Alberto Almeida and Flavia Bitteto, a happy encounter that became a joyful friendship to this day.

Working out of my home office more frequently than I would if the market had been normal, I was already preparing for a possible change: I was simply no longer sure whether the plan for setting a long term foot in the European market was sustainable for *TBM*. While I held on for clear directions, I kept managing the existing relationships. On a personal level, we got to fly a couple of times to The Netherlands; we also enjoyed traveling the country on weekends – Aveiro, Coimbra, Sesimbra and Lisbon, our favorite spots to gather with some distant relatives and close friends – and many times we got to go to Vigo, in Galicia, Spain, the region south of the *Camino de Santiago*, also known as "Pilgrimage of Compostela" or as the Way of Saint James. Many follow its routes as a form of spiritual path or retreat for their spiritual growth. The way was also popular with hiking and cycling enthusiasts and organized tour groups.

Amidst the present uncertainty, I began to assert myself and felt strong convictions as to the direction to go, at least in my mind. As William Bryant accurately puts it: "Between twenty-eight and thirty-five, thought begins to occupy the judgment seat, where it can overview the experiences that stormed the psyche in the previous period. Its light begins to cut away some illusions which festoon the personality, since we have by now plenty of experience which can be examined and assessed in terms of our ideals, goals, and conscience. So, all things considered, we should have a more thoughtful and realistic picture of ourselves by the time we reach thirty-five." Bryant's description of this period is precise. "This cycle," he proceeds, "for the most part, continues the major expansion begun at thirty. The conversion of our psychic potential into reality depends on our own efforts. Our development, the deepening of our humanity, is now a matter of fate or freedom – it is our choice."

I could see change coming and embracing it was the only way to go. After about a year on the job, now I knew that Byron Queiroz was no longer with *TBM* and that the president, Ivan Bezerra and his son were heads of the eighty-million-dollar industry in Fortaleza. Dr. Ivan's secretary called me up announcing that the president would be in Porto in the beginning of November. "Please prepare to visit our main clients during his stay," said she. Anticipating what could come as "Thanks for your services but we are extinguishing this position and no longer need you here," I had already started a process of sending resumes and interviewing with potential Portuguese employers: My friend Rui Peixoto Duarte, as my attorney, had been assisting me on the steps to become a citizen should the plan to remain in Portugal for several years went through, which also depended on my professional success at the Brazilian organization. Simultaneously, aware of a possible professional change, he had been advising me on the search for alternatives and emphasized that the ceramic industry in Portugal was strong and attractive.

Silvia prepared one of her delightful meals for dinner at home, which impressed both Dr. Ivan and Facchini, his financial director, an aspiring executive to fill Byron's shoes. Straightforward and charismatic, Dr. Ivan was also a warm-hearted and outgoing personality. Opposite to the exited VP - cold, secretive and calculating. It is interesting how leadership plays out, there's no good nor bad. *TBM*'s president was quick and decisive to let me know that he wanted me in the group; however, for obvious reasons there was no justification for me to be staged in Europe anymore since the 'anti-dumping' judicial muddle could take years to be resolved. A little over a year on the job, he gave me about a month to close operations and proposed that I managed the exports/imports division of the organization, to which I would report directly to him. "Take your time to think about the idea with Silvia and the girls. We will be happy to have you move to Fortaleza and take over the position. We have big plans and want you to be a part of them," he concluded with a smile as he looked at Catherine Bianca and GG – "your girls will love the beaches and the lifestyle."

# 14

# Back Home but Not Quite

*"I've looked at life from both sides now,
From win and lose, and still somehow
It's life's illusions I recall
I really don't know life at all."*
Both Sides Now – Joni Mitchell

GROWING ONE'S CAREER TAKES TIME, dedication and investment. Tom Betts, my first manager at Dow back in the days, and I, still communicate. We only worked together for about a year, but our connection is strong and there every time we bring it up to life. Still located in Porto, I reached out to him for advice on whether an MBA degree would be something to pursue at this time of my career. Curiously, a few years earlier during a seminar at *Fundação Getulio Vargas*, one of the top business schools in São Paulo, once I asked a professor about my wish to embark on an MBA program, he unabashedly said: "You are too old for this." Interesting, I think to myself, "Too old for learning?" Not convinced, I kept the idea in the backburner. In Porto, I took classes with an English teacher turned friend – Ray Charles, love the name – to prepare for a GMAT Exam. If I were to stay in Europe, I was going to seek a good MBA school – *Universidade do Porto* actually does have a good program, per my friend Rui Peixoto Duarte.

The focus now was divesting from all the stuff utilized to set up *TBM's* short lived operation in Europe. Car, apartment, furniture, computer, phone/fax – the home office itself – have to go prior to us flying back to São Paulo, where we will temporarily be at my parents' before the next move. The Belgium solar power company offer never properly materialized; now it was between the Portuguese ceramic industry to possibly cover for *TBM's* proposal already on the table. It was the first week of December, Christmas was coming and it would be wonderful to be with the family. As much as our parents would like us to settle back around them, it was out of question to stay in São Paulo. Moreover, our apartment had been rented to a French family as the mindset was to stay the course of our plan before going to Portugal – definitely, there's no going back to live in SP except for visiting. The ceramic job offer is good but not enticing enough for me to accept it. With the MBA idea still in mind, *TBM* has agreed that I could resume work in my new position in February – Silvia and I left the girls with my parents and were off to Phoenix, Arizona for a 4-week January winter class at the American Graduate School of International Management, better known as Thunderbird. An excellent school, the plan was to touch the waters and possibly chase the opportunity for a full MBA course venture within the next year or two time-frame – funds and arrangements yet to be determined based on potential discussions with *TBM's* higher management.

The girls properly looked after by their four loving grandparents, we got to L.A. for a three-day visit to our friends Nerenita's and Bruce's home before heading out to Phoenix. It was a day after New Year's, 1994. For my wife, it was Silvia's first time visiting the U.S. It felt like a mixture of another honeymoon combined with a good opportunity for continued education.

We had known our friends in California for years and spending time with them and their three girls was a delight – lots of fun during these few days – great hospitality and, of course, L.A. *We love it!*

## TREMBLING DAYS

Well designed, the class and the subject could not have been more interesting for me. An observer of international trade and trends, the perspective of seismic changes in commerce and international business in general was laid out for a productive 4-week program – *Challenges in a Borderless World* – was a study mainly focused on the influence of the 'Asian Tigers' – Hong Kong, Singapore, South Korea and Taiwan, which underwent rapid industrialization and maintained exceptionally high growth rates, especially in the 80s and 90s – and, of course, China and India, within the context of the Western economies when facing with their processes of waking up to become two giant participants in the shifting world of industry, commerce and technology.

Divided into two periods, the class was taught daily from Monday thru Friday. The schedule was split between class and group work, where at the end of the seminar the students were required to present a final paper. Silvia took the time to deepen her knowledge of English – a schedule that worked for both of us, as we gathered for lunch every day. During free time, on the first two weekends we drove around the area and got to visit the amazing Montezuma Castle National Monument, in Camp Verde, built by the Sinagua people, a pre-Columbian culture closely related to the Hohokam and other indigenous peoples of the southwestern United States, between 1100 and 1425 AD. And, of course, the unmissable Grand Canyon National Park, home of the immense marvel canyon of the same name, with its layered bands of red rock revealing millions of years of geological history.

The day was Monday, January 17th. Just about a couple of weeks through the program, we woke up in the morning with the news that at 4:30 a.m., the San Fernando Valley region of the County of Los Angeles had been brutally shaken up by what came to be known as the 1994 Northridge earthquake. With a magnitude of 6.7, its epicenter was in Reseda, a neighborhood in the north-central Valley. The quake had a duration of approximately 10–20 seconds, and was the highest ever instrumentally recorded in an urban area in North America. Strong ground motion was felt as far away as Las Vegas, Nevada, about 220 miles (360 km) from the epicenter. We learned about the quake as we were preparing for our day and quickly tried to reach out to our friends in California. To no avail, we found out that all communications were blocked and disabled with no estimate to get re-established.

Devastation across the region, the official death toll was placed at 57; 33 people died immediately or within a few days from injuries sustained; more than 8,700 were injured including 1,600 who required hospitalization. The Northridge Meadows apartment complex was one of the well-known affected areas in which sixteen people were killed as a result of the building's collapse. The Northridge Fashion Center and California State University, in Northridge also sustained very heavy damage — most notably the collapse of parking structures. The earthquake also gained worldwide attention because of damage to the vast freeway network, which served millions of commuters every day. The most notable was to the Santa Monica Freeway, Interstate 10, known as the busiest freeway in the United States, congesting nearby surface roads for three months while the freeway was repaired.

Our remaining time in Phoenix/Glendale was great, although concerning: we did not hear from our friends in CA until almost two weeks after the quake. Bruce was a big guy and was thrown off his bed by the upheaval's violence, with no injuries fortunately. Nerenita and the girls were also ok despite some damage in their home. As our journey ended, we could not make it back to L.A. via I-10 and therefore drove to San Diego via Interstate 8 and then north to catch our flight home.

The classic scary stuff which unfolds after major natural disasters. Once again, that was close.

## *PINDORAMA*, LAND OF THE PALMS

The *Tupi-Guarani* peoples – representing one of the most widespread families of South American indigenous languages – had a designation for the mythical place: *Pindorama*, which would be a land free from evils. In the early 1500s, the native people of this enormous country called it the *Pindorama* invasion. The Portuguese called it the Discovery of Brazil. The nation derived its name from brazilwood tree. This land is not only gigantic dimensionally but I like to think culturally as well. Brazilian culture is one of the most distinct and unique in the world. An eclectic blend of the old and the new combined with the mix of race and ethnicities work to create a diversity that gives this country its charm and welcoming atmosphere, for the most part. To broach the culture without mentioning its people is an exercise, only partially done. Brazil, besides its variegated number of indigenous tribes scattered throughout its land, is a nation of immigrants, an ethnically diverse land that has a heritage founded on Asian, African, European, Middle Eastern, and North American descent. A major accomplishment by the Portuguese was maintaining the one and only language in such a continental space; whether or not questionable, years of working toward the common goal of colonization and centuries of intermarriage have blurred ethnic lines and resulted in a unique culture that truly defines Brazil.

This country has found a way to create relative unity from diversity and to use a variety of cultural influences to build a nation that represents the qualities and characteristics of its people. The culture of Brazil differs vastly from the rest of the westernized world, and this is very evident in the nature and personality of the Brazilian people. Here are some of the aspects:

- At its best, one of the most distinctive characteristics of the

Brazilian people is generosity, which they show liberally, even to strangers.
- In spite of poverty and difficult circumstances, the Brazilian people are uninhibitedly optimistic.
- Relationships are more important than money or possessions. People take precedence and family is the very center of the culture.
- Brazilians are physically expressive and will often touch your arm, shoulder, or hand when speaking with you.
- The Brazilian people in general adhere to a much slower pace of life than what those from western nations may be accustomed to, although there is some exception to this in the more westernized cities such as São Paulo.
- The Brazilian people are generally friendly and social. They will engage you in animated conversations and especially enjoy talking about soccer, family, and children.
- Brazilians have a great appreciation for the arts including dance, theater, music, literature, and poetry, and use these as a way of documenting and celebrating the unique culture.

North, Northeast, Center-West, Southeast and South compose the regions of this nation. Having grown in the Southeast and about to re-engage back in the country, now in a different area, this meant a significant change for our household.

The Northeast was the first region to be settled by the Portuguese, and Brazil's Portuguese heritage is stronger in this region. Apart from the Portuguese, the coastal areas were also significantly influenced by the imported African slaves. Parts of the Northeast were also under Dutch rule for some time, which contributed to the diverse origins of the Northeasterners. The natives left a mark, but the large influx of Portuguese settlers and African slaves overshadows it somewhat.

The Southeast was the second region to be settled, and it has been for quite some time now the richest and most populous. Like the Northeast, its culture was largely influenced by the Portuguese settlers and African slaves. One difference, though, is that this one had a stronger influence from native cultures during the earlier stages of colonization. After gold was discovered in Minas Gerais, however, this region became the main focus point for European settlers. During the late 19th and early 20$^{th}$ century, this region was also heavily influenced by immigrants from other European nations, like Italians, Germans, and Poles. Japanese immigrants have their largest numbers in Brazil compared to other regions in the world. Later on, there was a significant influx of Koreans and Chinese, all of them vastly contributing to the country's development in the past 100 years.

## FORTALEZA, *LAND OF LIGHT*

Silvia had been to Fortaleza a number of times throughout her youth, which made the city a somewhat familiar place. Plus, she had a number friends – also, contributing to our decision to experiment with the new lifestyle. As for the girls, they would blend in as easily as they did in Porto – especially in an environment where the sun shined about 300 days/year and the sea was just across the street from where we were. For the first three months until the real estate unit was ready for us to move in, we stayed in a hotel at the sea shore. An area with lots of tourists and densely populated, I must admit, but pleasant: the ever present breeze makes all the difference in a city with an average temperature varying from 80 to 85 degrees Fahrenheit over the course of the year – rarely below 73 or above 89. Sounds heavenly, doesn't it? I will get back to this theme later in the next chapter.

Work was going well and about to get interesting. My task, in a nutshell, was twofold: on one hand, managing current international accounts via supporting reps and partners who promoted our products with targeted volumes; on the other hand, assisting higher management with appropriate information for sound decision making as it related to the acquisition of raw materials from all over the world. One exciting aspect of my job as a manager, as it was for all managers of this growing business, was the open access to and collaboration with higher management; therefore, especially contributing to our areas of expertise while understanding the direction where the organization was going – cutting layers of communication for agile and effective performance. The future was bright.

At this point in time, I had a good understanding of my potential and vision for my career: "*The thirties* are the years of hard work, of organization and continuity and of persevering in one's chosen field. The individual has to prove that he can hold his own. The ups and downs of this phase can be regarded in a soberer light. If there is any time of life when it is possible, this is the time for fighting for insights and results. From this there grows increasing assurance, including certainty about what the individual is incapable of and what he must give up trying to achieve. The working man in the second half of his thirties is at the peak of his performance capability in the quantitative sense. He knows his job, and he knows what he is worth and what he wants to achieve." – *Phases, Career Prospects and Personnel Policy, Bernard Lievegoed.*

The girls adapted quickly and making friends was a natural consequence. We were now in a brand new apartment located less than a mile from Iracema Beach, which we were able to rent it at a reasonable cost. My income was good and somewhat equivalent to being an expatriate while in Portugal, without fringe benefits; however, I myself had to adapt to being in a well-organized but yet manufacturing environment – much different from previous years, where I had no direct contact with the production line but only with the commercial segment of the textile sector. My first trip was scheduled to Memphis, Tennessee, where I accompanied the president on a critical mission: avoid arbitration and consequently try to resolve a dispute related to an undelivered number of containers of raw materials, i.e. cotton from the USA. Meeting with non-compliant vendors was challenging and involved negotiations that one party may not always be interested in coming to terms; hence, arbitration becomes a last resort.

Work days were alternated with lots of sun and sea shore exploring. The coast of Ceará is extensive and there are myriads of beaches to visit. Hotels and hostels are abundant and part of the landscape for tourism as a main economic activity. Lagoinha, Cumbuco, Morro Branco and Canoa Quebrada are must see beaches. The latter one, for instance, is a natural paradise. With access somewhat long and difficult, the scenario is composed of wooden boats, high dunes, the ocean nice and rough, miles of walking and the beaches feel good under your feet.

## A CHANGE OF HEART

My next work task, Europe: Switzerland's southernmost airport is located close to the Swiss cities of Lugano, Locarno and Bellinzona, and the Italian city of Como, where my next trip was taking place to discuss another delicate and possible arbitration matter. After meeting with a cotton agent in Lugano, a somewhat undependable individual, I was headed out to Geneva to gather along with Ivanito – Ivan Bezerra's son – and Montoro. The latter is a former executive of Rhodia who had joined the organization years back to manage the overall domestic yarn sales market. Montoro's performance had been stellar over the years as targeted sales were regularly achieved. Byron's departure had brought a vacuum of power which had been silently filled by the company's founder and his son; nonetheless, this was not meant to last. Followed by an unexpected strike in Fortaleza pursued and put in place by a portion of the production floor unionized leadership – coincidence or not, it started right at the time we were in Geneva – this one was not seen coming. The strike lasted longer than normal and contributed to temporarily eroding confidence throughout the factory environment. Higher management, not happy with the outcome, decided that it was time to fill the VP position and therefore used the experienced executive to deal with the unpredicted situation: Montoro, based in São Paulo, would spend three weeks in Fortaleza and one back home on a monthly basis, with the mission of 'sweeping the dust out of the floor.' Adding to his new responsibilities, while second tier management had transitorily enjoyed the proximity with the top executive-owners, this link would be broken by Montoro's management style, one that is territorial, controlling and would favor pragmatism and results only. To me, this posed a question mark and could prompt a major turnaround from the once well-developed connection among factory workers, mid-management and top executives. Montoro was there to break that bond, whether higher management knew it or not.

It was May, 1994. The opportunity to manage and organize T.B.M.'s Imports/Exports Dpt. was given to me and I embraced it wholeheartedly. This time I was bound to visit the Canadian market, which has been traditionally a key player and could well benefit from enhanced mutual development. Scheduled to be in Montréal and Toronto for about ten days, here was a great chance to spend the weekend with my brother-friend James. James' wife Patricia drove all the way from Waterbury, Vermont, to pick me up at Montréal-Pierre Trudeau International Airport. Along with Tricia – James had to be at work on that Saturday morning – there is beautiful 3-year old Gabriela. Her little brother Joseph stayed with grandma Wanda at home, where we headed for a two-and-a-half-hour drive. I couldn't wait to see my friend again and get to know his son and his new home.

Our weekend went by way too fast. Back in 1989, I had flown into Burlington and seen little of the landscape. Five years later, the drive from Montréal to Central Vermont gave me the occasion to appreciate the geography and perceive Vermont from a different perspective: "Where are the billboards?" I ask myself. In Waterbury, seated at Wanda's table for another round of gastronomy and laughter, I learned that in 1968 the State of Vermont passed a landmark anti-billboard law allowing the landscape to become billboard-free ever since. Outstanding mindset, I pondered. The law was the result of the extraordinary efforts of one man, Ted Riehle, a larger than life personality and political character, who was determined to preserve the natural beauty of Vermont. Its original goal: "We need to provide information to the traveler, but do not want to compromise our natural scenery. Tourism is the number one industry in the state. And the lack of advertising is one of the most commonly reported things that visitors appreciate about Vermont." The man, a visionary, was darn right.

## *JERICOACOARA*

Back in Fortaleza after a productive business trip in Canada and the opportunity to see my friends in Vermont, our little girls were ecstatic with the news of their grandparents' visit. To make things more exciting, it would take place during a fun time: The 1994 FIFA World Cup, starting in mid-June. A new hope for the sport since the tragic death of Ayrton Senna, the three-time Brazilian racing driver of the famous Formula One World Drivers' Championship, only six weeks earlier. Regarded as one of the greatest Formula One drivers of all time, Senna died in an accident in Imola, Italy while leading the 1994 San Marino Grand Prix. While the country still mourned his beloved race car driver's death, this time the FIFA tournament took place in the U.S., with chances for a good performance by the Brazilian Team. Back from North America, another three weeks went by until the Soccer Cup got started. Our daughters had spent close to a month earlier in the year with their grandparents while Silvia and I were in Arizona and now had another opportunity to share great quality time with them during their stay.

As for getting adjusted with the new lifestyle and for making new friends, Silvia, Laura Colirri and our respective offspring – Catherine Bianca and GG along with Sabrina, Amanda and Melissa – hit off immediately the first time they met at *Nautico Club's* pool, a social and sports club at the heart of *Praia de Iracema*. And so did Alberto Colirri and I, both from the same neighborhood back in São Paulo where we grew up but never met. Little did we all know that our families would become great friends during the time we would be in Fortaleza and beyond: this friendship was meant to last through multiple household moves and many years to come.

The climate at work was picking up, in an unpredictable way. As for myself and for most of mid-management, signs of change were looming and it was a matter of time until things got clearer as to which direction the organization was going to go. At home, Mom and Dad were in town and we all felt so blessed to have them around. They were both easy going individuals who had learned to appreciate diversity; and to do well away from their comfort zone. Speaking of which, our next trip – a spot which years later would be considered by the *Washington Post* one of the Top 10 most beautiful beaches in the world – clearly required everyone's understanding as to what a less than comfortable travel would mean. Unbeknownst of the Brazilian Soccer squadron bravely qualifying for the final World Cup match, we all planned to visit beautiful "*Jeri*," at the time a virgin beach hidden behind dunes of the west coast of *Jijoca de Jericoacoara*. The beach consisted of blue lagoons, calm seas and huge dunes. In *Tupi* language, Jericoaquara means "lair of turtles" (*iuruká* for "sea turtle" and *kuara* for "lair, hole"). Declared as an environmental protection area back in 1984, the distance to bigger cities such as Fortaleza and Teresina and the limited road access also helped to keep the beach and the village isolated throughout the years.

Getting to *Jeri* can be seen as an ordeal. A two to two-and-a-half-hour travel time, the road from Fortaleza to *Jericoacoara* is comprised of beaches and rustic villages; notwithstanding, the last 45 minutes of the trip becomes quite challenging. It was late evening and the journey now took place off-road, among dunes and along a beach. The ride was on what was known as a *Pau de Arara* – translated as "macaw's perch" – a flatbed truck, poorly adapted for passenger transportation, carrying about 40-50 people. The truck's bed is equipped with narrow wooden benches and a canvas canopy. The term referred to long metal rails extending lengthwise under the canopy where passengers would hang on when standing or while sitting on the benches – at the mercy of the cushioning of their buttocks. An experience for the girls and for us. As for Mom and Dad, they probably had an interesting time...As we got to the village, we learned that our hostel got electricity generated by diesel engines and street lighting was only provided by the moon and the stars. It was late and any horizontal surface resembling a bed was more than welcome.

The day was July 17$^{th}$ and the match took place at the Rose Bowl Stadium in Pasadena, CA: Brazil became the fourth time FIFA World Soccer Champion against Italy. The precarious TV utilizing power from a simple generator did the job bringing the images to a small but excited group of people who ventured to be in that part of the world during those days. And most excitingly, it felt good to be along with the family, especially Dad, a fan of World Cups, from an early age. In *Jericoacoara*, the day was winding down. It was one of several places in Brazil from which one could see the sun sink into the ocean – often viewed from the tall "sunset dune," just next to the village. A fascinating sight.

## UNFOLDING CHANGE FAVORS OPPORTUNITY

"Aw, you are so beautiful. I love your hair. Your earrings are lovely too. And you smell so good. And your skin...it's so soft but, your wrinkles don't look good..." Touching her face as if touching aged rose petals, she went on. "My darling. Awwww... it's too bad you are going to die soon..."

The words would come out as a shock if they weren't pronounced by this funny and bold little girl who happened to be our lovely daughter, Diana – GG, as we call her. *Dona Afif* was in her mid-80s but still in very good shape when she, Dr. Lazaro and a group of friends came to dinner at our apartment at *Rua Ana Bilhar*, the temporary place we were living. Whoever was paying attention to the conversation couldn't help but to blush and get embarrassed or just have a big silent laugh at the statement. Including *Dona Afif* herself. Good days of innocence and spontaneity depicting our girls in their full speed growth.

Less than a year after higher management had relinquished direct managing attributes to the competent but challenging-to-relate-to executive from São Paulo, the entire mid-management environment began to disintegrate. Coincidentally or not, I was the first of the managers to notice the trends shifting and to take a pro-active step towards change. My sense was that I should look for a different position since politics took center stage. Besides, my initiative in requesting a possible company's financial support for an MBA overseas does not resonate. Recapping the original proposition, the idea was that I'd stay in Portugal for at least five years and develop the company's exports while based in one of the main destination markets. Instead, one year down and I was sent back to Fortaleza. At the headquarters, things started well until the winds began blowing on the opposite direction. Clearly dissatisfied with new management, I ended up negotiating a good exit out. With the Bezerras, I left on good terms and continued to touch base occasionally for a lengthy period of time. What unfolded was a series of mid-management replacements as an outcome of politics in the workplace. Not my cup of tea, I felt sorry for my former co-workers as it could certainly have been a different experience.

## CATCHING UP WITH WHAT MATTERS

*"Friendship is unnecessary, like philosophy, like art...it has no survival value; rather, it is one of those things which give value to survival."* – C. S. Lewis

I had not seen my friend Fabio D'Onofrio, from my mid-to-late teenage years, since we got together for a few days in Sydney, Australia, back in 1992. With the temporary move to and back from Portugal, the quick stop in São Paulo, then Arizona and the immediately after travel to Fortaleza only allowed us to exchange a couple of letters and post cards. Now my friend was a proud dad of a beautiful little girl. As a single parent, he was determined to raise his child in common agreement with her mom; I thought he would be a terrific dad. Silvia and I were excited to host him in our home and so were the girls every time there's a friend or loved one to come visit and share our new lifestyle.

Fabio – besides having played handball as a teen – was a surfer himself. A lover of the outdoors, we managed to have a great time getting around Fortaleza and surroundings. Moreover, the ever sunny days of this region made things easier. As I was experiencing a hiatus at work – currently expecting a couple of words from potential employers – we found this a perfect time to catch up and enjoy each other's company. My lovely wife, always a companion and half of her day busy with the girls, joined us every time she could to show our friend a little bit of the area beyond the rich beach scenery: *Mercado Central* and *José de Alencar Theater* are neat places to drop by and get the essence of the local cultural landscape.

Cellular phones were beginning to pick up and were unavoidably there to stay. My newly acquired *Motorola* ringed; it was Roberto Matoso, a consultant and entrepreneur with whom I had developed a good relationship over the past year, asking if I would consider working as a Marketing Director for a local popular and well known producer of beverages. Founded in the mid-1800s – unusual for a company to withstand such longevity – *Ypióca* is a traditional and popular distiller of sugar cane brandy products with national presence and consistently pursuing the sales of its brand internationally. Very original in its approach to packaging a rather common beverage in Brazil – *pinga* or *cachaça*, made from fermented sugar cane – *Ypióca* already used distillation technology similar to European standards for the ageing of its brandy utilizing the traditional wooden barrels. More interestingly, its distinguished glass bottles are packaged with handmade straw – similar to wicker shells – made by multiple craftswomen, locally and regionally supplied.

Not a great fan of alcoholic beverages when used in excess,

I promised to consider the offer. The company has multiple product lines and is improving its farm products along with water distribution. In a few days, I interviewed with president and vice president which presented to me a compelling story of entrepreneurship as to where the company stands for, present and future. The proposition was impressive: the company was diversifying its products and saw in my experience a good fit, especially as it related to exports. Career perspective and compensation package discussed, I began work in a week.

## SELF-KNOWLEDGE IN A BOTTLE

> *"Which way are you lookin'? Is it hard to see?*
> *Do you say what's wrong for him is not wrong for me?"*
> *Which Way are You Goin'* – Jim Croce

It didn't take long for me to realize this job venture was going to be short lived. A family-run business, it took me only a few days to understand that the focus of my efforts was to solely revolve around increasing sales. But that was not the reason for my disappointment. Alcohol consumption in moderation could be fun and spice up one's time towards socializing and bringing people together. What I have a hard time accepting is that too great a percentage of the beverages, produced and sold, were directed to the local market, which helps me make the connection between the use of alcohol with the high percentage of social and family issues in the community, let alone accidents, violence and crime related events. It should have been obvious to me had I deepened my research on the company's numbers or simply asked higher management the hard questions. I must admit that for a head of a family it was always challenging to be out of work for long periods of time, which is why accepting the position seemed the right thing to do. But staying on the job and building a career in that industry was difficult to envision and therefore I had to re-evaluate my goals.

The company's VP walked into my office with a letter from

FIEC – the local industry entity which, among multiple activities, promoted professional development, technical and technological services with focus on innovation and executive education for the people of the State of *Ceará*. It was an invitation for *Ypióca* to point out a candidate for a scholarship in Japan. JICA – Japan International Cooperation Agency – a governmental agency that coordinates Official Development Assistance for the government of Japan, was chartered with assisting economic and social growth in developing countries, and the promotion of international cooperation. "What do you think?" the VP asks me. "Interesting" I replied. "With first steps given in the past to promote our brand overseas, we do have a presence in Japan but it is still very incipient. Wouldn't it be great to learn the intricacies of this market and substantiate our presence more efficiently? Would you be interested in applying?" As I understood the VP's approach, I found out that this was a scholarship provided by JICA on an annual basis for potential exporters to join a group of developing countries on a seminar about the distribution system in Japan. "Absolutely!" I doubled back. This could be an opportunity to utilize my skills on a more specialized effort, I reason. Why not give it a shot?

### *SAYONARA*

Days went by as I finished up the application for the JICA grant, and I wondered about the possibilities. "Once a year? Only one spot for applicants for the entire country? What are the odds?" I shared my thoughts with Silvia. If nothing else, it was an avenue to explore. As I thought about my exposure to the Japanese culture, I remembered the days in school when I had a number of classmates from Japanese background, and a couple of good friends, Roberto Takaoka and Wilson Tadashi, with whom I would share play time and music exchange, respectively. Having grown in a neighborhood with a strong Asian influence, mostly Japanese due to historic immigration initiatives, the food, the culture and *kanji – the ideographic symbols*

– at small business store fronts were somewhat familiar in my brain. For this reason, I felt comfortable filling out the extensive questionnaire in connection with the application package.

From vocabulary.com I got this: "*Sayonara* is a casual way to say goodbye, similar to phrases like "so long" or "see ya!" You might say sayonara to your traveling grandmother, or say sayonara to a terrible job at the end of a long summer. It's a Japanese word that has been a popular informal word in English since the late 1800s. It literally means "if it is to be that way," combining *sayo*, "that way," and *nara*, "if."

A couple of months on the job, the company received a letter directly from JICA informing that the application had been... accepted! The seminar was to take place during a 6-week time frame where I would be based out of Osaka, the third largest city in Japan after Tokyo and Yokohama. A package was on its way once acceptance was confirmed. Thrilled with the perspective, I saw that my wife was truly excited about the professional outlook this might bring up with the unfolding of events. The downside was the length of time away from home. I gladly took the chance and embarked on preparations for the trip.

China, India, Thailand, Malaysia, Indonesia, Philippines, Papua New Guinea, Egypt, Mexico, Peru and Brazil were the 11 guest countries invited to attend the seminar. With the idea of promoting trade and providing a comprehensive understanding of how the distribution system of this once isolated country worked, the seminar was designed to facilitate access to the Japanese market for products and services from their respective countries. Always aiming at bringing more equilibrium to its trade balance – Japan chronically exports more than it imports – this is an ongoing effort which was conducted was conducted multiple times a year, in multiple capacities.

## *NIHON*, LAND OF THE RISING SUN

I arrived in Osaka in mid-October, 1995. Its airport, Kansai International – KIX – is a masterpiece of architecture and engineering. In 1988, Italian architect Renzo Piano, already renowned for designing the Centre George Pompidou, in Paris, won an international competition for a new airport to be constructed on an artificial island in the port of Osaka. The main terminal he designed was extremely long, just about over a mile, with a very low profile, so that the controllers in the control tower could always see the aircraft on the runways. The frequent earthquakes in the Japanese islands required special building techniques; the structure is mounted on hydraulic joints which adjust to movements of the earth, by itself, an amazing challenge completed in 1994. Earlier in the year, on 17 January 1995, Japan was struck by the Kobe earthquake, whose epicenter was about 12 miles away from Kansai International Airport killing 6,434 people on Japan's main island of Honsh. Due to its earthquake engineering, the airport emerged unscathed, mostly due to the use of sliding joints. Even the glass in the windows remained intact.

Landing in Osaka promised to be the start of an unforgettable experience. Before take-off, I was advised by a friend from São Paulo, Kinya Kikuchi, that being in Japan and experiencing the lifestyle even for a short period of time, just over six weeks, would be very different from what we knew of the cultural heritage back in São Paulo. In fact, since the early 1900s, Brazil was home to the largest Japanese population outside Japan – in 1995, there were approximately 1.5 million people of Japanese descent scattered throughout the country. Street savvy at this point of my life, I liked to think, I was open for this project like any other one before. Besides, the amount of support offered by JICA was outstanding: fully covered accommodations, a generous cash advance, more than enough to cover for meals, transportation and mementoes, and the program itself which would encompass an extensive and galvanizing agenda.

## GRASPING JAPAN

Japanese culture and people are one of a kind. This ancient

land was historically characterized by great regional influence, especially Chinese, followed by periods of isolation from the West. Ruled during eight centuries by feudal military *shoguns* in the name of the Emperor, Japan entered into a long period of seclusion in the early 17$^{th}$ century, which ended in the mid-1850s when a US fleet pressured the country to open to the West. By the late 19$^{th}$ and early 20$^{th}$ centuries, the wars against China and Russia and World War I allowed the country to expand its empire during a period of increasing military action, only to succumb at the conclusion of World War II when the allies forced the country to surrender.

Adopting liberal democratic practices and granted membership in the UN in the mid-1950s, the country achieved phenomenal growth to become the second-largest economy in the world for decades, greatly due to Japan's education system which played central part in the country's recovery after WWII. Culturally, it has evolved greatly from its origins as contemporary culture combined by influences from Asia, Europe and North America. It is clear that over time the Japanese developed the ability to absorb, imitate and assimilate elements of foreign culture that complemented their own aesthetic preferences. While in the textile business, I had a chance to extensively work with a Japanese multi-national enterprise, *Kanebo*, from which I learned to observe their modus operandi of translating, transforming and creating art in textiles. This organization is no longer in the textile business and today is solely focused on the cosmetic industry – by far, a more lucrative business.

Ancient pottery, sculpture, ink painting, silk and paper calligraphy, woodblock prints, ceramics and origami are among the myriad art manifestations of the Japanese; however, it is in music that this people seem to thrive both in terms of creativity and consumption. The word for "music" in Japanese is *ongaku*, combining the kanji *on* (sound) with the kanji *gaku* (enjoy). Traditional or contemporary, combining the use of instruments such as *koto*, *biwa*, *shakuhachi* and *shamisen*, to name but a few, Japanese music differs markedly from Western music, as it is often based on the intervals of human breathing rather than on mathematical timing.

## KARAOKE

There's nothing like it. *Karaoke* in Japan is not what I thought and not what you think. Arguably a more important part of the Japanese culture than even the tea ceremony, nearly every Japanese has picked up the mic. Although we Westerners have a flare for the fun, *Karaoke* hasn't caught on in the West the way it has in Japan. It is...different. There's no stage or crowd assisting you and no room for embarrassment. *Karaoke* is meant to take place in a small, cozy venue with food and drinks accompanied by just good friends or peers aiming at enjoying a good time, singing and singing along – between sips of scotch or any other preferable drink. It is one of the spots where the Japanese manifest freedom and let it all hang out. With a group of foreign and variegated people which added up to eleven, plus the organizers, always a minimum of two individuals, our heavy schedule of visiting everything related to the 'distribution system in Japan' during certain days was crowned with a few spaced out tours to *Karaoke* rooms in downtown Osaka. Lots of fun, literally memorable. Each member of his or her country learned the cultural aspect of it: the reason why *karaoke* is so popular in Japan may be because of the high stress level in the work environment. Most Japanese are very devoted to their jobs and careers, and often are overworked and stressed out. As a result, most *Karaoke* lovers go for it for about 2 hours. And many can do an all-nighter in a *karaoke* box...

## THE PROGRAM

Our close to perfectly designed program of visiting all things in connection to learning the intricacies of doing business with Japan was at full fledge after the first couple of weeks. John Fahy, a lecturer in strategic marketing, School of Business Studies, University of Dublin, Trinity College and Fuyuki Taguchi, a professor of marketing, School of Business Administration, Senshu University brought a concise study through a good depiction of the momentum the country needed to undergo in order to open up for opportunities. In the words of the authors:

"Some see the pace of change in Japan as slow. The country has ingrained business practices, integration of the private and public sectors, and societal values that ensure that traditional systems will persist, at least in the short term. But there is little doubt that Japanese distribution, so long the target of Western criticism, is undergoing fundamental change. Signals are everywhere.

"Major structural shifts in distribution, such as the growing power of retailers and the decline of department stores, have already occurred in the United States and Europe. Innovative competitors in Japan are increasingly monitoring developments and adopting practices that have proved successful in other industrialized countries. This does not mean that Japan is suddenly an easy market to enter. But distribution is becoming less of a barrier, and recent commentaries have focused not on the difficulties of doing business in Japan but on the successes achieved there, particularly by U.S. companies. Manufacturers and retailers may want to take a second look at Japan to determine if the current signals of change present an area of opportunity."
– Source: *Reassessing the Japanese Distribution System* – *MIT Sloan Management Review*

Transportation, manufacturing, distribution channels, couriers, auction venues were all but a key portion of the knowledge one must dive into if serious about doing business with a country of such complexity. Most importantly, understanding *keiretsu*, the trading companies and their associations, was huge when working the puzzle around business practices and its effects on the system of imports. Corporate behavior and business climate were permeated by long-term relationships, loyalty, obligation, and their impact on decision of switching suppliers, for example. Personal contact would turn out to become a process and a lifeline for the success for developing business in that market.

## KYOTO, TOKYO AND THE CULTURAL EXPERIENCE

The time of the year is unfortunately not Spring time when the cherry blossom bloom takes place all over the land and make the scenery extraordinary. It is fall but it is just as interesting to experience the season. At both times of the year, there is little rainfall, skies are clear, and temperatures are mild. The vivid hues of autumn leaves are visually stunning. Visiting Tofuku-ji Temple in Kyoto and Tokyo's exquisite Gingko Avenue brought a special perspective to such a differentiated environment. Besides, the Autumn festivals in both places made for an auspicious time to be in the country. I could not have been more pleased with the opportunity and just wished my lovely wife and daughters could have been with me on this trip.

The locals. Mr. Fukuda and Mrs. Hata were fantastic hosts. Employed by JICA or acting as consultants for the governmental entity, their knowledge and passion about what they did made up for the journey. In both cities and with their help coordinating actions, the group was able to uncover the multiple layers of the Japanese culture during this voyage of discovery and contrast. In Kyoto, we experienced the privilege of a private dinner with *Geishas* followed by the ritual of an authentic tea ceremony, coupled with exploring the city's hidden garden's, which only locals could provide. From Kyoto, the group took the ride on the legendary bullet train and traveled to Tokyo at 130 miles/hour – *Shinkansen*, the first high-speed rail system. Today, through technical advances, the system has been upgraded to reach speeds of up to 199 mph – mind blowing! Tokyo's fierce modernity was quite a distinction from traditional Kyoto's soberness – temples, shrines, gardens and hiking – a city best known in Japanese history for being the former imperial capital of Japan for more than one thousand years. Energetic, huge, techy, nightlife-oriented and very expensive, Tokyo is, on the other hand, the ultimate urban environment.

If it weren't for a three-day pass out, my experience in Japan would have been beyond complete. Having been a vegetarian for many years had always been a relatively easy ride even in the most meat-eating oriented countries, starting with my own. What I did not see coming was that virtually every meal cooked in Japan has a fish-based recipe, which eventually contributed to some kind of stomach bug that knocked me down for a few days. Worth the trouble, I was never deterred by that and valued every minute of such a once in a lifetime opportunity. *Domo arigatogozaimashita*, Japan.

## NOW, SOLO

It's always good to come back. Having grown a goatee and lost a few pounds, I was back in Fortaleza. At the airport I experience that being away from my family for longer than usual always required some adjustment: GG spotted me through the customs' glass wall and I noticed that she looked at me, then to her mom and back to myself doubting as to whether I was really her dad. While Catherine Bianca had no issues recognizing her dad's new looks, GG took several minutes between tears and hugs only to find that her dad had changed just a little...but ended up admitting he was still the same.

With a short stop in São Paulo on the way back from Tokyo, I had lunch with my dear professor Antonio Carlos Borges, then the Assistant Superintendent to the President of the powerful FCESP – the commerce federation of São Paulo State. Borges was aware of my career transition potentially looming and advised me to consider a turn into consulting. Related thoughts already crossed my mind in the past several weeks while still in Japan, his words were a pass for me. Back in Fortaleza and after careful considerations along with my wife, I communicated my decision to resign my position at Ypióca and began a new professional cycle.

Probably one of the most rewarding professional achievements is for one to have the freedom to use creativity in the workplace – one thing some people may take for granted. Especially when the stars line up and conditions are favorable. Along with my wife, we designed the activity that would percolate into exceptional opportunities for the next four years. *R. Wakim Associates* opened doors for business for an intense new cycle of international experience, exposure and diversified action. The consulting firm partnered up with companies in the areas of developing business opportunities, strategic partnerships, worldwide outsourcing and foreign trade, as well as promoting cultural diversity in the workplace. It focused on improving the performance of entrepreneurs, managers and professionals dealing with foreign trade in the public and private arena, including marketing, finance and human resources people. Our efforts revolve around designing, organizing and accompanying multiple business delegations throughout the U.S., Europe, Asia and the Middle East, as well as creating and presenting seminars to executives on the multi-cultural aspect of international business.

Life is good, business is good. With a healthy and diversified portfolio, I was pleased to have my wife join efforts in the business as a smart and efficient partner. Our networking and consulting endeavors did not take long to pick up as we became a resource to our customers, both on efforts towards importing goods from overseas for subsequent commercialization and/or industrialization and on exporting local products and raw materials. The latter, a lot more challenging seeing that competitiveness is the major hurdle for regional companies accustomed to the comfort zone of supplying local and regional markets.

# 15

# A Change is Gonna Come

*"Come gather 'round people*
*Wherever you roam*
*And admit that the waters*
*Around you have grown*
*And accept it that soon*
*You'll be drenched in the bone*
*If your time to you*
*Is worth savin'*
*Then you better start swimmin'*
*Or you'll sink like a stone*
*For the times they are a-changin'."*
*The Times They Are A-Changin'* – B. Dylan

THE OVERNIGHT BREEZE combined with the warmth of the ocean steam made for a pleasant resting time almost every night. As a result, the quality of my sleep in Fortaleza was remarkable. At dawn, although our apartment is located a couple of blocks from the shore at *Praia de Iracema*, this allowed me to start my mornings at around 5:30 a.m. and drive over to *Praia do Futuro* for about fifteen minutes where the water tended to be cleaner. After a mild workout, there I bathed and engendered my thoughts for the day. Peter Gabriel's "Washing of the Water" lyrics often came to my mind and was symbolic of the momentum I was going through:

*River, river, carry me on*
*Living river, carry me on*
*River, river, carry me on*
*To the place where I come from*
*So deep, so wide, will you take me on*
*your back for a ride*
*If I should fall, would you swallow me deep inside*
*River, show me how to float, I feel like I*
*'m sinking down*
*Thought that I could get along*
*But here in this water, my feet won't touch*
*the ground*
*I need something to turn myself around*

Earlier in the previous chapter, I had referred to the number of sunny days in that part of the world – about 300/year. For many people, paradisiacal. I'm not so sure about that. To me, contrast is critical. From a design and artistic standpoint, contrast is defined as difference. "Difference between art elements like color, value, size, texture and so on can intensify the elements used. As a result, the elements used in a work of art can become more powerful. Although contrast is closely related with variety, it is usually considered a principle of art." – *The Virtual Instructor*. In other words, balance is what I seek. The nuances between extremes is what I try to grasp as if survival depended on it, the reason why working as a consultant and being able to travel the world works as an element of equilibrium in my system.

Silvia and the girls were happy living in that part of the country, Northeastern Brazil. As for myself, I liked it too. Not as geographically close to our parents as we and they would like us to be, this was the reality and the life we had chosen to live. Besides, Silvia and I had always believed that parents are the real ones to bring up their offspring. Relatives, friends, teachers and the communities in general all play a very important role, no doubt about it. But, ultimately, unless otherwise forced to doing it, there is no way one could transfer that core responsibility to third parties.

Approaching the end of 1997, our fourth year in Ceará, on average, the temperatures in Fortaleza are always high. The rainy season would fall in the months of February, March, April, May and June, whereas the city has dry periods in September, October and November. On average, the warmest month was January with the coolest month being July. It was past "winter" and the rain season was coming to an end. I got a call from the developer of the apartment we had purchased and have lived in the past couple of years, a comfortable 3-bedroom suite located a couple of blocks from the sea shore. "I have an offer on your apartment from a family moving from Southern Brazil that I think you would be quite interested in learning about," said the realtor with whom I had a pretty good connection. Months before, I had brought up the idea to him that if I had a good offer to my real estate property I would be open for discussions.

## JAMES, TRICIA AND THE DUNES

My wife and I had gone through a unique period in our marriage which required careful attention and a lot of love and understanding. Closure of this short phase coincided with the news that James and Tricia would be visiting us, which would be happening in the middle of another transition: simultaneously to the sale of our property, an offer we could not refuse, we rented an apartment in the same building complex and the move in date was to take place a few days after our friends' arrival in the country. Logistically favorable, this was also an opportunity: after spending a couple of pleasant days along with our friends, while James and Tricia headed to *Jericoacoara*, our household managed to vacate one space and move into the other one in a matter of hours.

Like the two other times in which James made to visit Brazil, this one was also special. James had just lost his mother; Also, it's Tricia's first time in the country and in South America. With Gabriela and Joe at home with Wanda, they took an extended vacation and joined us for a full two-weeks of sun and fun activity. Either at The Beach Park – the largest aquatic park in Latin America – or off to remote beaches, we had a great time driving up and down the dunes on buggy cars. The girls also had a blast as James and Tricia spent quality time with both Catherine Bianca and GG. Glad to see my friend and his wife exposed to a totally diverse part of the country this time around, we talked about all of us spending Christmas with their families the next year in Vermont. A real, White Christmas, like never before. The girls would certainly love it.

It's November 20$^{th}$, James' birthday. We baked a nice big strawberry and chocolate cake and invited a number of friends over. Of course I wanted to show off and introduce my best buddy from the North to my local friends, something that would happen, in my view, once in a lifetime. James seemed not that excited as he would rather enjoy the quiet, something I only realized during the party. Selfishly, I assumed he would enjoy the group without even asking him if he would feel the same way. Oh well, I thought indulgently, tomorrow will be another day and James is smart enough to understand my excitement. Besides, my friend Rui Peixoto Duarte from Porto, Portugal was also in town teaching a post-bachelor seminar, which completed my satisfaction. It is interesting how people, and I speak here for myself, go about their lives choosing the 'other family' they want to be around with, translated into friendships and nurtured relationships.

One of Brazil's most influential musicians, Milton Nascimento's compositions talk a lot about friendships and reveal beauty beyond words. Among his best are *"Maria, Maria," "Travessia"* ("Bridges") *"Bailes da Vida,"* and *"Coração de Estudante"* ("Student's Heart"). The latter, is a song about the funeral of Edson Luís, who was killed by police officers in 1968. The song became the hymn for the *Diretas Já* social-political campaign in 1984, was played at the funeral of the late President of Brazil Tancredo Neves the next year, and was also played at Ayrton Senna's funeral. While his reputation within Brazil was already firmly established with his *Clube da Esquina* works, Nascimento's international breakthrough came with his appearance on jazz saxophonist Wayne Shorter's 1974 album *Native Dancer*. This led to widespread acclaim, and collaborations with Paul Simon, Cat Stevens, George Duke, Quincy Jones and Earth, Wind and Fire. *Angelus* (1994), one of my favorite albums, features appearances by all-time amazing musicians and songwriters such as Pat Metheny, Ron Carter, Herbie Hancock, Jack DeJohnette, Naná Vasconcelos, Jon Anderson, James Taylor, and Peter Gabriel. Extraordinary music. As for one of Milton's highlights, there is one that speaks dearly to my vision of love and friendship:

SONG FROM AMERICA

*A friend is something to be kept*
*Underneath seven keys*
*Inside the heart*
*Thus spoke the song*
*I heard in America*
*A friend is something to be kept*
*In the left side of the chest*
*Even if time and distance might say "no"*
*Even forgetting the song*
*What matters is to listen to*
*The voice, that comes from the heart*

*No matter what happens, whatever happens*
*One day, friend, I will find you again*
*One day, friend, we will meet again.*

## A THOUGHT ABOUT COMPLACENCY

*Webster Definition: "Self-satisfaction especially when accompanied by an awareness of actual dangers or deficiencies. When it comes to safety, complacency can be dangerous."*

Fast forwarded to the present day, I must resort to bringing up complacency within the context of the Brazilian culture and its influence on it. Here are excerpts taken from an interview with Brazilian journalist William Waack: "A common element to tragedy is complacency. While the meaning may be also 'benign, tolerant, capable of facing adversity,' in Brazil complacency has a special meaning: the capacity to tolerate situations to the limit of the impossible. Which may present undesirable consequences." While I write this memoir several years after the sequencing of the current chapter, tragic man-made events such as *Mariana* in 2015, where the dam's disaster should have been a wake-up call to the world, this is the history of the world's third largest mine tainted by crimes against environment and local communities. Only to see history repeating itself after another announced tragedy: the rupture of another dam at *Corrego do Feijão*, in *Brumadinho*, three years after *Mariana*.

Crime and violence also seem to be in a perpetual state of complacency. More than 60,000 homicides, a macabre record across the country with increasing rates year after year. Corruption as well, a major topic. The belief within the Brazilian universe that things will get resolved by themselves, fast-forwarded to 2017, it takes about 20 years for things to start to change; only more recently addressed by courageous judges and a handful of public prosecutors through the well-known *Operação Lava Jato*, Car Wash, an ongoing mega criminal investigation being carried out by the Federal Police of Brazil. It has taken heavy weight politicians to jail and even a former highly popular president to incarceration. Great resistance may yet bring this fight to a fragile condition. Its success depends on the capacity of the society to support it relentlessly. Time will tell.

At last, inflation. One can assume that this beautiful and once promising country's biggest tragedy is complacency. A society anesthetized by subsidies, both in less developed geographical regions as well as to some of the most auspicious corporations in the private sector, it is the complacency and impotence to fight off inflation – and the acceptance to the point of hyper – inflation – that corroded the fabric of society for decades. Presently under control, one would hope this cycle is forever gone.

## "WHY HAS BRAZIL NEVER TAKEN OFF AS A COUNTRY?"

Mike Horn, Quora, 2019

"I would not say Brazil has never taken off as a country. I would say there is opportunity for improvement.

"Corruption is a scourge on the Brazilian economy, the extent of the damage it causes is difficult to ascertain. The country is starved for investment in education, healthcare and infrastructure. The path to improving Brazilian economic performance clearly involves ending corruption and increasing investment in these much needed areas.

"There is something else though that most people are not aware of, but that they should be. This is that Brazil faces significant natural obstacles related to geography and inflation.

"This is the conclusion reached in a fascinating article on the development challenges facing Brazil. The article was published in 2012 on the Stratford website.

"Inflation is Brazil's biggest problem. Economic growth is inflationary anywhere in the world. But in Brazil the scarcity of land, labor, transport infrastructure and capital mean that any economic growth almost instantly turns inflationary.

"Brazil has a serious case of inflation-phobia, as would any country with its history. In fact, the country's recent macroeconomic policy could be described as seeking low inflation at any cost, rather than growth at any cost.

"Much of Brazil is tropical. Tropical zones represent the most difficult sort of biome for human activity. Soils are poor, diseases are rampant.

"Central Brazil lacks navigable rivers. Moving goods on water costs about 10 to 30 times less than moving the same goods on trucks.

"Only 7% of Brazilian territory is considered traditionally arable. The vast Cerrado region can be farmed, but only at great cost. While 85% of US farms are 500 acres or less, 70% of Brazilian farms are 500 acres or more.

"The Brazilian interior is a raised plateau called the Brazilian Shield. The drop-off from the shield to the Atlantic Ocean is quite steep; most of the coast appears as a wall when viewed from the ocean. Cities are found on small, isolated pockets of relatively flat land where the plateau falls to the sea. The dirt of flatland means that, with the exception of São Paulo, cities cannot radiate out as they've done in the US and Europe, leveraging economies of scale.

"Brazil has few major highways and railways and lacks a major coastal road system. The seven largest Brazilian ports combined have less loading capacity than the top U.S. port, New Orleans.

"Of course, inflation and geography don't explain the way in which crime, of many kinds, has traditionally largely gone unpunished in Brazil. Criminal behavior sometimes appears to be a credential for office holders..."I steal, but I deliver!"

In considering Brazil's accomplishments and shortcomings, who are we to benchmark the country against? What if we compare Brazil to its peers in the Southern Hemisphere? From that perspective, the world looks different: included are the countries of South America and Africa that fall below the equator, Indonesia, Australia and New Zealand. From that perspective of a world of about 43 country-sized countries, Brazil comes in a respectable #10 in GDP per capita, as ranked by the IMF in 2015.

## COLLISION COURSE

The year was 1998 and my consulting business was doing quite well. In the past few years, although my activity was now more focused in helping organizations aggregate goods and services from overseas into the country – especially from Southeast Asia's Taiwan, Hong Kong, Singapore, Malaysia and Thailand – I began combining initiatives around promoting exports to multiple markets. This time, besides working with local and regional companies, I signed up to join a delegation to the Middle East. For the first time in more than a decade, São Paulo-based Arab-Brazilian Chamber of Commerce was organizing a business trip to three potential markets – United Arab Emirates, Kuwait and Saudi Arabia – in which investments were pouring in. Having visited Chile along with Silvia in the beginning of the year on a mission for a Carnaúba Wax customer, I saw that as an interesting opportunity and was now bound to the three Arab countries to try and develop business for Brazilian exporters – cashew nuts, apparel and textiles also in the mix.

Back in 1994, the *Plano Real* (Real Plan) was a set of measures taken to stabilize the Brazilian economy during the presidency of Itamar Franco. Its architects were led by the Minister of Finance and succeeding president Fernando Henrique Cardoso. The Plano Real was based on an analysis of the root causes of hyperinflation in the *New Republic* of Brazil, that concluded that there was both an issue of fiscal policy and severe, widespread inertial inflation. The Plano Real intended to stabilize the domestic currency in nominal terms after a string of failed plans to control inflation.

A new currency called the *real* (plural *reais*) was introduced in July of that same year aiming at substituting the short-lived *cruzeiro real* in the process. Then, a series of contracting fiscal and monetary policies was enacted, restricting the government expenses and raising interest rates. By doing so, the country was able to keep inflation under control for several years. In addition, high interest rates attracted enough foreign capital to finance the current account deficit and increased the country's international reserves. The government put a strong focus on the management of the balance of payments, at first by setting the real at a very high value relative to the U.S. dollar, and later (in late 1998) by a sharp increase on domestic interest rates to maintain a positive influx of foreign capitals to local currency bond markets, financing Brazilian expenditures.

The *real* initially gained value against the U.S. dollar as a result of the large amount of capital inflows in late 1994 and 1995. It then began a gradual depreciation process, culminating in the 1999 January currency crisis, when the real suffered a maxi-devaluation, and fluctuated wildly. And wildly it did.

# 16

# Why Not?

> *"You and I*
> *We were captured*
> *We took our souls and we flew away*
> *We were right*
> *We were giving*
> *That's how we kept what we gave away."*
> *Comes a Time* – Neil Young

THE DAY WAS JANUARY 17TH, 1999. The original idea of spending a White Christmas in Vermont did not exactly materialize since we decided to spend the holiday time along with our extended families in São Paulo; however, James had promised us to only decorate the Christmas Tree when we got to Vermont a couple of weeks later – a tradition he was surprisingly willing to break. As we arrived in New York, James was set to pick us up at JFK and drive us North where what we had pictured as Santa's home would be waiting for us.

"This is my friend Renato. He is from Brazil, where the nuts come from." Quite an intro to literally break the ice when introducing me to his friends. Working at Sarducci's in Montpelier as a bartender, James would join us in his break time to show us the area around amidst one of the harshest winters in decades. For us, with the excitement of being in such a different environment, the cold weather didn't quite make any difference; despite the temperature variation – we left Fortaleza at close to 90 degrees for a minus 15-degree Fahrenheit! Bundled up in layers, as Tricia would advise us to do, off we went to experience the next two weeks of a very unusual vacation in beautiful Vermont.

Wanda Persons, Tricia's mom, had been living at 16 Randall Street in Waterbury for many years. Her four girls were actually raised in the house where we would be spending our vacation time; A great hostess, Wanda graciously offered us the two rooms upstairs to accommodate the four of us. Surrounded by loving care and attention, there was so much to talk and laugh about. As for getting around, in Waterbury alone, we visited the art shops and glass blowing studios; the legendary Ben & Jerry's manufacturing unit, the Cold Hollow Apple Cider facility with its exquisite cider and donuts, as well as the many bagel and coffee shops housed in the 150-year old New England style buildings. James and Tricia took us to the Green Mountain Coffee Roasters shop, where we stopped by and warmed up at the beginning of the day with the many coffee and chocolate recipe drinks - Silvia, Catherine Bianca and GG couldn't get enough of. Tricia's sister Marianne and her husband Jeffrey owned Arvad's; with two locations, one in Waterbury and the other in Waitsfield, here was another nice spot for a great taste of the local food. Not to mention the ski areas, Sugarbush on one side and Stowe on the other, with plenty of the white stuff, which kept us enchanted at first sight.

Silvia, the girls and I left Brazil with the spectrum of a potential convoluted currency shake-up. The economy had already given signs of another transitional period ahead of us and it was a matter of time until we found out its precise intensity, this time around. From the day we arrived, I accompanied the news and via telephone I got the updates from customers and associates. The picture was not good. What had started out as a minor but consistent devaluation of the Brazilian currency in the beginning of January, escalated to 20%, then 30%, 40% and 50% in a matter of days. And climbing! In simple words, what that meant to my business is that, if the measures adopted by the government had the desired results, the trend would shift the focus of commerce activity from imports to exports in order to attempting to bring balance to the economy. Quite a lot to absorb, to say the least. I picked up the phone and sensed the tension on the other side from one of my main partners describing a grim near future to our partnership: the already ongoing cancelling of contracts and uncertainty of things. On the other hand, my customers, whose businesses were associated with exports, were exhilarated with the outlook.

What followed was an exercise of vision. Silvia and I, although concerned, would most of the time look at the bright side of the picture. "Well, we will have to intensify redesigning our business towards servicing exports." The upside was that we see the picture. The downside, we had no idea as to how long this would take to materialize. Opening export channels not only takes time but competence and trust from importers. We knew the battle was uphill, crystal clear.

> "THERE'S NOTHING IN A CATERPILLAR THAT TELLS YOU IT'S GOING TO BE A BUTTERFLY."
> – Buckminster Fuller

My identity with the lifestyle of the outskirts of Melbourne, Australia, would only pair up with what I see in the Green Mountain State. The greenery and views, the small town feel with small businesses and lots of nice cafes and restaurants were but a part of the whole experience. The idea of offering Silvia and the girls the opportunity to experience multiple cultures starts with building a solid knowledge of the English language. I had learned that a long time ago. With Chinese Mandarin being the mostly spoken language on the planet, it was a requirement that they got exposed, first and foremost, to an English speaking country and culture before they ventured into their own cultural exploration. It is said that nothing happens by chance. Little did we know that the last two weeks of January, 1999 would change our lives forever.

"What if we stay?" I asked James. To get to the point of asking my friend that question made me think of the latent state of my determination to change the status quo. I couldn't quite remember whether he had a couple of beers or a six-pack or simply had not drunk at all that day. His answer was an unequivocal: "Why not?" Long pause. Those two words were the key to the edification Silvia and I were willing to dive into. What revolved around "staying" would have implications we were not concerned at all at this point. At that moment, it really didn't matter. What was supposed to be a two-week vacation time in the Northeast of the USA emerged as a not so obvious intent to take a leap of faith.

"EVERY CAUSE IS THE EFFECT OF ITS OWN EFFECTS."
– Ibn 'Arabi

Here are William Bryant's thoughts on cause and effect that falls similarly to the crossroads I would be going through: "The remorseless drive of evolution engineered the awakening of the kind of consciousness responsible for the growing interest in human rights. This emergence is reflected in humankind's increasing use of its ability to think as separate individuals. The stronger the sense of Self became, the more individuals felt responsible for their own choice of action. Conversely, the more primitive the thought life, the more collectively dependent were the people. Obviously, the degree of self-awareness decides whether the process of cause and effect is ruled by fate or freedom."

William Bryant's thoughts describe his own process of making the decision to work in the United States as a "complex series of apparently free choices shaped by a mixture of ideals, the quest of experience, and available opportunities." Which, inevitably would lead him to a myriad of nuanced "line of events" between joy and sorrow. I could not relate more to those thoughts once we triggered the process of change. Were we prepared for that?

## ACTING ON

In a matter of days, James's signal resonated around Wanda's absorbing the idea and her daughters Theresa, Georgeanne and Marianne – and their respective husbands, Gordie, Don and Jeffrey – developing incredible support to bring our project to fruition. Not to mention Tricia's surprise turned into enthusiasm and creative ideas. We knew this was going to take a lot of stamina for it to become a sustainable ground plan. Nevertheless, we had to take the first steps.

Crossett Brook Middle School and Thatcher Brook Primary School were the first "touching the waters" initiatives we took in order to get a sense of how receptive this small community of less than 5,000 people would be towards our family and, especially, to our girls – Catherine Bianca and GG were 11 and 9 years old, respectively. For Silvia and me, having grown in a major city had never given us a sense of community other than the neighborhoods we were brought up in. Not really part of the cultural landscape since very little attention was given to the sub-municipalities, our experience was practically nil. The same thing would apply to our girls who had lived in São Paulo, Porto and Fortaleza at such early ages and were too young to discern. It is important to highlight that *The Lectorium* had provided us with a significant sense of community, although restricted to its philosophical teachings and orientation.

After purchasing a 1990 Black Volvo Station Wagon at the Greensboro Garage in Hardwick, the vehicle that seemed appropriate for the environment, the other critical aspect of the new undertaking was dwelling; after looking around at a scarce inventory of real estate options in Waterbury and Waterbury Center, we found a 1956 ranch-style house located at the highest part of the Village; a cul-de-sac area which looked appropriate and affordable. Grand View Heights is right behind Thatcher Brook Primary School, walking distance from the house for GG, right where she needed to be. For Catherine Bianca, she would catch a bus to Crossett Brook Middle School, roughly a 10-minute ride. Convenient and desirable.

## THE REAL WHY, YET TO BE REVEALED

"In fact, most of the time, things do not turn out as we expect. But the potential value of unexpected developments is rarely tapped. Instead, when things turn out contrary to our expectations, we go immediately into problem-solving mode and react, or just try harder – without taking the time to see whether this unexpected development is telling us something important about our assumptions. This more prepared mental state is really where a lot of the longer-term payoff is." – *Peter Senge, The Fifth Discipline.*

Life in Fortaleza was good. I mean really good. The temperature was paradisaically. Living nearby the ocean is remarkably healthy. Our professional lives were successful. Silvia and the girls loved the lifestyle. We had great friends and our relationship network was promising. As a middle-class family reasonably educated and with a good deal of exposure to the outside world, the future was relatively secured for our children – good schools, friends and opportunities. Moreover, we could afford to have maids – and even a driver – to support us in our day-to-day routine and tasks. Why move away?

## SIGNALS

The news of a new pregnancy came as a big welcoming surprise in the beginning of the Spring (Fall in the Northern Hemisphere) of 1998, a few months before going to our Vermont vacation. Ten years apart from GG's birth, Silvia and I intuitively had a sense that we could have a third child. Excitement in place, only to disappointingly experience a natural miscarriage at the early stages of her pregnancy. We took it well and accepted the experience serenely. A signal of change? Possibly, what did we know? The fact is that, as we made the move towards making a big change in our lives in a totally unknown environment, things seem to positively fall into place. With a minor deposit directly to the owner of the house we realistically saw ourselves living in, the next step was to tell our families of our intent and to plan my trip to Brazil in order to divest of our obligations and commitments. Not an effortless endeavor per se, we pictured that a decisive way to pursue this project would be enrolling the kids in school immediately. And throw ourselves into the new perspective. As Peter Senge, American scientist, director of the Center for Organizational Learning at MIT properly points out, "Courage is simply doing whatever is needed in pursuit of the vision." I had read Senge's *The Fifth Discipline* and one of the major breakthroughs for me when it comes to managing change was to make it happen while a certain situation does not require change, contrary to the reactionary move. It's almost as if change should be provoked as a means to enhancing opportunities. Yet again, what do we know?

## THE FAMILY STAYS

Flying by myself while the girls settled in to the new living possibilities gave me the chance to organize my mind. The move to Portugal years earlier was under different circumstances since I had the backing of a large company. Now, it's all new territory. The challenges were huge. As I arrived in Fortaleza and met with one of my partners, J. Martins – the same one who demonstrated great concern with the currency debacle and its unfolding of events – I experienced resistance. He did not take the news of 'moving to the US' lightly. In actuality, he reacted as if I had premeditated the whole move and that the currency situation was being used to justify our decision. Truth be told, one thing was to give wings to imagination. Another was to engender a plan without the proper foundation. The first one was always there. The latter, was never considered before the economic events took place. I respected his reaction but there was nothing I could do about the way he looked at the situation. Our decision had been made based on the opportunity presented and there would be no way back.

At the apartment, among my somewhat lonely preparations to substantiate the move - other than the obvious packing up of our stuff – it was time for releasing our dear helpers and employees from their responsibilities. As for saying goodbye to them and to our friends, there was a minus: Silvia and the girls would not have a chance to participate in that. My take was that, if we were all to come back and then organize the move from Fortaleza, the move would simply not happen. If back to the comfort of our home and with everyone's routine sinking in, we would probably get distracted and push back the opportunity. It had to be disruptive – much to Silvia's and the girls' realization. Even though we extensively discussed the seriousness of our intent as a family, we weren't sure they got a grip of its magnitude; therefore, the choice was to deal with the girls' feelings of being 'uprooted' once they fathomed that change would come accompanied with reality. Aware of that, we would have to deal with that at some point in the future.

"He who has a Why to live for can bear almost any How."
–Friedrich Nietzsche

# 17

# It's All About Them

*"And you, of tender years*
*Can't know the tears that your elders grew by*
*And so please help them with your youth*
*They seek the truth before they can die."*
Teach Your Children – Crosby, Stills and Nash

WORDS OF REFLECTION from Livegoed's "Phases" in the chapter "The Course of Life" were keen to describe that momentum of my journey: "And then the incomprehensible happens: into the middle of this world of assurance and planning there creeps a doubt, 'as a thief in the night', and indeed it usually is in the night. You wake up and can't get back to sleep. The events of everyday life run through your head: little irritations and things that have gone wrong stir up the emotions; you decide to tell so-and-so exactly what you think of him. Then drowsiness sets in, and suddenly you are obsessed: 'I'm nearly 40 - 25 years to retirement – my God, another 25 years of the same old grind!

I know there's nothing new to be expected – at the newest scenery for the same old problem... 25 years... Is there really anything new still to come?" – *Phases – The Course of Life – Bernard Lievegoed.*

By them, I mean the kids. Already turned 40, the drive and volition to see and make things happen were there and strong. But the focus started to shift more and more on the children. And in a big way. In our case, as much as we enjoyed living in Brazil, earlier in São Paulo and later in Fortaleza, with Portugal in between, the idea of expanding opportunities was always present.

With Fortaleza behind and some of our friends left with a mix of surprise and apprehension, I headed down to São Paulo where I got to spend time with my folks as well as with Silvia's parents before catching the flight back to Burlington. No less apprehensive and with added concern, here was my chance to make our case to our folks and try to ease unnecessary preoccupations. Not an easy task.

## BEN & JERRY'S TOWN

The first two months of the 1998/1999 Central Vermont winter had only seen nearly seven inches of snow, compared to over 35 inches in November and December of the previous year, only to experience a whopping dump of over 30" in January plus another close to 35" in the next two months, with 25" in March alone. What actually made that a cold winter was not necessarily the amount of snow but the low temperatures, which contributed to the lingering snow on the ground and the feeling of a longer winter, I learned from the locals. For our family, it was a whole new experience and we found fun everywhere. Except when...Silvia must have gotten excited and neglected the 'layers' factor. The result: a minor pneumonia that was enough to get us scared at the pleasures of outdoor activity at that time of the year.

Back in Waterbury, we made an affordable rental arrangement with Wanda: until we got approved for a mortgage loan and subsequently managed to go for a successful closing – with the unforgettable help of James and Tricia as our co-signers, our household stayed at the first floor of the Randall Street house. There, we used the two bedrooms and ½ bathroom; at ground floor, we shared the kitchen and the additional living space with Wanda as well as with Ginger, a lovely American Cocker Spaniel puppy which would turn out to be Wanda's companion for years to come. Our girls wasted no time looking back at what was left behind: GG, especially, did not hesitate to pick up the phone and call some of the neighbors' children and invite them to play – at that point she started making up sentences in English with the help of Gabriela and Joseph, the Meade's adorable children who, like their mom and dad, developed the same care and sympathy for our project. As for Catherine Bianca, she had always been a little more mature physically and looked older than she really was; therefore, a little self-conscious, she tried a bit harder to fit into the new lifestyle.

Silvia and I discussed for days how we thought that environment would adequately pace out our children's speed of growth. With many aspects to be considered – seasons, community life and the small town lifestyle itself all contribute to that. In Fortaleza, as in most coastal cities in Brazil, the culture revolves too much on beach life and consequently appearance; thus to a good extent, to the cult of the body, which we did not necessarily debate or oppose, but there was something terribly wrong about the early insertion of children into the lifestyle. The result: too much partying and distractions, possible precocious sexual activity, early exposure to alcohol and drugs and the loss of focus to the meaningful and simple things in life. From my and Silvia's perspective, the Greek aphorism 'know thyself' says it all: understand who you are, then nature, our role as human beings and how things work.

At the end of that day, I ran by a thought that helped dissipate some of the doubts that naturally come around the large path ahead of us:

"Confusion can be dissolved only through self-confidence, and this confidence cannot be gained through another. You have to undertake, for yourself and by yourself, the journey of discovery into the process of yourself, in order to understand it."– J. Krishnamurti

## THE VERMONTER

Just when you think you have enough on your plate, life comes to you and pushes you a little harder. "Now that you have enhanced your perspective to make a 180-degree change, here's another task for you," whispers that little voice deep down, unapologetically. And this one would have profound consequences. After Silvia's recovery from the mild pneumonia and as we were ready to focus on the upcoming multiple challenges – the major one, in our view, learning and navigating the new lifestyle as the foundation for this project – she surprisingly relapses showing signs of fatigue. Oh boy, here we go. "Pneumonia has not been properly healed and it's making its come back" we suspect. With no fever, this time her symptoms were accompanied by other signs. Pneumonia is gone, what now? Instead, it looked like our past year's experience is ready to re-manifest itself. The fatigue comes along with nausea and food cravings...a pregnancy test and yes, a new baby was on his way!

## THE WHY, EXPLAINED AND INTERPRETED

Ten years back, a friend or acquaintance had told us to try the ring gender test as soon as we found out our second baby GG was on her way. Of course we wouldn't know the baby's gender at that point nor did we care for what we thought could be one more superstition. Moreover, there was the element of surprise in our minds at that moment. In fact, we didn't pay much attention and waited until the 18-20-week ultrasound, the routine second trimester ultrasound, when the OB-GYN is able to investigate and possibly determine a baby's sex. Silvia and I gladly learned that another baby girl was coming to join us in a few months. The idea of the ring test started to sound intriguing when someone closer to us brought it up once again emphasizing its efficacy. "Why not give it a shot?" we considered. Passed down from generation to generation, we learned, the test got put in place. With a piece of thread attached to a ring, using Silvia's wedding band, she would lie on her back and I would dangle the thread over a couple of specific spots over parts of the body, such as palm hand, between the eyes and even over her belly button. The distance, 5-8 inches above the spots. What followed was a surprising and magnetized move of the ring: if it moves back and forth like a pendulum, the baby is a boy. If it moves in a circle, one's having a girl. Well, it doesn't stop there. Once we did it sequentially, both to Silvia and to myself, not only the ring moved but it did it twice as a circle. Then...a third time, now back and forth like a pendulum. Then it would stop even if we tried once more. After a minute or two, we would do it over again. "What?! Are we supposed to have...three kids?!"

Fast forward, it's flashback. We were thrilled and concerned at the same time. Never really planned, of course the baby would be most welcome. But it was hard to ignore that ten years had passed and here we are mortified with the outlook of having to deal with so many moving targets: new country, new language, new town, new home (actually, not even in our new house yet), new schools, new culture, new friends and...a new baby coming up. Not to mention, a new professional perspective, to which the present seems tenuous and the future still uncertain. All at once.

As we navigated this experience and devoted quite a lot of time making sense and connecting the dots, the whole process boiled down as to how we would interpret this new life equation. Aware of a number of past vivid impressions, our interpretation now was that this entity, which we call 'the new baby', wanted to be born in this stamping ground – Vermont. With the proper conditions created, manifestation was turned into reality. Did it sound too imaginative? It probably did. I stuck to it.

# GRANDVIEW HEIGHTS

"How could I, to whom the only significant things are civilization [Kultur] and barbarism, hate a nation which is among the most cultivated in the world, and to which I owe a great part of my own culture? In any case this business of hatred between nations is a curious thing. You will always find it more powerful and barbarous on the lowest levels of civilization. But there exists a level at which it wholly disappears, and where one stands, so to speak, above the nations, and feels the weal or woe of a neighboring people as though it were one's own." *Johann Wolfgang von Goethe*

Love for one's country is no small thing and cannot be neglected. After all, it's where you are born, raised and made a citizen along with loved ones and millions of other individuals. If one is lucky to be brought over in a prosperous and more balanced country, even better. Goethe's reflection has to do with France's occupation during and after one of Napoleon's wars, this one against his beloved Weimar. Asked to write negatively about his neighboring country after the war, he not only rebuffs the idea but highlights what he admires about the country next door. Not a perfect analogy to the moment we were living through but somewhat a valid one; deciding to experience a new lifestyle has nothing to do with abandoning one's roots. On the contrary, it is the very opportunity to add elements which enhance and bring meaning to one's existence. All that combined with the essential: the joy of learning.

Speaking of which, J. Krishnamurti's following thoughts helped me understand the centerpiece of learning by shedding light into the theme: "What do we mean by learning? Is there learning when you are merely accumulating knowledge, gathering information? That is one kind of learning, is it not? As a student of engineering, you study mathematics, and so on; you are learning, informing yourself about the subject. You are accumulating knowledge in order to use that knowledge in practical ways. Your learning is accumulative, additive. Now, when the mind is merely taking on, adding, acquiring, is it learning? Or is learning something entirely different? I say the additive process which we now call learning is not learning at all. It is merely a cultivation of memory, which becomes mechanical; and a mind which functions mechanically, like a machine, is not capable of learning. A machine is never capable of learning, except in the additive sense. Learning is something quite different…Learning is never cumulative; it is a movement of knowing which has no beginning and no end." – *J. Krishnamurti – The Book of Life*

The wooded area behind the Grandview Heights house is located at a steep portion of the lot. There, we had multiple species of maple trees along with birch trees surrounded by ferns and other types of vegetation. I found comfort in the quiet as Spring was well on its way to complete the thawing of the season. Smell, colors and textures were still unfamiliar but in a process of becoming part of our new experience. Catherine Bianca and GG were both doing well at school as we prepared to welcome our extended families. Both Silvia's parents and mine crossed the ocean and made sure to give us their blessings as we approached to receive the new member of our family, as I describe Eric's arrival in more detail on Chapter 20.

"Eric, I perceive the importance of your coming and assignment entrusted, bringing, at the end of this century of great crisis and transformations, your vibrations of love, wisdom and dedication with our humanity. Your family will offer you all the conditions so you can develop yourself surrounded by love, spirituality, care and understanding, providing all of the necessary energy for you to keep and defuse your light. We are happy with your arrival and can already sense the vibration of your presence." – Leonardo Villela – 11/8/1999

# 18

# Music, Lyrics & Lessons from Songwriters

*"We don't make music. It makes us."* – David Byrne

"It's funny. People will literally cross a room to confess to me that they don't like Jazz. As if Jazz is all I listen to; as if Jazz requires a secret handshake...they haven't mastered.

Then they'll tell me they adore (insert name here) that their dad played records of around the house when they were kids. Then they'll ask when Discover Jazz is going to bring (insert name of dead jazz musician who appeared here several times).

So I've decided to share a secret here: Jazz is just music. And as Ellington used to say, there are only two kinds of music... Good music and Bad music.

If it makes you cry or jump for joy or play air guitar and forget where you are... if it saves your life one day at a time - it's good music." David Beckett, *Jazz Broadcaster, Realtor.*

Within my circle of friends and family, it's no secret that my preferred music style has become Jazz for the past twenty-five years or so. Added to my own domestic musical upbringing, I had great exposure to Rock'n Roll, Pop and Classical genres from an early age; nevertheless, with so much to encompass within what is known as Jazz, I find immensely gratifying to follow the music of the musicians who have seemingly developed their careers mingling and sharing their talents with other musicians of similar - and not always so similar - styles.

Brazilian music is vast and allows for a multitude of influences and influencers. A unique blend of European harmony and melody, as well as African rhythms along with Native South American culture, it accounts for more than twenty original styles. From notable classical composers such as Heitor Villa-Lobos, Carlos Gomes and Cláudio Santoro, it is with Pixinguinha's *Choro*, Noel Rosa's and Ary Barroso's *Samba*, Dorival Caymmi's *Samba-Canção* and Tom Jobim's *Bossa Nova* that the legacy of the finest Brazilian music resides. This is doing justice to only a few of the many compatriots which became significant contributors to world music; for this reason, my appreciation to fusing these styles with Jazz is profound. My taste for instrumental music ranges from the previously mentioned forms to Jazz, where figures like Sergio Mendes, Oscar Castro-Neves, Eumir Deodato, Airto Moreira, Flora Purim, Naná Vasconcelos, Hermeto Pascoal, Sivuca, and Egberto Gismonti are some of the most significant exponents.

The German label ECM Records, an independent record label founded in 1969, is a unique and unparalleled promoter of Jazz from all corners of the world. The label has released a variety of recordings from which ECM's artists often refuse to acknowledge the boundaries between genres. It is at an ECM recording that I came across a musician who, from an early age, would become a major character to my musical liking: Pat Metheny. By far my favorite Jazz musician of all time, Metheny is a musical storyteller – one of the best. His curiosity to collaborate with other musicians is what makes him a giant in the genre. Needless to say that he as a bandleader has produced a meaningful body of music, especially after leaving the ECM label when he could devote more time to execute the studio recordings and be able to refine the sounds of the next albums.

It is contributing to defusing his talent with a myriad of great musicians, as a bandleader or as a sideman, that makes him unique. It is known that Metheny kept an apartment in Rio for several years during the mid-80s, followed by the ingenious collaboration with Naná Vasconcelos in records such as *Offramp*, in 1982. And it was there that the seeds for one of his most beautiful albums were first planted: *Still Life (Talking)*, released in 1987. "I played a lot of concerts there back then," he said in an interview with Jazz Improvisation Magazine. "There's a deeply musical sensibility everywhere." He also met and recorded with many of Rio's top musicians including Antonio Carlos Jobim, Celia Vaz, Toninho Horta and percussionist Armando Marçal. Broadly, Metheny's role here is his connection to Berklee College of Music and the generation of Brazilian Jazz musicians who studied there, including saxophonist Leo Gandelman, Jair Oliveira and Luciana Souza. Later on he would produce works with legends such as Gary Burton, Ornette Coleman, Jim Hall, Charlie Haden, Michael Brecker and Toots Thielemmans; a major collaboration with legendary Lyle Mays, evocative pianist, composer and orchestrator, who helped carve a new channel for contemporary jazz with The Pat Metheny Group, and most recently with younger talented musicians from a multitude of backgrounds – Antonio Sanchez, Cuong Vu, Richard Bona, Gregoire Maret, Anna Maria Jopek, Chris Potter, Ben Williams and Giulio Carmassi - with everything in between. His career is a phenomenal one and his legacy is what makes in my opinion this fascinating world of Jazz worth diving into.

Here I found myself lined up to buy the ticket of what would be the sixth time I would have the opportunity to see my favorite jazz player at the Flynn Theatre in Burlington, VT. Behind me, there was a guy wearing a Panama hat to which I was proud to communicate with the many times I had the chance to see Metheny. The year was 2002 and this would be the first time I would see him in Burlington, therefore my excitement – I had seen him in São Paulo, Portugal and New York, and most recently at the Hopkins Center for the Arts, in Hanover, New Hampshire. It's his first album after 9/11, *Speaking of Now*. When I asked the gentleman if he had seen the musician before, he unpretentiously and modestly says, "Yeah, a few times." Not happy with the answer, I asked for accuracy on the information. "I would say...probably about 25 times." Astonished, I was all ears to absorb the outstanding knowledge this guy must have gathered throughout his existence about Jazz and music in general. And my impressions were right. I learned that this now acquaintance and yet to become good friends with had a local radio program at St. Michaels College where he himself was a diffuser of Jazz and other co-related genres to our community and beyond. A great admirer of the many Brazilian music styles, David Beckett would invite me once in a while to join him at "Worry Later," his every other Wednesday Jazz Radio session on WWPV, which I gladly accept every time I can – what a wealth of knowledge, I'm so fortunate to have come across the man.

Wisdom abounds. Whether mythical or not, here I find inspiration on Yogi Berra explaining Jazz:

Interviewer: "Can you explain jazz?"

Yogi: "I can't, but I will. 90% of all jazz is half improvisation. The other half is the part people play while others are playing something they never played with anyone who played that part. So if you play the wrong part, its right. If you play the right part, it might be right if you play it wrong enough. But if you play it too right, it's wrong."

Interviewer: "I don't understand."

Yogi: "Anyone who understands jazz knows that you can't understand it. It's too complicated. That's what's so simple about it."

Interviewer: "Do you understand it?"

Yogi: "No. That's why I can explain it. If I understood it, I wouldn't know anything about it.

Interviewer: Are there any great jazz players alive today?"

Yogi: "No. All the great jazz players alive today are dead. Except for the ones that are still alive. But so many of them are dead, that the ones that are still alive are dying to be like the ones that are dead. Some would kill for it."

Interviewer: "What is syncopation?"

Yogi: "That's when the note that you should hear now happens either before or after you hear it. In jazz, you don't hear notes when they happen because that would be some other type of music. Other types of music can be jazz, but only if they're the same as something different from those other kinds."

Interviewer: "Now I really don't understand."

Yogi: "I haven't taught you enough for you to not understand jazz that well."

## LYRICS AND THE VOICES OF THE SOUL

"But it's the art that shapes life, not the artist. Art provides a template we apply to our lives—we pick up a song's central message and fill in any gaps or vagaries with our own personal information. Art tells us we are not alone in feeling how we do, connects us to our peers, and ties us back to particular moments in our lives." –*Anonymous*.

The beauty of instrumental music is undeniable. It helps us build our moods and states of being in which we transport ourselves to places that otherwise would not be available without those tunes; however, lyrics give meaning and once crafted with emotional balance they sometimes help us understand who we are and where we are going to. If I were asked to pick the best lyrics which significantly helped me – and continue to - get through this journey of ours, the list would be extensive; nonetheless, I want to name a few in which their influences have been profound. Some of them are translations from Portuguese to English and not always make the greatest sense. Others were written in English and may also not always make great sense.

One gets the picture.

*BOY* – Ivan Lins

*I cling to this boy, who has calm eyes,*
*The most beautiful eyes, the watery mouth*
*of tamarind*
*I cling to this boy, who lives healthy days*
*Who is fish in the river, a cornered animal*
*without my affection*
*I cling to this boy, who in thick fields has*
*A sealed and fiery bay, waiting for my Sundays*
*I cling to this boy, with glue and fig mink,*
*Who plays with me while my children are asleep*
*Will he grow up?*
*And take me for granted?*
*And forget me one day?*

Clearly, a reminder of where we once were – and may always revisit – our childhood. Growing up is painful but it doesn't have to be like that for the rest of our lives; therefore, resorting to the child inside allows us to pause and put a break on the ever demanding lives of adulthood. As if we could stop time every chance our mind allows us to do that. It is a mindset indeed and we can make it a spontaneous habit. It is exploring, always, the ability to be curious. Michael Jager, a well-known graphic designer based in the Burlington, Vermont area and a significant contributor to creative graphic design driven by the idea that design distinction matters most, is keen on pointing out the exponential world of technology impacting our ability to continue to be curious. Literally, too much information, too fast, too many expectations, unrealistic most of the time. "Saving curiosity," in Jager's own words, requires vulnerability and empathy - a quality often found in children, why not in the child in us?

Lievegoed's surgical eye to signalize one's developmental opportunities is deep: "The uncontrolled, chaotic experiences of 'trips' and being 'high' have nothing to do with personal development, which requires the conscious exercise of faculties that lie dormant in the majority of lives. I have already pointed out that man is born with very many possibilities, and that because of our modern culture only a very small proportion of these are required and hence exploited. It is for this reason that many people feel dissatisfied with the reduced world in which we live as reduced people. But what has to be developed?" – *Phases, Personal Development and Biography.*

It is clear to me that what needs to be developed is the balance between our inner being with the outside world, a certainty that only the individual can find through his/her own experience, whichever the outcome.

*ASPIRATIONS* – Gentle Giant

*As the dust settles, see our dreams,*
*All coming true*
*It depends on you,*
*If our times, they are troubled times,*
*Show us the way,*
*Tell us what to do.*
*As our faith, maybe aimless blind,*
*Hope our ideals and*
*Our thoughts are yours*

*In your hands, holding everyone's*
*Future and fate*
*It is all in you,*
*Make us strong build our unity,*
*All men as one*
*It is all in you.*
*Be our guide, our light and our way of life*
*And let the world see the way we lead our way.*
*Hopes, dreams, dreaming that all our sorrows*

*Gone forever.*

A track from a Gentle Giant classic and contextual album called *The Power and the Glory*, "Aspirations" is actually a song which the lyrics relate to when we experience a new ruler or politician being elected by the people. It obviously differs from country to country, and from culture to culture but, generally, people cast much if not all their hopes on him/her. They have voted for him/her so that he/she can deliver them from "troubled times" and all their problems. Their aspirations are enormous: "In your hands, holding everyone's/ Future and fate, it is all in you." Hopes for prosperity, unity and peace, dreams to be fulfilled. Here I introject the message to work towards finding the ruler not outside ourselves, but rather inside. It's not about not supporting honest people as I'm sure there are good intentioned individuals that join politics; though, the way I see it, what needs to be fixed starts with ourselves. And no one can do that for us. The waters ahead of us to be sailed, the ocean wide open for us to navigate.

## MILES FROM NOWHERE – Cat Stevens

*Miles from nowhere*
*I guess I'll take my time*
*Oh yeah, to reach there*
*Look up at the mountain*
*I have to climb*
*Oh yeah, to reach there.*
*Lord my body has been a good friend*
*But I won't need it when I reach the end*
*Miles from nowhere*
*I creep through the valleys*
*And I grope through the woods*
*'Cause I know when I find it my honey*
*It's gonna make me feel good, yes*
*Miles from nowhere*
*Not a soul in sight*

*Oh yeah, but it's alright*
*I have my freedom*
*I can make my own rules*
*Oh yes, the ones that I choose*
*Miles from nowhere*
*Guess I'll take my time*
*Oh yeah, to reach there.*

   I can't think of the innumerous times I had the blessing of playing and singing this song along with friends and in circles. In fact, this song is almost a prayer if seen from a liberation seeking standpoint. For one who pursues understanding and overcoming our limitations as human beings, this song can be interpreted as a reminder that we are just pilgrims in this physical realm, navigating through occasional pain and joy – and everything in between – a long way from the spiritual spheres. And yet, only to realize that our bodies are indeed the vehicles to achieve the doorway that may lead us to a higher and more integral life.

   *HEJIRA* – Joni Mitchell

*I'm traveling in some vehicle*
*I'm sitting in some cafe*
*A defector from the petty wars*
*That shell shocked love away*
*In our possessive coupling*
*So much could not be expressed*
*So now I'm returning to myself*
*These things that you and I suppressed*
*I see something of myself in everyone*
*Just at this moment of the world*
*As snow gathers like bolts of lace*
*Waltzing on a ballroom girl*
*You know it never has been easy*
*Whether you do or you do not resign*

*Whether you travel the breadth of extremities*
*Or stick to some straighter line*
*I'm porous with travel fever*
*But you know I'm so glad to be on my own*
*Still somehow the slightest touch of a stranger*
*Can set up trembling in my bones*
*I know, no one's going to show me everything*
*We all come and go unknown*
*Each so deep and superficial*
*Between the forceps and the stone*
*And the wax rolls down like tears*
*There's the hope and the hopelessness*
*I've witnessed thirty years*
*We're only particles of change I know, I know*
*Orbiting around the sun*
*But how can I have that point of view*
*When I'm always bound and tied to someone*
*White flags of winter chimneys*
*Waving truce against the moon*

Hejira meanings, according to The Free Dictionary by Farlex:
1. A journey by a large group to escape from a hostile environment. exodus, hegira. escape, flight – the act of escaping physically;
2. An Arabic word meaning emigration or flight, used to refer to any flight from danger but especially the flight of Muhammad from Mecca to Medina in 622.
3. Any flight or journey to a more desirable or congenial place.

The lyrics speak for themselves. The experience of travelling can be daunting for some individuals whereas liberating for others. But it's hard to deny that the idea of travelling is a means to fleeing from a state of mind before the physical experience takes place, only to be substantiated by the journey where the senses themselves take over from dreams and imagination. I have always liked the aspect of movement when planning and experiencing travelling, therefore my identification with this beautiful song. Joni's description of the law of the opposites seems incidental but yet intentional, especially when portraying her own clear views of love. Only to find herself deeply reflecting on life turning around and bringing her back over again to a starting point.

### *IF I WANT TO SPEAK WITH GOD*
### – Gilberto Gil

*If I want to speak with God*
*I need to be alone*
*I need to turn off the lights*
*I need to silence my voice*
*I need to find peace*
*I need to loosen the knots*
*Of the shoes, of the tie*
*Of the desires, of the fears*
*I need to lick the floors*
*Of palaces, of sumptuous*
*Castles of my dream*
*I need to see myself as sad*
*I need to find myself fearful*
*And despite a bad measure*
*Cheer up my heart*
*And if I want to speak with God*
*I need to risk myself*
*I need to rise to the heavens*
*Without strings to sustain me*
*I need to say farewell*
*Turn my back, walk*
*Decidedly, through the road*
*Which in the end will lead to nothing*
*Of what I thought I might find*

In a world full of certainties about God, the song is a crying out loud that works to awaken hearts and minds. Rather philosophical than religious, it talks about the mysterious and the unknown. Silence and solitude, acceptance of suffering and rejection of fear, humility and the emptying of our beings, the tools for the true pursuit of liberation. For this journey, the pass is a one-way ticket. And at last, if and when we find Him, we'll end up facing our foolish convictions. How can we, limited beings, understand the Unlimited?

# 19
# Mirrors and The Present

*"The human biography is a symphony which each individual personally composes." Phases* – Bernard Lievegoed

REFLECTIONS ON THE PHASES OF LIFE start for me from an early exposure to a workshop done at Artemisia, in São Paulo, during the mid-80s, by Gudrun Burkhard. Born in Brazil, she is a physician and therapist who, along with her husband Daniel Burkhard, runs seminars in biographic work, lecturing around the world and authoring many publications, among them the well-known "Taking Charge: Your Life Patterns and Their Meaning." As a physician, Dr. Burkhard's interest in human biography began by observing that when a physician did not pay attention to the biographical aspects of his patients, his understanding of the recovery processes would run the risk of relapsing due to incompleteness. Ignoring the roots of one's upbringing, especially considering the foundation represented by the early years of an individual, would only provide for partial results. The Burkhards made significant contribution to the biographical movement in Brazil and around the world, systematizing the methodology of working in biographical groups and through the publications of multiple titles.

Below, I list my notes of that life changing experience which would help me understand my own development process throughout the years:

0 – 3 Years – Fundamental formation of a child – Good Nutrition – Learning

At 3 Years – Conscience of the self – Seeking Self-Affirmation – Negation

0 – 7 Years – Development of the neuro-sensorial system. Absorption of the environment

7 – 14 Years – Beginning – Fairy tales – Fantasy – Perils of television and technology in general during this phase due to the steeling of fantasy (atrophy)

At 9 Years – Experiencing the self

At 12 Years – Pre-puberty

At 14 Years – Puberty – differentiation between man/woman knowledge/crisis

14 – 21 Years – Beginning – Freedom – Ideals – Danger of Idolatry Discrepancy between ideals and the "physical body charge"

At 19 Years – Development of own autonomous thinking

14 – 21 Years – Development of fineness - Resignation – Questioning
and - Emotional/Soul Phase – Ups and Downs - Experiences

21 to 28 Years - Wishing to become him/herself, coinciding with own autonomous thinking –Who Am I? What am I To Do About My Life?

At 28 Years – Talent Crisis

28 to 42 Years – Peak of Human Potentialities – Conscious Phase

## DEVELOPMENT OF THE SEVEN YEAR CYCLES

| 0 | 7 | 14 | 21 | 28 | 35 | 42 | 49 | 56 | 63... |
|---|---|---|---|---|---|---|---|---|---|
| Protection | Authority | Individual Judgment | Self Knowledge | Rational Phase Self-Acceptance | To Transform, The sky is the limit | Altruistic phase, imaginative | Morality, Inspirational phase | Abnegation, Intuitive or Mystic phase | Spirituality and Physical Decline |
| Love Warmth Faith Hope | Regular habits, Inclinations | Friends *Trouble of alcohol and drugs* | What? Technical Competencies | What? How? Organizational Competencies | Social Competencies | Conceptual Competencies | Creativity | Wisdom | *Obstacles, Losses, Health* |
| Imitation, Family | Example, School | Freedom | Seeking a Place | Conquering a Place | Consolidating a Place | Freeing up Thinking | Freeing up Feeling | Freeing up Acting | Doing Good |
| Life is Good | Life is Beautiful | Life is True | Life is Sensation | Life is Organization | Life is Organization | Life is Sensation | Life is True: *To Have or To Be?* | Life is Beautiful | Life is Good |
| Moral Sense | Aesthetics Sense | Critical Sense | Task Vision | Process Vision | Whole Vision | Strategic Vision | Holistic Vision | Holistic Vision | |
| Trust | Fantasy | Ideals | Ups & Downs | Reasoning › Impulses | Limits | Realism | Sexual Inversion | New Mission | TO SEEK |
| TO | LEARN | | | TO | FIGHT | | | WISDOM | |

At the end of the second decade in the 21st century, it is clear that for most of the civilized world, as well as for many parts of the developing world, life expectancy has been raised significantly when compared to fifty, forty or even thirty years ago, let alone doubled from the early 1900s. Whichever way we look at it, whether we live to being 70, 80, 90 years old or beyond, we may discern within that period the following three phases: "*a period of growth*, during which constructive development outweighs decline; a *period of equilibrium* between development and decline; and *a period of involution*, a time of increasing decline," says Lievegoed on *Phases, The Course of Life*. Therefore, the point is not how much longer can we live but how do we make good and better use of our short existence.

Martha Moers calls the fourth phase of life – 42 to 56 years – a time to encounter the challenge for a disposition towards crisis. It is almost like drawing an analogy with puberty, which is also preceded by a period of assurance, only to be suddenly interrupted by the discovery that we know neither ourselves nor life. From a biographical standpoint, this is what I mean by mirrors; when the sky is the limit – between 35 and 42 – and just when we thought that a certain path would prevail 'for the rest of our lives' we find a similar pattern of experience from the mirroring equivalent phase, the twenties in this case, only to deepen more forcefully at around 49, which coincides with around our $14^{th}$ year. Yet, the great difference is that 'our first puberty' occurs during an ascendant life-line, whereas the second happens during a descendant one. Our bodies change, our vision gets blurred, our joints hurt, our hormones act weird, etc. there are a myriad of scientific studies to testify for the contrasts.

With the aforementioned considered, comes menopause – OMG! – and I'm not only talking about the female menopause but the male menopause as well. Easier to be identified, female menopause is described by gynecologist Elizabeth Parker in *The Seven Ages of Woman* in three phases: pre-menopause, menopause, post-menopause. Whereas for women this reality is more vivid and physically evident, for men it takes a more elusive approach. Male menopause, or andropause, characterized by a gradual and variable decline in the production of androgenic hormones, the most known, testosterone, progresses slowly. As physical symptoms, the most notable are lack of emotional stability, a lump in the throat when dealing with more awkward situations, an every now and then tachycardia – all typically occurring during the work day. Good reasons to check with the doctor but rarely a reason to think one's life is being threatened.

For both men and women, Lievegoed describes: "the desire to be young again – as camouflage for the inner longing for something new in life – can lead to external projection of these needs." Something of the 'rooster in the man' becomes visible whereas women become a more frequent visitor to the beauty salon. The real question here is when this becomes conscious and how long it takes for both to understand that this is a temporary state of things, and then, to make a decision as to which way to embrace it or to let it go for the sake of "the real business in life, the realization of one's own *leitmotiv*."

# 20

# A Job is a Job is a Job?

*"Working all day, I'm digging up the roads, just working all day*
*Dig for my pay and spend it where I like. I've nothing to say*
*Drown in my sweat but money buys escape. I've got no regrets*
*Working all day."* – Shulman, Minear, Shulman

AMERICAN AUTHOR ROBERT GREENE'S VISION of work is fascinating: "The way to transforming yourself is through your work. Now, I know this runs counter to our prevailing cultural prejudices. Work is too ugly, too boring, too banal. Self-transformation, we think, comes through a spiritual journey, therapy, a guru who tells us what to do, intense group experiences and social experiences and drugs...but most of these are ways to run away from ourselves and relieving our chronic boredom. They are not connected to processes, so any changes that occur don't last. Instead, through our work we can actually connect to who we are instead of running away. And by entering that slow, organic process we can actually change ourselves from the inside out in a way that's very real and very lasting. This process involves a journey of self-discovery that can be seen as quite spiritual, if you like. And in the end of this process we can contribute something unique and meaningful to our culture – through our work, which is hardly ugly, boring or banal." *TEDxBriton, The Way to Transforming Yourself – Robert Greene*

There's no mystery in the significant distinction between the job we do and the work we do. Whereas a job is described as an activity, performed by an individual for a given objective, more specifically a task performed regularly for an agreed price, work refers to any kind of activity that involves physical or mental strain; work is performed by an individual as a duty or as a responsibility towards other people, like family, friends or even for self.

In a perfect world, there's no doubt that a job or employment should be treated as a vector of dignity in the workplace. Its definition is more or less like this: vector, commonly represented by a directed line segment whose length represents the magnitude and whose orientation in space represents the direction; combined with dignity, the quality or state of being worthy, honored, or esteemed. As I consciously avoid debating the merits or demerits of capitalism, we can't do much to support us and our loved ones unless we employ ourselves in exchange for money or use our talents to run our own income generation efforts. Nonetheless, whichever way we choose and the degree in which we are aware of the process, there ought to be key components to it: simply put, *purpose* and *no harm*.

When it relates to purpose, especially, I know it's no easy task. For some individuals, it comes fluidly. For others, it may take a lifetime. I am a firm believer that we all have the ability to find our purpose in the workplace and in life in general; and it may start with the most domestic but no less important things; like cleaning up our desk or decluttering our room, or yet clearing up our minds by getting rid of persistent habits and thoughts. To seek and find purpose is one of the best things we can do for ourselves. Once embraced, we have direction, peace within, the ability to stand up to any challenges that may come our way; most importantly, it brings character, self-awareness, and a greater understanding of our talents and abilities which can be applied, guess where? In the workplace! And beyond. In any work-related activity we do, be it as a volunteer, as an employee or as an entrepreneur, big or small.

## MAKING A LIVING IN THE GREEN MOUNTAIN STATE

Here is what American stand-up comedian Jeff Foxworthy has to say about Vermonters:

"Forget Rednecks .... If someone in a Home Depot store offers you assistance and they don't work there, you live in Vermont. If you've worn shorts and a parka at the same time, you live in Vermont. If you've had a lengthy telephone conversation with someone who dialed a wrong number, you live in Vermont. If Vacation means going anywhere south of New York City for the weekend, you live in Vermont. If you measure distance in hours, you live in Vermont. If you know several people who have hit a deer more than once, you live in Vermont. If you have switched from 'heat' to 'A/C' in the same day and back again, you live in Vermont. If you can drive 75 mph through 2 feet of snow during a raging blizzard without flinching, you live in Vermont. If you install security lights on your house and garage but leave both unlocked, you live in Vermont. If you carry jumpers in your car and your wife knows how to use them, you live in Vermont. If you design your kid's Halloween costume to fit over a snowsuit, you live in Vermont. If the speed limit on the highway is 55 mph, you're going 80 and everybody is passing you, you live in Vermont. If driving is better in the winter because the potholes are filled with snow, you live in Vermont. If you know all 4 seasons: almost winter, winter, still winter and road construction, you live in Vermont. If you have more miles on your snow blower than your car, you live in Vermont. If you find 10 degrees 'a little chilly', you live in Vermont. If there's a Dunkin Donuts on every corner, you live in Vermont. If you think everyone else has a funny accent, you live in Vermont. If you actually understand these jokes, and forward them to all your Vermont friends, you live or have lived in Vermont."

Early in the process of learning about Vermont in the context within New England, besides being the largest producer of maple syrup in the U.S., I knew Vermont was a unique place. Towards the end of Chapter 16, I mention the momentary slender professional perspective I am faced with in regards to the overall scenario of moving our family from the other side of the world to this great state. Unaware of the intricacies, my concern about subsistence, for a period of time, would be much less important than my intuitive certainty that this was the right thing to do. In mine and Silvia's mind, we would find the paths to substantiate the project. And my friend was there to help provide with the proper 'translation' from one culture to another. Lucky enough to have James guiding me through the process, I was also graciously granted the opportunity to run my plan by an immigration attorney who would help me figure out the equation to make this project materialize. Her name, Leigh Cole.

"EVERY JOB YOU'VE HELD AND EVERY RELATIONSHIP YOU'VE FORGED IS A KIND OF KEY THAT CAN UNLOCK A FUTURE OPPORTUNITY." – Anonymous

A thought on fear. Wisdom says that it starts with levels of anxiety, then it evolves to multiple stages of concern and ends up influencing and stressing out our system. Once the chain is unlocked, it escalates and it becomes prone to panic when we face ourselves, for example, with the unknown. With those three aspects being emotional states – deeply interconnected and a consequence of one another – it is imperative that cultivating awareness about the process helps us break and dissolve one or all three aspects. The rationale here is to avoid paralysis, from which fear is the mother of all failures.

With the unknown ahead of us, my challenge was clear: it was time for resolve. Leigh Cole was keen in bringing my potentialities to the table so she could design the right case for me professionally and, as a consequence, for my household, in order for us to live and enjoy the rights of legal individuals in this country. With the perspective of continuing to work with two of my most important clients in Brazil, now based in the U.S., my consulting experience enables me to set foot on the right path from day one. From which, in exchange, it helps Leigh gather the elements to build our legal case which could eventually culminate in the first steps toward immigration. I must emphasize that the idea of immigration had never seriously crossed our minds. Before even knowing of Eric's coming, what Silvia and I wanted was the option to provide a more thorough experience for the family. Now with the new baby, things could take that perspective to a whole new level.

Then, oh well, the undesirable. A few months before Eric was born, I learned that my exporter of Carnaúba Wax was going to pull the plug on his enterprise for selling his product directly to the market. Traditionally marketed through brokers, his initiative to promote me as his connection in the U.S. – aiming at limiting the influence of brokers – had been systematically undermined by the brokers themselves. I knew this could or could not work and now faced myself with a major obstacle: that monthly income was gone. To make things more interesting, or challenging if you will, my other client began having difficulties at his company. As a result, the steady income I had experienced since the decision to make the 180 degree move, as we get closer to the baby's coming, disappeared. You are on your own, man.

Once again, I encountered the ups and downs of the economy of my country of birth, which I thought could now take off, with the currency devalued and being more equated to the dollar. Not so fast. Besides, my initiatives toward promoting a large number of other goods could take many months and, in some cases, years until they could materialize. And unlike the other clients, none of the companies could afford to send me draws unless effective business got generated. Not a great place to be. Our savings would not last very long and the ticking of the clock put the pressure on.

## CARING FOR THE INDISPENSABLE

Eric's upcoming arrival was joyous. Pregnancy and the whole process throughout never being a simple undertaking, Silvia and I were blessed by her folks Mauricio and Elvira's visit a few months prior to his birth. Added to our good fortune and a couple of weeks apart, it was my parents turn now to spend several weeks with us through the baby's birth. With their four grandparents' presence, Catherine Bianca and GG had the rare opportunity to spend great quality time relating to them their new lifestyle – getting around to local and favorite travel sites, showing school grounds, introducing new friends, books and recently acquired skills. From our parents' perspective, other than their understanding of our decision and the enjoyment for watching the girls thrive, I can only imagine what might be going through our folks' minds – "Is this just a temporary thing?" "Will it last?" "Once the initial venture about being in a new country is germinated, will it grow to become permanent?" "Are they going to be alright?"

In their almost two months stay my Mom and Dad spent with us during Eric's birth, I never forgot one of my Dad's favorite observations: "Wow, those kids are young to be doing that." Everywhere he went and saw young men and women at work he would point out to me as if this had great significance for him. Especially, if the job would require skills not clearly associated with his own perception of one's learning process to perform a specific task. In other words, he was always positively amazed at seeing youngsters at work and yet being able to balance it out with school – something which was not culturally familiar for him, for example, a boy or a girl working at the supermarket after school.

Our experience with our folks at this time was different. While seven years earlier we thought about moving to Australia and faced significant resistance, the boundaries now were being fully respected. Additionally, our confidence had been building proportionally to our understanding of our role as parents and of what we wanted to offer our kids. We could sense our folks' silent emotional manifestation – a mix of admiration and uneasiness, intertwined. Most likely because what we as a household were doing had the powerful component of love, which is inevitably followed by intimacy – only found through true love between parents and offspring. Nothing strange to our folks, who were unquestionably supportive – a never to be forgotten partaking of their true love.

## FAITH, FREEDOM AND OPEN MIND

Our familial cell was complete. It's hands on and embracing the change is the name of the game. The universe will provide; The universe speaks in mysterious ways; You are not alone: these are not empty statements. Rather, they can be turned into powerful states of mind. It's all that it is. It's like acknowledging that the obstacles are there and that our understanding of time, space and matter is what makes the difference in the way we look and interpret them – obstacles can be the blessing in disguise, and they typically are.

With that steady income no longer there, the signals were evident that I would have to reinvent myself and my career. I had no problem with that and was open to go through the experience. If nothing else, another opportunity for learning. Passed the initial three-month adjustment after our loving little guy's arrival, I got a phone call from Mark Kelley for an interview. OE – Office Environments, a contract furniture organization, is an Integrated Interior Solutions company dedicated to the business, healthcare, education and government communities throughout Vermont and beyond its borders. This is quite a similar activity to what I used to do in the textile industry as a *converter*, to which design and customization were critical components. I succeeded in the interview. In a few days I got hired as a consultant, which would also perfectly match my work visa status. Forever thankful for that call, that job would become a significant milestone which would allow us to set a definitive step forward towards our goal.

Throughout the following years, I had more ups than downs and was able to build a consistent career in the industry. Aiming at shortening my commute, although I took great pleasure in being in Waterbury and next to my old friend James and his family, we were ready to move from Washington County to Chittenden County where we would be closer to Burlington, an area that offered more options to our household's preferable lifestyle, in multiple aspects.

# 21

# The Small Things.
# And The Big Things.

*"How does it feel, how does it feel?*
*To be without a home*
*Like a complete unknown, like a rolling stone."*
*Like a Rolling Stone* – Bob Dylan & Tom Petty

I PHONED MY FRIEND FABIO D'ONOFRIO in São Paulo and was glad to speak with his father after a long time. "Mr. Wilson, it's been years. How've you been? It's great to hear your voice!" After Eric's birth, it was time to catch up with the many friends who wrote warm welcoming words, via letters, emails and postcards. As we went through the initial bumpy three-month period where almost all the attention went exclusively to the new baby, I finally got time to reach out to one friend in particular. This was a friend I would love to have visiting us some time in the future, just like he did for a week in Fortaleza a few years earlier. The only chance I had to see Fabio D'Onofrio after that was when I stopped by in São Paulo on my way back to Vermont, exactly the year before. At that time, we got together for a few hours and I even picked on him: 'it's about time you quit smoking, man' – I had done that myself at least 18 years earlier. This is a typical attitude of former smokers toward dear ones, as if trying to 'save the world.' Amidst poking on my buddy's habit, my intention was obvious: "I want to see you in good shape, my friend."

It was late February, 2000 when I write the email to Fabio and had Dylan's lyrics in my mind. This was one of my favorite friends to hang out with, talk to and listen to great music during our teen years. He, a big *Yes* fan, myself a *Genesis* aficionado, we loved the prog-rock of the day. Not having heard from him in a while, I picked up the phone to call his home number in São Paulo. Fabio had built a nice house in Ubatuba a couple of years back, a beach town situated on the northern part of the coast between São Paulo and Rio. There he spent every weekend he possibly could along with his young daughter, Barbara. When in São Paulo, he dwells with his folks. A single dad, I wondered about his experience and how well he was managing the change.

Mr. Wilson briefly paused after my greetings and ardently began asking about our new life in Vermont. As a teenager, I would address older folks by their first names after Mr. or Mrs. I was extremely respectful to him in particular, most likely due to his always curious ways to approaching his son's friends, portraying himself as an equal and genuinely interested in our experiences as young men. After I enthusiastically exhausted the information to him, he calmly started to talk, almost as if narrating a story. The current month was April and he began to tell me that, in early March, Fabio went to the surrounding mountains of Campos do Jordão, in the *Vale do Paraiba*, State of São Paulo, to gather with a number of friends for their usual bike rides across the area. It was the end of summer, a beautiful and sunny Sunday, when the weather during this time of the year is typically stunning. "At some point of the itinerary, as the group speeded up, Fabio slowed down his rhythm after biking up a very steep portion of the trail and decided to take a break before continuing on the ride. There, as he tried to catch his breath, he parked the bike on the curb; very tired and after putting in the extra effort, he sat down on the sidewalk for proper rest. His legs partly folded on the trail line, his upper body stretched down by the lush green grass sidewalk." As I heard Mr. D'Onofrio's words, my brain was rapidly processing his words while looking for an answer as to why he was telling me all that and why I felt the way I did. Mr. Wilson, in a slow manner, placidly continued: "The extraneous effort, added to the heat of that day, and possibly not enough hydration, took a toll on his system, Renato. Unfortunately, he had a cardiac arrest and as he laid down, he peacefully passed away, right there..."

Standing up by the kitchen counter, my wife and kids watched me motionless, in shock and disbelief – and probably the first time, they saw their dad in tears.

"The shade of a cedar tree in the forest is not the same one as of a cedar tree which became a vessel mast, a temple cornerstone, or a gallows scaffold. Nor is that cedar tree's shade the same under the sun or at starlight, or at a twilight's rosy fog. Nevertheless, that cedar tree, no matter how much it has been transformed, lives like a cedar, although the other cedar trees no longer recognize it like one of them." *The Book of Mirdad, on Death* – Mikhail Naimy

> *"Close to the edge, down by the river*
> *Down at the end, round by the corner*
> *Seasons will pass you by*
> *Now that it's all over and done*
> *Called to the seed, right to the sun*
> *Now that you find, now that you're whole*
> *Seasons will pass you by"*
> – YES, Jon Anderson / Steve Howe

Farewell, my dear friend. It's been a pleasure and an honor.

# A JOB

The next three-plus years in the new career were very productive. Not always an easy industry to navigate, I successfully managed to learn the essentials of the contract furniture industry and counted on a good team of professionals. Moreover, leadership – savvy and skilled, but also demanding and somewhat impulsive at times – did a good job taking care of customers and employees. I was designated a large but complex account, which gave me the opportunity to ramp up my income and plan on moving closer to the Burlington area where Silvia and the girls saw as a more enticing area to live – schools, shopping, entertainment, restaurants, etc. and yet with a good feel for beautiful rural Vermont. With the real estate market tight, it was a seller's opportunity to make a profit. In our case, not much of an advantage since we were selling our house and buying a new one, anyway. Lucky on the sale and equally lucky on the purchase, our new house was larger, newer, more modern and our neighborhood seemed to be outstanding. Essex Junction has the reputation of having one of the best school systems in the state, which for us was one of the factors for moving into the area.

Experiencing the next couple of years in the contract furniture business, it was almost unavoidable to go through highs and lows. If the balance is positive, that's a bonus. As I've lived through before in my profession, I inevitably found out that the reality of living and working in Vermont has its downfalls too. While in Waterbury, taxes are lower and our mortgage a lot more affordable; In Chittenden County, taxes on the new house were higher and expenses in general would follow suit. The result, a gap in income. Besides, I had decided to finish up the house basement myself, which incurred additional investment - and more bills.

## TWO JOBS?

It was the year 2003 and Home Depot in Williston was the

sole box store in the region, selling truckloads of home improvement goods on a weekly basis. Besides being hands-on, my always available friend James gave me valuable tips in construction and on materials to acquire, whereas I hired a couple of contractors to help me with electrical and drop ceiling projects. For about 45 days, it was waking up at 5:30 a.m. and getting some work done followed by a full work day, only to get back home and do some more work in what would become a nice expansion to the house. The idea, to provide the kids a game/TV – room mixed with gym, office space and storage. With some boo-boos typical of an adventurous beginner, the basement was finished and it was time to enjoy – and also pay for the added value to the house. Perhaps I could add another source of income at the same spot I'm getting the supplies? It's a no-brainer and worthwhile going the extra mile to help pay for the work in the basement. Another 20 hours a week on top of my full time job? Hmmm, I think I can make it.

## 50 GOLDEN YEARS

"Fifty years of marriage, over 2,609 weeks together, 18,263 days of bliss, 438,321 hours of love, 1 blessed family, 1000s of laughs, countless happy memories, a never ending love story." I read that on a post card at a Hallmark store. So true. To watch a young couple in love is quite a thrill, but to closely experience your own folks aging and nurturing their love for one another is such a treat. Reaching that milestone is an achievement in partnership and such a moment is carefully lived with gratitude and joy. Although at a distance, I have always been very close to René and Jeritza and would not have missed their anniversary by any means. Silvia, Eric and I flew to São Paulo while the girls stayed at home. School and the high expenses at a time of cost control were the decisive factors. At 15 and 13 years old, we knew it was quite a responsibility and trusted them to take care of one another. Besides, it was only going to be for a few days and the Meades agreed to check on them on a daily basis.

I can easily state that my parents were the kind of parents many kids would hope to have as both always strived for harmony and understanding. Balanced and inspiring in their demeanor, they were not perfect, like no one is; however, they were perfect for us in the sense of their presence, love and support. Like any couple, both had hit a few rough patches but took pride in the learned knowledge to work through things as a team. As March 14$^{th}$ came, the celebration proceeds wonderfully. Gathering with people I hadn't seen in many years was worth the effort. For the three of us, as well as for many of our friends and relatives, that was the unique opportunity to get together and rejoice. Especially for our young boy, only 3 ½ years old, it was a rare chance to meet family and loved ones for the first time. Priceless moments.

## SUMMER 2003

My tenure at OE came to an end. An intense learning period now gave way to new opportunities. As I quickly joined another contract furniture player in town, BI – Business Interiors, with headquarters in Brattleboro, I kept my part time job at Home Depot until my bills were fully paid off. Conveniently located at less than half a mile from one another, the two jobs provide what my household needs for supporting the new lifestyle. With the girls already adapted to the new school system, it is now time for Eric to join pre-school activities. Not an inexpensive environment, Silvia visited Racquet's Edge to learn about their unique children's experience program running from ages 6-weeks to 12 years old. As we looked for a school atmosphere which prioritized a less academic program in exchange for a more ludic and child-centered activity, the school seemed to correspond to our expectations of an 'exploration-based philosophy environment,' as defined by the school. This seemed to be a good fit where our boy can also experiment a wide choice of sports, from tennis to climbing wall to swimming to basketball and several other options. That visit to the school opened up great possibilities: on one hand, Eric can get exposed to a different spectrum of interests that can well turn into healthy habits and give him a good sense of discipline and social interaction. On the other hand, this one was not expected: when wrapping up a discussion with one of the teachers, Silvia was encouraged to apply for a job where she could undoubtedly contribute with her great experience as a teacher and as a mom. And to make things more interesting, she could get tuition free for Eric. It was cakewalk, there are no second thoughts.

## A DARK CLOUD IN THE NEIGHBORHOOD

Life is good at Fairview Farm. Every Friday afternoon after work, from spring through fall, the neighbors gather and unwind in the backyard of a given household. Neighbors alternate hosting the gatherings in a casual but organized way, contributing to the sense of community in the area. Many are IBMers and have young kids, which also contributes to the familiarity among its members. A relatively new development, most of the houses at the upper part of the development have been there for only 5-6 years. Our family could not have chosen a better spot: internally, the house is just the right size for us, while our backyard is large enough to accommodate virtually any outdoor activity with a substantial number of people – from soccer to volleyball to frisbee golf to badminton, you name it.

Fall recently started along with the beginning of the school year, the day is Tuesday, October $7^{th}$. As I drove off to work first thing in the morning, I noticed a police car parked at one of our neighbor's driveway, located three houses down from ours. With one of our neighbors being a state police officer, that unusual scene was not necessarily intriguing since the police car resembles his work vehicle. Driving by at normal speed and with no action to be perceived, I took it as an uneventful situation. Notwithstanding, as I got in the office, I got a call from my wife. That tragic day would change the Halligan family's lives forever, and to an extent, our neighborhood's, our town's, our

State's and our country's too.

Ryan was the same age as GG, both classmates at Albert D. Laughton Middle School. He was described by his father John as a "gentle, very sensitive soul," who experienced some developmental delays affecting speech and physical coordination in his early school years. Although he overcame those difficulties by fourth grade, John went on to say "He still struggled; school was never easy to him, but he always showed up with a smile on his face, eager to do his best." At 10 years old, he suffered bullying at the hands of a group of students at his school because of his learning disorder, his passion for music (drums and guitar), and his love for drama. His father said that when Ryan told him he was being picked on, his initial response was to ignore the boys, as they were just bullying him with words. Nevertheless, the bullying continued for the next 2 years.

Like many kids of his generation, Ryan spent much of his time online, particularly on AIM and other instant messaging services. He did not tell his parents about that and used up a great deal of his summer in front of the computer. During this period, he was cyber-bullied by schoolmates who taunted him, thinking he was gay. His father later learned that on one occasion, Ryan ran out of the classroom in tears. Ryan had unintentionally archived online conversations on his hard drive when he installed DeadAIM, to which his father was able to read these discussions. Ryan had deliberately saved transcripts of online exchanges with a popular girl whom he had a crush on, who pretended to like him. Later at school, she told him that she was only kidding and that he was a "loser." According to an ABC Primetime report, she had once been his friend and defended him when the bullying first started, but as she became more popular, she left him behind. He found out she only pretended to like him to gain personal information about him. She copied and pasted their private exchanges into other IMs among his schoolmates, culminating in embarrassment and humiliation.

On that day, Ryan's dad was away on a business trip. Early in the morning, when the other family members were still sleeping, Ryan hanged himself with a bathrobe tie that belonged to his older sister, who later found his body. Although Ryan left no suicide note, his father learned of the devastating cyberbullying thread when he accessed on his son's computer.

Not close friends but close enough to deeply sympathize with their horrific and indescribable experience, I could only imagine what John, Kelly and the two siblings were going through. The bright side of this heartbreaking story, if there's one, was that John took it to a totally new level. After much grieving and forgiving of the characters involved, he soon began lobbying for legislation in Vermont to improve how schools address bullying and suicide prevention. Over the years, he has given speeches to schools in various states about the story of his son and the destructive effects of cyber-bullying among teens.

Vermont enacted a Bullying Prevention Policy Law in May 2004 and later adopted a Suicide Prevention Law (Act 114) in 2005, closely following a draft submitted by Ryan's father. The law provides measures to assist teachers and others to recognize and respond to depression and suicide risks among teens. Ryan Halligan's case has also been cited by legislators in other states proposing legislation to curb cyber-bullying.

Ryan's story was featured on a Frontline television program entitled "Growing Up Online," produced in January 2008, by WGBH-TV in Boston and distributed nationwide over PBS. In it, his father recounts his shock upon discovering the extent of the abuse his son endured, saying he believes that bullying on the internet "amplified and accelerated the hurt and pain he was trying to deal with, that started in the real world." Ryan's story has also been featured on Oprah in a report they did on a rise in homophobic teasing in schools. In addition, his father presented his powerful assembly to many schools across the country.

Ryan's story was also featured in the 2018 documentary, *Stories of Strength and Hope: Preventing Youth Suicide*, supported by an on-screen interview with John Halligan. Today John visits other schools to inform students about his son's death and how it has changed his life.

"EVERYONE WE MEET IS FIGHTING A BATTLE
WE KNOW NOTHING ABOUT."– Anonymous

Resilient, our neighborhood quickly joined in to support the Halligan's and to assist one another, especially the youngsters. There are always the angels who draw incredible strength from within to provide the so necessary help and comfort in times of despair. Despite the tragedy, the Friday gatherings resumed at the Halligan's request. We gathered for some time until another neighbor's passing occurred. Troy Siemen, a loving father of three, aged 43, of a sudden cardiac arrest. This would interrupt the work week's end get-together indefinitely but yet, kept our neighborhood tightly connected.

### HE'S GONE AWAY

April 23rd, 2004. We arrived a few hours earlier from a trip to Portland, Maine after a pleasant few days by the ocean. The weather was still a little cool but we were excited to have gone through another winter and now were ready to embrace spring time. Already in bed, I got a heavyhearted call from my sister Liliana from my parents' home: "Mom called me and I rushed over. I'm sitting next to Dad. He is not breathing. We've lost him."

Dad and Mom enjoyed watching movies on TV Friday nights. Scheduled to travel to the countryside to visit his brother Sergio in *Atibaia* the next morning, the plan was not to stay up late. Passed 9:00 p.m. and with the movie still running, he stood up and lightly complained about a minor discomfort on the left side of his mid-upper back. Stating it was nothing of a concern, as a customary habit he went to the living room, sat on his favorite Victorian-style high-back chair and prepared for a nap. Leaning on, he rested his cheek on his right back hand, elbow supported on the armchair, as if looking for a position of comfort. As Mom kept watching the movie to the end, it took her some time to picture he must have fallen deeply asleep on his chair. "Time for bed," she realizes. Yawning, she stepped out of the TV room. As she walked by the living room, all lights are atypically off. On the way to the kitchen area to reach for a glass of water, she sensed an incredibly unusual silence. Nothing she had ever experienced before. Her senses on the alert, back from the kitchen she attempted to wake him up, only to shockingly find out that he was already gone. Peaceful and serene, in the exact position as if he was taking a nap.

Here's a letter one of his friends wrote to my Mom after knowing of my father's passing:

*São Paulo, April 28th, 2004*

*Dear Jeritza,*

*For days I have been trying to write to you.*
*I would like to share with you my sensation of loss.*
*I want you to know that, besides my children and my brother, René was my best friend. I had for him special considerations and care, without limitations, more than any other human being.*
*I am sure it was reciprocated.*
*I played cards with René for many years, thousands of hours, and we never, never had anything that could alter our affection for one another, no word or gesture which was nothing but respect; and, you know, at card games, it is common to have misunderstandings.*
*It is a little silly but, the respect he had for me was so great that at times he would call me sir, most likely by the fact that I am a physician.*
*From all people in the world, if I could choose a partner for a given card game, I would always choose him, as I did while playing several tournaments, even out of our usual venue at the club.*
*The last time we were together, the Tuesday before his passing, while he was playing, I kept looking at him and thinking to myself: How extraordinary is René, how can he, with so many cards in his hand, and with only one functional eye, see so well all the existing possibilities.*

*It was at this day he told me that you had a vernissage, or an exhibition of some sort, and that he shouldn't have come to play, but yet he ended up making an effort to come. We made comments as to how sweet you are, a special person in my way of looking at you, and that you were probably very affectionate to him. We talked about that you two were a gift to one another, given how formidable you two were.*

*I joked and said that you are fabulous, but he was... just ok!*

*He laughed hard and said: "I know you are kidding but, I want you to know that actually I used to be more 'raw' and that it was my wife that made me a better person." With love, she taught me very much."*

*Then after, I took him home. He said – "My goodness, we will have six continuous days of 'tranca' (the card game), as Wednesday will be a holiday. It will be so cool!!!*

*As we got closer to your apartment building, he said – "You can drop me at the street corner."*

*I answered, "No way. I will drop you off at the door, and won't give chance a chance!!"*

*I waited until he got through the gate, he waived me goodbye, and that was the last time I saw him!!*

*What a pity!!!!"*

*Sammy Gois*

Dad was like...I could go on and on to try and describe the man. However, it's how one feels about someone or a loved one who departs that really counts. At age 19 or 20, Cat Stevens' "Father and Son" helped me shape, right or wrong, my understanding of that time of my life and my relationship with my Dad, and all the 'dads' in the world. The authoritative figure is at times uncomfortable and at that age it gets confounded with an authoritarian perception, in its worst sense. Here's a key verse of the song:

*"How can I try to explain, cause when I do*
*he turns away again*
*And it's always been the same, same old story*

*From the moment I could talk I was ordered*
*to listen*
*Now there's a way and I know*
*that I have to go away*
*I know I have to go"*

It would not take too long though, I would say probably at around 25, to reverse that image of authority and replace it with a deeper understanding of my Dad's relevance to me. And to neutralize the image of authority as a whole in its symbolism and myriads of forms. Many years passed, it's another song, this one written by Peter Gabriel, "Father, Son" that reveals parts of the reality between these two entities, so closely connected:

*Father, son*
*Locked as one*
*In this empty room*
*Spine against spine*
*Yours against mine*
*Till the warmth comes through*

*Remember the breakwaters down by the waves*
*I first found my courage*
*Knowing daddy could save*
*I could hold back the tide*
*With my dad by my side*

Such meaningful lyrics. Since I was a little kid, I grew up watching my Mom concerned about my Dad's diet and the consequences of him being a 'good gourmet.' The result throughout the years was that every now and then he would experience minor to major health issues such as stomach ulcers, gout, high blood pressure and cardiac problems. Gout, although not life threatening, was the worst of all. I had countless memories of him going through excruciating joint pains, every time he went through a crisis – shoulders, knees, wrists, knuckles, bunions just about every joint. During his late years, he would turn to a more moderate diet, which helped him put the darn gout away. Notwithstanding, his heart condition was there, unknowingly manifesting initially at his mid-to-late fifties. He would only learn that he had had a cardiac arrest probably ten years later. Physically strong, he simply took that acute pain and shrugged, ignoring that it would have been appropriate to consult a heart specialist, only to learn from more than one doctor years later the strong recommendation for a coronary artery bypass grafting, also known as open heart surgery. At 65, primarily against my will – I thought he should exhaust and try non-invasive methods of treatments first – he successfully underwent the surgery. The surgery was good for his heart but caused multiple side effects – prostate and bladder issues – it took him several months to recover. From there, he would live for another fourteen years. It makes me think that that period gave him the opportunity to balance out habits and better realize our fragility as human beings.

"Pai Grande", translated as Big Dad, a song by Milton Nascimento, deeply reflects the powerful relationship between these so tightly unified creatures:

*My big dad*
*I still remember*
*And how I miss you*
*Saying: "I already raised your father*
*Today I will raise you*
*Still have much living to do*

*My big dad*
*I wish I had the courage to tell*
*The history of the warriors*
*Brought from far away*
*Without their peace*

*Of my longing without your singing*

*From where I came from*
*It's good to remember*
*Every man of truth*
*Was strong and without malice*
*The day goes by*
*And the day comes by*

*Every son of yours*
*Following the steps*
*And a little corner to die*
*To where I've come*
*I will not cry*
*Don't want to leave anymore*

*This is my people now*
*If I'm here*
*I brought it from there*
*A love so far from lies*
*Wants whoever wants to love me*

The man, admired and respected by many – family, friends and acquaintances – had a good life altogether. A savvy and honest businessman, his curiosity also made him relish traveling. Joyful by nature, he loved a good joke and would often pull up a couple of good ones to entertain friends and family. His last moment was spent the way he liked the most: enjoying a good nap, for which he had no problems finding an adequate spot. This last one, an everlasting experience.

So long, my old man. I will always love you.

## THE JOURNEY SOUTHBOUND

Post-mortem procedures in Brazil are somewhat different than those in the U.S. Although the immediate family has the right to refuse or agree to a hospital autopsy of the deceased in both countries, embalming for funeral purposes, unless in very specific cases, is not typically an option in Brazil. Therefore, burials are accomplished the next day after an individual's passing, which gives no option to family members to attend the burial ceremony when required to travel a period that exceeds 24 hours after the passage. That was my case and the idea of not being around my Mom and sisters bothered me for not being able to see my Dad for the last time. As I processed the impact, I've come to realize that there is also a silver lining. The heartfelt memory of him, reserved but always laughing and smiling, would supersede by far that last moment. Moreover, I had no choice.

The next available flight to São Paulo was Sunday night, which would get me to Guarulhos Airport early in the a.m. As I landed in the big city, my goal was to approach my Mom to come stay with us in Vermont for a few months, then suggest that she could extend the trip to Mexico and spend some time with her sister Gloria and husband Nico. As I got picked up by my sister Cristina and my mother, she was immediately receptive to the idea and we already started making plans. Happy to see them both, they were equally glad to have me around, especially at that very moment. As much as a sudden death may likely benefit the deceased, as opposed to longer periods of illness which take a heavy toll on everyone, for the family it's always a difficult event to process. It has been a year since the 50-year anniversary celebration and I could tell that they saw me as a breath of fresh air. I promised myself not to disappoint them and made sure that during my short stay we would keep a positive vision from present to future.

"Why should suffering play so powerful and widespread a role in mortal life? What is its significance for personal development? Did we sow its seeds in a previous existence? If so, what fruit will it bear in the future? One way we can sense the value of pain is by viewing it as a catalyst, an agent of change and transformation." *The Veiled Pulse of Time – The Seasons of Immortality* – William Bryant

## A TALENTED ARTIST

*"You're an artist when you say you are. And you're a good artist when you make somebody else experience or feel something deep or unexpected."*
– Amanda Palmer

Jeritza has them all. Persistence, Patience, Passion, A Sense of Adventure and Discipline, the key attributes of successful artists. Years back, during her most active period when traveling through Europe and the USA participating at multiple exhibitions, Carlotta Clara Baukelmann, President of one of São Paulo's Visual Artists Associations described her profile:

"Jertiza Wakim is a person who strives for perfection. This immensely talented artist presents her very best work, even in the smallest details of her paintings. Her work touches the human spirit with its perfection. She shows extreme sensitivity in her use of themes and colors. A look at life through her diverse work shows a life that is a great work of art. Her pieces have the power to awaken artistic selves and open the eyes of the dreamer that lives in us all. The reality of the life we live is seen in the beauty, transparency and softness conveyed in her portraits, in which it seems Jeritza truly places her own soul. Her success and recognition are not simply results of accomplishments or challenges that Jeritza has met. They are truly deserved."

I remember once asking my Mom, "How do you do it?" Expecting a technical and most elaborate answer, she simply says: "I don't know, it just comes naturally." As I picked her up at the Burlington International Airport in mid-June 2004, a month and a half after Dad's departure, I was convinced that it would be a good option for her to experience a new environment and, if she deemed appropriate, to be able to continue developing her incredible artistic skills from a new perspective. Most of the time a positive personality, she cheerfully embraced the idea and we began discussions around the next steps.

Silvia and the children were happy to see grandma and to be able to help. Jeritza hadn't been in Vermont since Eric's birth, so the new house did accommodate her better and more comfortably. As the days went by, Mom's presence was delightful for us and the kids, especially for the little guy, who was now almost 5 years old. Her sweet voice and ability for story-telling had always been an enjoyment for the girls at their early infancy, when we were still living around our parents. Now, it was Eric's opportunity to experience grandma's loving more closely.

Mom has been a retired school teacher for many years. She has always been very active: in her lifetime, she painted more than 400 paintings, many of them from her mid-life age onwards. Be it for pleasure, commissioned or as give-away presents, she has also consistently attended multiple local, regional, nationwide and international events where her art could be exhibited along with renowned artists, or at her own exclusive vernissages. Vermont being a fertile ground for the arts in general, I had no doubt that she could keep herself busy and even possibly develop some commission work among acquaintances and friends, or even at galleries.

As I told our neighbors Renee and Brad of my Mom's upcoming visit a few days prior to her arrival, I learned that Renee's father is not doing well. Sadly, his illness was severe and he might not be around for much longer. Aware that Jeritza's specialty is portraits using oil on canvas, Renee let me know that Tony Citro had always wanted to have his portrait done. A former military official, he had in the past expressed his wish to be portrayed in uniform. As the idea matures on followed by a few days after Jeritza's arrival, she met with Renee and felt she could do the job. As they agreed on how he was to be pictured, Renee took a photo of her dad in uniform, already weakened by the illness, and also brought us another photo along. This one of her wedding day a few years earlier, where Tony has a big smile. In days, Jeritza drew the definitive blending of the two pictures and initiates the paint work on the portrait. No one could tell how much time Renee's dad would withstand his condition, therefore it became a race against time. In less than a month and working many hours every day, she pulled it out and delivers the portrait. Tony was very weak but still able to see the final product. He would only live for another two weeks after that. Saddened, yet we all felt some sense of accomplishment that his wish had been fulfilled.

## LEARNING TO NAVIGATE THE UNKNOWN

Grief is inevitable and can take unexpected forms, says the American Cancer Society: "Many people think of grief as a single instance or as a short time of pain or sadness in response to a loss – like the tears shed at a loved one's funeral. But grieving includes the entire emotional process of coping with a loss, and it can last a long time. The process involves many different emotions, actions, and expressions, all of which help a person come to terms with the loss of a loved one."

I was not sure how well Mom would navigate the process and wanted to be supportive to whatever her needs were. We respected her privacy at all times and, at the same token, we went out and did things to keep her heart and mind aware of the care she needed to provide to herself, physically and emotionally. Always protective of her, my Dad had been a provider throughout his life. And a nurturer, in its deepest sense. She sure missed that.

Our frequent gatherings with the Meades, along with Wanda's and her daughters' attention to her, were also key to her sense of feeling welcome during her stay in Vermont. Language being somewhat of a deterrent to plain communication, they always made sure to make her feel at home – especially when playing the card game *Tranca*, which my Dad had taught them all how to play. He is revered as the master, '*Le Professeur*', as James liked to address him. Another commission work and three other paintings kept my mother productive to the extension of her stay with us. Besides, we visited a large number of galleries throughout the state in order to get a sense of present and future opportunities. As our immigration status evolved to allow us the option to possibly sponsor our folks, we contemplated some professional activity in case she decided to spend longer periods of time with us in the future. After three mutually gratifying months, she was ready to go to Mexico where she would spend another month along with her beloved sister. Gloria and Nico, being world travelers and high-spirited individuals, would certainly provide her with love and cherishing before she returns home.

## REALITY SINKS IN

In essence, reality consists of our interactions with changing environments. Not until my Mom was back home to realize that the sense of loss was deeper in her own realm. As days went by, I stayed in touch with her frequently. At every phone conversation, I could grasp her struggles with the new reality. My sisters were happy to have her back, especially Liliana who lives closer to her. An accomplished psychologist, Liliana and her husband Marco, himself also a psychologist, along with their son René, are always supportive and know how to perceive Mom's moods. Being 5,000 miles away from her, I could not be more thankful for their love and affection. A wonderful family, they are a strong bedrock of care and assistance to her.

At home, the girls and Eric are thriving. Catherine Bianca, 16, begins to investigate the possibility for a Rotary Exchange Student program in the next school year, starting in September; it looks like Chile would be her destination. GG, 14, was growing up and enjoying her friends at school. Eric loved swimming and reveled in meeting and playing with new friends. My most admiration went to my wife as she flourishes in her profession. A year into the new job, kids and parents enthusiastically embrace her teaching style coupled with her extreme dedication to the young creatures in formation. I could not be more proud of her: hard work and courage, a key recipe for success, pays off anywhere. In any condition. Invaluable.

The year was 2005, it was school winter break in Vermont and summertime in the southern hemisphere. We all decide to run away from the last leg of that winter to spend a week with my Mom at her beach house on the northern coast of São Paulo, *Praia da Baleia,* Whale's Beach. Years back, my Dad had built a nice house located in a condominium where, if not spending weekends along with family and friends, this would be a good investment to generate income via daily or seasonal rentals. A magnificent beach area, this was, and still is, one of the few pristine and protected environments from real estate over-exploitation. From Antofagasta, Chile, Catherine Bianca flew over to join us during our vacation. We all had a great time and truly enjoyed being there – what a treat in the middle of the always cold weather at home. As our oldest daughter returned to Chile, GG and I flew back home earlier for school and work; Silvia and Eric remained in São Paulo for a few more days in order to spend a lengthier period with her family. Then, a big, unpleasant surprise: the day before flying back home, Silvia parked what used to be my Dad's car in front of Mom's apartment a few hours in the afternoon only to come back and find out that the car had...disappeared. Stolen, another way to call it, to be precise. Great, another infuriating experience in that mega city which I so despise when going through such miserable situations. It is not the first time, nor the second. A third experience that I can remember...

It was mid-April, almost a year after Dad's passing. Silvia and Eric were back, I was on the road and my cellphone ringed. Phone calls from Brazil to the U.S., especially when calling cellphones, are a lot more expensive that the other way around. Hence, my typical initiatives to call my Mom to spare her from spending unnecessarily. As I pulled over on Interstate 89 and picked up her unusual call, her voice did not sound good. Gloomy and disconsolate, she let me know that in the past week or so her stomach had not been well and her doctor asked her to run some tests with a certain urgency. "With the results at hand, my doctor calls me to give me the most surprising news." With a broken voice but yet accepting tone, she says: "I have cancer. Stomach cancer. The doctor wants me to go through surgery as soon as possible." I paused. Her news, as devastating as it sounds, had an interesting effect on me. For some reason, I seemed to have the answer figured out. With uncommon calm and conviction – what do we know about cancer and its unfolding consequences, right? – I said: "Mom, don't worry, you will be just fine. Has the doctor given you a date as to when the surgery will take place?" To which she replied: Next Saturday, April 23$^{rd}$. "Mom, stay cool. I will be there on Monday morning."

Cumulative grief, also known as grief overload is more common than we think. It should be obvious that "age can increase the risk of cumulative grief," says the blog WYG – What's Your Grief." "As individuals progress into their 70s, 80s, and 90s they most certainly find themselves experiencing the deaths of friends and family members more regularly than earlier in life. This can put them at a higher risk for cumulative grief. This is without even considering the other losses they are prone to, like loss of home, independence, and identity, as well as the fact that their grief may be minimized by society if those they lose are elderly."

At 75, although more fragile, Mom had always been healthier than Dad. More moderate by nature, she knows exactly what was appropriate for her, i.e., balanced eating habits or minimum to no-alcohol consumption, as good examples. She knows what should be avoided as her liver would unmistakably signal. "Now this?" she was asking herself. My trip to São Paulo, less than two months from my last visit, now had a sole purpose: I didn't think that her cancer had anything to do with her physical health but rather with her relationship with my father's death. Therefore, with a little research, I got that what is known scientifically as "broken heart syndrome" has more to do with the concept of not being able to live after your significant other is gone. Triggered by a devastating event, age and a pre-existing condition may play a vital role in combination with the syndrome. With all that in mind, I had one and only question for her: "Mom, do you want to go or do you want to stay?" Without any explanations to her, she intuitively knew what I was talking about. Her immediate response was: "I think I still have things to do here."

Of all the scientific road map coupled with mystical reasons to try and explain all that was happening, there's two that boggle the mind to this day and would define our experience: one, as it relates to the stolen car several weeks earlier, she learned that the insurance would finally pay the premium of about the same amount of the car's value, the total necessary to pay for her surgery with the doctor of her choice and trust – her current health insurance would not cover the specialist. The second, the more interesting of the two, the day of the surgery: April 23rd, would fall on the same exact day of her husband's one-year death anniversary. Coincidence? Maybe. Maybe not.

I couldn't stay for the extent of the surgery and its outcome as my flight back was scheduled to leave early that evening; however, I left with some sense of achievement: from the airport and just before my departure, I learned from Liliana that the surgery went exceptionally well. All of the cancer cells seemed to have been properly extirpated without affecting other organs, which brought us a great sense of relief. Now, with a fifth of her original stomach size, her life would not be quite the same. She would have to start over from an all new perspective.

## A STORY LIKE NO ONE

Having been away from relatives and friends for some time now did not necessarily mean I had forgotten them. Quite the contrary. My hope, on the other hand, was that they wouldn't find it too awkward if I reached out to them, like old friends for example, after a long period of time. "What is time anyway, if we squander it?" I had once read it. While in São Paulo, the day before my Mom's surgery and my travel back, I wanted to try to find an old friend I had known since kindergarten seeing that our lives took different turns.

Machi didn't get a chance to finish up college as his father unexpectedly passed away; his choice, more like necessity, was to take over the family business during his freshman year. It turned out that his life process speeded up and he ended up getting married to his high school sweetheart, both at an early age – the wedding that I never got to attend back in 1980. I knew they had had two children, whom I'd never met, one more reason I wanted to reconnect with my old buddy. My Mom had been in touch with him from time to time for repair, purchase or to sell off any given piece of jewelry. I wasn't sure if he had known about my Dad's passing the year before; in retrospect, I think I was probably looking for some identity around our experiences which could justify not letting the opportunity pass by without seeing him, while being in the city where we both had grown up.

It took two or three calls to find him: surprised to hear from me, we immediately set up a time to meet up at one of his stores, located at the famous *Rua Augusta*. I took a taxi and quickly get to the *Jardins*. Glad to see that handsome Italian smile, and immediately inquiring about one another, we walked out of the store to a nearby restaurant for a quick bite. Neither one of us had much time – it was Friday afternoon, traffic and the approach to close of business would soon make things hectic in the big city. As I ordered a light meal, Machi goes for a cup of coffee. "How are you man, so happy we could make it. How's life?" He played it back and asked about my life and family in the U.S. as we began the usual catch up process. Once my meal arrived, I basically stopped talking upon returning to my initial question. With his usual composed and calming voice, my friend would describe to me his hair-rising, life change, mind-blowing experience – something close to the unthinkable.

Several years back at age 13, his boy and oldest child contracted a very serious illness. A rare disease, leukemia is one of the most common cancers for people under the uncommon teenage years to become gravely ill. What I learned through the years is that it affects the body causing a number of problems and side effects. Starting in the soft, inner part of the bones – bone marrow – it often moves quickly into the blood. It can then spread to other parts of the body, such as the lymph nodes, spleen, liver, central nervous system and other organs. "We caught the problem at its early stages and addressed it swiftly. Nonetheless, its progression could be unpredictable as we didn't know how aggressive it would be. For an active teenager as he was, symptoms like fatigue, fever, bruising, headaches, nose bleeding, weight loss and frequent infections would become the new norm in his all-changed routine. As for myself and my wife, all we could do was to be supportive and caring at all times. His sister, a little younger than him, would experience the intensity of what her brother was going through the most." As I heard his words, I stopped eating and gave him my undivided attention. "School, friends and the normal activities we generally take for granted slowly begin to fade away from his ordinary life. The illness is now part of him and no doctor, or team of specialists, knew for sure if curable or, best case scenario, how long he would have to live with it."

I had seen my friend Machi lose his temper only once, during one of the many *handebol* games we played in college together. Now, while listening to him relate this story in such a calm manner, flashes of the time when he lost his dad came to my mind. As I remembered his demeanor, even though not being the oldest child, he was the one to hold his family tight together – mom and two older siblings. His balance and coolness could be decisive during hard times. Real hard times like this one. While I tried to make sense of his family ordeal, his phone ringed a couple of times. The first call was from his daughter, letting him know she would be going from point A to point B and would call again soon. The second call was from his son, now close to being in his early-twenties, asking for some information or advice. What a good dad my friend is, I quietly reflect on that with a sense of relief. It looked like things seemed to have taken a positive course, I sighed.

After hanging up, he proceeded: "The disturbing thing about

all this is that this situation didn't last only for a few months. It took nearly five years. In three occasions, it was as if we were going through a hurricane or a major natural disaster. I thought my son wouldn't make it and had already prepared for the worse. As a consequence, I thought his mom could have a break down and do something insane. In several occasions, we would hug each other so tight as if losing one another was imminent and inevitable." As much as I could grasp what he and his family went through, I had no idea of what the outcome could be.

Another call from one of his children, this time I could not tell who it was. As the quick phone call was over, Machi continued on the jaw-dropping unfolding of the story: "My son was already 18 when his health miraculously began to give signs of recovery. All this time, his immune system, previously compromised with side effects that would manifest through infections, slowly begins to improve. Unbeknownst to us, the several years of despair, coupled with relentless caregiving and exclusive dedication, would take a heavy toll on us in different ways. His mom, not surprisingly, the most affected. Powerless and desperate to run away from that maddening situation, my wife hadn't done anything stupid yet. But I could see the potential for damage. I just wouldn't know what she was capable of. Paradoxically to his health betterment followed by a successful transplant of his bone marrow, things would take a turn I could never have imagined. My daughter's boyfriend, a 15-year old young man, also a close friend to my son, had been accompanying the process throughout the years and was very close to all of us. Then, the unimaginable: my wife, derailed from her ground, would be the link that would break and rupture the family bond. Madly in love with one another, my wife and the young man simply vanished from our sight. To this day."

At that moment, my brain could not process much more. "How in the world could something like that happen?" I asked him trying to conceive of that unbelievable nightmare. "I've tried to find a reason or a philosophical explanation to it but I'm afraid I will never have an answer...other than moving on and being there for my son and daughter, unrestrictedly and unconditionally..."

# 22

# It Comes and Goes in Waves

*"I don't want a pickle*
*Just want to ride on my motorcycle*
*And I don't want a tickle*
*'Cause I'd rather ride on my motorcycle*
*And I don't want to die*
*I just want to ride on my motorcycle."*
The Motorcycle Song – Arlo Guthrie

MY FRIEND'S AND HIS FAMILY'S EXPERIENCE would stick to my mind for quite some time. His inner strength inspired me to look deeper into my own microcosm of values, people, ideas and places and inevitably become more assertive when it comes to covering the holes of my existence.

Freedom. In this country, where this memoir is being written, freedom has a special meaning. Probably more than any other nation on this planet. Dissidents in countries such as Sudan, Yemen, Afghanistan, Egypt and even Russia and China are perhaps the bravest people on Earth. It's no easy business to stand up to their governments despite the risk of imprisonment or death, thinking, doing and saying what they please. Kudos to such courage.

"That's it!" I nearly yell. Bill and Gordon are chatting, it's mid-to-late afternoon, we had had a good week and the day in the office is winding down. One of those things that, once you see it, smell it, taste it or hear it, helps trigger a dormant thing inside yourself you don't even know was there. Bill says: "If there's one thing that I regret not having done at this time of my life is having a motorcycle." Darn it. As I walked by their workstations and overheard Bill Flowers' words, that was a firecracker sound to my ears. "Are you kidding, Bill?" I interject. "Let's do it!" Both looked at me as if I had taken those words very seriously. "What's the plan?" I asked. He smiled and, between looking at Gordon and myself, he went: "There's a Motorcycle Safety Training class happening in St. Albans at the end of the month. If it weren't for Carol to certainly oppose to my initiative in that direction, I would have done it a long time ago."

It was July and the window for outdoor activity in Vermont would not last long. Ideally, we would have two full good months to enjoy the weather if we were to venture into that new project. As I got the details of the MST class, I immediately enrolled in it. Bill, skeptical but yet inspired by my move, raised the courage to do the same. "What the heck, let's give it a try. Besides, I don't have to tell Carol I am going to go for it until it's done." Whatever he had in mind, my plan was a little more aggressive and clearly defined: I was going to get a motorcycle, park it at home and start riding it right after the class was done.

Without asking for permission, I went ahead and did it. It only took a few days to get the 1300 cc Silver Honda VTX Cruiser in my garage. My wife's reaction was pretty cool: "Hmmm, I didn't know you liked motorcycling." To which I replied: "To be honest, I didn't know either." Bill was impressed and soon would embark on the same path. Gordon Edmonds, the senior of the three of us, seemed curious and likely pondered "What if I did it?" Curious, but not enough to make him experiment that route. An excellent and very resourceful tool, the MST class is invaluable for those who want to not only get a license but as an important hands-on experience before hitting the road. After all, it's a two-wheel vehicle and you don't want to fool around with it before having a critical learning exposure. Added to the practical knowledge, *Motorcycling for Dummies and Zen and the Art of Motorcycle Maintenance* are other premium compilations I included in my tool box before and through the process of getting in the fun but risky business of motor biking.

That turned to be a memorable summer/fall time as both Bill and I got to enjoy the scenery of the beautiful green mountains of Vermont. With plans already in mind to attend rallies out of state, such as Sturgis, Daytona, Laconia and Myrtle Beach, the first one in line would be next year's Americade, in Lake George, NY. That would help us acquire the taste for riding – a year later I would swap the VTX1300 cc with a VTX1800 cc – before we outbraved longer and more challenging distances. For now, we wanted to let it sink in. And just enjoy the rides.

It was also during this period that I had the jolly visit of members of my extended family that I hadn't seen in years. Not once, but twice we had a pleasurable time with my dear uncle Sergio to our home in Vermont. Sergio is my Dad's youngest brother with whom we both have nurtured a great relationship over the years. A talent for learning languages, Serjão, as I call him, speaks perfect English having worked for Ford Motors in Brazil for many years. He is an admirer of the American lifestyle and one of my greatest supporters on our life change project. In one of his visits, he came in 2007 along with cousin Bob, his youngest son, when we had a joyful and rare opportunity to do some traveling together and also see my preferred jazz musician at The Flynn Theater – Pat Metheny. Bob, a career judge, is also himself an electric guitar player and loves the same kind of music I cherish. Both were exhilarated to see Pat Metheny along with Christian McBride and Antonio Sanchez perform a great night in downtown Burlington – unforgettable!

## PROCESSING THE UPCOMING CHANGES

Mom was recovering well as the healing process has been successful. No sequels or consequences other than the substantial reduction of her stomach size, which for some time has been requiring extra care on her diet. The new concern is with Mauricio, Silvia's dad. This is a unique individual for whom I have much respect and appreciation. Incredibly intelligent, he would get irksome with frivolities and therefore would spend a great deal of his time by himself reading or playing chess with a few individuals of his predilection. Back in April, I had a chance to see him and Elvira and learn of a delicate heath issue he was battling with. Years earlier, a week or two before my Dad passed away, the four of them got together. When getting back nearby his apartment after the visit, Mauricio accidentally slipped, hit and broke his right arm in an awkward way. The pain lingered for several weeks. Without a doubt, in general men are much more casual about, and to an extent, disinterested in their own health. Not until the pain got critical did he finally see a doctor. After multiple exams, back and forth from clinics and hospitals, the undesirable suspected diagnosis: his arm had been broken not due to the fall but due to a much more complicated problem – he had bone cancer in scattered areas of his body, at an advanced stage.

Being away from our folks had invariably haunted my wife and me in past years. And I'm sure it does that to every immigrant family. Unless conditions are created for the extended family to join the migrating family unit for periods of time and vice versa, or for frequent travels between one end and the other, there will always be a struggle. We were aware of that and knew that we would have to come across that reality one way or another.

Few authors refer to the relevance of relationship like Krishnamurti: "Without relationship, there is no existence: to be is to be related... Most of us do not seem to realize this—that the world is my relationship with others, whether one or many. My problem is that of relationship. What I am, that I project; and obviously, if I do not understand myself, the whole of relationship is one of confusion in ever-widening circles. So, relationship becomes of extraordinary importance, not with the so-called mass, the crowd, but in the world of my family and friends, however small that may be—my relationship with my wife, my children, my neighbor"– *J.D. Krishnamurti, The Book of Life*

For the next two years, Mauricio would struggle with the lingering condition. As we would travel back and forth to try and be of minimum support, his health would deteriorate significantly in front of our eyes. To the point that he really wished he was...gone. Contrary to Vermont and eight other states in the U.S. where patients must meet stringent eligibility requirements for a physician-assisted suicide, there's not such a thing in Brazil. Nonetheless, he did his own research as to ways to provide himself with a dignified death. That research proved to become a useless effort since there was no legislation to support it. From our family's perspective, and especially from the couple's, the inability to change things began to take a toll on all of us, most significantly and not surprisingly, on his wife, Elvira. With us being physically distant, our sentiment of impotence grew as no significant improvement was experienced. Nor could he count on a foreseeable closure that will give him the final relief from the excruciating pain and discomfort.

Sergio and Ivone, Silvia's brother and sister-in-law, themselves busy and doing their best to raise their four kids, relayed to us their experience and overwhelming sense of frustration. A cancer diagnosis, followed by an unpredictable sequence of events, does affect family members where complex feelings and lifestyle changes caused by the illness become as difficult to family individuals as they are to the patient himself. A major effect on marriages and other long-term partnerships, the experience of sadness, anxiety, sometimes anger and many times hopelessness can put a major distress on a couple.

Never prepared for, we knew that the effects of the illness could pose challenges. Whether it would strengthen their relationship, create new problems and even worsen existing ones, our concern and strange desire from our end was that closure came sooner than later. With his condition not improving and the new diagnosis being such that if he didn't undergo a back surgery soon he would run the risk of becoming paralyzed from the waist down, Mauricio made the decision to move on with the operation. Not a great place to be, the surgery happened. As a consequence of his depletion, he entered a profound coma which would last for several weeks.

Silvia herself had already been in São Paulo twice in the past two and a half months. Firstly, when the whole household flew together. Secondly, for three weeks, before and after Mauricio's surgery. Split between her many roles at home and at work, she was frazzled with her parents' situation. We were relieved to hear Mauricio was doing ok since he had left the hospital a month earlier. At home, he was being assisted by his wife and an occasional caregiver. Not an easy task, given the complexity of his illness.

A phone call to her mom raised up the definitive flag in our minds: as I dialed it before passing it on to Silvia, I notice that Elvira's voice is not normal. Her speech seems somehow slurred, therefore more than just slightly affecting her communication. After my wife hung up the phone with her mom, I was adamant about what I had perceived: "Honey, let's talk. Your mom doesn't sound well. I think you should take the next available flight immediately and go see her." Our knowledge of delicate health situations is proportional to our exposure to it and from other's experiences. Just enough to add an intuitive component. "Really?" Silvia replied. "I'll go."

I dropped her off at Pierre Trudeau's Airport in Montréal the same evening. The next morning, she was in São Paulo and upon arrival she went straight to the hospital where Elvira was undergoing her ninth dialysis, the same institution where Mauricio had convalesced before. She was not well but looks luminous, cheerful and obviously happy to see her only daughter. Silvia and Elvira spent the whole afternoon catching up...That evening, though, bitter news once again ravages our family. Elvira had a major stroke and her state was critical. As for Silvia, an indescribable shock. After long and tormenting eleven days, with the grim picture of Elvira's state being irreversible, sadly, she was gone. Her big plans to come spend longer periods with us in Vermont are now forever in our hearts. Too soon, too fast. Life is funny when it isn't so harsh.

## CLOSURE

"In the Lakota/Sioux tradition, a person who is grieving is considered most waken, most holy. There's a sense that when someone is struck by the sudden lightning of loss, he or she stands on the threshold of the spirit world. The prayers of those who grieve are considered especially strong, and it is proper to ask them for their help. You might recall what it's like to be with someone who has grieved deeply. The person has no layer of protection, nothing left to defend. The mystery is looking out through that person's eyes. For the time being, he or she has accepted the reality of loss and has stopped clinging to the past or grasping at the future. In the groundless openness of sorrow, there is a wholeness of presence and a deep natural wisdom."
—*Tara Brach*

Several weeks went by. Silvia had already been back home after a hectic period preceding and following her mom's passing; Before she left, she and her brother Sergio had the burden to deliver the news to their dad. Angered and wretched to hear the mournful news, Mauricio would say: "Not fair. How come she gets to leave before I did?"

# STAYING WHOLE

Mauricio passed away only a couple months after Elvira had. *The Science of Longtime Couples Who Die Close Together*, by Melissa Dahl, is an intriguing article which speaks about "the widowhood effect." Considered by social scientists to be 'one of the best documented examples of the effect of social relations on health', the study commented on the article suggests that within the three months after one spouse dies, the chance that the other will follow is anywhere from 30 to 90 percent. In the case of my in-laws, who would have thought they would depart so close to one another?

At home, as much as we looked at 2007 as a year to forget, we managed to celebrate Elvira's and Mauricio's lives. As well, we gathered the kids and spent quality time camping and enjoying the outdoors like never before. The sense of 'life is too short' influences our appreciation for the true things that matter most. Among them, the simple fact of being well and alive and with the people we love. Precious.

Excerpts of the lyrics from James Taylor's "Secret 'O Life," say a lot:

*The secret of life is enjoying the passage of time*
*Any fool can do it*
*There ain't nothing to it*
*Nobody knows how we got to*
*The top of the hill*
*But since we're on our way down*
*We might as well enjoy the ride*
*And since we're only here for a while*
*Might as well show some style*
*Give us a smile*
*Isn't it a lovely ride?*
*Sliding down*
*Gliding down*
*Now the thing about time is that time*

*Isn't really real*
*It's just your point of view*
*How does it feel for you*
*Einstein said he could never understand it all*
*Planets spinning through space*
*The smile upon your face*
*Welcome to the human race*
*Some kind of lovely ride*
*I'll be sliding down*
*I'll be gliding down*
*The secret of life is enjoying the passage of time*

## BORN IN BELGIUM, A FRIEND OF THE WORLD

After Berkeley, Liège and Paris back in the days, I had one single opportunity to catch a train from Amsterdam and visit Françoise and her family again in Belgium during a trip to Europe, in 1984. She had just recently married a man from Senegal, the father of her first son. After that, our lives took turns and for some time we kept in touch but would never get together again. Yet, many years later, the group – Monica in Cyprus, Marie-Christine in Paris, Cecilia in Virginia, Marco in Brussells and Alejandra in Bali, manage to organize a surprise birthday party for our dear friend in Paris to celebrate her 50th. It was 2007, I could not make it but I got the glimpses of a great gathering with lots of wine, laughs, singing and guitar playing – once again, after a few decades, our friends had a lot of fun.

Françoise devoted her life to justice and human rights issues. Fluent in at least five languages, she worked for *Terre des Hommes* in Senegal before joining *L'Institut Panos Paris* (IPP), figuring prominently in the struggle to promote media pluralism, particularly among marginalized populations in Africa. In November 2000, she became the IPP's Executive Director, leading strategy to develop independent media, including in the Democratic Republic of Congo, Burundi and the Central African Republic.

This is a job that puts enormous pressure on her. With three children from two marriages, she traveled all over the world on an almost frenetic pace in order to keep up with IPP's cause and ambitious agenda.

I got a call from her at the end of summer in 2008 letting me know that she would be in Washington, D.C. for work and would love to catch a flight to visit us, even if it's for a few hours in the middle of the weekend. I was thrilled. Typical of herself, I would have done the same: she flew into Burlington on a bright early Saturday afternoon. Silvia and Eric seem happy to meet my glowing red-haired friend from the Old Continent about which they knew good stories. For only 18 hours, we got to spend a memorable time after such a long period. I could not forget that smile and her friendship – no one could resist such a cheerful and giving personality.

*November, 2008*

*Très cher ami,*
*At last some news from me!!!! I feel awfully guilty that I did not get back to you earlier, after the splendid if very short immersion you offered me in your new life and in Vermont. I came back with very fond memories and feel awful I've been so bad in sharing them. Silvia welcomed me like a sister, you were lovely good old Renato of the best ancient times, Eric reminded me so much of Pablo I felt just at home... And let's not say anything about the splendid day that the 'meteo' offered us.*
*Upon return from US my life went back to its usual madness, I love it but it really is a HUGE strain to manage a household of 4, each kid with his/her own challenges, pulling my organization forward and travelling so much. Since I visited you I went to Ireland, Greece, India, the Netherlands and Belgium. And that's without talking about in-house trips: last Thursday I inaugurated a colloquium my organization was co-ordinating in the Council of Europe, in Strasbourg. All well but .... oooooof, I wished things could be a little bit cooler.*
*I love the pictures you sent. I have a couple of you and Silvia which are just gorgeous, of course this coincides with a moment in which Pablo has*

*exhausted the battery of my camera, so I'll send them some other time.*
*Just wanted to tell you, better late than never, that it was just lovely and delightful to re-unite with you and get a quick glimpse at your new and very exciting life in Vermont. Making such a great step ahead, after Brazil and Portugal, is such a beautiful success story. Inspiring.*
*I'll be waiting for you, Silvia, Eric and your beautiful girls to visit me in Paris any time you get a chance. In the meantime, I am sending some random pictures of the kids, last shared times with Alejandra in Mexico, etc...*
*Be assured that your Belgian friend will always be around and remember you with the fondest memories.... Let's try not to wait another 25 years to re-unite again!*
*Much love and best of luck to you, thanks again for yours and Silvia's great welcome!*
*Je ne vous oublierai jamais,*

*Françoise*

## UPHILL BATTLES

From my sister Liliana, I learned the regrettable news that Mauro is fighting cancer. I knew my cousin well and could relate to his fight in a deep way. Doctors do have some ideas about why people may get cancer. Although the main reasons revolve around genetics and certain environmental influences, some behavioral triggers may be critical to contribute to its manifestation. Emotional and psychological factors may also increase the risk of developing cancer, although not fully scientifically proven. Bladder cancer is usually related to tobacco, which my cousin-brother hadn't given up until he found out about the disease. Here I am trying to find reasons for everything. The fact is, what do we know about it?

Since I departed the family business in 1992, my contact with Mauro had been restricted to occasional opportunities during my travels to São Paulo. Consequently, I kind of lost touch with him on a more personal level although our fraternal bond would always remain strong. I've always noticed a little melancholy in his demeanor and could understand why. After his divorce, I had the impression that he focused his energy strictly on raising his kids to the best of his ability. A great dad, I could tell that the last person he would be concerned about would be himself; therefore, his health was not a priority. Tobacco, and possibly alcohol, may have speeded up his predisposition to the number two killer in the world, after heart diseases.

It's early December, 2010. I left home knowing that his health was in a very delicate stage and nobody knew for sure how much longer he would be around. As I got to São Paulo 2010, besides focusing on spending time with my Mom, sisters and a few friends, I wanted to see my cousin Mauro as soon as possible on what could be our last opportunity together. Liliana and I got to the hospital and Ricardo was already waiting downstairs for us. Though always hopeful, the picture was somber. Visits would have to be alternated, so he had to step out of the room so that we could visit his brother. As we got into the shared patient room, Mauro was lying down the bed, half asleep. As he opened his eyes, he showed surprise and quietly opened a serene smile. One of the consequences of bladder cancer is that it has variable metastatic potential. Lung and brain, in his case, being two of the most affected organs. His brain had been compromised and, as a consequence, his speech was no longer functional. As I came next to him, I held his left hand with my left hand. With a strong, unusual and meaningful grip, it was as if everything we had left unsaid in the past years were in a process of getting caught up, energetically speaking. The little over an hour time I spent with my dear cousin, although Mauro could not speak, his energy was manifested in silence but very present.

It was time to get to the MRI room, to which I get to accompany him from one level of the hospital to another. As we get in the elevator, I cracked a joke about his height and how our basketball years made him a tall guy, nearly enough to almost not be able to fit in the platform. From the mirror door,

I could see his subtle smile which, for a moment, brought me a lot of hope. As we got in the MRI room, I prepare to say good bye to my cousin-brother of so many years and great times and experiences together. As I sympathized with his discomfort in being transported from his bed into the MRI machine, I whispered in his years: "Hang in there, man. We will get you out of here soon." His eyes semi-closed, I knew he got the message and thus showed a semblance of acceptance. That was the last time I saw the man.

Back home a few days after, I learned of Mauro's demise. His sister Sandra, always the rock among her siblings, told me they got him out of the hospital into a special memory care environment in the countryside, near the mountains, where he would like to be. There, he spent his final days, with dignity and peacefully, along with his loving family.

## GLOBAL *STURM UND DRANG*

Led by the 2007 financial crisis is the breakdown of trust occurred between banks the year before the 2008 financial debacle. Caused by the subprime mortgage tinderbox, which itself was caused by the unregulated use of derivatives. Despite efforts to fix the messy causes, the financial boiling point still led to the Great Recession of our days, affecting virtually every single household on the planet.

In the workplace, different industries would feel the repercussions of the crisis at different timelines, some during and immediately after; others, only after one, two or even three years following the crunch. At work, my company, and particularly myself, would feel the critical effects a couple of years after when some of the larger projects' completion took place while potential promising projects would be put in the drawer indefinitely. Downsizing and shrinkage determined the pace of things to come in the business realm. Like most industries, contract furniture and everything in between – e.g., design, architecture, construction – would feel the pain too. I had been working for

OM Workspace, an affiliated division of the giant office supplies retailer OfficeMax, which in recent years in Vermont had gone from a major player to a modest participant in the marketplace. Competition is fierce, especially in a small environment like the Green Mountain State. Reduced to two associates, I had to find a better position soon lest being the next one to go.

Graduating during and after the financial crisis would prove to be an ordeal to many students when it came to finding a position. College graduation, supposedly the start of something big, for millions of students who graduated in the middle of the Great Recession, was a big disappointment. My lovely Catherine Bianca was one of those students. Full of dreams and looking into the best employers in her field, it didn't take long for her to face the rough reality of the job market. The facts would speak for themselves: 8.8 million people unemployed where, according to numerous accounts, the Great Recession left many recent college graduates struggling to find jobs that utilized their education. The result, graduates found it increasingly difficult to secure a job, and those who did find work were often confined to low-wage positions. Let alone, being compelled to work jobs that had squat to do with their core field.

I successfully managed to find a position in one of the good contract furniture dealers in town. Based in Burlington, Creative Office Pavilion was a preferred vendor for Herman Miller, a world leader in design and high quality commercial grade furniture. An auspicious job in my opinion, if it weren't for the reality of the high end category of its product lines. Vermont, like Maine, is an idyllic state, that's undeniable. Beyond Chittenden County, the area which encompasses Burlington and sixteen other towns, the state is predominantly rural. Out of the seventeen towns, nearly seven have the capacity to absorb industries, jobs and consequently office units – the focus of the industry I'm involved with. Yet, I was pleased to join the organization and my team seemed fully engaged.

In Montréal for the past 4 ½ years, Catherine Bianca graduated at Concordia University in 2010 and was ready to fly high joining in a great player in her field of Design. With my exposure in the contract furniture industry, I had heard and seen many times of the benefits and hurdles designers encounter throughout their careers. On the pros side, one gets to use both the creative and analytical sides of his/her brain; freelance or in-house are key options that help define a working lifestyle; people typically appreciate your work, and it's a highly sought after skill in many industries. On the flip side, design is subjective and the real challenge is to appease your client; edits can become overwhelming and everyone tends to think graphic design is easy; at last, the field is a very competitive market to break into. Just enough to upset any recent graduate with so much to offer and so little experience.

## IN WAVES THEY COME AND THEY GO

*March, 2011*

*Dear Renato,*

*I don't know how to say it but it has to be said. Not sure if the news already came to you but...our dearest Françoise has been diagnosed with brain cancer...Yes, that's right. Alejandra told me last week and I have been devastated since. She is now home after many days in the hospital doing all sorts of tests.*
  *I just spent about 40 minutes with her on the phone...she starts chemotherapy tomorrow. She has difficulty speaking – it takes her time to find the words – she finds them but it takes time... Very strange at first but then I got used to it. But she is in great spirits which I believe, is also crucial in the healing process... she will also do radiation. As per what she told me – there is not really a way of being able to cure her type & size of cancer – (she told me there are several different tumors) they will do everything to prolong her living with it and make it, hopefully "dormant"... She's had this dormant melanoma for 18 years... from what I could grasp a pimple she had removed at the time – or so she thought – and the Dr. (asshole!!! I could kill him with my bare hands) did not do anything*

*else & this was actually a melanoma that has now metastasized....!!!!!
Fuck!*

*It's going to be a long and arduous battle. But Françoise is strong enough and with all the love & support from her friends from all over the world, I am sure she will have at least another 20 years!!! She will see grandchildren and all!!!*

*As I said, her spirits are great – she will not go back to her old job – (of course & she talks very calmly – "if I survive this and go back to work...I will take on a Board position and nothing else") I told her to focus on Françoise now & her kids... She is the center of the universe now and every ounce of energy is to be spent in getting better. Her memory is great, her laugh the same wonderful energizing sound... I was very moved and touched with our call. She has to survive this crap!!! She has to!!!*

*Of course as I write all this to you I am crying ..the tears I held behind during my phone call with her... I realize all the hell she is going to go thru with the chemo & all... But she said she will reconnect with everyone & one of her biggest regrets is not giving enough attention to all her friends...Imagine – she is going thru cancer & thinking she didn't give US enough time. She is getting tons and tons of calls obviously from all over and that is making her feel better too. She said every day she gets a "spark of goodness" and that my call was the one for today!!! She will create a personal email account and post her first picture with the wig she not only knows she will have to wear but has already ordered!!! She has amazing strength and I am sure we will be planning a trip to Paris soon to celebrate the decrease in her tumors...*

*All my love,*

*Monica*

"Every period of life has its own point, its own purpose. To find it and accept it is one of the most vital problems relating to life" – *Erich Stern*

Easier said than done, one would argue. The reality is that each individual, from whichever stratum and level of consciousness, has gone, is going, or will go through his/her own moment of truth. How graceful will that experience be?

On my every so often dynamic contemplation of my existence within the context of our world being subjected to the law of the opposites, I come across a thought that resonates deeply into my perception of things: "Life has no opposite. The opposite of death is birth. Life is eternal." – *Eckhart Tolle*. This powerful statement can be combined with another reflection: Miguel de Unamuno was an early existentialist who concerned himself largely with the tension between intellect and emotion, faith and reason. At the heart of his view of life was his personal and passionate longing for immortality. According to Unamuno, man's hunger to live on after death is constantly denied by his reason and can only be satisfied by faith, and the resulting tension results in unceasing agony. "My religion is to seek for truth in life and for life in truth, even knowing that I shall not find them while I live." Here, my intent is to depict a specific thought by one of Spain's most important authors, on one particular aspect of my reflections: Unamuno thought that history could be best understood by looking at the small histories of anonymous people, rather than focusing on major events such as wars and political pacts. I couldn't agree more, especially when I think of my dearest friend Françoise attempting to promote the plurality of voices and opinions to people in some of the difficult and complex African countries she and IPP had focused their efforts on. Too large a task, one would agree. Well, "a journey of a thousand miles begins with a single step," says the Chinese proverb...

Over the phone, I got to talk to Françoise for several minutes a month or so after she started her treatment. With difficulty to coordinate her speech, Françoise shared a thought that would sit deeply inside me: "If I am to get out of this there's one thing I will never do it again. I will never trade love for work, ever again." Our little Miss Sunshine had her friends in mind, thinking that she could have given more attention to them. That's why we all loved her. News and updates about her health traveled among her friends for months. It would take a little over a year for our friend to come across the line of her final battle. As for her friends, we wanted that her suffering could be minimized. At last, the sad news in early July, 2012. Marie-Christine Powels, a common friend from the Berkeley era and one of Françoise's closest friends in Paris, portrayed hers and others' last honors:

"It was indeed a very moving ceremony: picture yourself in a small room with about 50 seats, packed to capacity with about 200 of us, many standing in the back, Françoise's coffin in the front with her picture on top and rose petals all around, lovely music during the whole time...

"Several of Françoise's friends and colleagues, some in tears, then rose to speak a few words, and everyone, really every one of them kept saying over and over again just how truly incredible this great lady had been. An inspiration, a uniting force between people, a light and a smile, her generosity, her accessibility, her intelligence, her patience, ... I forget many things, but all of the speakers repeated how much she had touched them with her grace (and how good a salsa dancer she was too!).

"Then we all silently moved forward to spread a few rose petals on her coffin and lined up to sign the registers at the back. We hugged her sisters and we hugged each other.

"One last thing that struck me: I know it sounds corny, but I couldn't help noticing that before the ceremony, the sky was totally blue, the sun shining brightly, warming all of us waiting outside to enter the room. When the ceremony ended and we stepped outside again, the sky was overcast and dull, as if acknowledging that one of its stars had departed."

## PROJECT BONA FIDE

Earlier in the year, months before my Belgian friend left us, GG had embarked on an unusual program. After graduating in Nutrition and Food Science at University of Vermont, our second daughter took a pretty bold decision: she was bound to Nicaragua, Central America. After having worked at a local natural foods store, she comes across the perspective for a radical experience:

"Permaculture is a design system for creating sustainable human ecologies. The word itself is a contraction not only of permanent agriculture but also of permanent culture, as cultures cannot survive long without a regenerative agricultural base and land use ethic. The aims of Permaculture are to create systems that are ecologically-sound and economically viable, which provide for their own needs, do not exploit or pollute, and therefore are sustainable or even regenerative in the long term."

From its web page: "Project Bona Fide practices many different types of agro-forestry. Plantings of fruit, nut, and multi-use trees on contour are spaced so that "alleyways" are left for the inclusion of annual crops like cereal grains and annual legumes. Alley farming allows for multiple yields of tree and annual crops throughout the year. The use of vertical space is optimized when this type of poly-culture is employed."

Held on *Isla de Ometepe,* an island of twin volcanoes on Lake Nicaragua, GG attended Project Bona Fide's annual Permaculture Design Course (PDC), a 2-week hands-on training experience in permaculture design principles and practices. The curriculum is taught with a special emphasis on forest gardening in the tropics where, after its completion, she would remain on the island for another four to five months. In the wild and with very little comfort, her practical knowledge revolved around topics such as design for climate change, regenerative land management and stewardship, water catchment, storage, filtration, and distribution and organic horticulture among its core activities. Little did she know that that intro to sustainable agriculture would change her life in meaningful ways in the next few years.

## HITTING THE ROWDY ROAD

Conversely and during the same period, Catherine Bianca had already been back from her Canadian experience and was diligently pursuing a position in her field of Design. This would prove to be complex due to multiple factors: the job market was still recovering; the profession of designer can be limiting when it comes to certain segments, in her case, a highly competitive one, especially in a small state like Vermont; and not less important, just like her talent, her expectations were high, thus requiring flexibility that she didn't have yet given her experience. The result becomes challenging: she ended up combining her aim for independence with a lack of financial structure, which at the end of the same year would take her back to her roots in Brazil. There, she would spend a few years in search for her soul, in search for her *leitmotiv*.

## 23

# Oh, The Things We Do!

*"You'll be on your way up! You'll be seeing great sights!*
*You'll join the high fliers who soar to high heights."*
*Oh, The Places You Go!* – Dr. Seuss

UNDOUBTEDLY, ONE OF THE BEST CHILDREN'S BOOKS ever written and published. If someone asked me to highlight aspects about living in this country, I would say that besides the natural beauty of the National Parks, and the amazing music I've run by over the years, it is the blessing of having come across meaningful pieces of literature, such as the fabulous *Oh, The Places You Go!* by Dr. Seuss. Published in 1990, it was the last book he published during his lifetime. The plot starts with the storyteller describing the determination of the main character, depicted as the reader, to flee town in search of something he is not quite sure yet as to what to find.

Traveling through several geometrical and multicolored landscapes and places, the protagonist eventually hits the wall: "The

Waiting Place," the unpromising spot which represents a place where everyone is always waiting for someone to come and go, or something to happen. Encouraged to investigate and use his imagination, the main character is inspired by the thoughts of places he will eventually visit and things he will discover. With a magisterial completion, the book concludes with a highly positive open-ended note: *"Today is your day! Your mountain is waiting. So…get on your way!"*

I can't think of how many times I've read the book to my children, and especially, to Eric. In fact, besides being able to convey such wisdom and meaningful messages to the kids, I would interpret my fondness for this book as a catch up with my infancy and youth. This is a book for adults of all ages just as it is for young individuals. So much to be absorbed in every single word and illustration, its contribution to the humanities is beyond value. Talk about helping shape one's character, this is a book to be sitting on every household's bookshelf and read at least once a year. In a nutshell, a guide for the journey of life.

## TEACHING A PATH FOR DEVELOPMENT

*Sometime in the 21$^{st}$ century*

*"Miss Silvia,*
*Thank you for being such an important influential person in our lives. Early childcare and education is so important. We feel lucky and blessed to have had you for both Windham and Weston. Teachers are so important in our society. Thank you for being so loving, caring and committed to children. You are an absolute gift to the profession. We are grateful for all you've done for Weston this year. He absolutely adores you! We will miss you dearly! We love you! - Love, The Ellingsons."*

My wife is a unique creature. Not only to me, she is a special individual to a lot of people. At the beginning of every school year, she gets engulfed in a myriad of activities in preparation for the new period in which she will be embracing the lives of

15 to 20 new students. It's no small feat. Students, especially the young, can only grow and learn in an environment they feel is safe and honest. For many an underrated profession, teaching is still one of the most respectable jobs in a society, even at the pre-school and elementary levels. In reality, it's during that time that teachers ought to be valued the most for it's when the foundation of an individual is set out. To take the job is a high responsibility as it is to parents to entrust more than half of their children's daily lives with someone they wish will do a good job.

To be proud of her dedication to her profession is an understatement. Notes like the one above flow in at the end of every school year. That's when the sum of all of the aggregated efforts kick in to substantiate the recognition for the kind of work she has been performing for almost two decades. All of that, combined with being a mom, a wife and a manager of her own destiny, is no bed of roses. After being in Vermont for many years, on top of her B.S. in Music, she even took time to add a two-year degree in Early Education. I find myself asking, how does she do it? The answers are multiple: she thrives on the idea of potentially transforming lives; she is constantly exposed to chances of being creative in the workplace; it feels like she gets better every year at what she does; it keeps her feet on the ground, as teaching is ultimately a humbling profession; finally, she finds satisfaction everywhere there's proof of every child's little progress. What else could one wish for? Well, some would still argue that teachers are underrated. It's probably because they are.

## BECOMING A NATIONAL

Mumina Abdille wiped tears from her eyes as she stood on the front lawn of the main house at the Ethan Allen Homestead Museum. Her daughter, Ayan Mohamed, had asked State Rep. Joanne Cole for voter registration paperwork moments after her U.S. Citizenship and Immigration Services naturalization ceremony. Both mother and daughter emigrated from Somalia and now live in Burlington. "I am so very proud of my daughter,"

Abdille said.

Canadian-born Marc Joncas of Danville is married to an American. "Taking my family through the border has always been nerve-wracking," he said. "This citizenship means I can cross without being detained, or fear being deported."

The day was July 4th, 2014. Burlington's Ethan Allen Homestead was declared a federal courthouse for an Independence Day Naturalization Ceremony where 10 people, each from a different country, took an oath of citizenship. Chief U.S. District Judge Christina Reiss administered the Oath of Allegiance during the ceremony. Along with myself from Brazil, candidates originated from Canada, Haiti, Ireland, Japan, Poland, Somalia, Sweden, Ukraine and United Kingdom.

A big day, indeed. On that year, U.S. Citizenship and Immigration Services welcomed approximately 9,000 new U.S. citizens during more than 100 naturalization ceremonies across the country from June 30th to July 4th. Burlington's apt setting, the historic farm house surrounded by bright orange tiger lilies, was built in 1787 by revolutionary hero General Ethan Allen. Gen. Allen was an early inhabitant of Burlington who made a significant contribution to Vermont history. A meaningful day for me and my family. With Catherine Bianca and GG in São Paulo and Bellingham, WA, respectively, it is James and Tricia that join Silvia and Eric to attend the ceremony, which made the celebration even more special.

## IF IT'S NOT FUN...

Jerry Greenfield...Jerry of the Ben & Jerry's myriad lines of exquisite ice cream, coined the phrase which became an inspiring motto for legions of people – *"If it's not fun, why do it?"* I would say that only once or twice as a professional I had the luxury to think and act with that idea in mind. The rest is, well, "swallowing the frog." And, "if there are two frogs," per Mark Twain, "swallow the big one first." Parents know that well: mortgages, bills and the whole enchilada in between. According to a recent VTDigger post, Vermont's population is stagnating and the reason is that residents keep leaving. Although lawmakers have tried to attract new workers with a strategy of offering cash incentive for people to move to the state, a recent study suggests that it's working-class and middle-class residents that beautiful-but-difficult-to-afford Vermont is at risk of losing. Besides the fact that hard earned money will go further elsewhere, winter time requires snow plowing, by itself a fun activity that gets old pretty quickly once you do it the second time around during the season. Truth be told, coupled with low wages, it's property taxes that hurt the pocket. Especially, when the kids leave high-school. It's a double whammy: you pay more taxes proportionally and the kids need some kind of help making it through college.

Shaun Boyce, Designer, Illustrator and Artist chimes in: "Economies of scale is the Achilles heel of small town Vermont. Public schools, policing, fire depts, roads, and every other public service are all financial burdens that disproportionately impact the costs of living in this state because of the sheer lack of people that live here. Top all this off with extreme weather, harsh winter conditions, salting and plowing roads, heating your home, etc. Combine this with an ever growing real estate tax, and yes, no surprise people are moving out of state. We are over educated and underpaid in this state as well. Most carpenters get paid more than I do with a bachelor's degree and 15-year experience. The market for jobs in Vermont is not progressive, and tech forward, yet that is where the jobs pay best wages out of state. After college it's easier to move outside the state than to find an employer that pays a livable wage."

Therefore, when local national exponent politicians like Bernie Sanders say that "in my State people are working two, three jobs" he is not making it up. And, it's no different in my household. Even before Eric went to college, my wife and I were already putting a lot of extra hours to our weekly work assignments. As much as we loved the state, its beauty and the people we have encountered throughout the years, the challenge was how to keep up with a balanced lifestyle, preserve our career perspective and yet, hopefully, make time for some...fun?

## ELEMENTS OF THE EQUATION

"Someone I know works at the Burlington International Airport for one of the airlines. She says it's not necessarily an easy job and the pay is nothing special. But the perks seem to be good." I listened carefully to my wife and was open for new possibilities. "Interesting, I will check it out." I reply. Four years down and not quite happy at my full time job, perhaps it's time to diversify both income and job perspectives. Moreover, it may be a matter of time until I drop out of the contract furniture industry altogether. After fifteen years, it's time.

I got hired in a heartbeat. I knew little about the industry but could learn fast. DGS is a service provider for Delta Airlines in Burlington. A lot of the work evolves around servicing the aircrafts and passengers traveling out to and from three main hubs, namely Atlanta, New York and Detroit. With two categories, below wing and above wing, there's a team scheduled to service the multiple daily flights, to and from the already mentioned locations. The perk? Well, you fly for free. Or almost for free. Where to? Anywhere Delta Airlines flies to. What? True. The next step was training, online and hands on. Then learning the system.

## WEST BOUND

GG was back from Nicaragua after an outstanding experience in Permaculture. With swift moves, she begins working as a hostess, then as a waitress at one of the best restaurants in downtown Burlington, *Trattoria Delia*. Added to her responsibilities, GG was also attracted to working and embracing the restaurant's own garden's activities in Charlotte. There, organic fresh herbs and veggies are grown and used daily at the ingenious menu of this Italian fine eatery. At the same place, she met Matthew, one of the restaurant's topnotch chefs, himself a lover of the outdoors and appreciative of the great cuisine. Both lived in Burlington and as they shared the same interests, a promising relationship was developed within the course of a year, or even less.

"We're moving West," GG and Matthew brought up during a dinner gathering at home. "Come again?" Silvia and I reply, startled with the announcement. In a flash, Kahlil Gibran's *The Prophet* immediately takes charge in my mind when the author describes the tenuous relationship between parents and their offspring:

*"You may give them your love*
*but not your thoughts,*
*For they have their own thoughts.*
*You may house their bodies but not their souls,*
*For their souls dwell in the house of tomorrow,*
*Which you cannot visit, not even in your dreams.*
*You may strive to be like them,*
*But seek not to make them like you.*
*For life goes not backward nor tarries*
*with yesterday."*
The Prophet
– Kahlil Gibran

The plan had substance. Most importantly, it had consistency as both GG and Matthew were on the same page and aiming at a common goal: "We are going to dive into organic farming." The destination, Washington State. Bella, Matthew's inseparable chocolate lab, would be joining them on their journey across country. We gave them our full support and soon started planning our visit to Bellingham, where their lives would eventually get established. An exciting moment, we were happy for them.

Viva Farms is a non-profit Farm Business Incubator and Training Program. GG and Matthew would be beneficiaries of a project which has the foundation on helping beginning farmers and creating opportunities for success. Its mission statement: "to empower aspiring and limited-resource farmers by providing bilingual training in holistic organic farming practices, as well as access to land, infrastructure, equipment, marketing and capital." With the perspective of Western Washington facing a generation crisis, and the number of farms, produce processing facilities, and acreage of farmland all decreasing, young farmers like GG and Matthew were more than welcome to join in. It would depend on them to embrace the program and their new lifestyle wholeheartedly.

## ON THE RAMP, OFF TO THE SKIES

After a few weeks of intensive training, I was ready to hit the ramp. The job is not for everyone; I learned that quickly. Turnover is significant and it drives managers and supervisors nuts as it relates to hiring and retaining work force. What's the relevance of this job? A commercial airplane wouldn't properly operate on the ground, without the help of a team of airport ramp agents. Guiding airplanes to their gates and backing them up for take-off, handling heavy equipment such air stair units, belt-loaders, push back tugs, de-icing planes in cold weather, transporting baggage to passengers in a timely and speedy fashion, and cleaning the aircraft are just a few of the important duties of this position. Glamourous? Hell, no. Working under pressure and in a tight time frame, airport ramp agents must work diligently to make sure that the airplane is ready to go for its next flight. With great emphasis on safety, which is paramount as regulations get significantly more stringent every so often. Last but not least, airport ramp agents work in the thick of 175,000 pound airplanes moving around the tarmac at incredible high decibels.

When properly staffed, ramp work is perfectly doable. The nature of the job is fast paced, which requires coordination and it can be challenging at times. I wouldn't feel the harshness of the job until wintertime kicked in. We see part of the staff walk away for multiple reasons, but Vermont's merciless weather can put a great strain on the body when working on the ramp. Thinking that I could handle the job for some time, the requirement for constant vigilance about airplane traffic and attention to safety procedures is imperative for this position. A lot of things can go wrong even when doing things right.

Withstanding inclement weather, fumes, extreme noise, dust and dirt are all expected to be encountered from day one; however, not everything was bad news. One of the fun aspects of the job is teamwork and how diversified labor is: whereas most men and women are rather young, some still in college, others recent graduates, there are a number of people from multiple nationalities from all continents working both above and below wing. That makes the environment very interesting from many angles of observation. But I can't deny the main reason for working this job: the benefit of flying for a fraction of the cost is astronomical. Although traveling stand-by, I learned to be humble and not feel entitled to fly until the condition and opportunity is presented. Here resilience plays a role. If not this particular morning, it may happen in the afternoon or the next day.

It took me a while to learn the system. Yet, I began traveling that summer and after a couple of domestic flights I made it to my first international destination: São Paulo. After years without being able to afford time and resources, I got to see my family and spend joyful moments. So worthy. Extended to my wife and son, the perks of flying almost for free would take us several times around the country, South America, Europe and beyond. Surviving the job is the name of the game.

## REJOICING THE DAY

Along with the toughness of this job there are moments of joy. Especially when you can be of service to those who need an extra hand. Like Shirley. I was requested by one of my above-wing teammates to take this elderly lady through the gate on a wheel chair. At the counter, her son Ken asked my name, introduced himself and told me that Shirley had just turned 99 years old. She would be traveling by herself to Atlanta. As she prepared to sit down on the wheelchair, I noticed that she reached her purse in search for a tip, which I thankfully refuse. She told me 'he's my baby son,' to which he can't hide his pride. Looking groomed and much younger, but not surprisingly frail, I can't help but remember that soon my Mom will be 90. Like Jeritza, I figured that it would most likely make her feel good to give her a compliment: "Shirley, you look fantastic." Her natural tension in preparation for the travel was momentarily eased as she gladly smiled and unabashedly blew me a kiss. As I said goodbye to Ken wishing him "safe travels" to Grand Isle, I took her through the airport security, where we inevitably have to go through the whole security ordeal process: ticket showing, along with driver's license; backpack, jewelry, shoes and jacket taken off; laptop - yes, Shirley has one and uses it for e-books! - metal detector forth, then back and forth again, putting on her shoes, picking up her stuff and finally getting back on the wheelchair to be rolled over to the gate. Whoa, amazing operation seamlessly performed by this conscious, grounded and savvy lady. A real joyful moment, I couldn't help but give her a hug and wish her a good journey.

## WITH TRAVELING REVISITED, A FRESH LOOK AT THINGS

Prior to settling in Vermont in the late 1990s, my professional life was quite demanding when it came to regular travels abroad. Back then, as our lifestyle completely changed in a matter of weeks, and then even more in a space of months with Eric's arrival, I basically settled to be fully present at home and drove my efforts to finding a career in the local arena. Passed almost two decades, with Catherine Bianca and GG out of college and Eric about to finish up high-school and embark on his college experience, the opportunity to join an airline position opened new possibilities. Besides, with family members scattered around and out of the country and the perspective of offering Silvia and Eric the option to make their lives more exciting, the effort was worth the trouble.

Back from São Paulo, Catherine Bianca's experience re-assessing her roots in Brazil had come to a conclusion, at least for the time being. She was back in the country and our family cell was now re-united. It also felt right to see her decision to come back as one being spontaneous. Although she much enjoyed being around friends and family, with the economy tanking and, as a consequence, her professional outlook not looking very promising, her resolution was welcomed. We looked forward to her finding better winds at this new phase of her life.

In Texas, our friends Laura and Alberto Colirri had always insisted that we checked out the lifestyle and job perspectives in the Dallas-Fort Worth area, where they have been settled for the past ten years or so. Silvia truly likes the lifestyle and Laura is like a sister to her. It was June 2015 and, as I was about to disengage from my current full time position and looking for a fresh start, I began to nurture the idea that Vermont, although home for us for quite some time now, had already given us enough of its lifestyle. Very graciously, our friends offered me to stay with them while going through interviews and probing the job market. I would go to Dallas a number of times to attend multiple job opportunities. I got very close to being hired twice and had to turn down a couple of job offers as well. However, nothing really came out of the connections. On the West Coast, GG and Matthew would like to see us moving over to their area too as they seem truly committed to making their project successful. There I went to Washington State and got to interview a couple of times – one of them, again very close to getting hired. The same outcome in Texas repeats in Seattle. After a couple of months of flying back and forth, I would find the situation intriguing if it weren't for its annoyance. "Is this going to happen or not?" "Here I am all open to embrace change, now what?" I caught myself asking these questions silently, over and over again.

Lievegoed's *Phases* in its encompassing knowledge and wisdom has a message for me: "It is now high time to prepare for what one still hopes to achieve, what one will have to drop, and what one may still be able to finish. There is a growing anxious realization that this is less than one had thought up to now. The past passes in review. It is incredible that one has wasted so much precious time on trifles – if only I had more time *before* me, time which I let slip through my hands like sand! There is no longer a long future for me in this life, but what, despite this, might prove to be enduring?" Lievegoed on *Phases* points out that at about the age of 56, my exact age at this moment, "new clouds begin to form on the horizon. In the same line of thought, he proceeds reflecting: "the high plateau on which life unrolled provided a good view in all directions, but it was chiefly a view directed at the outside world. The gaze is now again turned inwards. It is as though all the values of life must be relieved existentially."

## A NEW CAREER – 1

While working on landing a new full time job opportunity, whether or not related to my contract furniture background, I couldn't afford not to have income flowing in. The work at the airport had great benefits but the pay was modest. Besides, my wife worked hard and we wanted to keep up with our household demands. Hence, the same way I had once to resort to a 'big box' store job for a temporary cash inflow, I did not hesitate to apply for a Lowe's position that I thought will go well with my skills and the ones I looked into developing further. With a design component, I would work with customers developing custom doors and windows - plus the whole ball of wax related to millwork. The best part of the job? Certainly, helping people improve their living spaces, homes where they are supposed to spend quality time with loved ones. With two jobs on the calendar, I was still looking for a full time position, Monday thru Friday, 40 hours, give or take.

# VERMONT COUNCIL ON WORLD AFFAIRS

"In a rapidly changing world, the VCWA is committed to fostering cultural understanding, strengthening international diplomacy, and engaging Vermont with the world and the world with Vermont."

A few months following naturalization, Leigh Cole invited me to join the VCWA, an entity affiliated with the Lake Champlain Chamber of Commerce. "The Vermont Council on World Affairs works to promote awareness and understanding of the world and its people, places and cultures through education and engagement. In cooperation with the public and private sectors, the VCWA helps develop an understanding of the world and its people through public forums, hosting speakers, ambassadors and other international visitors and working with educational institutions to develop programs for students, faculty, staff and community." I had always admired Leigh's involvement with international affairs and the opportunity to volunteer at the VCWA brought me a sense of community I had not experienced before. Working two jobs, with a third in the works, it was challenging to juggle all those balls. I like to think that when there's teamwork involved, two are always better than one; diverse people with complementary skills and committed to a good purpose can achieve great heights. Always with the interest of the State of Vermont in mind, this group of individuals is remarkable. I wish I could dedicate more of my time and add to the efforts...I'm working on it.

# MR. AMBASSADOR

On the brightest side of social media, I got to reconnect with a former middle school colleague I hadn't seen in a gazillion years. Carlos Den Hartog's daughter lives in Northern Massachusetts, where he makes an effort to flee from his busy agenda to visit her once a year. As he had not been in Vermont before, he drove over to Burlington for the afternoon as we were set to meet for lunch at the Farm House, along with my daughter Catherine Bianca. Carlos had been recently named the new Ambassador of Brazil to Jamaica, after having spent his diplomatic career roaming around the world in multiple positions. It was a treat to see him as we caught up with just about everything from family, lifestyle, world affairs, sports and, of course, music – yes, he is also *Mr. Led Zeppelin*, the young teenager who introduced their music to a generation of schoolmates. And, most importantly, he would become the link I had lost with a dear group of people after being away from my birth country for twenty years. Being a part of one of the best times of my adolescence, in seconds I was on the WhatsApp group from *Colégio Bandeirantes* which gathers once or twice a year. I vowed to join them the next year at the same time Carlos would be taking his vacation in São Paulo. "Great seeing you Carlito, and thanks for making to Vermont. Until next year, my friend!"

## A NEW CAREER – 2

It is undeniable that the workplace revolves around technology. With advantages and disadvantages, it has transformed the planet in the past 4 or 5 decades – its influence is literally everywhere. Although the contract furniture industry has been delving into more and more technology in the past decade, only major players can handle a wide variety of solutions incorporating technology, such as audio-visual solutions and what not. As I looked into joining a globally oriented technology company, I ended up getting an offer from Ricoh – a major Japanese organization specialized in office imaging equipment, production print solutions, document management systems and IT services. Quite a change from my previous career, I embraced the opportunity and began to learn the new gig.

## JOYFUL REUNIONS

Well over a year into the job, as I reconnected with Mr. Ambassador Carlos Den Hartog in December 2016, one of my unforgettable classmates from the 1970s, I promised that I would join him and the group in São Paulo next time he went to São Paulo on vacation from his diplomatic duties in Jamaica. The group of about 20+ members kept an active channel of communication through WhatsApp, so reconnecting became not only a fact but a continuous real time experience. I had not seen most of those guys since high school and wondered how this encounter would take place and what effect it would have on me. As the period was set up for the end of March 2017, it was now time to make it happen.

The flight time from Detroit to São Paulo takes about 10 hours. Luckily, I got to travel executive as my stand-by condition sometimes allows me to get good seats. Besides the planned reunion, I would certainly see my Mom, sisters, and other family members I hadn't seen in years. Traveling for a few days made things a lot more intense and every minute became precious.

On my way to my destination, I couldn't help but to reflect on the history of human migration being as old as history itself. The act of moving from one place to another, particularly different countries, denotes an intention that only the individual can explain. On one hand, my observation of involuntary migration as it encapsulates forced displacement – in its various forms such as deportation, slave trade, trafficking in human beings, – and flight – in its forms of war refugees and ethnic cleansing, – made me realize how fortunate one is when being capable of making choices. On the other hand, my voluntary experience was unique and can be considered a successful one. The fact that our family arrived before 9/11 probably contributed favorably towards a smooth immigration process. Therefore, I never felt like an immigrant myself but, rather, one that had the opportunity to choose his own destiny. The same is not reflective of our current times, where so much has changed and polarization has taken over the discussion around immigration. The Constitution of the United States is the only legitimate resource to bring things to normalcy and this country has gone on a tangent when it comes to dealing with this issue, at least temporarily. Better days ahead? Who knows – I'm an optimist and wish that this subject can be dealt with intelligence, wisdom and common sense.

Gathering with the group of schoolmates from *Colégio Bandeirantes* was of significance for me as memories of an important time – my teenage years – resurfaced. What else can be more meaningful than reconvening with our own biography and being able to settle past experiences? And yet, set the stage for continuous growth? Lievegoed's observations on the approach of our 60th year and beyond is remarkable: "In a certain sense the development of the individual's life has come to a temporary conclusion at the age of 63. Toddler, schoolchild and adolescent – together they make up the youth in which much was granted us. And as usual the gift of the world is always a mixture of joy and sorrow, of helping and hindering experience. Vital-mental, objective and spiritual strivings have made of the expansionary phase a period in which much could be given to the world in the form of work, friendship and enmity, commanding and obeying, but in which it was also possible and necessary to interiorize and appropriate past experiences."

Seeing my schoolmates after decades, 17 of us altogether, even for a couple of hours, was simply magic – Barollo, Rottman, Lerner, Almir, Castillo, Arnaldo, Victor, Ruy Mondolfo, Sergio Gallo, Ronaldo Filet, José Emilio, Caribé, all along with my dear old Elementary School classmates – Homero, Murano and Walter. So glad I took the time, so glad they were there, thanks to Mr. Ambassador, Carlos Den Hartog. A timeless treat.

## SURPRISE, SURPRISE

My sense of accomplishment after getting together with meaningful people from my past was short-lived by the news coming from the office: Arriving in Burlington from São Paulo on a Friday, the last day of March, I got an email from Steve Casale, my manager at Ricoh, letting me know that I would be receiving a Fedex packet first thing in the morning on Monday to be followed by a meeting at the office. Interesting, I pondered. My afterthought when using the word 'interesting' has so many meanings that it's almost overwhelmingly difficult to describe. It's one of those words that one can associate both synonyms and antonyms – and everything in between – to describe exactly the opposite of its real meaning: from absorbing, to breathtaking, to provocative, to enchanting, to mesmerizing, to curious, to weird, to surprising, and to...concerning, dreary and discouraging.

Come Monday morning, the inevitable: Ricoh's 10% of the salesforce nationwide were being laid off on that very day, April 3$^{rd}$ 2017. For me, it's the first time I experienced an involuntary professional break-off. Less than 18 months on the job, bummer... No hard feelings, I guess we could all see this coming sooner or later as Ricoh needed urgent adjustments. The rest of my senior team would get the pink slip just a few weeks later. This meant that I needed to increase hours on the other two jobs until I got a solid full-time position. Again.

## BOUND TO AMSTERDAM, *VENICE OF THE NORTH*

It didn't take long to re-arrange my professional life but I wanted to spend the rest of the time I had off in May and take advantage of my flying benefits before starting the new position in early June. I had told Tom Severino, o Tomané, one of my good Portuguese friends from the period we had lived in Porto, that one of these days I would show up and visit him in his adopted country: The Netherlands. As I got from *Amsterdam Airport Schiphol* to *Amsterdam Centraal Train Station*, I picked up the phone and called my friend; Tomané knew I was going to come at some point but knew not when. Well, the way I travel, I never know if I am going to catch a specific flight until the last minute prior to boarding. Sounds weird? I know it does and that's the way it is. Never a dull moment, I tell myself and my wife – no entitlement, low expectations, and great results when we make it to our destination.

I was lucky to find my friend with a flexible schedule the day I got to Amsterdam. Tomané is an excellent musician from Faro, Portugal, who had moved to The Netherlands along with his wife Maria and their children Alex and Ines, around the same time my family and I moved to Vermont. Jazz and folk music have always strongly influenced his musical life where Tomané worked as composer, arranger and producer in Lisbon and in the last two decades in Amsterdam. The man has a great character and I wish I had traveled to see him earlier. Although we stayed in touch consistently over the years, we had so much to catch up after over twenty years. Among laughs and multiple discussions around our highly similar musical preferences, we enjoyed an espresso at one of the many coffee spots located by one of the hundreds of canals in downtown before heading to a multicultural-cuisine restaurant nearby.

As we walked through the myriads of bicycles and around the people of this small but very populated European country, I recalled previous experiences of visiting Holland, one of the ways this country is known for. I have always been impressed by the Dutch people as being disciplined and conservative, hard-working, practical and organized – and yet very private and progressive in many ways, which to me explains their respect for diversity. Among many of the attributes of this fun people, I like to think that the Dutch are just as serious as the Germans but own a greater sense of humor rarely seen in the Germanic culture. No offense to my German friends or to the people of that outstanding country.

Based in Hoorn, a 30-minute train ride from Amsterdam, Tomané graciously invited me to stay at his house where Maria and Alex would be joining us later on for dinner. With Ines living in Norway for the past couple of years, we had a great musical time together – father and son are wonderful composers and performers, on piano and guitar, respectively, and put in such a treat for me with some of their exquisite repertoire. The next day we walked around historic Hoorn, a small town with a heyday in the 17th century, with rich maritime history where I can get a feel of the flair of the 'Golden Age,' as they call it. It is a magical little harbor town near IJsselmeer Lake, with a beautiful atmosphere, natural surroundings and historic sailing ships. After a quick peek at one of the many studios and galleries, Tomané and Maria took me to *Schiphol* where my flight to JFK would be leaving soon. One of those moments where time is less important than the intensity of the bond we build around loved ones. An ode to friendship, cheers to my friend and to his beautiful family!

## THE EVERGREEN STATE

It was the last week of May and my new job will be starting soon. Yet, in an effort to maximize time and opportunity, Silvia and I managed to fly over to Vancouver, Canada aimed at spending a few days in Washington State to get together with GG and Matthew, and their choc-lab Bella, now living in a larger house they purchased, located at about an hour north of Seattle and 25 minutes south of Bellingham, where they used to live when first moving to WA. More spacious and perfectly located to facilitate their commute to the farm, the house is located on a plain, green and open farmland with views to an astonishing glacier – Mount Baker. After Alaska, I learn that Washington is the second most glaciated state in the US, with a high square mileage of glaciers and perennial snow and ice features. A magnificent sight.

We got to have a pretty good idea of GG's and Matthew's organic farming activity and were thrilled with future perspectives for them. GG's and Matthew's combined unique backgrounds give them the diverse skills, passion and hard work ethic to operate their small farm and accomplish their goal of producing high quality and nutrient dense food.

The Crows Herbfarm's main focus is on producing, among 175 species, a wide selection of fresh culinary herbs, Italian crops such as, fennel, radicchio, heirloom tomatoes, as well as fall brassicas and winter squash. Using the best available practices, The Crows Herbfarm is Certified Organic and the quality of the produce starts with the soil: "We practice crop rotations to eliminate disease pressure and plant cover crops to add nutrients and maintain healthy soil structure throughout the year. Beneficial insects and pollinators are attracted to our fields, mainly due to our diverse fresh cut herbs and flowers, which allows our farm to maintain a balanced ecosystem. We take pride in our role as environmental stewards for our small farm. The Puget Sound Food Hub enables us to reduce our carbon footprint while reaching expansive markets."

GG's and Matthew's hard work is on the right path to supporting sustainability and the environment. Organic farming is and will continue to be on the rise in the U.S., with more than 14,000 certified organic farms, according to the USDA. It still represents a small share of the total agricultural area in the country – just about 1% only; however, can anyone doubt that this is where the future is when it comes food being healthier and fresher for consumption as compared to conventional food?

While in Washington, we took the time to see our good friends Matt Eagens and Geanie Young and their son Peyton, in Yakima. Located at around 2 ½ hours southeast of Seattle, we drive over for a day and get to spend a delightful time with our friends in the Yakima Valley – I hadn't seen Matt in a couple of years since they moved from the Stowe, VT area. Matt and I have a strong connection and share the same values and beliefs, especially as it relates to our vision of freedom and spirituality. Such a treat to reconnect with him as we both look forward to strengthening this great friendship.

## READY FOR A NEW BEGINNING

Back home and at the start of my new job in early June, it was at Conway Technology Group, a Xerox Company, that I found a group of individuals and leadership seemingly committed to the marketplace. With an excellent training program coordinated by Jim Hodge in Nashua, NH, Chris Sterzinar manages our Vermont office under Steve Barrett's, Brett Heffernan's and Carl Tourig's leadership; along with Chad "CJ" Woods' recent move to Burlington and Brian Cameron's joining the group a few months later, we made a good team. With superior document management hardware and software solutions, I could apply my top customer service practices and help organizations streamline document workflow and processes – all that without having to change industries. I would do well by offering my customers the utilization of technologies and tools to help them become more efficient and productive in the workplace. Life getting better, I'm pleased with joining this organization and with the possibility of building the blocks for a renewed career foundation.

## DREAMING OF VENICE, THE REAL ONE

"I'm a musician, and part of what I do is jazz, but I always have some idea that's larger than just playing a gig." For over two decades, George Petit has performed at the iconic Burlington Discover Jazz Festival and, as a product of his encompassing mindset, he creates the Stowe Jazz Festival in 2017 after gathering enough community support to kick start his new project. It is at the lush green lawn at the Alchemist, the award-winning IPA-specialized brewery, that the festival takes place. A Friday evening in September, I got together with my jazz buddy Dave Beckett to attend the presentation of Chico Pinheiro, guitarist, composer and arranger from São Paulo, now established in New York City. I once chatted with Brad Mehldau, one of the most respected piano jazz masters of his generation, after one of his concerts at the Flynn Theater, in Burlington, and learned of his admiration for the Brazilian musician. Chico Pinheiro studied at Berklee College of Music in Boston and is undoubtedly a leading figure of modern jazz in Brazil today. The opportunity to see and chat with the musician corroborates the reviews – a truly phenomenal musician, I was instantly struck by his superior virtuosity and musicality.

Music and travel seem to go together in my mind and I tend to look at them as part of the same structure that confers benefits to my system – I guess one leads to another and vice versa. After a few weeks of coming across great music in Stowe, it was the beginning of October and still time to get on the road before wintertime kicked in. For years, I had promised to take Silvia to Italy for a visit to Venice. Even though this one would have to be a short trip, we committed ourselves to do it and put the plan to work: a direct flight from JFK, if we get to leave Burlington without delays. Knowing the advantages of packing light, it turns out that getting to JFK is a non-issue but getting to Venice directly was a no-go option. One possibility is flying directly to Zürich, which we promptly book the tickets and set our minds to decide how to get to Venice when we get in Switzerland.

From *Flughafen Zürich*, we figured that a good move would be to try and visit my dear cousin Marcelo Hamam and his wife Adriana near Geneva, on the other side of the country. I hadn't seen Marcelo in years although we talk over the phone on a regular basis. Besides, it's a chance to meet Adriana as both have been living in Switzerland for about ten years. In a couple months, they would welcome their first baby and could not be more thrilled. We drove over to Paudex, near beautiful Lake Geneva, and catching up with Marcelo and Adriana for just a day was a delightful moment before heading for a great time in Venice.

Quite a contrast from the gloomy Venice I had visited during the same time of the year back in 1980, we get to "The Floating City" in the beginning of October on a sunny and pleasant day with temperatures resembling a mild summer in the Adriatic Sea. My wife was truly excited to be there whereas I was a little more conservative on the expectations. We know that the city faces challenges such as an excessive number of tourists and problems caused by pollution, tide peaks and cruise ships sailing too close to the historic buildings. Yet, it is a lifetime experience to visit Vivaldi's birthplace and be able to contemplate its art, history, architecture and romantic waterways – an eternal source of inspiration for authors, playwrights and poets - undoubtedly, the most beautiful city built by man.

## HIGH LIVING COSTS AND COLD WEATHER: TIME FOR CHANGE?

It was February 2018 and we were ready for some warm weather. Besides, we wanted to look up other areas in the country that may offer alternative lifestyles. It was during a probing trip to Tampa, Florida, before the end of Vermont's winter and after visiting my old friend and former manager Tom Betts in the Naples area, that Silvia and I began to mature the idea that at some point we ought to be thinking that moving out of Vermont is just a matter of time. Where to? Not clear yet.

After three months back in town, with due diligence about what we wanted, I raised the courage to come to my Senior VP, Brett Heffernan, explain the rationale behind the idea and shoot him the question: "Brett, would you support me if I reached out to one of our sister companies – also affiliated with Xerox - out of state?" A young, energetic and competent professional, Brett shoots back: "Wow, that's quite a change from Vermont and New England. I envy you. If you think that that's best for you and your family, I will give you my full support. Go ahead and tell HR of your idea so they can make the proper connection. Best of luck to you."

More than just investigating possibilities, I had been to North Carolina before and knew that the State is a natural destination for Northeasterners. Not only for the weather, but property taxes are a lot more affordable. Besides, more than two neighboring families had already gone through the move and were encouraging us to do the same. I picked up the phone and called a friend, Samantha Baumgardner, in Charlotte. A former colleague at OM Workspace, I relayed the plan on to her. "You are going to love being here!" she said enthusiastically. Sam offered to introduce me to her network and, to make things more exciting, her husband Brian is a realtor and can certainly drive me around the area in order to deepen the knowledge of the housing market.

Things began to take shape. With the blessings of my current employer, it felt that I could make the transition appropriately. Now, it was hands on preparing our house and list it for sale. With the way we had been maintaining and improving our home over the past sixteen years, we knew it could go fast, especially with the market being seller prone. The delicate equation would be the kids: Eric would be going to college in Montréal at the end of summer. As for Catherine, having been back in the country for a little over a year and still managing the transition, it wasn't clear yet if she would want to go with us. On the job seeking side, I had arranged for two interviews and scheduled them up for the second week of July.

Silvia and I were excited with the outlook and willing to give it a shot.

# 24

# A Hard Rain's a Gonna Fall

*"Oh, every day you gaze upon the sunset with such love*
*and intensity. Why?*
*It's ah, it's almost as if you could only crack the code*
*then you'd finally understand what this all means."*
*Calling All Angels* – J. Siberry

JULY 3RD, 2018. My house is burning down. The minutes I take to drive from downtown Burlington to Essex feel like days. As I cross Five Corners and drive by The Essex Agency right by the train tracks, I remember to call my insurance agent, John Handy. Not sure if John is still in town as it's the eve of Independence Day, I find out that he is not yet aware of the ongoing situation. As I continue through Main Street prior to approaching the Fairview Farm neighborhood where soon I will be facing my house in flames, I can see the dark smoke on the sky from afar. A wrecking sensation. Once again, I can't avoid the thought that crosses my mind while reality and disbelief inevitably collide: "Is this really happening?"

Years back during my journey as a young man through Europe, I looked for answers following my reflections on how the continent survived the dark times during the major continental wars of the 20<sup>th</sup> century. Especially, as it relates to the suffering of millions of people during the Holocaust. Viktor Frankl's *Man's Search for Meaning* is known to be one of the most important books of our time. Here's an excerpt of the book's foreword that is emblematic: "Typically, if a book has one passage, one idea with the power to change a person's life, that alone justifies reading it..." From my perspective, the following is the passage I need to embody at this very moment:

"Forces beyond your control can take away everything you possess except one thing: your freedom to choose how you will respond to the situation. You cannot control what happens to you in life, but you can always control what you will feel and do about what happens to you." – Victor Frankl

Yet from my past and in a flash, another reflection resurges from one of the best advices I had ever received, this one from Nathalia Kolosuki just a few weeks before my wedding: "I am a firm believer that life does prepare us for the difficult things." These two glimpses of awareness were there to guide me through the next several hours and beyond, following the life adversity experience my family would have to endure.

## ONE MAN AT THE STATION

"At roughly 1203 hours on Tuesday, July 3<sup>rd</sup>," says the Essex Junction Fire Department report, "one of our members happened to stop by the fire station during his day. As the firefighter was in the station, he answered the station phone to find a female shouting that her garage was on fire at 12 Juniper Ridge Road in the Village of Essex Junction. The firefighter immediately contacted Essex Dispatch in order to have Essex Fire and Essex Junction Fire be dispatched to the call. Before leaving the station, personnel requested mutual aid from Williston Fire with a Tower as well as Saint Michael's Fire with an Engine.

"Ladder 3 was en route to the fire with a crew of three within three minutes of dispatch. As Ladder 3 turned onto Main Street, a significant column of black smoke could be seen towering over the Fairview neighborhood. Seeing this, Lieutenant Gragg (the officer on L3), requested working incident tones be put out for both departments for a working fire.

"Ladder 3 arrived on the scene moments later to find a two story, wood frame, single family dwelling with significant fire showing from the garage. The garage was so well involved it had begun to collapse and the fire was spreading into the attic of the residence.

"The crew of L3 immediately went to work; the lineman stretched an attack line and made a quick knock on the garage while the Lieutenant prepared to make entry into the residence and pulled a second attack line. The operator of L3 assisted in stretching a line and then established a water supply utilizing a (conveniently) nearby hydrant. The lineman and Lieutenant on L3 then made entry into the residence to the second floor in an effort to stop progress of the fire through the attic.

"As the crew made entry, Essex Fire Car 10 arrived on the scene with Captain Sheeran establishing command. Engine 5 arrived moments later, with the Lieutenant on E5 immediately taking the second attack line to continue working on the garage and side of the neighboring residence.

"As the crew from L3 worked on the second floor, the fire progressed through the rest of the attic, breaking out of the roof in multiple spots. At this point, the operator of L3 had thrown ground ladders for egress and was working to place the aerial to the roof. The decision was made to briefly pull personnel out of the building and let the aerial master stream knockdown the remaining fire in the roof due to staffing and crew exhaustion.

"As this was occurring, Williston Fire Tower 1 arrived on the scene and was positioned so that they could utilize their aerial master stream for the gable end of the home, also to assist in knocking down a large amount of the fire. Also, Essex Fire apparatus as well as Saint Michael's were arriving on the scene with fresh personnel. Underhill-Jericho Fire was also requested to the scene with an engine and manpower due to the extreme heat.

"The bulk of the fire was extinguished within the first 20 minutes on the scene. One resident was transported to the UVMMC by Essex Rescue for a burn injury.

"Crews would work for the next four hours extinguishing hot spots, overhauling the structure and salvaging what belongings we could. Fire damage was contained to the garage, attic and second floor. The first floor and basement sustained severe water damage from firefighting efforts.

"Your EJFD respond with Engine 5, Engine 21, Ladder 3 and Utility 61 with a total of 11 personnel. EJFD was assisted by Essex Fire Department, Williston Fire Department, Saint Michael's College Fire and Rescue, Colchester Center Volunteer Fire Fighters' Association Inc. CCVFC, UJFD, Essex Rescue, Inc., Essex Police Department and investigators from the Vermont State Police. A big shout out to ERS members and EPD officers who assisted with ensuring firefighters were hydrated and had an area for rehab in the front yard!

"The cause of the fire is believed to have been accidental at this time.

"This was also a great reminder to call 911 and NOT your local fire station in case of an emergency. Most departments in the State of Vermont are volunteer, meaning no one is at the fire station at any given time. EJFD is a "paid on call" department, meaning that members are compensated for their time when they respond to fire calls. Our members carry radios and pagers and must respond to the station for emergency calls in order to get their gear and an apparatus. Had our firefighter not randomly been at the fire station, the delay in our response could have been much longer."

## THE THIRTY-YEARS PHASES - II

The next several hours following our household misfortune

seemed unreal. Or surreal, if I may. I can't imagine what multiple households go through when entire neighborhoods burn down in California and on the east coast of Australia, and inevitably draw an analogy with our own mishap. As Silvia accompanies Catherine Bianca to the hospital, James arrives at the scene. From the steps of my neighbors' house across the street, we watch the sheer number of people coming out of nowhere to try and fathom the proportions of the accident – firefighters, neighbors offering immediate support, friends dropping everything they're doing to help, police, the insurance representative, potential builders assessing the damage and, finally, the abundant usual curious individuals. All there for a reason, somewhat connected to the event, looking at someone else's moment in time in an effort to make sense of their own.

On Chapter 11, there is a citation of William Bryant's *The Veiled Pulse of Time*, about the potential for conspicuous changes that may affect individuals during the thirty-years life cycle. Bryant is clear on his idea that significant episodes may occur that may alter rhythm, course and priority when it comes to the next learning lesson to be apprehended. From how I see my own experience, during the years surrounding my first thirty-year phase, my life took a very different direction from what I had in mind, i.e., having to undergo the process of reinventing myself professionally after my family business gradually, but yet dramatically, shrunk. This time, now at 60, with the event of seeing and living the burning and destruction of our home, "an adjustment to jerk us back on course, a course known only to the psychic center of our being," the analogy is there and the process had been laid out in front of my eyes to navigate.

With a note to The Essex Reporter, I make a statement preceding the sailing of the new waters:

*"On behalf of our family, I am writing this note to express my deepest appreciation for all the more than 50 firefighters that worked to extinguish the fire that brought our home in Essex Junction to a complete loss on July 3rd. We always hear about that volunteer firefighters are dedi-*

*cated, hardworking, and brave men and women. But that Tuesday, at Fairview Farm, as part of one of the many incredible communities in Chittenden County, we experienced this first hand. These brave, smart, strong, heroic, selfless firefighters from Essex Junction, Essex, Williston, Colchester, Jericho-Underhill and Saint Michaels College, fought fearlessly. Our house, unfortunately, is virtually destroyed by the fire and the water used to fight the blaze. Most importantly and remarkably, one of our family members only suffered minor injuries and is fully recovering. As well, we are very thankful that no properties were affected by the side effects of the fire – we must say that our next door neighbors had part of their siding melted due to the intense heat – fighting the fire on that 90+ degree temperature day was a herculean effort. We are saddened but will get through this challenging time. Our most heartfelt gratitude goes for these crucial members of our community, who are almost all volunteers, for their amazing effort, dedication, and their display of professionalism. God bless them all.*

*Sincerely,*

*The Wakim Family"*

## "WHAT WISDOM CAN YOU FIND THAT IS GREATER THAN KINDNESS?"
– Jean Jacques Rousseau

James and Tricia's new lifestyle – housesitting across the country and across the world – required that, after selling their house in Waterbury, they scattered several of their functional things such as some clothing, sentimental valuables and documents around friends' and family homes. Although we could fortunately salvage some of the contents they had entrusted us to store, a lot got destroyed. I felt bad about that and wished they didn't get damaged. Our friendship of decades would only get stronger as he and his wife too felt the occurrence personally.

The Red Cross was at the house during and after the efforts to extinguish the fire were completed. A wonderful and principled organization, our household received immediate emotional support followed by financial assistance to our new immediate needs such as food, water, clothing and shelter.

It is on the next few days after the accident that the experience sinks in. The day after being the 4$^{th}$ of July, our neighborhood is putting the pieces together to try and hopefully enjoy the holiday. The scene is not pleasant to the eyes as I come to the site to assess the destruction and what could possibly be salvaged out to the rubble. The fire itself had flattened the garage and, as it tried to fight into the house, it encountered the firewall and the fireproof door. From there, it went up to the attic and followed a sequential line around the perimeter of the house destroying the attic completely. Had the firefighters not acted swiftly, the house itself would have been annihilated. However, the crashing volume of water – the hard rain, as I see it - virtually ruined the inside. Furniture, floors, walls, carpet, clothing, fixtures, almost everything gone.

In the backyard, as I contemplate the image and begin to order my mind, one of our neighbors, Teresa Reed, had spotted me from her backyard and comes to comfort me. Teresa is in tears and almost inconsolable. For a moment, the situation reverses as I see myself comforting her. As we men look at things with some perspective, I perceive that women are so much more attached to their living spaces and feel the pain in a totally different way. "I'm so sorry for you guys, I can't imagine what you're going through right now," Teresa wipes her eyes amidst her broken words. "Teresa, we are doing alright. Silvia is doing ok and Catherine Bianca is recovering well. Eric is getting great support from his friends and GG and Matthew, on the other side of the country, are sad but doing alright. I'm sorry you guys have to go through this. I know it affects the entire neighborhood in one way or another." Teresa's son, TJ, had been Silvia's student in pre-school. TJ and Eric basically grew up together and were good buddies for a significant period of their childhood. "We want to help, please tell me how we can help." Teresa walks away and we wave good bye. I was touched with such genuine and loving manifestation of true friendship.

A few days go by, slowly as we try to go about our lives. By then, we had already moved from one hotel to another and feel fully supported by the insurance company. Scheduled to do my regular shift at the airport on Saturday, I get a break from management on that day to try and organize things. It's mid-morning, when I get a call from my friend Ben Russell inviting us to join him and Leah for pizza later in the day. We gladly accept and plan, accordingly. Although sidetracked from my work routine, it pops in my mind the job interviews I had previously scheduled in Charlotte, NC early in the week following the hazard. "Should I go, honey?" We both agree that the plan to research into the project we had kick started should take place and I would take the flight to Charlotte, first thing Sunday morning. Having gathered with Ben and Leah the evening before, individuals with smart and thoughtful insights given their personal experiences in life, would help us frame up our thoughts and possibilities under the new circumstances.

## CHARLOTTE, NC

Samantha is a former colleague from a previous position at OM Workspace, where we met years back in Chicago. Still in the contract furniture business, she had arranged for her husband Brian to pick me up at the hotel so he would educate me around the livable areas in and around Charlotte, NC. Himself a successful realtor, they are a sensitive couple and offer their invaluable support during the two days I'm in town. Strangely, I can't say the same about my experience in the interviews. In my mind, I thought I should not share my ordeal with the potential employers and decide to keep it strictly professional. I must admit that my preparation prior to the interviews ends up being basic and that my concern was to keep myself somewhat balanced without pushing it too hard, given the recent episode. The result is that nothing happens. "We are slow to hire and quick to fire" was the signal I got from one of the interviewers, something that at this time of my life I don't relate well listening to. Immediately after the interview, I email the HR person thanking for the opportunity. "Unfortunately, not a good fit for me."

## UNPULLING THE TRIGGER

*"In any moment of decision, the best thing you can do is the right thing, the next thing is the wrong thing, and the worst thing you can do is nothing." T. Roosevelt*

Back in Vermont, my mind is set. The idea of moving out of State as we had envisioned should be going to the backburner, at least for the time being. Silvia and I agree that the focus should be setting forth with the insurance company the next steps to determine whether to walk away with cash or to rebuild the house. The proper lingo, ACV or RCV, Actual Cash Value or Replacement Cost Value, respectively. A tough nut to crack given the mode we were in towards changing our lifestyle. To move or not to move, to rebuild or not to rebuild. The questions that would take up our sleep for some time.

## ACTS OF LOVE – I

Peggy Eagan is a dear friend who immediately reached out to Silvia once she learned about our house. An incredibly funny, outgoing and giving creature, the next day she invited my wife to have lunch – which, to Silvia, meant the world at that moment. After lunch, Peggy told Silvia she had something for her in the car's trunk. There, Peggy picks up a packaged frame, gives it to Silvia and let her know that she wanted her to have it. "I know what this is Peggy, why?" We had given our friends Peggy and Brian Eagan one of my Mom's paintings for their house in Grand Isle, years back. Now, she wanted us to have it back knowing that we might have lost everything in the fire. With both sharing a great sense of humor even in difficult times, Silvia in tears still found the mood to ask Peggy: "Unless, you don't like it, yeah I would take it!" Among tears and laughs, Peggy went: "Oh no, I love it, I just wanted to help you guys with your starting over." Of course, the painting went back into the car's trunk. At last, Peggy handed over to Silvia a couple of envelopes. A gift card and a check from Brian addressed to myself. A real act of love, in real life.

## ACTS OF LOVE – II

Silvia got a call from Teresa Reed on Friday evening asking if she could come over to her house the next morning. Promptly scheduled, Silvia showed up at her door prior to going to work. Silvia couldn't help but to drop tears as she drives by our house, which she hasn't done it in over a week since July 3$^{rd}$. Both comfort one another and share their inner fears and sadness around what occurred. Passed that moment, Teresa brought Silvia a bag of envelopes. A product of Teresa's and her son TJ's initiative of dropping a sheet of paper at every house in the neighborhood, ninety-nine in total, with the following content:

<u>"Help Support the Wakims!!"</u>

"The Wakims, 12 Juniper Ridge Road, were left homeless after a fire consumed their home on Tuesday, July 3$^{rd}$. Although they have insurance that will assist them in getting back close to where they were before this devastating loss, our neighbors need us, their friends, like never before!"

<u>"Join Our Gift Campaign!"</u>

- "They literally need EVERYTHING…so our goal is to provide them with donations they can use at their own discretion."
- "Cash, checks (made out to Silvia Wakim), gift cards*, will all be welcome and most appreciated during this interim time!"
- *Gift card suggestions: price Chopper, Hannaford, Bed Bath and Beyond, Amazon or a Visa GC.

"Please send or bring donations to: Teresa Reed, 8 Juniper

Road, Essex Junction, VT 05452 by Friday, July 13th."

"If you come by and we are not home, please leave it between two front doors on the porch and then leave me a text message so I know it's there. You can also email me as well."

"The Wakims have loved living in our neighborhood for over 15 years! They already know it – but let's really show them what Fairview Farms is made of! THANK YOU SO MUCH."

### ACTS OF LOVE – III

Ben Russell and Leah Mital call me that same Saturday afternoon in the middle of my shift at the airport. "Hey Renato," says Ben, "Leah and I were thinking about setting up a GoFundMe on your behalf. Are you ok with that?" Here's what we have in mind, see if you agree:

"Help Wakims Rebuild After Fire"

"Our dear friends, Renato and Silvia Wakim and their family, had the tragic experience of their home accidentally catching fire in the 90-degree heat. Their home was destroyed and they are living in a hotel as they go back to work and find a path forward. Please help us raise money for this wonderful family in their time of need. Below is a link to the news story:

https://www.burlingtonfreepress.com/story/news/2018/07/03/fire-house-ablaze-90-degree-heat-essex-junction/755437002/"

Speechless, how could we refuse such an outpouring manifestation of love, friendship, empathy and kindness?

# 25

# Where Do We Go? What Do We Do? Things Will Never Be the Same

*"Oh, but if you could, do you think you would trade in*
*All the pain and suffering?*
*Oh, but then you'd miss the beauty of the light upon*
*this earth*
*And the sweetness of the leaving."*
Calling All Angels – J. Siberry

BILL FRISELL IS, IN MY OPINION, undisputedly one of the best guitar players in the jazz realm. His eclectic output as a bandleader has emphasized folk, country music, blues, classical and Americana, as a reference to some of the more meaningful genres he's been successfully playing throughout his career.

Around since the early 1980s, it is in the early 1990s that Frisell makes two of his best-reviewed albums: first, *Have a Little Faith*, an ambitious survey of Americana of all stripes, from Charles Ives and Aaron Copland (the entirety of Billy the Kid)) to John Hyatt (the title song), and Bob Dylan ("Just like a Woman"); and second, *This Land*, a complementary set of originals.

The musician has exquisite and vast collaborations with the likes of Paul Motian, John Zorn, Marc Johnson, Elvis Costello, David Holland and Hank Jones, to name just a few. Plus, a large number of works along with other fantastic musicians such as Greg Leisz, Ron Miles, Kenny Wollesen and Vinicius Cantuaria.

As I'm always drawn to find inspiration in music, it is in his album named *Blues Dream* that I find solace to go through this moment in time. William Layman gives a keen description of the album: "It is a movie for your ears, a soundtrack for your passage through a daydream, a kind of classical music even: a set of most careful compositions that orchestrate sounds beyond our imaginations. *Blues Dream* moves from beautiful to strange and back again. But it's a classic."

Three of the multiple album's tunes are displayed as the title of this chapter, a suggestive depiction of the questions roaming my mind.

## NAILING DOWN OPTIONS

"Do you think you want to go through the agony of rebuilding?" Yvonne asked me, a former general manager of Lowe's, now a Key Bank Branch Manager, after I tell her about my experience. For days and weeks, Silvia and I questioned the relevance of rebuilding versus a potential decision to walk-away with the depreciated amount from the insurance company.

We were aware of the fact that this had the potential to be a long rebuilding process. We hear that fire victims opt to pull up stakes after living through the fire's emotional trauma or due to unpredictable rebuilding costs. For us, this could be a struggle; we all knew that. At every stop by the house, now fully gutted, the memory of the damage and its mess was vivid in our minds. Whether it's the water damage soaking into the walls and floors, or the big hole in our roof allowing for the hot sun to get through, it's there.

Now, forgetting about the actual mess for a moment, what is to come needed to be equated: we have to rearrange our whole life around this muck. "You will have to have all kinds of strangers in your home: experts to evaluate what they will do to fix the problem and rebuild it. And, most importantly, you will want to be in the house every day during the process. That's the only way you will get to build the house you want to build, as opposed to building the house the contractors want to build...," said my mortgage holder, Joe Gallagher, warning me of the upcoming experience should our decision be to rebuilt the house.

To make things more interesting, I came across one of those intriguing thoughts, just like when people come up out-of-the-blue and always seem to be present when we need them: "Life will give you whatever the experience is most helpful for the evolution of your consciousness. How do you know this is the experience you need? Because this is the experience you are having at this moment." – Eckhart Tolle

# 26

# Taking Action as The Universe Conspires

*"The size of your problems is nothing compared with your ability to solve them. Don't overestimate your problems, and underestimate yourself."* – Anonymous

CELTIC MUSIC HAS TOUCHED MY HEART for many years. Both Ireland and Scotland have produced distinctive styles of Celtic music, which makes me naturally and magnetically attracted to that region of the world. Although knowing little about the two countries, I have pledged to visit those cultures for some time. Taking advantage of my perk, we managed to take a few days off, just twenty days after our house burned down, to at least visit Dublin.

With both countries sharing a common Celtic ancestry and

consequently, a common music heritage, these styles are known because of the importance of Irish and Scottish people in the English speaking world, especially in Canada and mostly in the U.S., where they had a profound impact on American music, especially bluegrass and country music.

Making the decision and thus flying to Dublin, even for a few days, went a long way for Silvia and myself. It did bring the impressions about our relationship with our new environment at home to be more real and clearer as it helped us overcome more quickly the impact we had gone through. In Dublin, we both fell for the city instantly and were lucky to have a couple of sunny days on the forecast. Getting around, it was pleasantly surprising to see colorful and flowerful buildings, the charming locals are friendly and of course, it was quite a treat to hear the *sing-song* Irish accent. With not much time under our belt, we got to walk long walks by The River Liffey and get a good feel for the city.

Our genuine and unexpected gastronomic experience is in contrast with our preconceived view of Dublin as a food destination – what a pleasant surprise! And, of course, the no-brainer and not-to-be-missed walk to and around Temple Bar: spread over cobbled pedestrian lanes, the spot is crowded with pubs hosting live folk music with the quirky boutiques and crafts making up for a delightful glimpse of Ireland's capital. This old city was once stage of a Viking settlement more than a thousand years ago with so much history to explore. With lots to see, learn and experience, we promised one another to come back. For now, this trip brought us inspiration and an invigorating sense to embrace and deal with the reality at home.

Back in Vermont, we felt that we could make decisions and move forward with our plans. Yes, we thought we were ready to navigate the 'agony' of rebuilding and have decided that we would make the best out of the experience. With the support and recommendations of the insurance company and the fine tuning communications with the builder, we would embark on a trip that could be bumpy but, at the same time, a journey which would allow us to see the light at the end of the tunnel.

## SILVER LININGS

My hardworking wife and I, despite the heavy hours of work we put in on a weekly basis, are open to embrace the bright side of things. As we moved out from a hotel into an apartment in Colchester, life became more simple: in a two-bedroom apartment, maintenance is faster and easier, there will be no mowing the lawn for the rest of the season and the upcoming winter won't see me shoveling or plowing. Not a bad break that I wholeheartedly cherish as we approach year's end.

*"I have just three things to teach: simplicity, patience, compassion. These three are your greatest treasures".*
—Lao-Tzu

Work too was going well as I was fully committed to perform on all three of my jobs; As well, to help as I can at the VCWA and be present at the house as reconstruction takes place, virtually a fourth job. The latter is by far the most challenging of all, as it became an exercise of endurance. With the job market heated as it was, labor was scarce everywhere and the construction industry is no exception. Coupled with the builder's modus operandi, there was no way I could get a set schedule for completion of the project, a source of many of the frustrations that need to be handled in order to keep sanity afloat.

## STEPHEN

At the beginning of this book, I allude to my decision of working on this memoir as a meaningful element for ordering my mind around the experience my family and I were going to go through. In fact, dedicating time and attention to this process at a very busy juncture in my life may seem unfathomable – three jobs, a volunteer function, the rebuilding of the house and...writing. However, my commitment to this project as a means to healing from the experience becomes unparalleled. Therefore, first and foremost, I promise myself not to pay too much attention to the outcome as much as I would engage in the process of telling the stories I had dormant in my system.

Saturday afternoon, winter time, early 2019. As I find myself writing during break time, warmed up and waiting for the next flight arrival at my airport gig at Delta/DGS, I run by Stephen Gragg. We both work at the Burlington International Airport in different capacities – besides being one of the key Operations Specialists, he is one of the few volunteers at the Essex Junction Fire Department. Stephen lives next to my neighborhood, Countryside. He was at his house fixing his wife's car when two of his co-volunteers happened to stop by the station on that wicked hot Tuesday in July. By pure chance, one of them picked up my daughter's call desperately reporting the beginning of the fire. Along with his colleagues, Stephen is the first firefighter to arrive at the house. Idealistic about community work and service, Stephen, like other firefighters, always wishes that their contribution when fighting a fire gets to be as impactful as it possibly can to the usually anonymous household. As we come across one another and often chat around the events of the day on the ramp, it is only a few months after the accident that he confides me that when he saw me arriving at the driveway during the disaster scene he felt that his responsibility had multiplied exponentially. Now, not only his ideal was at stake, but being able to cause an impact to someone's family he knew due to the proximity, did change the way he looked at his commitment to service. I could not be more grateful for Stephen's statement and for what he did on that day. He is a truly special individual, not only for what he does, but for who he is and represents to his community.

## FOR THE LOVE OF ACTING

Eric's last two years of high school were busy as he had a chance to stand out on what had become his passion: acting. Musicals such as *Urinetown, The Boy at the Edge of Everything, Les Miserables and Three Kinds of Wildness* are plays where Eric had found great joy in participating. Besides, the Essex High School Theater Group did offer the necessary structure for talents to manifest. Eric did encounter a great group of kids who are not only talented, but very determined to bring big projects into fruition. With excellent leadership and management, he finds purpose in what he does, a recipe for success in whichever career he decides to delve into. Come fall, he is gone to his freshman year in College, in Montréal. Excited with his new perspective and lifestyle, there's a lot to celebrate.

## ACQUIRING THE TASTE

"I think I'm going to London," says Eric out of the blue. "Wow, that's great buddy," I reply, caught by surprise. In my mind, I pause: Where in the world can you do this with a snap of a finger? You are either wealthy or one of your family members work for an airline company... Anyway, I'm glad to hear that. It was almost the end of another winter in good old Vermont. Eric's first initiative to fly on his own is a definitive step to learn the taste of adventure. His plan was to leave Monday and come back Saturday, as he has to be back to work on Sunday, first thing. Weather related, after not being able to fly out of Burlington on Monday, I arrange to pick him up and get back again to the airport on Tuesday. Before getting home, we text one another:

*E: "There're four seats on the plane"*
*R: "JFK's?"*
*E: "Yes, 14 seats left, ten standby"*
*R: "Yeah, because of the cancelled flights yesterday. 13 seats left on Delta,*

*not bad. It's 11:30 a.m, I should be home in 15 minutes"*
E: *"What time are we leaving? I'm still in bed!"*
R: *"12:20 p.m...."*

As I rush to drop him off, I wish him safe travels and we continue our text messages:

E: *"No chances on Delta flight"*
R: *"Hmmmm"*
E: *"I'm waiting to check JetBlue's, it looks like people are already boarding"*
R: *"Did they say overbooked by how many? Stay on, I am still at the airport"*
E: *"I didn't say overbooked but it's full and everyone is cleared"*
R: *"Yeah, you have to talk to someone"*
E: *"Yes, at Delta - he said it's a no-go for sure"*
R: *"K. You may want to ask about LaGuardia's"*
E: *"JetBlue will know in 10 minutes"*
R: *"Ok"*
E: *"The LaGuardia one at 6:30 is overbooked by one"*
R: *"Wow, only one. Wait, LaGuardia leaves at 4:52*
E: *"No, it leaves at 6:30. Oh sorry, you're right it arrives at 6:30. Total available seats is minus one: it's overbooked"*
R: *"Tough. Yesterday's weather messed up with everyone's schedules. Once you have a definitive word, look up tomorrow's chances. Even if it's a couple of days it's worth it"*
E: *"Not sure it is"*
R: *"Let's wait"*
E: *"The girl at JetBlue here is going to let me know, she thinks it might be possible"*
R: *"Fingers crossed!"*

Eric texts me the screen's snapshot:

E: *"What does this mean, should I go back to Delta? Is there room available?"*

R: *"Yeah, go ask the person at the counter. No chance with JetBlue at this point"*
E: *"It says there is a seat available in the image I texted you but he said no"*
R: *"Yeah, I don't know what to say"*
E: *"He's talking to someone right now but I'm gonna try to talk to him after"*
R: *"K"*
E: *"All checked in for LaGuardia. I wish the guy didn't tell me it was an absolute no for the first time I checked with him"*
R: *"I know, he could've asked you to stick around"*
E: *"Sucks. Hopefully I'll be lucky later"*
R: *"It sure does. Yes, you will"*

An hour later:

E: *"It's really unlikely given the stand-by passenger status. I will stay because it's better than staying in the apartment"*
R: *"Oh man, don't give up yet"*
E: *"This is my final option today with Delta, I checked every option online. How much is a ticket with United or something?"*
R: *"Not sure United flies New York City"*
E: *"Ugh, flights are like $300 plus. There's an American Airlines flight that goes to DC and then to JFK for $470"*
R: *"Yeah, that's a lot and it kind of defeats the purpose."*
E: *"Yeah, just to DC is $360, still too expensive "*
R: *"Yeah"*
E: *"I'm probably not going to get on this flight"*
R: *"Let's see, have you checked tomorrow's availability?"*
E: *"No, I don't think it's worth going tomorrow"*
R: *"Why not? You've got nothing to lose"*
E: *"I don't know. It just doesn't feel worth it. The only way I can get on this plane is if seven people don't show up and that's not possible"*
R: *"I've done short trips before, if you fly Delta One it's worth it"*
E: *"I have to cancel my hostel again. Besides, I'm looking at tomorrow's schedule and it doesn't look good"*

R: *"That's a bummer. We can look at JetBlue again"*
E: *"I don't want to, honestly. I don't think spending another entire day at the airport is worth only one night in London. Is there a Delta in Montréal? Montréal to New York City is a lot more likely to work, Burlington is just too tiny"*
R: *"Yeah, but that's part of the process. Don't get discouraged. You've learned to navigate the Delta booking real fast, I'm so impressed. It's just finding the right moment"*
E: *"I'm trying to find other places to go today but there's literally no flights out of Burlington. Right now there's 17 on standby for the already overbooked flight there's 10 seats and I'm the only non-rev"*
R: *"Boy, that's tough"*
E: *"I'm at the bottom"*

At this point, I'm back on the road:

R: *"I'll drive to the airport and wait for you, just in case"*
E: *"Five seats, 11 people standby"*
R: *"Shoot, there are no more flights today"*
E: *"Nope"*
R: *"K, on my way"*
E: *"There's one seat left. If six people don't get here within 20 minutes, then I can get on the plane"*
R: *"Stay on it"*
E: *"Hold on, I think I might get on this plane. Someone is in here and the guy at the desk called his number and the guy thought he'd cancelled"*
R: *"OK, whatever happens just take it"*
E: *"I'm ON!"*
R: *"Yay! That's awesome buddy, it pays off to be patient and persevere - I'm so happy for you!"*
E: *"How did this happen? This makes no sense"*
R: *"Awesome, stay in touch!"*
E: *"Yes, I also have to check in"*
R: *"Right, safe travels, let me know when you get to NY"*
E: *"Finished up check-in. Love you, thanks so much!"*
R: *"You got it, love you too bud, have a great trip!"*

*"Man cannot discover new oceans unless*
*he has the courage to lose sight of the shore"*
— Andre Gide

## MODENA, LAND OF ENGINES

GG and Matthew worked very hard during their 2018 harvest season. Come February, they were ready for a top-notch vacation in Italy. Both talk us into getting on a plane to Milan to join them in what becomes a memorable visit to this special region in Northern Italy. Once again, the opportunity to run away for a few days from our long winter would pay off. This time, joining our daughter and her fiancée has a special meaning. Their travel plan included an Italian cuisine experience, as both are organic farmers dedicated to the cause of superb quality food. Silvia and I went along and had a great time. Below is Matthew's notes on Instagram depicting their experience, to which we were enthused to be a part of for a couple of days:

"MODENA"
"Our biggest goal for the 2018 season was BALANCE! Sharing a business together and being in a relationship has its ups and downs. No matter how big the "chore" list was, we took at least one day off a week throughout the entire season. Balance for us includes, planning a season-end trip in the wintertime to celebrate, reset and continue finding inspiration.

"We've spent the last few days in Modena, a town of fast cars and slow food. A town that reminds us in life, hard work needs balance to prosper.

"Alongside a heavy meal of lasagna, parmigiano-reggiano and cured meats, a glass of fresh, sweet and bubbly Lambrusco cleanses the palate.

"When using balsamic to create a vinaigrette you must add salt, oil, and sweetness to achieve a BALANCED umami flavor.

"After a rare, unexpected earthquake rocked the region 7 years ago and destroyed thousands of aging parmigiano wheels, producers implemented racks that could sway to achieve BALANCE!

"During the balsamic production, the product ages in 5 barrels of different woods to achieve a complex, BALANCED final product.

"I have so many more but you get the point. @giwakim and I were very fortunate to be joined by her folks for this leg of the trip. We toured and tasted our way through this special region.

"Although we didn't get bumped up from the waiting list @ osteria_francescana, we did eat an amazing lunch Franceschetta 58! Trip highlight for sure!

"Do yourself a favor and try some of the quality products coming from this region, not grated Parmesan from a plastic tube or balsamic from Cali. Get the real deal stuff, made with love and passion.

"Ciao for now Modena! @ Emilia-Romagna."

## PUERTO RICO, THE ISLAND OF ENCHANTMENT

As paradoxical as it may seem, our convoluted recent past experience also brought us exhilarating opportunities for temporary relaxation and enjoyment along with some of my colleagues at work. With outstanding teamwork accomplishment and having been awarded as one of the three most successful members of my company's sales team in 2018, Silvia and I were honored to participate of Conway's President's Club trip to Puerto Rico at the beginning of April 2019, weeks before moving back into the house. Staying at a first-class hotel by one of the sandy beaches of this historic and delightful island, the palm trees and tropical breeze were an absolute delight in contrast to what the people of this country had gone through back in September, 2017, when Hurricane Maria made landfall causing awful and devastating damage. Weeks earlier, the island had also been hard hit by Hurricane Irma which provoked the electrical grid to be largely destroyed. As a consequence, the island went through the largest power outage in American history experiencing a painfully slow recovery process.

Being in San Juan and able to talk to some of the island's residents about their experience had a humbling effect on our visit. We learned that after the storm, massive landslides and downed trees blocked main roads, cutting many towns from the rest of the island for weeks. Nearly two years after the most recent hurricanes hit the island, many residents are still recovering from the storm. A number of its inhabitants simply had not rebuilt their homes and many roofs were still covered with blue tarps. The island's residents have been resilient and only time will bring this beautiful enchanted island back to better days.

# 27

# Where is home?

*"Wond'ring aloud*
*Will the years treat us well...?*
*Wond'ring aloud will a son one day be born to share in*
*our infancy in the child's path we've worn.*
*In the aging seclusion of this earth that our birth,*
*Did surprise. We'll open his eyes."*
*Wond'ring Aloud, Again* – Ian Anderson

THREE HUNDRED AND TWENTY-EIGHT DAYS. Just about an 11-month gestation, is what it takes us to move back into our house since the event of July 3rd, 2018. Without much effort, another book could have been written on all the stories behind the reconstruction of the house alone. What's the lesson to be learned? Why did we have to go through that experience? Other questions did also come about which brought me to reflect further: Is suffering a necessary part of the human condition? To what extent does hardship make a person more resilient? What for?

"I'm impressed with the way you guys handled this whole process, from day one of the fire through the entire experience until moving back into the house." Coming from one of your kids, especially from your oldest, that's quite a compliment. Catherine Bianca is a sensitive woman and this whole experience hasn't been easy on her. Yet, she is resilient and is bouncing back for great days ahead.

## BERLIN, *PAPER CITY*

Our passion for traveling keeps on giving. It was early August, 2019, two months after we moved back into the house when Silvia and I decided to take a few days off and fly to Berlin, a city that I did not have the opportunity to visit way back during my youth years. This is a special time for the city, for Germany, for Europe and for the world as it anticipates the celebration of the 30$^{th}$ anniversary of the fall of the Wall in November – the end of the massive border complex that left Berlin divided into East and West for 28 years, tearing apart families, friends and neighbors.

As usual, we only had a few days to spare and wanted to make the best out of this travel experience. We learn that Berlin is geographically huge. To put into perspective, Berlin is actually nine times bigger than Paris and therefore, we had to be selective in choosing what to see and where to go. Besides, jetlag plays a role and it's easy to succumb to sleep deprivation when running a tight schedule. Although we were interested in visiting some of the spots in town that represent the most relevant historical events – such as East Side Gallery and its sections of the Berlin Wall for street art, Brandenburg Gate, Reichstag Building, Checkpoint Charlie and some of the incredible museums, we typically go for the local take on things. Berlin being an extremely safe city despite its magnitude, walking around parks such as Tiergarten or visiting the Zoo Berlin are other great outdoor options. Not to mention the food diversity, which we have the opportunity to relish around and along with one of Silvia's old friend, Isis Martins. Isis had moved to Berlin many years ago from Brazil and loves the German capital – with her local insight, we got a taste of the upcoming events and certainly the clues for another travel experience in the future.

Being in Berlin and getting a glimpse of what the people of this city had gone through decades earlier, I could not help but to think of Viktor Frankl's *Man's Search for Meaning*. Frankl argues that we cannot avoid suffering but we can choose how to cope with it, find meaning in it, and move forward with renewed purpose. Berliners have come a long way and the city today is a reflection of their resilience.

9.0

> *"So if you're walking down the street sometime*
> *And spot some hollow ancient eyes*
> *Please don't just pass 'em by and stare*
> *As if you didn't care, say, "Hello in there, hello."*
> *–Hello in There*, John Prine

"You know, I'm going to be 90 and I'm still doing ok..." For several months, or I should say, ever since Jeritza turned 89, my Mom started the countdown to her 90$^{th}$ birthday and would not be shy about bringing up her plans for the upcoming event on October 22, 2019. Of course, she was excited, who wouldn't be? My Mom's side of the family has good genes. With some previous history of other long living members in the family, both her mother and her grandmother lived up to 90 and 100, respectively. Not surprisingly, living up to that length of time comes with the usual hurdles of inevitable decline and frailty. Jeritza seemed to have withstood her latest years fairly well, despite the cancer which had her going through surgery to remove a great portion of her stomach fourteen years earlier. In remission for all these years, she kept prioritizing balance in everything she does – from diet to sleep to some walking around the neighborhood, she has always been focused on avoiding excesses and using moderation in just about everything. Celebrating her 90th birthday was quite a milestone and we all looked forward to the day. From my end, the five of us made sure to put the effort towards joining the extended family for the celebration at Cristina's. While Matthew could not disengage from the ongoing attributions at the farm, GG flew from Seattle to Chicago to São Paulo and Eric from Montréal then JFK to São Paulo. From Burlington, Silvia, Catherine Bianca and myself made to JFK and São Paulo without surprises. We gathered ourselves almost around the same arrival date on the third week of October ready for celebrating such a memorable landmark. The party? Oh well, extraordinary. Mom could not be a happier human being as having all of her loved ones reunited meant the world to her.

## THE DOT

From my school years, Carl Sagan's work has been the inspiration of mid- and high-school dreamers at the time and, without a doubt, to this day. American astronomer, cosmologist, astrophysicist, author, science popularizer, and science communicator in astronomy and other natural sciences, Sagan has been a great influence to hundreds of millions of people. On "The Dot" his description of home is unique and I keep it close to my heart:

"We succeeded in taking that picture, and, if you look at it, you see a dot. That's here. That's home. That's us. On it, everyone you ever heard of, every human being who ever lived, lived out their lives.

"The aggregate of all our joys and sufferings, thousands of confident religions, ideologies and economic doctrines, every hunter and forager, every hero and coward, every creator and destroyer of civilizations, every king and peasant, every young couple in love, every hopeful child, every mother and father, every inventor and explorer, every teacher of morals, every corrupt politician, every superstar, every supreme leader, every saint and sinner in the history of our species, lived there—on a mote of dust, suspended in a sunbeam.

"The Earth is a very small stage in a vast cosmic arena. Think of the rivers of blood spilled by all those generals and emperors so that in glory and in triumph they could become the momentary masters of a fraction of a dot. Think of the endless cruelties visited by the inhabitants of one corner of the dot on scarcely distinguishable inhabitants of some other corner of the dot. How frequent their misunderstandings, how eager they are to kill one another, how fervent their hatreds. Our posturing, our imagined self-importance, the delusion that we have some privileged position in the universe, are challenged by this point of pale light...

"To my mind, there is perhaps no better demonstration of the folly of human conceits than this distant image of our tiny world. To me, it underscores our responsibility to deal more kindly and compassionately with one another and to preserve and cherish that pale blue dot, the only home we've ever known."

## SOIL VS. SOUL

Pico Iyer is a British-born American essayist and novelist best known for his travel writing. He has been based since 1992 in Nara, Japan, where he lives with his Japanese wife, Hiroko Takeuchi, the "Lady" of his second book, and her two children from an earlier marriage. Iyer's family home in Santa Barbara burned down due to a wildfire in 1990, a biographical landmark that may have had a deep impact on his peripatetic (itinerant) perspective on 'being at home' in general. In his literary essays and TED-Talks, he repeatedly said: "For more and more of us, home has really less to do with a piece of soil, than you could say, with a piece of soul."

## "PHOENICIANS..."

My greatest admiration goes to this ancient people. The

Phoenician culture originated in the Easter Mediterranean region of the Levant (Southern Syria, Lebanon and Northern Israel) in the second millennium Before Common Era. More than necessarily associating the Lebanese people with the Phoenicians, my identification with the latter is on the way this Semitic-speaking Mediterranean civilization saw their existence and consequently applied their beliefs into their behavior and *modus vivendi*. Below, a summary of how they have been perceived along the centuries:

"In the ancient world, the Phoenicians were famed for their miraculous ability to create awe-inspiring comebacks from devastating loss. Their legend spanned over 4,000 years and still lives on today, teaching contemporary civilization about resiliency, transformation and peace.

"Phoenicia was an ancient Semitic Canaanite society located in the land now called Lebanon. This area is part of what has come to be nicknamed "The Cradle of Civilization" and is more properly known as the Fertile Crescent, a region that contains the fertile part of the Middle East, and the Nile Valley and Delta of Northeastern Africa. The major Phoenician cities were situated on the coastline of the Mediterranean Sea, and their people created an enterprising maritime trading culture that spread, among other things, the alphabet from which all major modern alphabets are derived."

### "...THE LEGEND OF THE PHOENIX..."

"The legend of a mysterious bird known to us as the phoenix was popular in Ancient Egypt and later became part of the culture of Ancient Greece. As the story has it, the phoenix is a magnificent bird with red and gold plumage that lives for 500 years before suddenly bursting into flames and being consumed by the fire. From the ashes, a young phoenix then arises and begins anew. The Phoenix Rising legend came to be shaped by, and associated with, the long history of the Phoenician people.

"The evolution of the legend began in 3,600 BC when the

Phoenicians were building cedar boats in order to facilitate fishing and trading within a half-day's journey from one of their most important cities, Byblos. They soon ventured farther down the coast and by approximately 3,200 BC had forged a lucrative trading partnership with Egypt that brought them great wealth. Over the next two centuries, the Phoenicians developed cities up and down the coast of Lebanon, including Byblos, Tyre and Sidon, as well as a multiplicity of other colonies and cities along the Western Mediterranean, such as Santorini, Sicily, Crete, Corsica, Carthage, and as far afield as the Atlantic coast of Spain and Morocco. They continued to amass wealth while exploring new lands, people and customs."

### "...LIVING THE LEGEND"

"Unsurprisingly, their success attracted hostility, and by 2,000 BC other cultures were intent on conquering the Phoenicians and the surrounding area. Every couple of hundred years, invaders would set upon a prominent hub such as Byblos or Tyre, taking whatever they could before burning it to the ground and leaving. Such annihilation was common throughout the ancient world, a part of the way that life was lived and fought over at the time. However, the Phoenicians' extraordinary response to the devastation of their cities set them apart from other ancient peoples: They would return to their routed land and, as a unified force, rebuild it within five or ten years. Their cities would literally rise out of their own ashes and become even richer than before, and this miracle was repeated countless times over the centuries.

"A peaceful people, the Phoenicians weren't interested in conducting conquests or engaging in warfare. They valued family, spirituality, Mother Earth, women, relationships with trading partners and privacy. People within their society and those from other cultures were treated with respect. As explorers of exotic shores, they were known for blending in, admiring the customs, traditions and religions of all they encountered, and developing lasting relationships. It was simply the Phoenician way of being to appreciate people for who they were rather than focus on how they were different.

"The inspiring resurrection of their cities was closely tied to how they dealt with an impending attack. The Phoenicians were skilled in the art of diplomacy and sought at all times to avoid conflict. When they learned that outsiders planned to attempt to conquer them, they took action before the invasion occurred. They initiated a peace process that began with the Phoenicians lavishing their would-be attackers with gifts and concluded with the negotiation of a settlement that was equally advantageous for both parties. Their diplomatic finesse enabled them to thwart attacks and maintain sovereignty over their lives many times over.

"On the occasions when diplomacy failed and thus an invasion loomed, the Phoenicians would leave their city by boat, taking their material treasures with them. After the invaders had looted whatever was left and burned the city to the ground, they would retreat and the Phoenicians would return to the ruins with all of their people and wealth intact. Then, in a staggering show of resiliency, will and unity, they accomplished the miracle of rebuilding their home. They were known for placing high value on partnership and cooperation – principles clearly put into practice time and again. Each and every family shared in the prosperity generated through trading ventures, and therefore everyone contributed to resurrecting their city from ashes. Working as a collective unit with an impassioned purpose, and thereby rising from repeated trials by fire, made the Phoenicians remarkable in their own time and their legacy has been celebrated in the centuries since."

## SEVEN WOMEN

"I think women are foolish to pretend they are equal to men. They are far superior and always have been. Whatever you give a woman, she will make greater. If you give her sperm, she will give you a baby. If you give her a house, she will give you a home. If you give her groceries, she will give you a meal. If you give her a smile, she will give you her heart. She multiplies and enlarges what is given to her. So, if you give her any crap, be ready to receive a ton of shit!" –William Golding

Seven key individuals have been the doorway to my soul searching and development, directly at times or indirectly when geography and circumstances have changed over the years. Mom, my sisters Silvia Regina, Liliana and Cristina, my wife Silvia, and my daughters Catherine Bianca and Diana Louise (GG). William Golding, British novelist, playwright, and poet, pays a tribute to women very few individuals are capable of. With a few exceptions, there's no doubt that the role of women in our modern times still varies from country to country, especially when considering religion being a central focus of multiple cultures. Throughout history, the central role of women in society has ensured the stability, progress and long-term development of nations. Art, Agriculture, Education, Caretaking and Business, are but a few of the critical roles in which women, when empowered, provide excellence.

It's no different in a household environment and in the workplace. I'm very fortunate to have had the grace of coexisting with these seven individuals, for they have provided me the ability to see things as they really are and supplied the love one needs to continue to be an aspiring decent human being.

## "SCHOOL-PLANET"

Early in my life, I came across the idea that our planet was designed to provide humans the conditions for self-knowledge and ascendance to higher spheres – a concept as old as humanity itself. At some point in my journey, the discovery of a missing link becomes a quest in itself. According to Plato, Socrates believed that the value of self-knowledge consisted in "one's ability to recognize the limits of what they know," which Socrates ultimately thought, was nothing. That's been a good start for me and I think it may be the case for any individual, from any perspective, at any given time.

The text below is almost poetic and reflects much of how I see and experience our planetary field:

"To this day, scientists have not discovered any planet like Earth. Maybe it exists, maybe not. In any way, we face an absurdly important fact. Planet Earth has been the perfect habitat for myriads of living creatures until we've come to human life.

"We depend on it to live: the physical body, the sunlight, the air we breathe, the food we eat, the water we drink, the clothes we wear, the energy that makes everything move, the house we live in, the instruments we play, in conclusion, everything. Even the ships and space stations are built with materials from Earth, where the space travelers carry its oxygen for survival.

"The majority of human beings, however, spend life lost in thoughts and emotions, stepping on Earth without the least clue of the miracle it represents, as if everything was normal and natural, as if the world spun around his/her own being and only existed to realize their innumerous desires. The Earth is the perfect stage for the theater of life, it is so stunning in its magnificent and mysterious completeness that no religious being, scientist, politician or artist has ever achieved to fully understand it, to this day.

"It has been conceived to be a Life School-Planet, a Field of Experiences, a Privileged Place for the flourishing of our Soul, for the learning of our Being, the evolution of our Consciousness. What does it all mean? What is our role in this theater? What do we need to learn? These are fundamental questions for all those who begin to awaken from a world of fantasies and dreams, and to recognize that there is an invisible reality. Something that transcends us, and that life on Earth makes part of a Divine project of unimaginable importance and dimension. Reflecting over these questions has the power to rise us from darkness to a Light principle, from ignorance to an initial and truthful Knowledge experience." – Carmem Carvalho and Marian Bleier

# THE WILLOW TREE

For years, I have grappled with finding a solution for the puddles that accumulate from time to time in my backyard when it rains too hard. It's not that I was not warned by the previous owner who sold me the house in the early 2000s and honestly disclosed the issue. I guess I was not prepared to tackle the problem until after the completion of the reconstruction when, on laying out the landscaping project, the solution seemed more simple than I thought: To plant a Willow Tree, which I did. It is about 25-feet tall, located right in the middle of my backyard, visible from all angles of the house.

The willow, besides utilizing it as a great consumer of water for the practical purpose of draining the drenched areas in my backyard, has a symbolic meaning. With a little research, I learn that it reminds us to let go and to surrender completely to our innermost selves. And, to gain a deeper understanding of our subconscious. Another powerful symbolic meaning of the willow tree is its adaptability. The willow tree's ability to not only survive but also thrive in some of the most challenging conditions. We can also look at how the willow tree encourages the expression of deep emotions, including grief and sadness through tears and teaching us the value and consequences of love and loss. One of the greatest symbolic meanings of the willow tree is that even through adversity we have the ability to grow and there is potential for something new.

# WRAPPING UP

Mário de Andrade, a Brazilian poet, novelist, musicologist, art historian and critic, and photographer, had an enormous influence on modern Brazilian literature. As a scholar and essayist—he was a pioneer of the field of ethnomusicology—his influence has reached far beyond the Brazilian frontiers.
Here is my favorite of his poems, "My Soul Has a Hat":
"I counted my years and realized that I have less time to live

by, than I have lived so far.

I feel like a child who won a pack of candies: at first he ate them with pleasure, but when he realized that there was little left, he began to taste them intensely.

I have no time for endless meetings where the statutes, rules, procedures and internal regulations are discussed, knowing that nothing will be done.

I no longer have the patience to stand absurd people who, despite their chronological age, have not grown up.

My time is too short: I want the essence, my spirit is in a hurry. I do not have much candy in the package anymore.

I want to live next to humans, very realistic people who know how to laugh at their mistakes, who are not inflated by their own triumphs, and who take responsibility for their actions. In this way, human dignity is defended and we live in truth and honesty. It is the essentials that make life useful.

I want to surround myself with people who know how to touch the hearts of those whom hard strokes of life have learned to grow, with sweet touches of the soul.

Yes, I'm in a hurry. I'm in a hurry to live with the intensity that only maturity can give. I do not intend to waste any of the remaining desserts. I am sure they will be exquisite, much more than those eaten so far.

My goal is to reach the end satisfied and at peace with my loved ones and my conscience. We have two lives and the second begins when you realize you only have one."

*My Soul Has a Hat* – Mario de Andrade

# Epilogue

Much to our chagrin, we are yet to see the rise of real serious leadership when it comes to tackling and solving the pressing issues of the planet today and for the years to come: noticeable and measurable, the unraveling of climate change and its effects on nature. Leaders must have the courage and sensibility to scale up and think big. The pale blue dot, our home, or should I say our house, the place where we all live, is hurting and we need change. Soon.

Nevertheless, where is home in the grand scheme of things?

With my mindset geared around one of a peregrine or even a nomad, I'm still working on a complete and definitive answer. Until I get there, part of me tells me that home is...us. Yes, we ourselves. Like every snowflake which takes up a peculiar shape as it plunges through the chaos of the atmosphere, we are all unique. An extraordinary entity capable of finding enjoyment, of creating happy moments, of partaking laughs and learning. An unequaled individual with our own fingerprint, fitted to accommodate love, care and respect. An inventive, one-of-a-kind figure suitable for sheltering a constellation of thoughts and dreams and yet, for harboring the simplest microscopic reasoning. A distinct creature who spends most of our time taking pieces from the places we have been, from the places where we are now and from the places we would like to be.

Traveling is a key part of our social system. Along with movement, the beauty of traveling stands on the possibility of looking at the world from multiple perspectives, therefore changing the world inside, changing ourselves intimately.

As I conclude this memoir, while severe traveling and movement restrictions have been put in place, with consequences yet difficult to ascertain, the world is engulfed in a complex open-ended health and human crisis of unpredictable magnitude: a pandemic afflicting all peoples in every continent. The virus has been spread, firstly through international travelers: tourists, peregrines, lecturers and members of the entrepreneurial elite. As of this date, the international community is struggling hard to understand such a havoc of monumental proportions. With many more questions than answers as to how to cope with it. With the challenging periods our civilization goes through from time to time, we are at a crossroads.

Traveling will continue to be a crucial part of our moral, cultural and social fabric. Call it traveling, a journey accompanied by a physical dislocation, or reading a good book, or listening to a great classical or jazz masterpiece. Or yet, simply, the use and limits of imagination. To what extent the COVID-19 pandemic could make existing problems worse or it could be a once-in-a-generation chance to build a better future is up to us to decide. Inevitably, we will all grow jointly from this experience. What we do with it, from a personal and collective spiritual reset perspective, only our sovereignty as individuals will determine the outcome.

Yet, where and what is the meaning of home?

Home is what we look after. It has less to do with a roof and several walls, with our last name and what we have and don't have; It has little to do with what we look like, where we come from and where we live; Instead, home does have everything to do with us fitting in our own skin.

It has always been a liberating thought for me to think that nobody knows us better than ourselves. Life provides us with all the tools, it leads us to the right directions, it pushes us to come across the right people, at the right moment and place. It offers us the chance to come through our own paths. Especially, when we give room to create those sparkles for navigating the flow of the present moment, for letting go of the unnecessary, for embracing quiet and solace in order to come closer to our own selves, to listen to our own inner voices, to seek and find purpose.

Home is us. Truly, the only home we will ever know.

Why not?

# Acknowledgements

So much is said about how we grow, as individuals and as a group, every time we come across and overcome obstacles that life inevitably throws our way. Therefore, I start acknowledging adversity as a significant contributor to this book. Without having gone through one or two meaningful experiences, this memoir would not have happened.

I am deeply grateful to my wife and children for the love, patience, understanding and companionship during the travel experience of writing this memoir. Especially, as it got conceived and executed during a delicate time of our history as a family.

I am forever thankful to my extended family for being a constant source of inspiration throughout my existence.

I am indebted to James and Patricia Meade for being who you are: your true friendship and presence, especially at critical crossroads, have been beyond value.

Many thanks to all of my friends, in particular to Edison Machiaverni for being an inspiration, as well as relatives mentioned and not mentioned in this book. You were and continue to be an essential piece of my journey.

My gratitude to Sue Mehrtens and Ann Markle, and to my 'sister' Barbara Kelleher for their suggestions, expertise, time, patience and dedication in polishing my manuscript.

A special thanks to my daughter Catherine Bianca for her invaluable contribution using her outstanding graphic design and compositing skills throughout the editing and publishing process.

Words cannot express my gratitude to Steiner Books Anthroposophic Press in NY and the Rudolph Steiner Press in the U.K, and to the The Krishnamurti Foundation for allowing me to use the many inestimable quotes throughout this literary work.

My profound thankfulness to Teresa, Rob, TJ & Maria Reed, Ben Russell & Leah Mittal, Marcelo Hamam & Adriana Verdier, Gordon & Carol Edmunds, Brian & Peggy Eagan, Ken Kowalewitz & Jenn Bunker for their friendship and amazing support. True acts of love.

My deepest appreciation to Leigh & Chris Cole, Bill Mares and Eric Hanson, and to Ed McMahan, Patricia Preston and to all of the members of the Vermont Council on World Affairs; To all of the higher-management members and my colleagues at Conway Technology Group; To all of my colleagues and former colleagues at Delta Global Services, with special thanks to Pete Soons, Abby Kenney, Kathy Jean and Maple Dan Truso, as well as to my former co-workers at Lowe's in Essex, VT, Jason Pierson, David Foster, Geoff Tolo, Aneez Haniffa and Todd Rushlow.

I also want to express my gratitude to Seth Blanchard, Jason DuBois, Aimee Cronin, Chris Sterzinar, CJ Woods, Carol & Arnie Russell, Heather Allard, Wanda Arce, Brendan Walsh, Rhonda Jordan, Marla Paul, Monique Morneault, Steven Casale, Catherine Printon, Bill Flowers, Tim Harris, Ron Padgett, David French, Kate Soons, Sergio Wakim, Janet Carlson, Colin Lucas, Dylan Ravdin, Carolyn Smith, Daniel Woodworth, Jean Sirois, Judith Hines, Kim & Shawn Garrett, Stephen Frey, Robyn Ledoux, Theresa & Gordie Wood, Georgeanne & Don Baker, Maryanne & Jeffrey Larkin, Yves Bradley, Stephen Lotspeich, Annie Cooper, Deb Hazel, Raghavendra Krishna, Cheri Morgan, Jane Goodman, Annette Rexroad, Dongdong Lin, John Ferris, Elizabeth, Peter, Jasper and Ella Skinner, Laura Chadwick, Adriana Hamam Ohlmeyer, Luis Wakim, Maya Provost, Cindy Provost, Monica Gavrielides, Susan Hess, Michelle Guyette, Ellen Emery, Michael and Ute Kleiner, Dawn McGinnis, Mary Ann Haar, Zuzana Brochu, Becky Stowe, Matthew Eagens, Lynn and Geordie Braceras, Courtney Cutler, Tatiana Santillo, Sandra Zelaz, Eric & Elke Reichelt, Meghan & Ryan McCormick Audette, Dave, Audrey, Jordan, Kirsten, Cailey & Tobey Appenzeller, Gordon Watson and Joanne Brooks, Greg, Melissa & Camille Tomasulo, Melissa & Marc Lamarche, Dan & Jessica O'Neil, Tom & Lisa Heins, Ethan, Alicia, Piper & Violet Goodkind, Tim Jerman, Karen Lounsbury & Jody Edwards, Jen & Adam Ashe, Susan & Pinhas Zajdman, Eileen, Jay & Hannah Shepard,

Michael & Tyler, Shane & Nicole Leggett, The Gilbert Family, Jason & Sarah Riedinger, Linda, T.J., Tom & Joe Jackman, Dave, Carla, Kyle & Drew Riesters, Mike & Jill Sullivan, Sarah Davis, The Gookin Family, Terry, Sue & John Woods, Nikki & Brett Clace, Jim & Sue Girouard, Chris & Anna Laucius, Ash & Vidula Srivastava, Sandra & Noel Pinto, The Smiles Family, The Todias Family, Renee & Bradley Shedd, Robert & Deborah Ennis, Kris & MJ Merchant, Kristen & Brynn Carris, Daniel & Stephanie Weiss, Richard & Jennifer Celia, Donna & Greg, Ernest & Laura, Gary & Anna Malle, Lilly & Jim Fiore, The Turners Family, Andy & Kathleen Legg, Theresa & Mike Dwyer, The Dunbar Family, The Austin Family, Heather Henessey & Matt Butterly, Rebecca & John Sharkey, Sarah Chamberlain, Essex Kids & Fitness Staff Members. Susan Moore, Susan Brice, David & Flavia Bazoon, Marina & Sergei Shpaner, Lee & Sarah Chamberlain, our dearest friends Alberto & Laura Colirri and to all of the help of multiple anonymous supporters.

For the readers who wish to communicate and exchange ideas about this book, feel free to email at: **whynotamemoir@yahoo.com**

# Background Reading

1. Lievegoed, Bernard - Phases – The Spiritual Rhythms in Adult Life. Sophia Books, 2003, 2008, 2014
2. Bryant, William - The Veiled Pulse of Time – An Introduction to Biographical Cycles and Destiny. Lindisfarne Books, 1993/2018
3. Muir, John – The Yosemite – The Century Co., 1912
4. Huizinga, Johan – Homo Ludens – Random House, 1938
5. Carroll, Lewis - Alice's Adventures in Wonderland – Macmillan, 1865
6. Ferguson, Marilyn – The Aquarian Conspiracy: Personal and Social Transformation in Our Time, J.P. Tarcher, 1980
7. Einstein, Albert – The World as I See It – Nova Fronteira, 1979
8. Orwell, George – Down and out in Paris and London, Mariner Books, 1972
9. Harvard-Student-Travel-Guide – Let's Go: Europe - 1980 Edition
10. Fromm, Erich – The Art of Loving, Harper & Brothers, 1956
11. Huxley, Aldous – Brave New World, Chatto & Windus, 1932
12. Konig, Karl - Brothers and Sisters, a Study in Child Psychology, Steinerbooks 1991
13. Burkhard, Gudrun - Taking Charge: Your Life Patterns and Their Meaning – Floris Books, 2007
14. Stepan, Alfred – Authoritarian Brazil, Yale University, 1973
15. Thoreau, Henry D. – On the Duty of Civil Disobedience – Minerva Publishing, 1849
16. Furtado, Celso – Mito do Desenvolvimento Economico - Paz e Terra, 1974
17. Aurelius, Marcus – Meditations – Penguin Random House, 2006
18. Seneca – On the Shortness of Life – Penguin Books, 2004
19. Parham, Vishara – What's Wrong with Eating Meat? Ananda Marga Publications and Barbara Parham, 1979

20. Frankl, Viktor E. – Man's Searching for Meaning – Beacon Press, Boston 2006
21. Seuss, Dr. Oh, The Places You'll Go! Random House, 1990
22. Lao-Tzu – Tao Te King – Random House USA Inc., 1972
23. Pessoa, Fernando – O Eu profundo e os outros Eus, Ed. Nova Fronteira 1980
24. Gibran, Khalil – The Prophet - Alfred Knopf, 1923
25. Naimy, Mikhail – O Livro de Mirdad – LR, 1999
26. Krishnamurti, Jiddu – Freedom - Harper One, 1996

## References

(1) Being There – Wikipedia - Content is available under CC BY-SA 3.0
(2) Crater Lake – Wikipedia - Sacred Significance – Content is available under CC BY-SA 3.0
(3) History of Vegetarianism – Wikipedia - Content is available under CC BY-SA 3.0
(4) Museu do Ipiranga – Wikipedia - Content is available under CC BY-SA 3.0
(5) Homo Ludens - Wikipedia - Content is available under CC BY-SA 3.0
(6) Misfit – Alternate Dimensions (Belonging Chapter)
(7) Guaíra Falls, Sete Quedas - Wikipedia - Content is available under CC BY-SA 3.0
(8) Lectorium Rosicrucianum - Wikipedia - Content is available under CC BY-SA 3.0

## Favorite Tunes

There are many, but here is the essential sampling on their categories:

### Prog-Rock Albums
(1) Selling England By The Pound – Genesis
(2) Thick As A Brick – Jethro Tull
(3) Close To The Edge – Yes
(4) Dark Side of The Moon – Pink Floyd
(5) In the Court Of The Crimson King – King Crimson

(6) Octopus – Gentle Giant
(7) Brain Salad Surgery – Emerson, Lake & Palmer
(8) Utopia – Todd Rundgren
(9) Pawn Hearts – Van Der Graaf Generator
(10) Per Un Amico – Premiata Forneria Marconi

**Brazilian Jazz Musicians**
(1) All of Pixinguinha's
(2) All of Tom Jobim's
(3) All of Elis Regina's
(4) All of Baden Powell's
(5) All of Airto Moreira's
(6) All of Egberto Gismonti's
(7) All of Milton Nascimento's
(8) All of Marisa Monte's

**Jazz Albums**
(1) Kind of Blue – Miles Davis
(2) A Love Supreme – John Coltrane
(3) Time Out – Dave Brubeck
(4) The Incredible Jazz Guitar – Wes Montgomery
(5) Mingus Ah Um – Charles Mingus
(6) The Shape of Jazz to Come – Ornette Coleman
(7) A Quiet Time – Ahmad Jamal
(8) Infinity – McCoy Tyner
(9) Nearness of You – Michael Brecker
(10) Like Minds – Gary Burton
(11) Portrait in Jazz – Bill Evans
(12) Facing You – Keith Jarrett
(13) Just me – Clare Fischer
(14) The Sound of Summer Running – Marc Johnson
(15) American Dreams – Charlie Haden
(16) Highway Rider – Brad Mehldau
(17) Black Market – Weather Report
(18) The Imagine Project – Herbie Hancock
(19) Good Dog, Happy Man – Bill Frisell
(20) Season of Changes – Brian Blade
+ All of Pat Metheny's & Collaborations

Plus, a fantastic new generation of musicians in all genres is already in place and keeps brewing. To be uncovered.